Th

Zanzibar

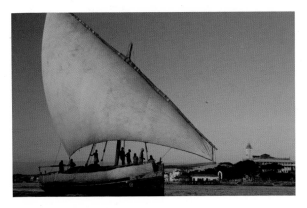

written and researched by

Jens Finke

916. 781

NEW YORK · LONDON · DELHI

www.roughguides.com

Contents

Zanzibar and the Slave Trade insert following p.112

Zanzibar and the Sea insert following p.208

◄◄ Dhow, Stone Town waterfront ◄ Girl entering Tippu Tip's House, Stone Town

Introduction to
Zanzibar

> This is the finest place I have known in all of Africa ...
> an illusive place where nothing is as it seems. I am mesmerised.
>
> David Livingstone, 1866

Lying in the Indian Ocean 35km off the coast of mainland Tanzania, and just six degrees south of the Equator, the archipelago of Zanzibar is one of Africa's best-known and most enticing destinations. Comprising the islands of Unguja and Pemba, along with a number of smaller isles and coral atolls, the very name evokes images of an exotic laid-back paradise replete with coconut palms, multicoloured coral reefs and, of course, miles and miles of white sands lapped by warm, translucent turquoise waters.

The image is not without justification, of course, but there's a whole lot more to Zanzibar than beaches and tropical languor. Its **history**, for a start, is one of the most turbulent and fascinating in East Africa, having seen more than its fair share of invasions, empires and intrigues, as reflected in the colourful architecture and monuments of Stone Town and the scatter of ruined cities and palaces spread across the islands. Zanzibari culture reflects this eclectic mixture of influences too, most obviously in its language, **Kiswahili**, where Arabic, Portuguese, English and Hindi words have been grafted onto Bantu and Cushitic roots. Zanzibari **gastronomy** also reflects the blend, quite deliciously too, as do a wealth of annual **festivals** that range from dhow races and Islamic celebrations to bull fights on Pemba and the world-renowned Festival of the Dhow Countries – a showcase for film and music at which you're as likely to hear traditional *taarab* as you are rap, reggae and sacred Sufi chants.

Where to go

The archipelago's biggest and most important island is **Unguja** (confusingly also called Zanzibar Island), 1651 square kilometres of low-lying fossilized coral separated from the mainland by the Zanzibar Channel. The capital **Stone Town**, on the west coast, is one of the world's most alluring cities, centred on an Arabian-style labyrinth of crooked narrow alleyways packed to the rafters with nineteenth-century mansions, palaces and bazaars. The town itself has enough of interest to merit several days of aimless wandering, and also provides a good base for visiting the rest of the island.

The wetter, western side of Unguja is where most of the island's famous **spice plantations** are located, easily visited on an organized tour, as are

▲ Stone Town street

Fact file

• If Zanzibar feels like a different country to mainland Tanzania, it's because it is – or at least it was until 1964, when it linked up with mainland Tanganyika to form the present-day United Republic of Tanzania. However, **Zanzibar remains semi-autonomous** and has its own parliament and president. Both have been multi-party democracies since 1995, although the ruling CCM party receives the lion's share of media coverage. On Zanzibar, CCM's powerbase is Unguja Island; the majority of Pemba's islanders favour the opposition CUF.

• The Isles' population is just under one million, most of whom subsist on a dollar a day or less, making Zanzibar **one of Tanzania's poorest regions**.

• In the nineteenth century, Zanzibar's sultanate controlled the East African **slave trade**, on which it grew immensely wealthy – as witnessed by Stone Town's profusion of opulent palaces and exuberant mansions.

• **Zanzibari Independence**, in December 1963, was followed a few weeks later by a bloody Revolution, putting an end to the Sultanate and kicking off a turbulent period of political unrest that has yet to settle completely.

• Most Zanzibaris are **Muslim**. Religious fundamentalism, whilst rare, is on the increase; respect local sensibilities by covering your legs and shoulders when in urban areas.

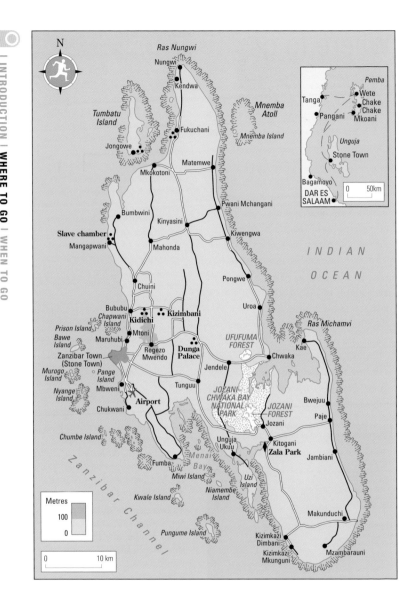

a number of other attractions including ruined Omani **palaces**, **Persian baths**, a cave used to hide slaves, and a number of **uninhabited islands** off Stone Town whose surrounding coral reefs are ideal for **snorkelling**. Another viable

Pemba's main attraction is its fringing coral reef, which offers exhilarating scuba diving and snorkelling

▲ Performance by Watmon Cultural Club

day-trip is **Jozani Forest**, Zanzibar's largest tract of indigenous evergreen woodland, which shelters several endemic species including the endangered red colobus monkey, and is usually combined with a boat excursion off Kizimkazi on the south coast, in search of the resident **dolphins**.

But Unguja's main attraction after Stone Town is its **beaches**. The most beautiful are on the east and northeast coasts, and either side of Unguja's northernmost tip, **Ras Nungwi**. Although parts of the coast, notably the northeast, have been

> **Stone Town, on the west coast, is one of the world's most alluring cities**

swamped by all-inclusive package resorts, development remains for the most part low-key, and **beach accommodation** ranges from homely bun-

▲ Boats moored off Prison Island

galow-style set-ups to plush five-star resorts with all the creature comforts you could wish for. As well as standard watersports, **scuba diving** is offered by an increasing number of PADI-accredited dive centres and schools, some at the beach hotels, others in Stone Town.

◄ Children on the beach, Jambiani

Unguja's sister island of **Pemba**, 48km to the north, is quite a contrast. Few tourists come here and facilities are limited, while the beaches are less numerous and less accessible than Unguja's – though you're at least likely to have them to yourself. The island's main attraction is its fringing **coral reef**, which offers exhilarating scuba

Fruits

"A patient person eats ripe fruit", say the Swahili. And what a choice. Millennia of trade and contact with other peoples has blessed Zanzibar with an extraordinary variety of delicious and often fragrant fruit – a good thing too, as surprisingly few fruits are actually indigenous, the main exceptions being watermelons and, despite their names, Indian plums and tamarind (Arabic for "Indian fruit").

The **Arabs and Persians** introduced pomegranates, dates and muskmelons. Far more industrious in their fruity endeavours were early traders from **southeastern Asia**, particularly Indonesia and Malaysia, who brought with them coconuts, sugarcane, giant pungent jackfruits and breadfruits (both originally Polynesian), bananas, mangos, Malay apples, orange-like mangosteens, and ineffably delicate durians, lychees and related rambutans. Either directly or via other traders, **China** contributed a welter of citrus fruits including diminutive kumquats, as well as loquats (rose apples) and mulberries, originally cultivated as a food source for silk worms. The **European** influence is represented by "exotics" such as grapes and apples, and by **New World** species introduced by the Portuguese, among them guavas and papaya, pineapples, passion fruit and custard apples (sweet sops and sour sops).

So, *karibu matunda* – enjoy the fruit!

Hey, Mzungu!

Mzungu (plural *wazungu*) is a word white travellers will hear all over East Africa – children, especially, take great delight in chanting the word whenever you're around. Strictly speaking, a *mzungu* is a white European, although Afro-Europeans and Afro-Americans need not feel left out, being known as *mzungu mwafrikano* (Asian travellers will have to content themselves with *mchina*, and Indians *mhindi*). The term was first reported by nineteenth-century missionaries and explorers, who flattered themselves to think that it meant wondrous, clever or extraordinary.

The real meaning of the word is perhaps more appropriate. Stemming from *zungua*, it means to go round, to turn, to wander, to travel, or just to be tiresome. However weary you may grow of the *mzungu* tag, you should at least be grateful that the Maasai word for Europeans didn't stick: inspired by the sight of the trouser-wearing invaders from the north, they christened the newcomers *iloridaa enjekat* – those who confine their farts.

diving and snorkelling, especially at **Misali Island**, whilst terrestrial attractions include the pristine **Ngezi Forest**, and a host of medieval **ruins** dating from the height of the Shirazi trading civilization.

When to go

Zanzibar's **climate** is typically tropical, making for hot and humid weather most of the year. There are two rainy seasons. The long *masika* rains (dubbed the "Green Season" by some hoteliers) fall from March to May, and are especially heavy from April onwards, when some of the larger hotels close. The lighter and shorter *mvuli* rains

▲ Women farming seaweed, Bwejuu

▲ TV Corner, Stone Town

come between October and early December. The end of both rainy seasons is heralded by blustery winds. The rest of the year is hot and dry, with temperatures gradually increasing from July until the onset of the short rains. **Ramadan** (see p.000 for dates) is not the best time to visit, as most restaurants are closed by day and the atmosphere, especially in Stone Town, is not at its brightest.

Zanzibar's average temperatures, hours of sunshine and rainfall

	Temperature (ºC/ºF)	Sunshine (hours per day)	Rainfall (mm/inches)	Rainy days
January	22–32/72–90	8	75/3.0	5–7
February	24–32/75–90	8	60/2.4	5–6
March	25–32/77–90	7	150/5.9	8–12
April	25–30/77–86	5	350/14	11–19
May	23–28/73–82	6	280/11	10–14
June	23–28/73–82	8	55/2.2	3–4
July	22–27/72–81	7	45/1.8	2–6
August	22–28/72–82	8	40/1.6	2–6
September	22–28/72–82	8	50/2.0	3–6
October	22–30/72–86	8	90/3.5	4–7
November	23–31/73–88	8	170/6.7	9–14
December	24–31/75–88	8	145/5.7	8–12

18

things not to miss

Whilst it's possible to see a lot of what Zanzibar has to offer in one trip, it won't leave you much time to indulge in that perennially favourite sport – beach lounging. So, what follows is a selective taste of the country's highlights, arranged in five colour-coded categories. All highlights have a page reference to take you straight into the guide, where you can find out more.

01 **Dhows** Page **186** • The largest lateen-rigged dhows – East Africa's maritime emblems – are gradually giving way to coasters and freighters, but the smaller *mashuas* still provide perfect photo-ops as they sail into view, and messing about on a dhow with a drink or three as the sun sinks beneath the waves is a perfect end to a lazy day's beach lounging.

02 **Misali Island** Page **201** • An idyllic beach, fascinating mangroves, coconut crabs, flying foxes, great snorkelling and exhilarating scuba diving – a trip to Misali Island (where Captain Kidd once buried treasure) is one of Pemba's highlights.

03 **Ngezi Forest** Page **211** • Pemba Island's largest surviving patch of primeval forest, a luxurious tangle of tall hardwoods and vines, scattered here and there with sacred clearings, gives the possibility of seeing flying foxes, owls and monkeys.

04 **Arts and crafts** Page **118** • Some of Aladdin's tales are said to be based on Zanzibar, and Stone Town is an Ali Baba's cave for shopaholics, with plentiful paintings, carvings, fabrics and antiques.

05 Jozani Forest

Page **147** • Ideal for escaping the tropical heat, this soothingly cool and shady primeval forest contains troops of endangered red colobus monkeys, and has adjacent mangroves which are well worth a visit, too.

ICE CREAM

06 Stone Town

Page **81** • Africa meets the Orient in the labyrinthine heart of one of Africa's most atmospheric towns, its narrow alleyways, mansions and palaces positively oozing historical decadence.

07 Forodhani Gardens

Page **110** • Town's nightly waterfront street food market offers a lavish spread of freshly cooked seafood that would spoil a sultan, all wrapped up in a magical twilight atmosphere.

08 **Snorkelling and scuba diving** See *Zanzibar and the Sea* colour section •
Lapped by warm equatorial currents and blessed with a plethora of coral reefs, Unguja and Pemba are great for snorkelling and scuba diving, getting you eyeball-to-eyeball with a myriad of weird and wonderful locals: clouds of multicoloured fish, lobsters, and perhaps even dolphins, turtles or sharks.

09 **Music festivals** Page **117** • Stone Town's two annual music festivals are reasons in themselves to visit. You can hear anything from formal Swahili *taarab* and African drum-based *ngomas*, to sacred Sufi chants and contemporary rap and hip-hop from all around East Africa.

10 **Spice tours** Page **129** • See, touch, smell and taste Zanzibar's famous spices on a farm, followed by a slap-up lunch – a veritable feast for the senses.

11 **Beaches** Pages **157, 177** & **188** • Broad powder-soft white sandy beaches, warm turquoise water, wavering coconut palm trees – Zanzibar's beaches are close to picture postcard paradise. Among the best are at Jambiani, Pongwe and Kendwa.

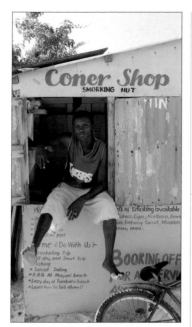

13 **Dolphin tours** Page **150** • In the protected waters of Menai Bay Conservation Area, Kizimkazi's fishermen have created a veritable dolphin-spotting industry.

14 **Seafood** Page **246** • With fresh ingredients often within swimming distance, eating out on Unguja is a real pleasure, with many restaurants excelling in the art of Swahili cuisine and blending the best of African and Arabian with Indian and Far Eastern traditions.

12 **Nungwi** Page **181** • Zanzibar's liveliest beach destination, and among the more personal too, with lots of seafood restaurants (great views), bars, and heaps of activities, including a natural tidal aquarium filled with turtles.

15 **Mwaka Kogwa festival** Page **154** • Every July, the sleepy fishing community of Makunduchi gets together for a colourful four-day shindig in celebration of the Persian New Year; a weird and definitely colourful way of getting rid of the old one.

16 Giant tortoises

Page **133** • Changuu Island (or Prison Island) is home to a colony of giant Aldabran tortoises, cantankerous relatives of the dinosaurs, some of whom live to over one hundred years old. Pet them if you wish, but watch out for those beaks ...

17 Slave cells, Stone Town

Page 104 & *Zanzibar and the Slave Trade* colour section • The claustrophobic underground cells where slaves were kept before market day provide a harrowing reminder of the inhumanity of the slave trade, the East African version of which was controlled by the Zanzibari sultanate.

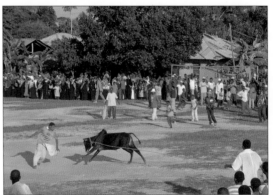

18 Bull-fighting

Page **206** • The most entertaining reminder of two centuries of Portuguese rule, and with no violence other than that inflicted on the hapless bullfighters. The time: September to February. The place: southern Pemba.

Basics

Basics

Getting there

Most tourists visit Zanzibar as part of a package holiday, often following on from a wildlife safari on the Tanzanian mainland or in Kenya. Arranging things yourself gives you more freedom, and is cheaper if you're on a modest budget. There are no direct flights to Zanzibar other than from mainland Tanzania and Kenya, though most international airlines offer through-tickets using local companies for the short hop from the mainland.

Flights to Zanzibar from outside East Africa require at least one stop, usually two or three. The only **direct flights** to Unguja are from Dar es Salaam, Arusha, Kilimanjaro and Tanga, all on the Tanzanian mainland, and from Mombasa and Nairobi in Kenya. For Pemba, the only flights are from Dar es Salaam and Tanga. Most international carriers flying into Tanzania or Kenya can issue **through-tickets** to Zanzibar, but be aware that the short hop is usually in single-propeller planes operated by local companies. If light aircraft give you the heebie-jeebies, opt for Air Tanzania (partnered with South African Airways), who have a Boeing 737, or consider catching one of several daily **ferries** from Dar es Salaam to Stone Town. There are no ferries from Kenya.

If you're looking for a "beach and bush" style vacation in Tanzania and on Zanzibar, **package holidays** are recommended, as they avoid the awkward and time-consuming process of piecing together the various practicalities required of wildlife safaris, but don't offer all that much more for Zanzibar other than booking hotels and scuba diving – something you could easily do yourself. That said, if you're planning to stay in upmarket hotels, a tour operator might get you discounts that would not be available were you to book directly. Most offer set departures, but their main expertise is in **tailor-made trips**. Either customize a sample itinerary, or work out exactly what you want in terms of so many nights here and there, submit the itinerary to several operators and compare the results. **Costs** depend largely on where you stay, and on the style of safari you choose: camping safaris are cheaper than staying in wildlife lodges, which in turn cost less than "mobile tented camp" safaris. Approximate costs for a two-week trip with five days on safari and the rest in Zanzibar, excluding international flights, are at least £700/$1200/€1000/Can$1450/Aus$1600/NZ$1700 at budget level, around £1500/$2500/€2100/Can$3000/Aus$3400/NZ$3600 mid-range, and up to £2400/$4000/€3400/Can$4800/Aus$5400/NZ$5700 upmarket.

Getting there from the UK and Ireland

Coming from the British Isles, Zanzibar is best approached via Dar es Salaam or Nairobi. Quickest is **British Airways**, daily from London Heathrow to Dar, with connections from other UK airports and Ireland. **KLM**'s daily flight from Amsterdam to Dar goes via Kilimanjaro in northern Tanzania,

Plane tickets

Before **buying a plane ticket**, find out how easy it will be to change your flight dates, and what refund you'll get if you need to cancel. **Fares** for July, August and December are the most expensive; the best prices are usually obtained well in advance, meaning six or even eleven months before travel. Shop around: the cost of the exact same seat will vary between agents. **Discount flight agents**, the majority of them online, generally have the best prices but their tickets may be non-refundable and non-changeable. Some agents offer reductions for **students and under-26s**.

and has good connections from the rest of Europe, but isn't too handy for Zanzibar as it arrives in Dar at night. Better is KLM's daily flight to Nairobi, with the onward leg to Zanzibar operated by Precisionair/Kenya Airways. Despite the longer distance involved, flying with **South African Airways** from London via Johannesburg doesn't take all that much longer; they use Air Tanzania for the flight from Dar es Salaam. Other airlines may be cheaper but take considerably longer: **Ethiopian** (via Addis Ababa, with a stopover up to 30hr); **Emirates** (via Dubai – long flights but comfortable planes); and **EgyptAir** (weekly to Dar via Cairo; arrange the onward flight to Zanzibar yourself – see p.76 for contacts).

Flight times from London to Dar are eight to nine hours direct, eleven to fifteen hours for most one-stop flights, and up to twenty hours for most two-stop routings. To this, add a two- to three-hour wait for the connection to Zanzibar, and twenty minutes for the flight itself. In low season (roughly September–November and April–June), the airlines can come up with great deals, with return through-tickets to Zanzibar costing under £500 (€900 from Ireland), but count on around £1100 or €1900 in high season (roughly July–August, December–January and possibly on to March). The most competitive airlines tend to be Emirates, EgyptAir and KLM (from London City, not Heathrow).

Airlines

British Airways UK ☎0870/850 9850, Republic of Ireland ☎1800/626 747, ⊛www.ba.com.
EgyptAir UK ☎020/7734 2343, ⊛www.egyptair.com.eg.
Emirates UK ☎0870/243 2222, ⊛www.emirates.com.
Ethiopian Airlines UK ☎020/8987 7000, ⊛www.flyethiopian.com.
Kenya Airways UK ☎01784/888 222, ⊛www.kenya-airways.com.
KLM UK ☎0870/507 4074, Republic of Ireland ☎1850/747 400, ⊛www.klm.com.
South African Airways UK ☎0870/747 1111, ⊛www.flysaa.com.

Flight and travel agents

Apex Travel Republic of Ireland ☎01/241 8000, ⊛www.apextravel.ie.

Co-op Travel Care UK ☎0870/112 0085, ⊛www.travelcareonline.com.
Joe Walsh Tours Republic of Ireland ☎01/676 0991, ⊛www.joewalshtours.ie.
McCarthys Travel Republic of Ireland ☎021/427 0127, ⊛www.mccarthystravel.ie.
North South Travel UK ☎012/608 291, ⊛www.northsouthtravel.co.uk. Friendly and competitive; profits support projects in the developing world, especially the promotion of sustainable tourism.
Rosetta Travel Northern Ireland ☎028/9064 4996, ⊛www.rosettatravel.com.
STA Travel UK ☎0870/1600 599, ⊛www.statravel.co.uk. Worldwide specialists in low-cost flights and tours for students and under-26s; other customers are welcome. Several branches.
Top Deck UK ☎020/8879 6789, ⊛www.topdecktravel.co.uk.
Trailfinders UK ☎0845/0585 858, ⊛www.trailfinders.co.uk; Republic of Ireland ☎01/677 7888, ⊛www.trailfinders.ie.
usit NOW Republic of Ireland ☎01/602 1600, Northern Ireland ☎028/9032 7111; ⊛www.usitnow.ie. Student and youth specialists with seven branches across Ireland; good fares on KLM.
⊛**www.ebookers.com** Low fares from the UK and Europe.
⊛**www.expedia.co.uk** Discount and standard fares.
⊛**www.gohop.com** From Ireland.
⊛**www.kelkoo.co.uk** Price comparisons.
⊛**www.opodo.co.uk** Low fares on BA and KLM.
⊛**www.travelbag.co.uk** Efficient site with alluring deals and masses of search results.

Specialist tour operators

Abercrombie and Kent UK ☎0845/070 0610, ⊛www.abercrombiekent.co.uk. Branch of the upmarket US company; see p.22.
Africa Travel Resource UK ☎01306/880 770, ⊛www.africatravelresource.com. Leading upscale company for Tanzania and Zanzibar trips, with a superlative website.
Baobab Travel UK ☎0870/382 5003, ⊛www.baobabtravel.com. Responsible, ethical and affordable, favouring locally owned ground operators. Cultural tourism features strongly.
Encounter Zanzibar UK ☎020/7514 5836, ⊛www.encounterzanzibar.com. This lot are nuts about Zanzibar: their detailed website, with commendably impartial hotel reviews, stands as proof.
Gane & Marshall UK ☎020/8441 9592, ⊛www.ganeandmarshall.co.uk. Upmarket small-group tours using well-chosen ground operators, whether on Kilimanjaro or walking in the Rift Valley.

Limerick County Library

IntoAfrica UK ☏0114/255 5610, ⓦwww
.intoafrica.co.uk. With none of the neo-colonial
trimmings vaunted by many others, this fair-trade
company is one of few to run their own Tanzanian
operations. Lots of hiking and community-based tourism, and very affordable.

Kuoni UK ☏01306/747 731, ⓦwww.kuoni
.co.uk. Long-established, well-regarded long-haul
specialists with several Zanzibar-only options, or
combinations with Kenya and mainland Tanzania.

Simply Tanzania Tour Company UK ☏020/8986
0615, ⓦwww.simplytanzania.co.uk. Ethically sound
specialists for less-travelled areas, including southern
Tanzania, and visits to cultural tourism programmes.

Tanzania Odyssey UK ☏020/7471 8780, ⓦwww
.tanzaniaodyssey.com. Tanzanian experts offering
good tailor-made trips at cost; their profit lies in
agents' commissions.

Zanzibar Travel UK ☏01242/222 027, ⓦwww
.zanzibartravel.co.uk. Does what it says on the
can, plus safaris and Kilimanjaro climbs. Budget to
mid-range.

Getting there from the US and Canada

There are **no direct flights** from North
America to East Africa, so change in
Europe or South Africa, and again in Tanza-
nia or Kenya. Taking under twenty hours is

Northwestern/KLM from JFK to Nairobi
via Amsterdam, from where there's a good
connection on Precisionair/Kenya Airways
to Zanzibar. Journey times are similar for
KLM's flight to Dar es Salaam, but it arrives
at night so isn't particularly helpful for
Zanzibar. Also taking under twenty hours
is **British Airways** via London to Dar, from
where there are good onward connections.
Taking around thirty hours are **Ethiopian
Airlines** via Addis Ababa (also from Toronto
at Christmas), **EgyptAir** (via Cairo), and
South African Airways (via Johannesburg), which code-shares with Air Tanzania
for Zanzibar.

High-season **return fares** from JFK to
Dar cost $2000 to $5000 depending on
season and availability. If you're late in booking and prices are high, you could make an
overall saving by **flying to London**, stop-
ping over for a day or two, and picking up
a last-minute (or Internet) flight from there.
New York–London returns can be had for
under $500: try Virgin Atlantic. Coming from
Canada, single-ticket fares can be hugely
inflated compared to buying two separate
tickets: one from Canada to Boston or JFK,
the other from there.

Airlines

British Airways Canada and the US ☏1-800/AIR-
WAYS, ⓦwww.ba.com.
EgyptAir US ☏1-800/334-6787 or 1-212/315-
0900, Canada ☏1-416/960-0009, ⓦwww
.egyptair.com.eg.
Ethiopian Airlines US ☏1-800/445-2733 or 1-
212/867-0095, ⓦwww.flyethiopian.com.
Kenya Airways Canada and the US ☏1-866/
KENYA-AIR, ⓦwww.kenya-airways.com.
Northwest/KLM Canada and the US ☏1-
800/447-4747, ⓦwww.nwa.com, ⓦwww.klm.com.
South African Airways Canada ☏1-800/387-
4629, US ☏1-800/722-9675, ⓦwww.flysaa.com
Virgin Atlantic Canada and the US ☏1-800/862-
8621, ⓦwww.virgin-atlantic.com.

Flight and travel agents

Air Brokers International ☏1-800/883-3273,
ⓦwww.airbrokers.com.
Flightcentre US ☏1-866/WORLD 51, ⓦwww
.flightcentre.us; Canada ☏1-877/478-8747,
ⓦwww.flightcentre.ca.
STA Travel US ☏1-800/329-9537, Canada

☎ 1-888/427-5639, ⊛ www.statravel.com. World-wide specialists in independent travel.
Travel Cuts US ☎ 1-800/592-CUTS, Canada ☎ 1-888/246-9762, ⊛ www.travelcuts.com. Popular, long-established student-travel organization, with worldwide offers.
Travelosophy US ☎ 1-800/332-2687 or 1-248/557-7775, ⊛ www.itravelosophy.com.
⊛ **www.expedia.com & expedia.ca** Discount and standard fares.
⊛ **www.orbitz.com** Returning lots of relevant results with better connections and prices than most, and great customer service.
⊛ **www.qixo.com** US-only: a rather lazy search engine (only KLM/Northwest for Tanzania), but competitive fares.
⊛ **www.skyauction.com** Auctions tickets and travel packages using a "second bid" scheme, like eBay.

Specialist tour operators

See also the reviews for UK-based companies (p.20), most of whom accept overseas bookings.
Abercrombie & Kent US ☎ 1-800/554-7016 or 1-630/954-2944, ⊛ www.abercrombiekent .com. Major long-haul upmarket operator offering a comprehensive and flexible Tanzanian programme operated through local subsidiaries. Group sizes can be large however.
African Horizons US ☎ 1-888/212-6752, ⊛ www .africanhorizons.com. Mid-range to bush luxury, including walking options; particularly strong on Tanzania's less well-known wildlife parks.
Africa Travel Resource US ☎ 1-866/672-3274 or 1-831/338-2383, ⊛ www.africatravelresource .com. Sales office for the UK company; see p.20.
Bestway Tours & Safaris Canada ☎ 1-800/663-0844 or 1-604/264-7278, ⊛ www.bestway.com. Small-group cultural forays, better value and more off-beat than most. Also covers family travel, voluntary working holidays, and other Indian Ocean islands.
Born Free Safaris US ☎ 1-800/372-3274 or 1-720/524-9683, ⊛ www.bornfreesafaris.com. Covering Tanzania since the 1970s, this lot offer camping to ultimate bush luxury for both group departures or private tours. Excellent online safari planner.
Good Earth Tours US ☎ 1-877/265-9003 or 1-813/615-9570, ⊛ www.goodearthtours.com. Tanzanian and Kenyan tailor-made specialists, slow in replying to emails but good at delivering the goods. Competitive prices.

Getting there from Australia and New Zealand

There are **no direct flights** from the Antipodes to Kenya or Tanzania – all require stopovers in Asia, southern Africa or the Middle East. From Australia, the best deals are on **Egypt-Air** via Bangkok and Cairo. More direct but more expensive would be to go via Harare with **Air Zimbabwe** (A$2500–3000/NZ$2500–3500) or to Johannesburg on **Qantas** (A$2500–4000) and change there. None of these airlines provide through-tickets for Zanzibar, so unless you prebook the connection to Zanzibar (see p.76 for local airline contacts), aim to get to Nairobi or Dar es Salaam early in the day to give you time to buy a ticket and avoid staying over.

Airlines

Air New Zealand Australia ☎ 132 476, New Zealand ☎ 0800/247 764, ⊛ www.airnewzealand .com.
Air Zimbabwe Australia ☎ 02/8272 7822, New Zealand ☎ 09/309 8094, ⊛ www.airzimbabwe .com.
British Airways Australia ☎ 1300/767 177, New Zealand ☎ 09/966 9777, ⊛ www.ba.com.
EgyptAir Australia ☎ 02/9241 5696, ⊛ www .egyptair.com.eg.
KLM/Northwest Australia ☎ 1300/303 747, New Zealand ☎ 09/302 1792, ⊛ www.klm.com, ⊛ www.nwa.com.
Qantas Australia ☎ 131 313, New Zealand ☎ 09/357 8900 or 0800/808 767, ⊛ www.qantas .com.
South African Airways Australia ☎ 1800/221 699, New Zealand ☎ 09/977 2237, ⊛ www.flysaa .com.

Flight and travel agents

Holiday Shoppe New Zealand ☎ 0800/808 480, ⊛ www.holidayshoppe.co.nz. General travel agent.
OTC Australia ☎ 1300/855 118, ⊛ www.otctravel .com.au. Online flight and holiday agent.
STA Travel Australia ☎ 1300/360 960, ⊛ www .statravel.com.au; New Zealand ☎ 09/309 9273, ⊛ www.statravel.co.nz. Worldwide specialists in independent travel.
Trailfinders Australia 1300/780 212, ⊛ www .trailfinders.com.au. Well-informed efficient agents for independent travellers.

@ www.travel.co.nz Comprehensive site for flights.
@ www.travel.com.au The same from Oz.

Specialist tour operators

See also the reviews for companies based in the UK (p.20) and in North America (p.22), most of whom accept overseas bookings.
Abercrombie & Kent Australia ☏ 02/9241 3213, New Zealand ☏ 0800/441 638, @ www .abercrombiekent.com.au. Branch of the upmarket US company; see p.22.
The Adventure Travel Company New Zealand ☏ 09/379 9755, @ www.adventuretravel.co.nz. Agents for some of the specialist tour companies reviewed here and many more.
African Wildlife Safaris Australia

☏ 1300/363 302 or 03/9696 2899, @ www .africanwildlifesafaris.com.au. Specialists in tailor-made safaris to southern and eastern Africa, from budget to luxury.
The Classic Safari Company Australia
☏ 1300/130 218 or 02/9327 0666, @ www .classicsafaricompany.com.au. Luxury, tailor-made safaris to southern and eastern Africa.
Gecko's Holidays Australia ☏ 02/9290 2770, @ www.geckos.com.au. Wide range of trips in all price ranges.
World Expeditions Australia ☏ 1300/720 000, @ www.worldexpeditions.com.au; New Zealand ☏ 0800/350 354, @ www.worldexpeditions.co.nz. A reasonable choice of Tanzanian and Kenyan options to tack on to Zanzibar, including a "twin peaks" attempt on Kilimanjaro and Mount Kenya.

Red tape and visas

Most foreign nationals require a Tanzanian visa to enter Zanzibar. Ensure your passport is valid for six months beyond the end of your stay. Yellow fever vaccination certificates are no longer required, though it's probably best to get the jab anyway, especially if you'll be travelling elsewhere in Africa. However, rules regarding visas have a habit of changing, so check requirements with a Tanzanian diplomatic mission beforehand.

Zanzibar's ill-defined semi-autonomous status means that at times of political turmoil (usually around election times; the next are due in 2010), petty official pride may oblige you to go through immigration formalities twice, once on the mainland, and again when arriving in Zanzibar. Be patient and polite and you'll have no trouble.

Visas

Single-entry **three-month visas** can be bought beforehand from any Tanzanian embassy, consulate or high commission, or on arrival at Tanzania's land borders and international airports. They cost $50 (or £50 for Britons if bought in London). If buying on arrival, it's best to pay in dollars cash,

as euro and sterling prices are significantly higher. It's helpful to have a pen to hand. There are two forms: one for the visa, the other for immigration.

Tanzanian embassies, consulates and high commissions

Tanzanian **diplomatic missions** are listed on @ www.tanzania.go.tz/embassies.htm. Opening hours for **visa applications** are generally Monday–Friday 10am–12.30pm (closed on Tanzanian public holidays; see p.45). You'll need two passport-size photos and – sometimes – an air ticket out of the country. Processing takes 24 hours, although same-day processing can be obtained for a small additional fee.

Australia See ⊛www.tanzaniaconsul.com for the list of Honorary Consuls.
Canada High Commission, 50 Range Rd, Ottawa, ON K1N 8J4 ☎1-613/232-1509, ✉tzottawa@synapse.net.
Ireland – see UK.
Italy Embassy, Via Cesare Beccaria 88, 00196 Rome ☎06/3600 5234, ⊛www.tanzania-gov.it.
Kenya High Commission, 9th Floor, Reinsurance Plaza, Taifa Rd, PO Box 47790, Nairobi ☎02/331056–7, ✉tanzania@africaonline.co.ke.
New Zealand – no representation.
South Africa High Commission, 822 George Ave, PO Box 56572, Arcadia, Pretoria 0007 ☎012/342 4371, ⊛www.tanzania.org.za.
UK High Commission, 43 Hertford St, London W1Y 8DB ☎020/7499 8951, ⊛www.tanzania-online .gov.uk.

US 2139 R St NW, Washington DC 20008 ☎1-202/939-6125, ⊛www.tanzaniaembassy -us.org.

Customs and duty-free

The **duty-free allowance** for visitors entering Tanzania is one litre of spirits, 200 cigarettes, 50 cigars or 250g of tobacco and 250ml of perfume. Unless you're carrying a mountain of gear, items for personal use, like binoculars, cameras and laptops, pose no problem with **customs**. At worst you'll just have to sign (and pay) a bond which is redeemed when you leave the country with all your stuff. If you're taking items as presents, however, you're likely to have to pay duty if you declare them.

Information, maps and websites

Tanzania's embassies have a few government-produced brochures to hand out, but aren't much help otherwise. Neither the Tanzanian nor the Zanzibari tourist boards have overseas offices.

Maps

The most accurate map of **Zanzibar** is harms-ic-verlag's *Zanzibar* (ISBN 3-9274-6818-5, 2nd edition 2004), which shows Unguja at 1:100,000 and has insets of Pemba and Stone Town. Prettier but not as detailed is the hand-painted 1:156,000 *Zanzibar & Stone Town* map by Giovanni Tombazzi (Maco Editions; no ISBN), which has two insets for Stone Town (1:35,000 and 1:3500), and useful paintings of local plants and fishes. **Zanzibar's dive sites** are nicely presented on Giovanni Tombazzi's *Zanzibar at Sea* (also Maco Editions). The best general **maps of Tanzania** are Reise Know-How's waterproof *Tanzania* (1:1,200,000; ISBN 3-8317-7126-X, 2004), and – almost as detailed and just as accurate – harms-ic-verlag's *Tanzania, Rwanda and Burundi* (1:1,400,000; ISBN 3-9274-6826-6, 2nd edition 2004).

Buying maps

Giovanni Tombazzi's maps are sold in bookstores in Stone Town, Dar es Salaam and Arusha, but can be hard to find outside Tanzania – the following are more likely to stock them. You should be able to buy the other maps through your local bookstore using their ISBN numbers.
110 North Latitude ⊛www.110northlatitude .com: 4915-H High Point Rd, Greensboro NC, USA ☎336/369-4171. Awkward search engine; search by map title.
harms-ic-verlag ⊛www.harms-ic- verlag.de: Industriestrasse 3, Kandel, Germany ☎07275/957440. Sells its own output.
Map World (Australia) ⊛www.mapworld.net .au: Jolimont Centre, 65 Northbourne Ave, Canberra ☎02/6230 4097; 136 Willoughby Rd, Crows Nest, Sydney ☎02/9966 5770; 280 Pitt St, Sydney ☎02/9261 3601; 900 Hay St, Perth ☎08/9322 5733. No online shopping.

Map World (New Zealand) ⓦ www.mapworld
.co.nz 173 Gloucester St, Christchurch
ⓣ 0800/627967. No online shopping.
NetStoreUSA ⓦ http://maps.netstoreusa.com: US
& Canada ⓕ 1-800/329-6736 or 1-602/532-7038;
UK ⓕ 020/7681 1463; Australia ⓕ 02/9475-0047.
International orders accepted.
Omni Resources ⓦ www.omnimap.com; 1004
South Mebane St, Burlington NC, USA
ⓣ 1-336/227-8300. Comprehensive Tanzania
coverage; international orders accepted.
Stanfords ⓦ www.stanfords.co.uk: 12–14 Long
Acre, London ⓣ 020/7836 1321; 39 Spring
Gardens, Manchester ⓣ 0161/831 0250; 29 Corn
St, Bristol ⓣ 0117/929 9966. Stocks all the maps
we've reviewed.

Zanzibar online

Governmental travel advisories

Australian Department of Foreign Affairs
ⓦ www.dfat.gov.au.
British Foreign & Commonwealth Office
ⓦ www.fco.gov.uk.
Canadian Department of Foreign Affairs
ⓦ www.dfait-maeci.gc.ca.
Irish Department of Foreign Affairs
ⓦ www.irlgov.ie/iveagh.
New Zealand Ministry of Foreign Affairs
ⓦ www.mft.govt.nz.
US State Department ⓦ www.state.gov/travel.

News and current affairs and magazines

Africa Confidential ⓦ www.africa-confidential
.com. Online presence of the highly respected
broadsheet for African current affairs; it doesn't
beat about the bush when covering corruption and
other political shenanigans, and is consequentially
usually banned in its paper form. A few articles
are posted online, together with summaries of the
main news.
allAfrica.com ⓦ http://allafrica.com/tanzania.
Comprehensive and up-to-date news portal for the
continent, collating articles from both mainstream
and not so common sources, including UN agencies.
Most articles are available on-site, and the enormous
archive is fully searchable.
Amnesty International ⓦ www.web.amnesty.org
/library. What the government won't tell you, and so
especially useful for the background to Zanzibar's
political woes.
BBC News ⓦ http://news.bbc.co.uk/1/hi/world
/africa. Reliable daily coverage of Africa, with a useful
search engine for older stories.

The East African ⓦ www.nationaudio.com
/eastafrican. The main articles and features from the
week's issue of one of Africa's leading newspapers,
plus an archive going back to 2001.
IPP Media ⓦ www.ippmedia.com. Home of Tanzania's *Guardian* newspaper and the Kiswahili *Nipashe.*
The Norwegian Council for Africa ⓦ www
.afrika.no. Brief summaries of the day's news with
links to full versions, a searchable archive, and free
email news service providing a more or less daily
selection of articles from papers around the continent.
There are also four thousand good-quality African
weblinks covering most subjects.

Tourism

Internet addresses for recommended tour
companies are given in the "Getting there"
section at the start of this chapter. Don't
necessarily believe recommendations on
interactive websites or newsgroups.
Africa Travel Resource ⓦ www
.africatravelresource.com. Travel "outfitter" offering
not just bookings and holidays but a staggeringly
comprehensive and mostly accurate website for most
of Tanzania, with detailed and copiously illustrated
accommodation reviews plus a good deal of useful
background reading too.
Commission for Tourism ⓦ www
.zanzibartourism.net. Zanzibar's official tourism
portal, with plenty of searchable listings (not all up to
date), information on upcoming events, photos, and
visa information.
rec.travel.africa The best newsgroup for advice
from fellow travellers and self-appointed experts.
Tanzania Tourist Board ⓦ www
.tanzaniatouristboard.com. Comprehensive travel
showcase covering all the main destinations and
towns, lists of licensed safari operators and many
hotels, but not much on culture – at least for now.
Zanzibar.net ⓦ www.zanzibar.net. A good portal
dedicated to Zanzibar with loads of links, sections
on tourism and the arts, and some books available
through Amazon.

Music and culture

Dhow Countries Music Academy ⓦ www
.zanzibarmusic.org. Zanzibar's musical pulse, this
doesn't yet have an awful lot online, but does briefly
cover the Isles' main sonic styles, and provides
information on courses and the annual Sauti za
Busara festival.
The Gutenberg Project ⓦ www.gutenberg
.org/catalog/world/search. Over sixteen thousand
freely downloadable public domain books. Type
"Zanzibar" in the "Full Text" field of the advanced search

to dig up works by explorers Livingstone, Baker, Burton, Speke and Stanley, and books on Islam and history.

The Kamusi Project ⓦ www.yale.edu/swahili. An immense online English–Kiswahili and Kiswahili–English dictionary, also downloadable, plus lots of language resources and excellent links covering East and Central Africa.

Rhythms of the Continent ⓦ www.bbc.co.uk /worldservice/africa/features/rhythms. A short and limited if well done and visually attractive introduction to African music from the BBC World Service, complete with sound clips. East Africa is represented by a good page on *taarab*.

Swahili Language and Culture ⓦ www.glcom .com/hassan. A modest selection of linguistic resources, including kanga proverbs, poems, and short lessons.

Swahilionline.com ⓦ www.swahilionline.com. Modest but growing site related to Swahili culture: music (with some Real Audio clips), language, history and cuisine being among its themes.

ZIFF ⓦ www.ziff.or.tz. Digital home of the fantastic Festival of the Dhow Countries, formerly the Zanzibar International Film Festival.

Insurance

It's essential to take out an insurance policy before travelling to cover against theft, loss, illness or injury. Before paying for a new policy, however, check whether you're already covered: some all-risks home insurance policies may cover your possessions when overseas, and many private medical schemes include cover when abroad. In Canada, provincial health plans usually provide partial cover for medical mishaps overseas, while holders of official student/ teacher/youth cards in Canada and the US are entitled to limited accident coverage and hospital in-patient benefits. Students will often find that their student health coverage extends during the vacations and for one term beyond the date of last enrolment.

After checking out the possibilities above, you might want to contact a specialist travel insurance company, or consider the travel insurance deal Rough Guides offer (see box below). A typical policy usually provides cover for the loss of baggage, tickets and – up to a certain limit – cash or cheques, as well as cancellation or curtailment of your journey. Most of them exclude so-called **dangerous sports** unless an extra premium is paid: in Tanzania this can mean bush walks, Kili climbs and scubadiving, though probably not standard game-drive safaris. Many policies can be chopped and changed

---

Rough Guides Travel Insurance

Rough Guides has teamed up with Columbus Direct to offer you **travel insurance** that can be tailored to suit your needs. Readers can choose from many different travel insurance products, including a low-cost **backpacker** option for long stays, a typical **holiday package** option, and annual **multi-trip** policies for those who travel regularly. Rough Guides travel insurance is available to the residents of 36 different countries with different language options to choose from via our website – ⓦ www .roughguidesinsurance.com. Alternatively, UK residents should call ☏ 0800/083 9507; US citizens ☏ 1-800/749-4922; Australians ☏ 1-300/669 999; and all other nationalities ☏ +44 870/890 2843.

to exclude coverage you don't need. If you take **medical coverage**, check whether benefits will be paid as treatment proceeds or only after you return home, and whether there's a 24-hour medical emergency number (note that you can't make reverse/collect calls from Tanzania). When securing **baggage cover**, ensure the per-article limit – typically under £500/$750 and sometimes as little as £250/$400 – will cover your most valuable possession. If you need to make a claim, keep receipts for medicines and medical treatment; in the event you have anything stolen, you must obtain an official statement from the police.

Health

As long as you protect yourself against malaria, Zanzibar isn't particularly dangerous healthwise and, with sensible precautions, you're unlikely to suffer anything more than minor tummy trouble – just as well, given the paucity of well-equipped hospitals and clinics (if you can, it's best to get treated in Dar es Salaam or back home). For further information, the *Rough Guide to Travel Health* offers a comprehensive and practical account of the health problems which travellers face worldwide.

Medical resources for travellers

Websites

ⓦ **www.cdc.gov/travel** Precautions, diseases and preventive measures by region, from the US government's Center for Disease Control.

ⓦ **www.fitfortravel.scot.nhs.uk** From the Scottish NHS – travel-related diseases and how to avoid them.

ⓦ **www.istm.org** The International Society of Travel Medicine lists clinics, publishes outbreak warnings, suggests inoculations and precautions, and provides other background information.

ⓦ **www.tmvc.com.au** Lists all travellers' medical and vaccination centres in Australia and New Zealand, plus general information on travel health.

ⓦ **www.travelvax.net** Everything you probably didn't want to know about diseases and vaccines.

ⓦ **www.tripprep.com** Comprehensive online database of necessary vaccinations for most countries, plus destination and medical service provider information.

ⓦ **http://health.yahoo.com** Information and advice on specific diseases and conditions, drugs and herbal remedies.

In the UK and Ireland

British Airways Travel Clinics ⓦ www.britishairways.com/travel/healthclinintro/public/en_gb: 213 Piccadilly, London W1J 9HQ (℡0845/600 2236; walk-ins Mon–Fri 9.30am–5.30pm, Sat 10am–3.30pm); 101 Cheapside, London EC2V 6DT (℡0845/600 2236; by appointment, Mon–Fri 9am–4.30pm). Vaccinations and travel health-care products.

Glasgow Travel Clinic 3rd floor, 90 Mitchell St, Glasgow G1 3NQ ℡0141/221 4224. Advice and vaccinations; walk-in clinics Wed–Fri 10am–6pm, otherwise by appointment .

Hospital for Tropical Diseases Travel Clinic 2nd floor, Mortimer Market Centre, off Capper St, London WC1E 6AU ℡020/7388 9600, ⓦ www.masta.org. Mon–Fri 9am–5pm by appointment only; consultations £15, waived if you have your injections here.

Liverpool School of Tropical Medicine Pembroke Place, Liverpool L3 5QA ℡0151/708 9393, ⓦ www.liv.ac.uk/lstm. Walk-in Mon–Fri 9am–noon, otherwise appointments .

Nomad Travel Stores and Medical Centres ⓦ www.nomadtravel.co.uk: 3–4 Wellington Terrace, Turnpike Lane, London N8 0PX ℡020/8889 7014; 40 Bernard St, Russell Square, London

WC1N 1LJ ☏020/7833 4114; Terminal House, 52 Grosvenor Gardens, London SW1W 0AG ☏0207/823 5823; 43 Queens Rd, Clifton, Bristol BS8 1QH ☏0117/922 6567. Vaccinations, medication and equipment.

Travel Health Centre Department of International Health and Tropical Medicine, Royal College of Surgeons, Mercers Medical Centre, Stephen's St Lower, Dublin 2 ☏01/402 2337, ⊛www.mwhb.ie. Pre-trip advice and inoculations.

Travel Medicine Services 16 College St, Belfast BT1 6BT ☏028/9031 5220. Pre-trip medical advice and help afterwards.

Tropical Medical Bureau Grafton Buildings, 34 Grafton St, Dublin 2 ☏01/671 9200, plus thirteen other locations in Ireland; call ☏1850/487 674 or visit ⊛http://tmb.exodus.ie for details. Advice and vaccinations.

In the US and Canada

Canadian Society for International Health 1 Nicholas St, Suite 1105, Ottawa, ON K1N 7B7 ☏1-613/241-5785, ⊛www.csih.org. Distributes a free pamphlet, *Health Information for Canadian Travelers*, containing an extensive list of travel health centres in Canada.

Centers for Disease Control 1600 Clifton Rd NE, Atlanta, GA 30333 ☏1-800/311-3435 or 404/639-3534, ⊛www.cdc.gov. Publishes outbreak warnings, suggested inoculations, precautions and other background information for travellers. Useful website plus International Travelers Hotline on ☏1-877/FYI-TRIP.

International SOS 3600 Horizon Blvd, Suite 300, Trevose, PA 19053, USA 19053-6956 ☏1-800/523-8930, ⊛www.intsos.com. Members receive pre-trip medical referral info, as well as overseas emergency services designed to complement travel insurance coverage.

MedjetAssist ☏1-800/963-3528, ⊛www.medjetassistance.com. Annual membership programme for travellers that, in the event of illness or injury, will fly members home or to the hospital of their choice in a medically equipped and staffed jet.

Travelers Medical Center 31 Washington Square, New York, NY 10011 ☏212/982-1600. A consultation service on immunizations and disease treatment.

In Australia and New Zealand

Travellers' Medical and Vaccination Centres ⊛www.tmvc.com.au: 27–29 Gilbert Place, Adelaide, SA 5000 ☏08/8212 7522; 1/170 Queen St, Auckland ☏09/373 3531; 5/247 Adelaide St, Brisbane, Qld 4000 ☏07/3221

9066; 5/8–10 Hobart Place, Canberra, ACT 2600 ☏02/6257 7156; 270 Sandy Bay Rd, Sandy Bay Hobart 7005 ☏03/6223 7577; 2/393 Little Bourke St, Melbourne, Vic 3000 ☏03/9602 5788; Level 7, Dymocks Bldg, 428 George St, Sydney, NSW 2000 ☏02/9221 7133; Shop 15, Grand Arcade, 14–16 Willis St, Wellington ☏04/473 0991. Vaccination, general travel health advice, and disease alerts; call ☏1-300/658 844 for details of travel clinics countrywide.

Inoculations

Whilst a **yellow fever vaccination certificate** is no longer required for entering Zanzibar (or Tanzania), if you're planning to visit other African countries except Kenya and Uganda, it would be wise to have a jab – and the certificate – just in case. Recommended inoculations are **typhoid, tetanus, polio** (booster), and **hepatitis A**. For the latter, Havrix is commonly prescribed – it lasts for ten years if you have a second, booster jab within six months. The much cheaper gamma-globulin (or immunoglobulin) shots are only effective for a few months, if at all. The series of **rabies** jabs is painful and cases of the disease are extremely rare. Start taking **malaria tablets** before departure (see p.29). In **Britain** your first source of advice and probable supplier of jabs and prescriptions is your GP. Family doctors are often well informed and are likely to charge you a (relatively low) flat fee for routine injections. However, for yellow fever and other exotic shots you'll normally have to visit a specialist clinic.

Malaria

Malaria is endemic in tropical Africa and accounts for at least one in seven deaths among children under five, and is the second-biggest cause of death amongst Tanzanian adults after HIV/AIDS. The disease, which is not infectious, is caused by a parasite carried in the saliva of female *Anopheles* **mosquitoes**, which tend to bite in the evening and at night. Malaria has a variable incubation period of a few days to several weeks, so you can develop the disease some time after you've been bitten. The destruction of red blood cells caused by the *Plasmodium falciparum* strain of malaria prevalent in East Africa can lead to **cerebral malaria** (blocking of the brain capillaries) and is also the cause of **blackwater fever**, in which the urine is stained by excreted blood cells. Malaria can be avoided by taking prophylactics and trying not to get bitten, although no method offers one hundred percent protection.

The disease is most prevalent in low-lying areas and around bodies of still water, meaning along the coast, on Zanzibar, around lakes and in areas of heavy banana cultivation, as the plants hold pools of stagnant water. The risk of infection increases during the rains, peaking in April.

Avoiding bites

You can greatly reduce bites by sleeping under a **mosquito net**, provided by virtually every hotel and guest house in the country, and by burning **mosquito coils**, which are readily available locally. After dark, keep your limbs covered if there are mosquitoes, and consider using mosquito repellent. Most repellents contain **DEET** (diethyltoluamide), a nasty but effective oily substance that gets everywhere and corrodes most artificial materials, especially plastic (it's supposedly harmless to humans). If you're bringing a net, it's worth impregnating it with insecticide as well. If you don't like all this synthetic protection, natural alternatives based on **pyrethrum** flower-extract also work. Other repellents (which do not appear to have been clinically tested) are **citronella** or **lemongrass** oil; be careful: too much and you'll sting your face.

Prophylactics

At home, get started on a course of **anti-malaria tablets**. They're freely available in the US, but require a prescription in the UK. Prophylactic drugs are rarely used by Zanzibaris, though generic versions of all the main drugs are readily available in larger towns without prescription.

The cheapest and most-often prescribed drug is **mefloquine** (tradenames **Lariam** or Mephaquin), which can cause nasty psychological side effects ranging from mild depression and sleep disturbances to full-blown hallucinations and paranoia, together with mild bouts of nausea,

dizziness and rashes. Mefloquine is unsuitable for pregnant women, scuba-divers, people with liver or kidney problems, epileptics, or infants under 3 years. The dose is one 250mg tablet per week, starting two weeks before entering a malarial zone and continuing for at least two weeks after leaving. Test your reaction to the drug by taking it three rather than two weeks before departure. Some travellers report that side effects can be minimized by taking half a tablet at four-day intervals, though this hasn't been clinically tested. In Dar es Salaam or Stone Town, a pack of four tablets costs under $10.

The antibiotic **doxycycline** (tradename Vibramycin) is recommended by some doctors, but the major side effect is that it causes an exaggerated sensitivity to sunlight in both skin and eyes, so use a strong sun cream. It can also cause thrush in women, reduces the effectiveness of contraceptive pills and is unsuitable for children or during pregnancy. Tablets are taken daily, starting one day before arrival and ending four weeks after you leave.

The newcomer to this inglorious pharmacopoeial collection is **Malarone**, a combination of atovaquone and proguanil. The known side effects are benign compared to the competition, and Malarone's newness means that no strains of malaria resistant to it have yet developed. In addition, you only need to start taking the tablets one day before entering a malarial zone, and for just seven days after. The disadvantage is that it costs a fortune, cannot be used by children, and should only be taken for a maximum of four weeks. It's extremely expensive locally, at upwards of $10 a tablet.

If you can't or won't take any of the above, a combination of **chloroquine** (2 weekly) and **proguanil** (2 daily) provides a modest level of protection, although chloroquine on its own is useless. Take the first pills a week before arriving, and the last four weeks after returning. The dose is best taken at the end of the day, and never on an empty stomach, or it will make you feel nauseous. Proguanil, bought locally, is expensive at around $0.50 a tablet; chloroquine is no longer sold in Tanzania.

Medicine bag

There's no need to take a mass of drugs and remedies you'll probably never use, and can buy in local pharmacies in any case. Various items, however, are worth buying in advance, especially on a longer trip.

Alcohol swabs For cleaning wounds and infections.

Antibiotics Given the often disease-specific recommendations for the dozens of antibiotics out there, buying a course beforehand isn't recommended unless you're allergic to penicillin, in which case ask your doctor for a general-purpose "broad spectrum" course.

Antihistamine cream To treat insect bites. Or simply spread toothpaste on the bite. You heard it here first.

Antiseptic cream Avoid metal tubes – they risk springing leaks. Mercurochrome or iodine liquid also work but dye wounds brown or red.

Aspirin Mild pain, inflammation and fever relief. Not to be taken if you're prone to bleed easily, as it thins the blood.

Codeine phosphate Emergency anti-diarrhoeal pill, in some countries only on prescription. Loperamide (tradename Imodium) is also useful.

Iodine tincture or **water-purifying tablets** The chlorine-based tablets make water taste horrific; iodine is quite delicious by comparison, much cheaper, and can also be used to disinfect wounds and keep fungal infections at bay. Some people are allergic to chlorine, others to iodine (especially if seafood gets to you); neither are recommended for long-term use.

Lip-salve/chapstick

Natural alternatives You can avoid some of the other stuff in this list with the following natural products: tea tree oil (fungicide and disinfectant); fresh garlic (natural antibiotic and vampiricide when taken daily); menthol-and-camphor-based essential oil (eg Olbas oil; for colds, relieving headaches, and aromatic pick-me-up); olive oil (for keeping skin trim).

Sticking plaster (fabric rather than synthetic, as it sticks better and also lets the wound breathe), steri-strip wound closures, sterile gauze dressing, micropore tape.

Zinc oxide powder Useful anti-fungal.

Treatment

Common **symptoms** of malaria include waves of flu-like fever, shivering and headaches. Joint pain is also characteristic, and some people also have diarrhoea after the first week. If you think you've caught malaria, get to a doctor as soon as possible and have a **blood test** (note that using mefloquine as a prophylactic can lead to an inconclusive result). Most cures are based on **quinine**, found naturally in plants, but to avoid malarial parasites becoming resistant to it, pure quinine is only ever used in dire emergencies. Instead, there's a welter of competing remedies. **Sulfadoxine pyrimethamine** (SP; sold under various names including Fansidar, Malostat, Falcidin, Crodar, Laridox and Metakelfin), has

long been used by Tanzanians. Severe side effects are rare, but you shouldn't take it if you're allergic to sulphur. An alternative treatment is **amodiaquine hydrochloride** (brand names: Basoquin, CAM-AQ1, Camoquin, Flavoquin, Fluroquine and Miaquin) – take 600mg to start, then 200mg after six hours, and 400mg daily on each of the two following days. Do not administer amodiaquine to children. **Malarone** (four tablets a day for three days) is also effective if you haven't been taking it as a prophylactic. An effective local remedy is a foul-tasting brew made from the quinine-rich leaves of the **muarabaini** tree.

All these treatments will leave you feeling very much under the weather: take plenty of fluids, and keep eating, but avoid milk-based products.

Sexually transmitted diseases

HIV is easily passed between people suffering relatively minor, but ulcerous, sexually transmitted diseases, and the prevalence of these is thought to account for the high incidence of heterosexually transmitted HIV: at least one in ten Tanzanians is infected. Zanzibar's traditionally strict Muslim society means that the rate on Zanzibar may be considerably less (possibly one in a hundred), though both society and government have been extremely reticent in broaching the disease. Female visitors especially should be aware that most holiday fling partners romance for a living. Standard advice is to avoid sexual contact or use **condoms**. A reliable local brand, sold in pharmacies in Stone Town and on the Tanzanian mainland, is Salama.

Water and bugs

Zanzibar suffers regular outbreaks of cholera, and Stone Town's sewerage system – installed a century ago – isn't leak proof, so **tap water** should not be drunk without being sterilized. If you're only staying a short time, it makes sense to be scrupulous, especially as locals happily quaffing tap water will have acquired some resistance to the most common bugs. Bottled purified water is sold everywhere. A cheaper, and environmentally sound alternative (no plastic bottles) is to purify drinking water yourself, either with iodine tincture (four drops per litre), or – giving a vile taste – chlorine tablets. For longer stays, **re-educate your stomach** rather than fortifying it; it's impossible to travel around Africa without exposing yourself to strange bugs from time to time. Take it easy at first, don't overdo the fruit (and wash it in clean water) and be very wary of salads served in cheap restaurants, as well as the pre-cooked contents of their ubiquitous display cabinets. That said, the fruit and vegetables in most Zanzibari restaurants, even the cheapest, is generally perfectly fine.

Travellers' diarrhoea is the most common affliction, best weathered rather than blasted with antibiotics. Twenty-four hours of sweet, black tea and nothing else may rinse it out.

The important thing is to replace your fluids. Make it easier on your body by sipping a **rehydration mix**: four heaped teaspoons of sugar or honey and half a teaspoon of salt in a litre of water. Commercial rehydration remedies contain much the same, and flat Coca-Cola is quite a good tonic, too. Avoid coffee, strong fruit juice and alcohol. Most upsets resolve themselves after two or three days. If you continue to feel bad, see a doctor. If you have to travel a long distance, any pharmacy should have anti-diarrhoeal remedies, but these shouldn't be overused. Avoid jumping for **antibiotics** at the first sign of trouble: they annihilate your gut flora (most of which you want to keep), don't work on viruses, and may result in long-term bacterial disequilibrium in your digestive system.

If you catch **giardia** (from water polluted with faecal matter) you'll know – apart from making you feel generally ill and drowsy, it makes you pass wind – from both ends of your body – that smells worse than a sewer. The bug generally works itself out after two or three days, but may recur a few weeks after. The definitive treatment for it, and **amoebic dysentery**, is **metronizadole** (tradename Flagyl).

You're most unlikely to catch **cholera**. Zanzibar's annual outbreaks, coinciding with the long rains (March – May or June), affects a few dozen to a hundred people a year, mostly in the overcrowded suburb of Ng'ambo east of Stone Town. The cholera **vaccine** is ineffective. The symptoms are fever and chronic diarrhoea; most attacks are relatively mild, and clear up naturally after a few days, but if left untreated the sudden and severe dehydration caused by the disease can be fatal. **Treatment** is simple: lots of oral rehydration therapy (salt and sugar in water; as above) or, in severe cases, rehydration fluid administered through a drip. Antibiotics (usually tetracycline or doxycycline) can also help, but are not essential.

Injuries, bites and stings

Take more care than usual over minor **cuts and scrapes**. In the tropics, the most trivial scratch can quickly become a throbbing infection if you ignore it. Take a small tube of antiseptic with you, or apply alcohol or iodine.

Otherwise, there are potentially all sorts of bites, stings and rashes which rarely, if ever, materialize. The handful of **dogs** on Zanzibar are usually sad and skulking, posing little threat. **Scorpions and spiders** abound but are hardly ever seen unless you deliberately turn over rocks or logs: scorpion stings are painful but almost never fatal (clean the wound and pack with ice to slow down the spread of the venom), while spiders are mostly quite harmless. **Snakes** are common, but again, the vast majority are harmless. To see one at all, you'd need to search stealthily; walk heavily and most species obligingly disappear. Victims of snake bites should be hospitalized as quickly as possible in case the bite is venomous, but whatever you do don't panic: more snake bite deaths are caused by shock rather than the venom itself. Venomous snake bites are usually treated with hydrocortisone and an anti-inflammatory and, in an emergency, with adrenaline injections.

Marine stings from sponges, corals, fish (including catfish) and jellyfish can usually be treated with vinegar, or sometimes tiger balm. Don't use alcohol to treat the wound. For stings from cone shells (which have neuro-toxic darts), immobilize the limb, apply a non-constrictive compress, and seek medical attention immediately. Spines from sea urchins, crown of thorns starfish, stingrays and surgeonfish are treated by applying scalding water (just under 50°C) to break down the poison.

Other complaints

Fungal infections can be avoided by not using used soap in cheap hotels, or towels if unwashed, badly washed or still damp. Antifungal cream is the best treatment for infections; alternatively, douse affected skin in iodine, though this will likely only keep the infection in check, not eliminate it. Many people get occasional **heat rashes**, especially after arrival between December and March. A warm shower (to open the pores) and cotton clothes should help. It's important not to overdose on **sunshine**; The powerful heat and bright light can mess up your system, and a hat and sunglasses are strongly recommended. Some people **sweat** heavily and lose a lot of salt. If this applies to you, sprinkle extra salt on your food.

To alleviate **sunburn**, aloe vera cream, calamine lotion, yoghurt, or a mixture of olive oil and lemon juice helps. **Coral ear** – an inflammation of the ear canal and tympanic membrane – is treated with antibiotic drops or an antiseptic solution.

One critter you might catch is a **jigger**, the pupa of a fly that likes to burrow into your toes. More horrible than it sounds, this is best treated by physically removing all of the bug, and then repeatedly dousing the cavity with iodine or other disinfectant. The cavity should heal itself in three or four days.

Finally, make sure you get a thorough **dental check-up** before leaving home, though there are reliable dentists in Dar es Salaam and Stone Town. For **acute tooth-ache**, the antibiotic Ampicillin works well, plus paracetamol for pain. Diclofenac helps reduce swellings. If you have a history of tooth inflammation or pain, take a course of the analgesic and anti-inflammatory nimesulida (tradename Aulin) with you.

Money and costs

Tanzania's currency is the shilling (abbreviated to "Tsh"). Kiswahili words for money are colonial legacies: pesa (from Portuguese), hela (on the mainland; from German times) and bob (from the Brits). Cash comes in denominations of Tsh500, 1000, 2000, 5000 and 10,000 banknotes, and Tsh5, 10, 20, 50, 100 and 200 coins. Exchange rates have depreciated steadily over the years, to your advantage. In February 2006, exchange rates were: £1 to Tsh2000 (up from Tsh1300 in 2002), $1 to Tsh1150 (Tsh900 in 2002), €1 to Tsh1400, Can$ to Tsh1000, Aus$ to Tsh850, and NZ$ to Tsh800. For the latest rates, see the Bank of Tanzania's website, ⓦwww.bot-tz.org.

Virtually all tourist services, from accommodation, tours and vehicle rental to plane and ferry tickets, have two prices: the **"non-resident" rates** for tourists quoted in US dollars, and the (often substantially cheaper) **"resident" rates** for locals, priced in Tanzanian shillings. Try to think of it as positive discrimination rather than the daylight robbery it too often feels like. Some hotels, too, are less than honest about payment modalities: despite signs to the contrary in some receptions, tourists can pay in shillings (albeit at bad conversion rates), as the law that insisted on payment in dollars was repealed years ago. Throughout this guide we've given prices in whichever currency they're quoted in.

Average costs

Zanzibar can be surprisingly expensive, especially compared to mainland Tanzania,

and can't be visited on a shoestring. That said, most things in Zanzibar – like accommodation, tours and souvenirs, but not food – are bargainable. The cheapest hotels charge $20–30 for generally very basic double rooms, while better hotels ask upwards of $50–100 for a room that might actually add some value to your holiday, for example one with a sea view.

On top of accommodation, you should also budget for **activities**: $15–20 for a half-day's spice tour or snorkelling, $35–50 for full-day trips, fifteen minutes' water-skiing or a dolphin tour, $70–100 for a couple of scuba dives if you're already qualified, and $350–400 for a four- or five-day PADI Open Water diving course. On the other hand, **car rental** is cheap by Tanzanian standards, costing little more than $50 a day – roughly half what you'd pay on the mainland. **Restaurants**, too, whilst certainly not cheap

Carrying money safely

First off, carry as little cash as possible and put whatever money you are carrying in several different places: a money belt tucked under your trousers or skirt is invisible and thus usually secure for travellers' cheques, passports and large amounts of cash. The best money belts are cotton or linen, as nylon ones can cause skin irritations if you sweat a lot. For the same reason, wrap up your things in a plastic bag before placing them in the belt.

Make sure that your money belt lies flat against your skin; the voluminous "bum bags" worn back-to-front by many tourists over their clothing invite a mugging, and are only one step short of announcing your stash with flashing neon lights. Equally dumb are pouches hanging around your neck, and ordinary wallets are a disaster. Put the rest of your money – what you'll need for the day or your night out – in a pocket or somewhere more accessible.

(around $5–10 for a main course, $15–25 with lobster), can be very good value given the quality and, often enough, paradisiacal location. **Drinks** are reasonably priced: $0.50–$2 for sodas and juices, a little more for beers, and $3–5 for cocktails.

Excluding activities, **budget** travellers should count on at least $30 per person per day for a bed, two simple meals, some drinks and public transport. The same on the mainland would cost roughly half. Staying in better, **mid-range** hotels and eating in more upmarket restaurants, count on $50–100 per day, again excluding activities. **Upmarket** travellers can easily blow $200–500.

Youth and student discounts

The various **student/youth ID cards** may get you reductions on flights, but won't get you discounts in Tanzania, and there are no student rates for entry fees, accommodation or transport. Full-time students are eligible for the **International Student ID Card** (**ISIC**; ⓦ www.isiccard.com); for Americans it also comes with up to $3000 in emergency medical coverage and $100 a day for 60 days in hospital, plus a 24-hour emergency hotline. The card costs $22 in the USA; Can$16 in Canada; Aus$18 in Australia; NZ$20 in New Zealand; £7 in the UK; and €13 in the Republic of Ireland. The **International Youth Travel Card**, available to anyone aged 26 or under, costs the same.

What to take

The US dollar reigns supreme on Zanzibar, more so than on the mainland, and as most tourist services are priced in dollars, it's the currency to take. Travellers' cheques are accepted in very few places, their main use being to change money in Stone Town – they're much more useful for longer journeys on the Tanzanian mainland. Credit cards can be used to pay bills from some upmarket hotels, air tickets, and sometimes scuba diving, but they are not widely accepted and may need prior arrangement with the company in question. You might also be stung with a ten to fifteen percent mark-up. Stone Town has a couple of ATMs that cough up shillings on

international credit cards; there are more in Dar es Salaam.

It's wise not to rely on one source of money alone: take along a mixture of dollars in cash, dollar or sterling travellers' cheques, and a credit card with PIN number. **US dollar** banknotes are widely accepted and generally rapidly changed. $100 denominations attract better rates, but **$500 bills and old-style notes** (prior to 1995–2000 depending on the denomination) may be refused, given the risk of forgery. **Sterling** and **euro** cash are less useful, and you'll lose out on the conversion into dollars. You'll need some Tanzanian shillings to pay for purchases in local shops, daladala fares and the like: try to avoid carrying mainly Tsh10,000 notes as they're difficult to change outside tourist areas.

Travellers' cheques

Travellers' cheques – either American Express or Thomas Cook – are the safest way to carry money, and the lower rates you get for changing them compared to cash are the price you pay for peace of mind. Be aware that to get dollars in cash, you lose out twice, first in the conversion to Tanzanian shillings, then back into dollars.

The best rates for changing cheques are on the Tanzanian mainland. You'll get around ten percent less in Stone Town, and twenty to twenty-five percent less in Nungwi, the only other place they're accepted. When changing cheques, you'll need to show your passport and the **purchase receipt** you received when you bought them (the one that includes serial numbers). Make photocopies and stash them and the original away in separate places. In the event that cheques are lost or stolen, the issuing company expects you to report the loss immediately – details are given when you buy the cheques; both American Express and Thomas Cook claim to replace lost or stolen cheques within 24 hours.

Credit cards and ATMs

Whilst it's theoretically feasible to use only **credit cards** while on holiday in Zanzibar, blips in the electronic verification system mean that plastic should definitely not be relied on as your primary means of accessing money. That said, by far the quickest means of getting cash (shillings only) if you have a card and PIN number is through one of Zanzibar's two **24-hour ATM machines**, both in Stone Town (NBC and Barclays). There are more machines in Dar es Salaam, Arusha, and in over thirty other towns elsewhere on the mainland, most operated by NBC Bank. The ATMs accept international Visa, MasterCard, JCB and Delta, but not American Express. The maximum daily withdrawal is Tsh400,000, approximately $360. **Additional costs** levied by your card supplier for ATM withdrawals should be no more than £2–3/$3–4 on a £200/$300 withdrawal.

Over-the-counter **cash advances** through the banks mentioned above are possible, if for some reason your PIN doesn't work, as long as your account has not been blocked (remember to set up a standing order to cover monthly charges and interest repayments before you leave home). You can usually withdraw up to your card limit, although large transactions may entail an interrogation to screen for potential fraud, and note that the credit card company will charge you for the service: anything up to four percent including a "conversion fee" included in the exchange rate.

Credit cards are less useful for **direct payments**, though some upmarket hotels and restaurants, travel agencies and tour companies may accept them, usually attracting a premium of up to fifteen percent. American Express users often pay an additional fee, if they're accepted at all. **To avoid abuse**, make sure that payment vouchers specify the currency before you sign, and fill in any empty boxes on the slip with zeroes. Be careful not to let the card leave your sight.

A compromise between travellers' cheques and plastic is **Visa TravelMoney**, a disposable pre-paid debit card with a PIN that works in the ATMs mentioned above. You load up your account with funds before leaving home, and when they run out, you simply throw the card away. You can buy up to nine cards to access the same funds – useful for couples or families travelling together – and it's a good idea to buy at least one extra as a back-up in case of loss or theft. The card is available in most countries from branches of Travelex (ⓔcardservices@travelex.com); for more information, see ⓦhttp://international.visa.com/ps/products/vtravelmoney.

Changing money

The best rates for changing hard currency into **shillings** are on the Tanzanian mainland, especially Dar es Salaam. Rates on Zanzibar are at least ten percent less. In Zanzibar, you can cash travellers' cheques at the airport, at NBC and Barclays banks in Stone Town (count on at least an hour). There are also a number of foreign exchange bureaux ("forexes") in Stone Town and Nungwi in the north, which have faster service, but worse rates. On **Pemba**, the only place that changes money – cash only – is NMB bank in Chake Chake, which can take half a day. Upmarket hotels may oblige, but at bad rates, and locals may be willing to exchange cash informally, but **do not change money on the street** – there's no need for a black market, and you're guaranteed to get swindled. In theory you should keep exchange receipts until you leave the country, though they're rarely – if ever – asked for. **Opening hours** for banks are Monday–Friday 8.30am–3pm and Saturday 8.30am–midday; forexes have slightly longer hours, and may also open on Sunday.

Getting around

Most Zanzibaris get around by shared pick-ups called daladalas, which cover pretty much every part of Unguja and Pemba, and are a good way of mixing with locals. To get between the islands, or to and from the Tanzanian mainland, most people catch a ferry, though it's not all that more expensive to fly.

Daladalas

Public **road transport** is by daladala, also known as *gari ya abiria* ("passenger vehicle") on Zanzibar. The older ones are delightfully converted Bedford lorries with wooden bodies; the newer and smaller Toyota and Isuzu pick-ups are in a similar style, with wrought-iron sides and wooden roofs. Passengers sit on wooden benches, between which go legs, baggage, goats and chickens, sacks of fruit and everything else. They operate during daylight hours only. Short journeys cost a few hundred shillings, the longest no more than Tsh1500 (roughly $1.40). **Useful routes** are detailed throughout the Guide, and overviews are given on p.122 for Unguja, and p.215 for Pemba.

Taxis

Rather more comfortable are **taxis**, which are also a safe way of getting around Stone Town at night. They lack meters, so settle on a fare before getting in. Tourists are invariably charged top dollar – bargaining prowess is very useful here, and if you don't get anywhere, try another driver. However, prices are inevitably higher than in other places such as Dar es Salaam. Those with average negotiating skills can expect to pay at least Tsh3000 for a short journey, Tsh10,000 from the airport into Stone Town, and anything upwards of Tsh30,000 for a ride from Stone Town to the east coast. When haggling, bear in mind that drivers have to pay a hefty slice of the day's takings to the vehicle's owners, who are the real con artists.

Car and motorbike rental

Renting a car has the advantage of flexibility, both in terms of where you want to go and at what time, as daladalas on less obvious routes may only run once or twice a day. Stone Town's tour operators, and one in Nungwi, can fix you up, as can a handful of hotels on Pemba. Taxi drivers are also happy to negotiate a day's fare. There are no multinational franchises. **Prices** are reasonable by Tanzanian standards, with a day's saloon car rental or use of a taxi costing no more than $50–70 including driver and fuel. You can also **self-drive**, but you'll need to be confident: what few vehicles there are in Zanzibar tend to be driven fast and dangerously, whilst people and animals are potential on-road hazards, particularly at night.

A cheaper way to get around is by **motorbike** or scooter. Called *pikipiki*, they're not recommended for safety reasons unless you have previous experience, and fully understand Zanzibar's vehicular pecking order, which determines who can run who off the road: at the bottom are chickens, who scatter at the approach of people. Then come bicycles, then *pikipikis*, then cars, daladalas, and finally trucks. So, stay alert and pull off the road where necessary. *Pikipikis* can be rented informally through hotels; see also "Listings" (p.121) in the Stone Town chapter. The cost averages $25–30 a day excluding fuel. Ensure you get a decent helmet.

Permits and paperwork

Drivers and motorbike riders must be between 25 and 70 years old, have held a licence for at least two years, and possess an **international driving licence**, available from motoring organizations back home; see the box on p.37. It needs to be endorsed by police; the rental company will arrange this, and the **temporary permit** (Tsh6000, roughly $5.50) if you've only got a national driving licence. You'll also need a **daily**

Motoring organizations

Australia AAA ℡02/6247 7311, ⓦwww.aaa.asn.au.
Canada CAA ℡613/247-0117, ⓦwww.caa.ca.
Ireland AA ℡01/617 9999, ⓦwww.aaireland.ie.
New Zealand AA ℡0800/500 444, ⓦwww.nzaa.co.nz.
UK AA ℡0870/600 0371, ⓦwww.theaa.com; RAC ℡0800/550 055, ⓦwww.rac
.co.uk.
US AAA ℡1-800/AAA-HELP, ⓦwww.aaa.com.

permit for travel outside Stone Town, which costs Tsh2500 – the rental company will fill you in.

With most companies, the arrangements are quite informal, and **deposits** not normally required. Most claim to have full **insurance** too, meaning that if you somehow total the vehicle, you'll have no "excess liability" to pay, unlike on the mainland. Check this beforehand though, and ensure that whatever is promised or agreed is stated on the contract. Going with a driver makes insurance arrangements irrelevant.

Driving regulations and the police

Traffic drives on the left. The **speed limit** is 50kph in populated areas and 80kph on highways; keep your speed down as limits aren't marked. A curious throw-back to the bad old days of the paranoid republic that followed independence is the requirement that all vehicles halt outside **police stations**, even when there isn't a cop in sight, where you'll have to wait until you're waved (or shrugged) on. You must also stop, evidently enough, at police **roadblocks** (marked by low strips of spikes across the road or concrete-filled barrels), where your papers are inspected – though their main purpose is to hinder the smuggling of cloves to the north of the islands, from whence they're shipped out by dhow to Mombasa in Kenya. However, there were reports a few years ago of tourists being robbed at **fake roadblocks**, which is a good reason to use a local driver.

If you're pulled over, the usual reason given is that you were speeding, although the notoriously corrupt cops are quite capable of finding something, anything, wrong with your car (broken wing mirror, flat spare tyre) so that they can fine you. Tourists are not immune. Do not let them keep your passport or driving licence, as it gives them a most unfair advantage when negotiating the fine. **Spot fines** are officially Tsh20,000, less if you're happy foregoing the receipt (ie a bribe). This might reduce the fine to a few thousand shillings but is, of course, illegal.

Driving hazards and etiquette

When driving, **expect the unexpected**: rocks, ditches, potholes, animals and people on the road, as well as lunatic drivers. It's accepted practice to honk your horn stridently to warn pedestrians and cyclists of your approach. Beware also of mostly unmarked **speed bumps**. Avoid **driving after dark**, but if you must, be alert for stopped vehicles without lights or hazard warnings, and also for one-eyed vehicles: when what looks like a motorbike suddenly turns into a truck at full speed. It's common practice to flash oncoming vehicles, especially if they're leaving you little room or their headlights are blinding you, and to signal right to indicate your width and deter drivers behind you from overtaking. Left-hand signals are used to say "Please overtake" – but don't assume that a driver in front who signals you to overtake can really see whether the road ahead is clear.

If you **break down** or have an accident, the first thing to do is pile bundles of sticks or foliage at fifty-metre intervals behind and in front of your car. These are the red warning triangles of Africa, and their placing is always scrupulously observed (as is the wedging of a stone behind at least one wheel). Mending punctures is very cheap (Tsh500) and can be done almost anywhere; local mechanics (*fundis*) can work miracles with minimal tools. Settle on a price before work begins.

Flights

Reasonably priced **internal air services** connect Unguja (Zanzibar International Airport) with Pemba (Karume Airport), and both to various mainland airports, including Mombasa and Nairobi in Kenya. It's well worth seeing the coastline from above at least once: the spice and coconut plantations, reefs, sandbanks and creeks are beautiful. Flight **schedules** are given at the end of the Stone Town and Dar es Salaam chapters, and at the beginning of the Pemba chapter. The best local airlines – all operating propeller planes – are Coastal Travels, Precisionair and ZanAir, and can usually be relied on to keep to schedule. Coastal Travels and Precisionair tend to use single-engine planes, although these companies have good reputations regarding safety. The national carrier, Air Tanzania (ATC), has – since its takeover by South African Airways – finally shed its "Any Time Cancellation" nickname, if only because it currently only flies four routes. It owns one 737 and leases a couple more. **Baggage limits** are usually 15kg, with additional weight carried at the pilot's discretion (and possibly at extra cost).

Fares for tourists ("non-residents") are quoted in dollars but payable in shillings if you prefer. If you've been around for a while, you may be able to wangle significantly cheaper "resident" fares – it all depends on the guy or gal in the office, as resident status is not checked at the airports. Fares vary little between the airlines; the twenty-minute hop between Dar es Salaam and Unguja averages $50–60; Unguja to Pemba costs $70–80; and Pemba to Dar es Salaam is $90–100. An **airport tax** of $5 (or Tsh5000) and a $1 **airport safety tax** are payable on domestic flights – bring cash, as they're rarely included in the fare.

Ferries

There are several daily **ferries** between Stone Town and Dar es Salaam, and sailings most days on to Pemba. There's also an unreliable weekly service between Pemba (either Mkoani or Wete) and Tanga on the mainland, close to the Kenyan border. The ferries are particularly useful for getting to and from Dar es Salaam, as the journey only takes a few hours and the ports at both ends are centrally positioned, but ferries are less useful for Pemba, as most sail overnight and aren't that much cheaper than catching a plane. As with flights, there are two kinds of **tickets**: ones for "non-residents" (tourists), which are priced in dollars but can be paid in shilling equivalent, at bad exchange rates; and "resident" ones for locals, which are cheaper and priced in shillings. A $5 **port tax** should be included in the fare. In Dar es Salaam and Stone Town, **ticket offices** – most inside or just outside the port – open daily until 6pm, though tickets for night ferries can be bought until departure time. Ensure it's you, and not the commission-hunting "fly-catcher" or *papasi* (hustler) who will undoubtedly have latched on to you, who does the talking when buying. **Bookings** are not necessary, even during peak tourist season, but it's wise to buy your ticket half a day in advance to avoid last-minute shenanigans.

Beware of **scams**. The usual trick involves someone selling you a non-resident ticket, sometimes at the tourist price; once on the ferry, cometh the ticket inspector, bent policeman and assorted heavies, you'll be made to buy another ticket at the full price, plus a bribe to smooth things over. A variation is to be offered a ticket at the discounted price paid by tourists travelling with overland trucks, with the same outcome. Even cruder is to be sold a ticket for a departure that doesn't exist – especially the "night ferry" from Dar to Stone Town (there isn't one, but there is an overnight sailing in the opposite direction). All these scams are easily avoided by buying your ticket at the tourist rate at the ferry company's office.

Dhows

Though discouraged by the authorities, getting passage on a commercial **dhow** is a legal and feasible – if adventurous and potentially dangerous – way of getting from the mainland to Zanzibar. Be aware, however, that dhows occasionally capsize, and there's little chance of being rescued should that happen. It's virtually impossible to arrange dhow passage from Dar es Salaam; more likely are towns further north, namely **Bagamoyo** (for Kizimkazi, possibly also Stone Town), **Pangani** (for Mkokotoni or Nungwi) and **Tanga** (for Wete on Pemba). The easiest of the three is probably Pangani; enquire there at *Pangadeco Bar & Lodge*. Catching a dhow in **Mombasa** is difficult, but things are easier in the opposite direction if you start at Wete, whose officials – beyond doling out schoolmistressy advice on not using dhows – will give you an exit stamp without much fuss. A good place for information there is *Sharook Guest House*. All routes take at least five or six hours, and considerably longer if there are problems with motors or the weather – so take plenty of food and water, and remember that although the thought of a dhow trip is undeniably romantic, the reality can be rather different, with choppy seas, cramped seating and rudimentary toilet facilities – often cantilevered over the side.

The main hassle though is dealing with **officialdom**. In theory, the irksome paperchase this often entails shouldn't be required as Zanzibar is of course part of Tanzania, but in practice – and depending, it seems, on the current political situation in the Isles or the clove harvest (during which time smuggling to Mombasa is common) – you may need to navigate obstructive and/or corrupt officials. The usual sequence is first to enquire with the harbour master for what ships might be heading your way, then agree a fare with the captain; anything up to $20 is reasonable for tourists. Once settled, you'll need to confirm things once again with the harbour master, then move on – pointlessly – to immigration, who might stamp your passport and may expect a little something in return (the price of a beer, or a much less reasonable $25). Final stop is customs, which shouldn't pose any problems. If for some reason you're given an exit stamp, on arrival in Zanzibar you'll need to head straight to the nearest immigration office – these are at the ports in Wete and Mkoani on Pemba, and at Stone Town on Unguja.

Accommodation

Zanzibar has a wide range of accommodation to suit all tastes, but nothing really cheap: even the most humble establishment charges tourists $20–30 for a double room, though this should be bargainable, especially if you're staying for more than a couple of days, or are coming out of season. Given Zanzibar's increasing popularity with tourists, it's worth trying to book any kind of accommodation in advance in high season, especially July and August, and from December to February. Camping is illegal on Zanzibar, but is permitted on the mainland.

Single bedrooms have one bed (*kitanda moja*). A **double** has a larger bed suitable for couples, or two beds (*vitanda viwili*), which we've called a **twin**. A **common** room (or *siselfu*) shares showers and toilets with other guests, whilst an **en-suite** or **self-contained** room (self-container or *selfu*) has a bathroom containing shower and Western-style toilet. More expensive places may have bathtubs, but please be sparing in your use of water. A **suite** has a lounge as well as a bathroom, often with a horrid three-piece suite and sometimes also a TV and fridge. Some suites also have a kitchen or kitchenette. A **banda** is any small cottage, usually with a thatched roof; a **rondavel** is similar but round. Both may contain several guest rooms, so it's not necessarily a guarantee of privacy.

Types of hotel

Most people staying in Stone Town take a room in a **guest house**. which tend to occupy characterful three- or four-storey

Seasons and prices

Many of Zanzibar's mid- and top-range hotels have **seasonal rates**, with low- or mid-season discounts knocking around twenty percent off high-season rates. However, Zanzibar's increasing popularity means that some hotels now charge the same all year, with the exception of Christmas and New Year, when peak season surcharges are levied.

Low season: From Easter until the end of May or June, sometimes also March, coinciding with the long rains, or the "Green Season", as some hoteliers prefer to call it. October, November and sometimes early December, coinciding with the short rains, may also be considered low season, depending on the hotel.

High season: July to September or to mid-December, sometimes also January to March or Easter. Mainly hot and sunny, though there's a chance of rain between October and December.

Peak season: Mid-December to early January; rates may be quoted as Christmas and New Year supplements over high-season rates.

buildings dating from the nineteenth century. Their condition varies greatly, from damp and mildewed dumps with shared bathrooms colonized by cockroaches, to majestic and stylishly restored former palaces stuffed with antiques. Stone Town also contains a number of more upmarket **hotels**, decked out in similar style but with considerably more services and mod-cons. Rooms invariably have ceiling fans, and a good many also come – at additional cost – with air conditioning, which can be essential from December to March when the heat and humidity is sapping. In the cheaper places, you'll pay more for a room with a private bathroom, usually a Western-style WC and shower, or for cable/satellite TV. In humbler places, before signing the register, test lights and fans (and the electric socket if you need it), hot water, and the size and condition of mosquito nets – it's amazing how many

don't cover the whole bed, or have more holes than a Gruyère. It's also a good idea to bring toilet paper, a towel and soap, as well as pillow cases and two thin cotton sheets (a *kanga* or *kitenge* will do) to replace the ubiquitous nylon ones.

Outside Stone Town, most beach hotels are **"bungalow resorts"**, consisting of a number of low, thatched, whitewashed cottages (*bandas*) usually containing two or more guest rooms, and a main building housing a restaurant and bar. These places are all fairly quiet, laid back, and can be enjoyably personal in feel. It's worth spending a little more for a **sea view**, if there is one – lounging in a hammock or deck chair on a private verandah while watching the sun rise or set over the ocean as a dhow glides by is all part of that ineffable Zanzibari magic. Do be sure you're paying for a proper view, and not just a distant glimpse through trees.

Accommodation price codes

All hotels on Zanzibar have two tariffs, one for **"non-residents"** (tourists) priced in dollars but also payable in shillings (albeit at bad rates), the other for **"residents"** (Tanzanians and expatriates), usually quoted in shillings and invariably much cheaper. All accommodation listed in this guide has been graded according to the **price codes** given below, based on the cost of a **standard double or twin room** charged at non-resident tourist rates in high (but not peak) season. Breakfast is almost always included in room rates.

- ❶ under $25
- ❷ $25–40
- ❸ $40–55
- ❹ $55–75
- ❺ $75–110
- ❻ $110–150
- ❼ $150–200
- ❽ $200–300
- ❾ over $300

A **garden view** is a polite way of saying no sea view; the gardens themselves are mostly boring lawns with a few palm trees.

A completely different kettle of fish are the all-inclusive, package holiday **beach resorts** – mostly Italian – mushrooming along Unguja's northeastern coast and in one or two places elsewhere. Whilst they pay fleeting homage to "Swahili style" via vast, *makuti*-thatched vaulted roofs, to call them brash would be an understatement for many. Most are not reviewed in this book, both on environmental and ethical grounds. They do however come with big swimming pools, several bars and restaurants apiece, and a raft of activities including discos, and can be very good value if you just want a beach holiday with minimal local interaction. Most need to be booked and paid for in Europe.

Eating and drinking

Zanzibari cuisine is a highlight of many a holiday, effortlessly blending flavours, styles and ingredients from around the Indian Ocean: African, Arabian, Indian, Far Eastern and even Chinese. Rice and seafood prevail, characteristically sauced and seasoned with any number of herbs and spices, tamarind and coconut milk. Most restaurants have good selections of vegetarian dishes too, whether pasta, pizza, curries or Chinese. Tourist restaurants tend to stay open all day, except during the month of Ramadan; see p.45.

Breakfast is almost always included in the price of a room. At its most basic, you'll get a thermos flask of sweet milky tea or instant coffee, a doorstep of white bread spread with margarine, scrambled eggs, and fruit – papaya, pineapple and mango. If you're staying in a luxury hotel, look forward to a lavish expanse of hot and cold buffets that you can't possibly do justice to. Zanzibaris themselves begin the day with *supu*, a light and spicy broth made from gristly pieces of meat, chicken, fish or sweetmeats that's eaten with chapatis, doughnuts (*mandazi*) or fried rice cakes (*vitumbua*). Also good for breakfast are **snacks**, including samosas (*sambusa*; sometimes vegetarian), stuffed chapati rolls (*mantabali*, nicknamed "Zanzibari pizza"), and "chops", being battered meat or egg balls coated in mashed potato.

Lunch is typically served from noon to 2pm, and **dinner** no later than 8pm. Naturally, seafood is the favourite, commonly fish (*samaki*) or octopus (*pweza*) served with coconut-flavoured rice. Many places also offer prawns (*kamba*), and lobster features on upmarket menus. Chicken and goat meat are also commonly available, but beef is rare. Restaurants attuned to tourist tastes feature Indian and Italian dishes on their menus, including pizzas and pasta, and you can find chips and fried chicken virtually everywhere. Increasingly popular among Zanzibaris is *ugali*, a thick cornmeal porridge that is the mainland staple. In Dar es Salaam, don't miss out on a **nyama choma** ("grilled meat") feast, a speciality of many a local bar, served with grilled bananas or *ugali*. Some typical Zanzibari **recipes** are given in Contexts at the back of this book.

Street food is best in Stone Town and Chake Chake, particularly in the evenings when grilled fish (*samaki*) and octopus (*pweza*) are commonly found, together with grilled cassava (*muhogo*) or maize cobs (*mahindi*), and small skewers of grilled goat meat (*mishkaki*). Most vendors offer optional chilli sauce (*pilipili hoho*), the best laced with tomato, onion and lemon. In Dar es Salaam, *mishkaki*, fried chicken, chips and *chipsi* *mayai* (Spanish omelettes made with, yes, chips) are the stock in trade.

Lastly, don't forget Zanzibar's glorious **fruits**. Bananas, avocados, papayas and pineapples can be found in abundance all year round; mangos and citrus fruits are more seasonal. Look out for passion fruit (both the familiar shrivelled brown variety and the sweeter and less acidic smooth yellow ones), tree tomatoes, custard apples (sweetsops), lychees, rambutan and guavas – all distinctive and delicious. **Coconuts** are filling and nutritious, going through several satisfying changes of condition (all edible) before becoming the familiar hairy brown nuts.

Non-alcoholic drinks

The national beverage is **chai** – tea. Drunk at breakfast and as a pick-me-up at any time, it's a weird variant on the classic British brew: milk, water, lots of sugar and tea leaves, brought to the boil in a kettle and served scalding hot. Its sweetness must eventually cause diabolical dental damage, but it's curiously addictive and very reviving. Variants are laced with ginger (*chai tangawizi*) or other spices (*chai masala*). A more traditional morning cuppa is an infusion of **lemongrass** stems (*mchaichai*), a wonderfully refreshing and aromatic way to start the day – ask the day before to be sure your hotel has it. **Coffee** is normally limited to instant, though fresh Kilimanjaro Arabica – if you can find it – can be an utter delight.

Sodas are cheap, and crates of Coke and Fanta find their way to even the smallest shack. Local varieties worth tasting are Krest bitter lemon, and the punchy Stoney Tangawizi ginger ale. Fresh **juice** is available in towns and in tourist beach areas. Passion fruit is excellent, though it may be watered-down concentrate; you might also find orange juice, pineapple, sugar cane juice, watermelon, mango, and sometimes tamarind (mixed with water) – very refreshing, and worth seeking out.

Mineral or purified **water** is expensive, but can be bought everywhere. Avoid drinking tap water on Zanzibar; on the mainland, tap water is usually fine if you're up to date on inoculations (especially typhoid), but heed local advice.

Alcoholic drinks

Zanzibar is Muslim, so **bars** are limited to Stone Town and the tourist areas. Being drunk in public is not too clever, so catch a taxi on the way back. The biggest-selling **lagers**, all from the mainland, are Kilimanjaro, Safari and Tusker. More distinctive is Ndovu, with a sickly-sweet smell not to everyone's liking. Foreign brands, either imported or brewed under licence, include Pilsner Urquell, Miller, Carlsberg and Heineken. There are two **stouts**: a head-thumping take on Guinness resembling fizzy soy sauce (often mixed with Coca-Cola to conceal the taste), and the more palatable Castle Milk Stout.

Most bars stock a limited range of imported **spirits**, and the popular Tanzanian **Konyagi**, made from papaya. It's usually drunk with bitter lemon, Indian tonic or soda water, and features in cocktails. **Liqueurs**, where you can find them, are pretty much the same as anywhere else in the world, though it's worth seeking out a chocolate and coconut liqueur called Afrikoko, and the South African Amarula, similar to Bailey's. More upmarket restaurants have good **wine lists** of mainly South African bottles.

Communications

The best way to keep in touch is by email. Post is not fantastically reliable, and phoning can be expensive. It's not possible to make collect calls (reverse charge), but cellular coverage is good, and foreign GSM handsets can be made to work with a minimum of tinkering.

Mail

There are **post offices** in Stone Town, Jambiani and in Chake Chake, Wete and Mkoani on Pemba. Opening times are Monday–Friday 8am–4.30pm, and Saturday 9am–noon. **Airmail** takes at least five days to Europe, and ten days to North America and Australasia. For stuff you don't want to lose, use a **courier** – DHL has branches in Stone Town and Dar es Salaam; see "Listings" for details.

Telephones

Zanzibar's terrestrial telephone network is patchy and unreliable, so most Zanzibaris use **mobile phones**. The best coverage is offered by Zantel, partnered with Vodacom on the mainland. Celtel is also good. You should be able to use your own handset by buying a SIM card on arrival, as long as your phone is not locked to one operator. Top-up scratch cards (ask for a *vocha*, a voucher) can be bought at kiosks in Stone Town and Dar. Roaming services are very expensive.

Calling abroad is cheapest via the Internet at a number of Internet cafés in Stone Town and Dar es Salaam; costs average Tsh500/minute to terrestrial lines and Tsh1500/minute to mobile phones. Costing up to four times more are card-operated public phones in Stone Town and in Pemba's three towns, and "assisted call" offices in Stone Town and Nungwi. Avoid hotel phones unless you're absolutely sure of the rates.

Email

Stone Town, Nungwi, Chake Chake and Dar es Salaam are blessed with surprisingly fast broadband **Internet**, accessible to tourists through Internet cafés. You can also get online at one or two hotels in Jambiani, Paje, Kiwengwa and Kendwa. Prices average Tsh1000 an hour. The downside is that most computers are infested with viruses, spyware, trojans and the like, so don't use them for things like Internet banking.

Phone numbers

Land lines have seven-digit subscriber numbers plus a three-digit area code, which doesn't need to be dialled if calling from the same area: 024 for Zanzibar and 022 for Dar es Salaam. **Mobile phone** numbers have ten digits that must be dialled wherever you are. **Calling from outside Zanzibar** or mainland Tanzania, omit the initial "0". **Tanzania's country code** is 255, unless you're calling from Kenya or Uganda, in which case dial ℡004.

Phoning abroad from Zanzibar, or Dar es Salaam, dial ℡000 followed by the country code, followed by the subscriber's area code (minus the initial "0" if any) and the number itself. The exceptions are Kenya (℡005 followed by the area and subscriber number) and Uganda (℡006). Some **country codes**: Australia 61, Canada 1, Ireland 353, New Zealand 64, UK 44, USA 1.

Useful numbers
℡101 National operator (English)
℡0101 International operator (English)
℡135 Directory enquiries (and general queries)
℡112 Emergency services (but don't expect them to come in a hurry)

The media

Journalists on the Tanzanian mainland enjoy wide freedoms by African standards, unlike their Zanzibari cousins, where independent press and media have to contend with officialdom's sporadically repressive whims. Zanzibari radio and television are state-controlled, so mainland stations are popular, as is satellite or cable TV.

English-language newspapers are only available in Stone Town. The leading dailies are *The Guardian* (and *Sunday Observer*), whose independence relies on the financial and political clout of tycoon Reginald Mengi, and *The Citizen*, which can at times be more incisive, but at other times ruined by its reliance on dubious pieces culled from the Internet. The other big daily is the *Daily News* (and *Sunday News*), strong on eastern and southern Africa and with some syndicated international coverage, but spoiled by its slavish bias in favour of the ruling CCM party.

Best of the **weekly papers** is *The East African*, sadly only rarely available in Stone Town (but always in Dar), whose relatively weighty, conservatively styled round-up of the week's news in Kenya, Uganda, Tanzania, Burundi and Rwanda is shot through with an admirable measure of justified cynicism. Its reporters and columnists are consistently incisive, articulate and thought-provoking, and it also carries the cream of foreign press news features. Less substantial but equally impartial is *The African*, combining an admirably combative and occasionally scurrilous editorial line with syndicated articles from Britain's *Guardian* newspaper. *The Express* is more downmarket but still entertaining.

TV and radio

Zanzibar's government-run television station is a particularly noxious example of state control, and has a weakness for interminable religious sermons. Much better is Tanzania's government-run channel, **TVT** (Televisheni ya Taifa), which – though staid and amateurish at times – is the country's most popular thanks to its blend of political propaganda, religious material (Muslim on Friday, Christian on Sunday), Nigerian and home-grown dramas, interviews, and all kinds of Tanzanian music. Its main competitor, **ITV** (Independent Television) screens locally produced soap operas and syndicated American sitcoms, and carries BBC and CNN newsfeeds. **Satellite TV** is ubiquitous in hotels and restaurants, piping up to sixty different channels from BBC World and Discovery to Iranian stations featuring Islamic clerics and sermons, and a ton of Bollywood action flicks and musicals.

Radio Tanzania Zanzibar broadcasts in Kiswahili and is good for getting to know traditional music, including *taarab*. Frequencies for the **BBC World Service** and **Voice of America** are given on ⓦwww.bbc.co.uk/worldservice and ⓦwww.voa.gov.

Opening hours, public holidays and festivals

In Stone Town and Dar es Salaam, shops usually open Monday–Friday from 8.30am to 5pm, sometimes to 7pm, and sometimes with a lunch break; they're also open on Saturday mornings. Supermarkets may open later, as will local stores and kiosks. Government office hours are generally Monday–Friday 7.30am–2.30pm (or 8am–3pm).

Public holidays

Christian and Muslim **public holidays** are observed, as well as secular national holidays. Government offices, banks, post offices and other official establishments are closed at these times. **Public holidays with fixed dates** are as follows: January 1 (New Year); January 12 (Zanzibar Revolution Day); April 26 (Union Day between Zanzibar and Tanganyika); May 1 (Workers' Day); July 7 (Industrial Day); August 8 (Farmers' Day); December 9 (Independence Day); December 25 (Christmas); December 26 (Boxing Day). If a holiday falls on a weekend the holiday is taken the following Monday. Another special day, if not yet a holiday, is October 17, which marks the death of Tanzania's much-loved first President, Julius Nyerere. **Public holidays with variable dates** are: Good Friday, Easter Sunday and Easter Monday, and the Islamic festivals of Idd al-Fitr, Idd al-Haj and Maulidi (see dates below).

Islamic festivals

The lunar Islamic **Hegira calendar** is followed in Muslim communities throughout Tanzania. The Muslim year has either 354 or 355 days, so dates recede in relation to the Western calendar by ten or eleven days each year. Precise dates for Islamic festivals are impossible to give as they depend on the sighting of the moon; if the sky is cloudy, things are put on hold for another day.

Only the month of fasting, **Ramadan**, will have much effect on your travels. This holy month is observed by all Muslims, who may not eat, drink or smoke between dawn and dusk during the whole of the month. Visiting Zanzibar at this time might leave a slightly strange impression, as most stores and restaurants are closed by day, though the evenings are much livelier than usual, and stores and restaurants stay open late. Public transport and official businesses continue as usual, however, and you can usually find a discreet non-Muslim restaurant serving food but you'll offend sensibilities if you're seen eating, drinking or smoking on the street by day. **Idd al-Fitr** (or Idd al-Fitri), the two- to four-day holiday that follows the sighting of the new moon at the end of Ramadan, is a great time to be in Zanzibar, with feasting, merrymaking and firecrackers. Another good time to be around is for **Maulidi** (or Maulid an-Nabi), the Prophet Muhammad's birthday. Also fascinating, so long as the sight of blood leaves you unfazed, is the **Idd al-Haj** (or Idd al-Adha) – the one-day feast of the sacrifice – during which every family with the means sacrifices a sheep or goat to commemorate the unquestioning willingness of Ibrahim (Abraham) to sacrifice his son Isaac for the love of God. Rooms fill up quickly for these festivals, so arrive a few days early or book in advance. Approximate dates for these events over the next few years are as follows:

Maulidi April 11, 2006; March 31, 2007; March 20, 2008; March 9, 2009; February 26, 2010.

Start of Ramadan September 24, 2006; September 13, 2007; September 2, 2008; August 22, 2009; August 11, 2010.

Idd al-Fitr October 24, 2006; October 13, 2007; October 2, 2008; September 21, 2009; September 10, 2010.

Idd al-Haj December 31, 2006; December 20, 2007; December 9, 2008; November 28, 2009; November 17, 2010.

Scuba diving and snorkelling

Caressed and nourished by the warm South Equatorial Current, Zanzibar's fringing coral reefs offer exhilarating scuba diving and snorkelling, with an abundance of colourful and sometimes heart-stopping marine life to be seen within a short boat ride of most beaches. Scuba diving is most spectacular off Pemba, though the strong currents that add spice to so many dives also mean it's safer for novices to learn the ropes in Unguja. Snorkelling is best off Unguja, whose eastern barrier reef encloses a series of shallow and sheltered tidal lagoons.

Pemba is generally considered the country's best dive centre, offering vertiginous drop-offs, largely unspoiled reefs and a stupendous variety of marine life; Misali Island is a particular gem. The waters around **Unguja Island (Zanzibar)** are shallower and sandier, and visibility is less, especially outside the November–March peak season. On the plus side, the corals here are excellent, there are many sheltered sites suitable for novices, and also a few wrecks within reach. Often forgotten, but also good, are the handful of islands – protected as Marine Reserves – off the coast **north of Dar es Salaam**, though some of the reefs were badly damaged in the 1990s by dynamite fishing. There are also some good coral-fringed islets off Bagamoyo. To the south of Dar, the reefs around **Mafia Island** rival Pemba's, and are reckoned by some connoisseurs to be among the world's most beautiful: they're protected as Mafia Island Marine Park. In the far south, **Mnazi Bay–Ruvuma Estuary Marine Park** on the border with Mozambique is barely known, and its reefs are in superb condition. For more information, contact Tanzania Marine Parks & Reserves, Olympio St, Upanga West, PO Box 7565, Dar es Salaam (☏022/215 0621, ⓦwww.marineparktz.com).

Diving is possible all year round, although the *kusi* monsoon (strongest June–Sept) is accompanied by choppy seas and strong currents that make the more exposed reefs inaccessible. There can also be strong winds in December and January. Visibility is best from November to March, before the long rains set in. Except for the east coast of Pemba, you'll always find good reefs for beginners (and most dive centres offer PADI-certified courses), whilst experienced divers can enjoy night dives, drift dives and deep drop-offs. On any dive you can expect to see a profusion of colourful tropical fish in extensive coral gardens, together with giant groupers, Napoleon wrasse and larger pelagic gamefish, including barracuda, kingfish, tuna and wahoo. Dolphins are frequently sighted, as are marine turtles (mainly green and hawksbill), blue spotted rays, manta rays and sometimes even whale sharks. Blue whales, though rarely seen, are sometimes heard on their northward migration towards the end of the year.

Scuba diving

Scuba diving is especially good around Pemba, with a stupendous variety of marine life and superb visibility, while Unguja's waters are shallower and sandier, with lower visibility but good coral variety, and sheltered sites suitable for novices. **Experienced divers** can enjoy night dives, drift dives, deep drop-offs and a number of wrecks. On any dive, you can expect to see a profusion of tropical fish in extensive coral gardens, together with giant groupers, Napoleon wrasse, and larger pelagic (open water) species like barracuda, kingfish, tuna and wahoo.

In general, the **best months** for diving are from October to March, before the long rains kick in. Visibility at most sites peaks in January. Following the end of the long rains, the *kusi* monsoon (usually June to September) can bring with it choppy seas and strong currents, rendering more

Responsible diving and snorkelling

B

Coral reefs are among the most fragile ecosystems on earth, consisting of millions of individual living organisms called polyps. Solid though it seems, coral is extremely sensitive, and even a small change in sea temperature can have disastrous effects – such as the mass coral bleaching that accompanied the 1997–98 El Niño, killing up to ninety percent of coral in places. You can minimize the impact that you have on a reef when diving or snorkelling by following these common-sense rules:

Dive and swim carefully. Never touch the corals. Some polyps can die merely by being touched, and all suffocate if covered with silt or sand stirred up by a careless swipe of fins (flippers). For this reason, some companies don't provide fins for snorkellers. If you do wear fins, always be aware of where your feet are, and use your hands to swim when you're close to anything. If you're inexperienced, keep your distance from the coral to avoid crashing into it if you lose your balance. If you haven't scuba-dived for a while, take a refresher course and practice your buoyancy control in a swimming pool first.

Do not touch, handle or feed anything. This is both for your own safety (many corals and fish are poisonous or otherwise dangerous) and to avoid causing stress to fish and interrupting feeding and mating behaviour. Although several companies encourage it, do not feed fish. In some species, feeding encourages dependence on humans and upsets the natural balance of the food chain.

Do not take anything. Collecting shells, coral and starfish for souvenirs disrupts the ecosystem and is illegal, both in Tanzania and internationally. Getting caught will land you in serious trouble. Similarly, do not buy shells, corals or turtle products. With no market, people will stop collecting them. Taking a beautiful seashell might also deprive a hermit crab of a home, and certainly deprives other visitors of the pleasure of seeing it after you.

When mooring a boat, ensure you use established mooring points to avoid damaging corals. If there are no buoys, drop anchor well away from the reef and swim in.

---

exposed reefs inaccessible. December and January, following the short rains, can also be windy. **Dolphins** are sighted year-round, as are marine turtles (mainly green and hawksbill). The southward migration of blue and humpback **whales**, though rarely seen, is sometimes heard. The best months for chancing on this are August and September for Pemba, and September or October for Unguja. **Whale sharks** are occasionally reported off Pemba from June to August.

For **further information**, Anton Koornhof's *The Dive Sites of Kenya and Tanzania* (New Holland, 1997) is a little dated if still highly recommended, and also covers a number of snorkelling sites; Delwyn McPhun's *East Africa Pilot* (Imray, Laurie, Norie & Wilson) is intended primarily for sailors but contains a mass of useful diving-related information, from Kenya to South Africa. A great **map** of diving and snorkelling sites is *Zanzibar at Sea* by Giovanni Tombazzi (Maco Editions), which details the main reefs together with contextual and practical information. Buy it in Stone Town, or through international map suppliers; see p.24.

Dive sites

The best dive sites are reviewed throughout this book. Zanzibar's **Pemba Island** (p.196) ranks among the western Indian Ocean's best diving locations; visibility is excellent, averaging twenty to sixty metres, peaking at seventy, but the strong ocean currents that make for such exciting drift dives, especially at depths below twenty metres, can also be dangerous.

Fish life is not as profuse off **Unguja**'s shallower and calmer coastline, and visibility is considerably less, too, averaging ten to thirty metres, but that's plenty enough for enjoying Unguja's wonderfully colourful coral gardens. The dive sites off Unguja's **west coast**

47

(p.128), accessed from Stone Town, consist of many small islands, sand banks and submerged reefs. Underwater visibility averages a modest ten metres, however, though several reefs give good odds on spotting marine turtles, and there are a number of diveable wrecks for experts. Unguja's entire **east coast** (p.146) is fringed by a barrier reef one or two kilometres offshore, which encloses a series of sheltered lagoons – ideal for novices. In the **northeast** (p.171) is Mnemba Atoll, Unguja's subaquatic highlight, whose wide depth range and variety of reefs makes it perfect for all levels of experience. Dive centres on Unguja's **north coast** (p.182) also offer trips to Mnemba Atoll, and to the spectacular if potentially dangerous Leven Bank, between Unguja and Pemba.

Courses, costs and dive centres

Both Pemba and Unguja have numerous **dive centres**, generally based at beach hotels – most will pick you up for free in the morning if you're staying elsewhere. At the time of writing, all centres reviewed in this book were accredited by **PADI** – The Professional Association of Diving Instructors (Ⓦwww.padi.com). PADI-accreditation doesn't guarantee safety or quality, but does set minimum standards for **courses**. The standard one for beginners is a four- or five-day **Open Water** course ($300–400), completion of which gives you the right to dive to 18m with any qualified diver worldwide. It can be followed up with a three- to five-day **Advanced Open Water** course ($200–300). If you're not sure about whether diving is your thing, most centres offer single or double dive tasters, such as the PADI's "Discover Scuba". Details of other courses are given on PADI's website.

Safety (meaning the reliability and experience of a diving company) rather than price, should be your overriding concern, as even with the best preparations, instructors and equipment, things can go wrong. Scuba diving is inherently dangerous, and kills a higher proportion of participants than any other sport. Be aware also that standard **travel insurance** won't cover scuba diving, so you'll need to pay a supplement. Not that it'll help you if you catch the bends, as the nearest decompression chambers are in

Kenya and South Africa; for this reason most dive centres wisely refuse to take clients down further than 25–27m. When comparing the offerings of several centres, check for maximum group sizes (the smaller the better), and also on the style and fittings of their **dive boats**. Some are state-of-the-art inflatables equipped with oxygen, radio and powerful engines; others are converted dhows; whilst many are just normal boats with an outboard motor. The especially safety conscious should check for life jackets, an HF radio link, and whether boats have two motors (better than one). In theory, a **medical certificate** is necessary before taking a beginner's course, though few companies ever ask for one.

Costs are never cheap, and you'd do well to be sceptical of cut-price outfits not reviewed in this book: corners will invariably be cut. In general, divers with Open Water qualifications can expect to pay $40–70 per dive, or $70–100 for a double-tank dive. Things work out cheaper if you buy a package, usually six or ten dives, which can cut the price to $30–50 a dive depending on where you're going. When comparing prices, read the **small print** carefully: some exclude VAT (twenty percent) on their quotes, and most charge supplements on reefs that require longer boat trips. You don't need to bring **equipment**, though there's usually a discount if you do. In-house equipment is generally fine, but bring specialist gear like dive computers and waterproof cameras or camera housing as renting them locally can be expensive, if you can find what you want at all. Warm water (27ºC average) means that wetsuits aren't essential, though most companies routinely offer them and some recommend a thin wetsuit from June to September. For **Nitrox facilities** (for deeper and longer dives, averaging forty minutes at 30m), ask at Sensation Divers at Nungwi.

Snorkelling

If the idea (or cost) of scuba diving scares you, **snorkelling** is an excellent and cheap way of discovering the fantastic underwater world of East Africa, especially off Unguja, where some east-coast reefs are close enough to swim or wade out to. Nonetheless, it's worth using a boat to reach the more beautiful but less accessible reefs. On **Pemba**, Misali Island and Ras Kigomasha in the north are good spots, and there are a number of nice reefs accessible by boat from Mkoani. **Unguja** has many suitable locations, the undoubted highlight being **Chumbe Island Coral Park** off Stone Town, a day-trip to which costs upwards of $70, including lunch. Day-trips to other islands off Stone Town can also feature snorkelling, though the water isn't always clean. Unguja's eastern and northeastern snorkelling reefs are subject to huge tidal variations but have plenty of variety. An alternative is to combine snorkelling with **dolphin spotting**; see p.150.

Other than trips to Chumbe Island, **prices** for a combination of boat and equipment rental should be negotiable. If arranged through a dive centre or a mid-range or upmarket hotel, expect to pay $20–30 for two or three hours off Unguja, and $30–50 off Pemba. You can cut costs by arranging things through a cheaper hotel (in Pemba, this means *Jondeni Guest House* in Mkoani), or by talking directly with local fishermen – in both cases, you shouldn't end up paying more than $10 per person including equipment and use of an *ngalawa* outrigger. To avoid feeling short-changed, be clear before paying on how much time you expect to spend actually snorkelling, as some boatmen assume that a ten-minute once-over suffices. If you plan to do much snorkelling, you'll save money by bringing your own gear.

Shopping

Stone Town is heaven for shoppers, and the isles' eclectic heritage means you're as likely to find Moroccan leather slippers and lampshades as you are Omani stained-glass lanterns, colourful Indian fabrics inlaid with mirrors, "ethnic" jewellery from the Far East, and kitsch colonial antiques. Homegrown souvenirs aren't lacking either.

In both Stone Town and Dar es Salaam, **traditional crafts** from the mainland are very much in evidence, including weapons, shields, drums and other musical instruments, stools, headrests, and Maasai beadwork jewellery. With the notable exception of Makonde "helmet masks" representing an evil spirit called *mpiko*, most **masks** are reproductions based on Central and western African designs, and even the oldest-looking examples may have been made for the tourist market, no matter how much congealed cow dung appears to fill the crevices. A Zanzibari speciality is a **kibao ya mbuzi** ("goat board"), a kind of foldable wooden stool with a serrated knife at one end that's used for grating coconuts. Rather less portable are brass-studded Ali Baba-style **Zanzibari chests**, as small or as large as you like. **Woodcarvings** are ubiquitous, including walking sticks, Maasai spears (put the metal heads in your hand luggage when flying home!), combs and animals, and – most famously – intricate and abstract **Makonde figurines**, named after the largest tribe of southern Tanzania and northern Mozambique. Also well worth buying are the colourful **Tingatinga paintings**, found anywhere there are tourists; see the box on p.119. Tanzania's distinctive **toys** also make good souvenirs: most worthwhile are beautifully fashioned buses, cars, lorries and even motorbikes made out of wire or beer cans.

Typically Tanzanian, too, is the riot of colourful **fabrics and clothes** to be found in any market. Notable among these are printed women's cotton wraps called *kangas*, which bear intriguing Kiswahili proverbs, and heavier versions without proverbs called *kitenges*, which come in matching panels, so that you could use half as a skirt, and the other as a shawl. For men, try a dapper embroidered *kofia* cap, although the best are inevitably made by mothers for their sons or grandsons and are not for sale. International food and safety regulations mean you can't take a selection of Zanzibar's wonderful fruit back home, but local **honey** (*asali*) is well worth buying – scented as it often is with cloves – as are any number of **aromatic oils and essences**, which make far better presents than the packaged spices sold in every tourist shop, which are no different to those available in any supermarket across the globe.

Lastly, please remember that purchasing or exporting **ivory**, **turtleshell** ("tortoiseshell"), **seahorses** and **seashells** encourages the destruction of wildlife and is in any case illegal, both in Tanzania and abroad – penalties include heavy fines or even imprisonment. Similarly, avoid anything like animal skins or game trophies; possession of these is illegal in Tanzania without the requisite

paperwork, and may be completely illegal in other countries.

Bargaining

Bargaining is an important skill to learn, since every time you pay a "special price" for goods or services, you contribute to local inflation (or, rather, to tourists after you having to pay inflated prices). This is especially prevalent on Zanzibar, where even basic foodstuffs are first offered on a "hey, my friend" basis. It's impossible to state prices in this guide for everything, so before splashing out ask a few disinterested locals about the real price – as what's sometimes initially offered may be literally ten times what the vendor is prepared to accept. The bluffing on both sides is part of the "fun"; don't be shy of making a big scene, and once you get into it, you'll rarely end up paying more than twice the going rate. Where prices are marked, they're generally fixed. Finally, a bit of philosophy: if you're happy paying a certain price, then it's a good price, irrespective of what locals would have paid.

Trouble

Outside election times, Zanzibar is largely safe and peaceful, and Stone Town probably Africa's safest capital. Crime levels are low by any standards, and outside the main tourist areas you're unlikely to come across much or any hassle. Specific advice is given in this guide: p.86 for Stone Town, and p.64 for Dar es Salaam.

Hassle and misunderstandings

There's virtually no **hassle** outside Stone Town and Dar es Salaam, but in those places, trouble generally takes the form of young men trying to get you to buy safaris or tours, or failing that, pay for their dubious guiding talents, sexual "favours", drugs, or even, it seems, their grandmothers. On Zanzibar, these wonderful creations are aptly known as **papasi**, meaning "ticks", whilst on

the Tanzanian mainland they're called **flycatchers**. The rather more charming shoreline species are called **beach boys**; women looking for a holiday fling should take care, as these guys romance for a living.

Your **appearance** goes a long way in determining the extent to which you'll attract attention. It's impossible not to look like a tourist – but you can dress down and look like you're been travelling for months, so that people will assume you're streetwise. Avoid wearing anything brand-new, especially white clothes or safari suits, and make sure your shoes aren't overly shiny. Some tourists swear by sunglasses to avoid making unwanted eye-contact; while this usually works, it still marks you out as a tourist and also puts a barrier between you and everyone else, not just hustlers.

But appearance isn't everything: **attitude** counts as well. While most tourists try to ignore *papasi*, the latter have developed stoic persistence as a countermeasure, and being trailed by one throughout town quickly becomes tiring. If you're being bugged by someone whose "help" you don't need, just let them know you can't pay anything for their trouble. It may not make you a friend, but it's better than a row and recriminations. Once you get past the initial "buy this, buy that" stage, some *papasi* can actually be helpful and even pleasant to be with. That said, you shouldn't assume anything they do is out of simple kindness. It may well be, but if it isn't, you must expect to pay something. If you have any suspicion, confront the matter head on at an early stage and either apologize for the offence caused by the suggestion, or agree a price. What you must never do, as when bargaining, is enter into an unspoken contract and then break it by refusing to pay for the service.

Beggars

Beggars are rare on Zanzibar but fairly common in Dar es Salaam, albeit to nowhere near the same degree as London, for example. Most are visibly destitute; many are cripples, lepers or blind, or are homeless mothers with children, and are regularly harassed by police and *askaris* (security guards). Some have regular pitches; others keep on the move. Giving Tsh100 is generous; Tsh200 will often delight.

Politics and the threat of terrrorism

The ugly scar on Tanzania's self-portrayal as an "oasis of peace" is, unfortunately, Zanzibar, where **political unrest** has been a constant theme since Independence. The violence, which tends to peak around election times (the next bout is pencilled in for 2010), is most unlikely to affect you directly, unless you're partial to attending political rallies. However, the use of several **homemade bombs** in the aftermath of the 2000 elections against electric transformers and the like is unsettling, particularly in the post-September 11 context. With the distinction between politics and religion becoming ever vaguer, and given that Al-Qaeda struck twice in East Africa, once in 1998 against the US embassies in Dar es Salaam and Nairobi, and again in 2002 against a Kenyan beach resort and Israeli plane, there's a small but real risk of international **terrorism** striking Zanzibar. Other than being one of the few tourists to heed the polite requests posted in every hotel about covering up legs and shoulders in town, there's little you can do to minimise such a vague risk. Any large tourist hotel could be a target, as would any place selling alcohol. Lastly, be aware that whilst you can get away with publicly airing your own **opinions** about local politics on the mainland, it isn't such a grand idea on Zanzibar.

Drugs

If you spend any time in tourist areas, someone will probably offer you **marijuana** (*bangi*) which, despite being illegal, is widely smoked and remarkably cheap. The use of, and attitudes to it, vary considerably, but you should be very discreet if you're going to indulge, and watch out who you get high with – if you're caught in possession, you'll be hit with a heavy fine, and possibly imprisoned or deported.

Whatever you do, never buy marijuana on the street in Stone Town or Dar es Salaam – you're almost guaranteed to be shopped to the police, or approached by fake "policemen" anything from a few minutes to a few hours after buying, who will shake you down for everything you have. Buying in beach areas, where a good many men have adopted Rastafarian-style braids and laid-back lifestyles, if not the religion, is probably safer, not least because there are few if any police around. However, as with alcohol, being seen to be high in public is a bad idea.

Police – and bribes

Though you might sometimes hear stories of extraordinary kindness and of occasional bursts of efficiency that would do credit to any constabulary, in general the **police** are notoriously corrupt, and it's best to steer clear of them. If you need to deal with them, patience and politeness, smiles and handshakes always help, and treat even the most offensively corrupt cop with respect. Having said this, in unofficial dealings the police can go out of their way to help you with food, transport or accommodation. Try to reciprocate; police salaries are low and they rely on unofficial income to get by.

If you know you've done something wrong and are expected to give a **bribe**, wait for it to be hinted at and haggle over it as you would any payment; Tsh2000 or so is often enough to oil small wheels. Be aware, of course, that bribery is illegal – if you know you've done nothing wrong and are not in a rush, refusing a bribe will only cost a short delay until the cop gives up on you and tries another potential source of income. If you're really getting nowhere, you can always kick up a loud fuss – it usually works wonders.

Robbery and theft

Your chances of being **robbed** in Zanzibar are minimal, and even in Dar es Salaam you'd need to be pretty slack or unlucky to be robbed, but you should nonetheless be conscious of your belongings and never leave anything unguarded. In addition, be careful where you walk, at least until you're settled in somewhere, and stay alert at crowded bus stations and ferry terminals.

The best way to avoid being **mugged** is to not carry valuables, especially anything visible. It should go without saying that you don't wear dangling earrings or any kind of chain or necklace, expensive-looking sunglasses or wristwatches; even certain brands of sports shoes (sneakers) can be tempting. Similarly, try to avoid carrying valuables in those handy off-the-shoulder day bags or even small rucksacks, as these provide visible temptation. Old plastic bags (nicknamed "Rambo", courtesy of the dim-witted action hero whose likeness is printed on millions of them) are a much less conspicuous way of carrying cameras. If you clearly have nothing on you, you're unlikely to feel, or be, threatened. If you do get mugged, don't resist, since knives and guns are occasionally carried. It will be over in an

instant and you're unlikely to be hurt. You'll have to go to the nearest police station for a statement to show your insurance company, though you may well be expected to pay a "little something" for it. You can usually forget about enlisting the police to try and get your stuff back. As angry as you may feel about being robbed, it's worth trying to understand the desperation that drives men and boys to risk their lives for your things. Thieves caught red-handed are usually mobbed – and often killed – so when you shout "Thief!" ("Mwizi!" in Kiswahili), be ready to intercede once you've retrieved your belongings.

Thefts from locked **hotel bedrooms** are extremely rare. That said, you could – judiciously – deposit valuables with the hotel management (get a receipt), and minimise temptation by not leaving things lying about openly. Hiding stuff between a mattress and bed frame is also usually safe.

Cons and scams

Some new arrivals get **ripped off** during their first day or two. Most scams are confidence tricks, and though there's no reason to be paranoid (indeed, one or two scams play on a tourist's paranoia), a healthy sense of cynicism is helpful.

One old favourite is the offer to **change money** on the street at favourable rates. Given that the Tanzanian shilling is floated against hard currencies, there's no reason for a black market, so it doesn't take a genius to realize that by changing money on the street you're just setting yourself up to get ripped off. In its most obvious form, the money-changer simply dashes off with your money, sometimes aided by the timely appearance of a "police officer". Much more subtle – and common – is to trick you by sleight of hand: the scammer lets you count the shilling notes, takes your money, then proceeds to roll up the shillings and tie them with a rubber band. When you open the bundle it's been switched for one containing only low-value notes or even paper.

Approaches in the street from "school children" or "students" with **sponsorship forms** are usually also scams and best shrugged off, and if a man who has just picked up a wad of money in the street seems oddly willing to share it with you down a convenient nearby alley (a favourite in Nairobi), you'll know you're about to be robbed... Lastly, several travellers report having had **marijuana planted** on them and then being nabbed by cops, real or fake, with hefty bribes being the way out. So, check your pockets in Dar and Stone Town if a stranger started chatting to you in the street, and if you do get "caught", insist on going to the police station to sort things out, where you'll be able to kick up a fuss with the officer's superior, threaten legal action and so on – a rigmarole that hopefully won't be worth the corrupt cop's time, or his job if he gets shopped.

Customs and good manners

With the exception of *papasi*, Zanzibaris are well known for their tactfulness and courtesy, qualities that are valued right across the social spectrum. As such, you'll be treated as an honoured guest by many people, and if you make the effort, you'll be welcomed to a side of Zanzibar that only few tourists see. The vast majority of Zanzibaris are Muslim, belonging to the pragmatic and tolerant Sunni branch, but the line is drawn at mosques, which should only be entered by Muslims.

Appearance and behaviour

There are no hard and fast rules about **public behaviour** as long as you respect local customs, cultural and religious beliefs – it's really up to you, as most Zanzibaris are too polite to publicly admonish offensive tourists. The main thing you should be aware of is the **dress code** for towns and villages, where both women and men should cover their legs and shoulders. For women, the most elegant solution is a cotton *kanga* or *kitenge*, which makes a wonderful souvenir in any case. On **beaches** frequented by tourists, the only rules are no nudity or going topless, both of which are in fact illegal.

A few other things are likely to cause mild offence. These include a man and woman **kissing or hugging** in public, though holding hands is fine, as indeed it is between two men or two women, and **immodesty**, whether verbal or material (don't flaunt wealth). Open displays of **bad temper** or impatience won't endear you to anyone either. There are exceptions to the latter, of course: if you're a woman being pestered by a man, an angry outburst should result in embarrassed bystanders coming to your rescue. Lastly, it is insulting and invasive to take **photographs of people** without their permission. Always ask, and respect their refusal, or cough up if they ask for money in return.

Greetings

Throughout Tanzania, lengthy **greetings** – preferably in Kiswahili – are extremely important, and people do value your efforts to master them, no matter how garbled the attempt. On Zanzibar, elderly men and women are invariably treated with great deference. The most polite greeting for them is the stock Islamic phrase, *Salaam mualaikum* ("Peace be on you"), to which the reply is *Mualaikum salaam*. To vary a bit, you can distinguish yourself by being one of few tourists to use *Sabalkheri* (good morning) and *Masalkheri* (good evening), though the person you're greeting will likely assume you speak fluent Kiswahili. For **other greetings**, see the "Language" section on p.255.

As well as the verbal greeting, younger women do a slight **curtsy** when greeting elders, while men invariably shake hands both at meeting and parting. Among younger people especially there are a number of more elaborate handshakes that anyone will be happy to teach you. You should always use your right hand to shake or to give or receive anything; it's especially polite to clasp your right forearm or wrist with your left hand as you do so. Incidentally, if someone's hands are wet or dirty when you meet, they'll offer their wrist instead. It's impolite to discuss a man's work or financial standing unless you know him well.

Gifts

When invited into someone's home, it's usual to bring small **presents** (see box below). If you're staying longer than for just a meal, slightly more elaborate presents are in order. Increase the amount of practical stuff you bring (a few kilos of sugar, more tea), and bring a *kanga* or *kitenge* for the mother and grandmother. Ballpoint pens and writing pads will always find a use, and the kids will love books (Tanzania's literacy rate, though down from a peak of ninety percent-plus which it reached in the 1980s, is still high by African standards). The better bookshops in Stone Town and Dar es Salaam stock some gorgeously illustrated children's books in Kiswahili. For other gift ideas, ask your host before coming – and insist beyond their polite insistence that the only presents you need to bring is your own presence.

Lastly, **do not give coins, sweets or pens to children**: it encourages begging, as you'll notice in the chorus of "Mzungu give me money/pen/sweet" that accompanies you anywhere where tourists ignoring this rule have been in the past. If you really want to give something, hand it to an adult who will share it out, or – even better – make a donation to the local school. If you'll be travelling or staying for some time and really want to prepare, get a large batch of photos of you and your family with your address on the back. You'll get lots of mail.

Sexuality

In contrast to mainland Tanzania's uncluttered mores, Zanzibari attitudes to **sex and sexuality** are difficult to pin down, particularly given the many traditional "veils" that serve to shield private lives from public view. As might be expected, however, unmarried Zanzibari men consider themselves free to embark on romances with foreigners, unlike Zanzibari women – the exception being a number of ill-regarded prostitutes who frequent Stone Town's handful of bars and night clubs.

Plenty enough **female tourists** arrive expecting sexual adventures to make flirtatious pestering a fairly constant part of the scene, irritating or amusing as it strikes you. If you are a woman looking for a holiday affair, be aware that your cute dreadlocked lover

Being invited to eat at home

If you're invited to a meal at someone's home, do accept – it's something of an honour both for you and for the people whose home you visit. Taking small gifts for the family is in order. Elder men often appreciate filterless "Sigara Nyota" cigarettes, nicknamed *sigara ya babu* – grandfather's cigarettes. Women appreciate anything that helps keep down their household expenses, be it soap, sugar, tea or a few loaves of bread. Kids, of course, adore sweets – but give them to the mother to hand out or you'll end up getting mobbed. Make sure you leave a big hole in your stomach before coming: your hosts will probably make a huge play out of the fact that you're not eating enough, even if you've just gobbled up twice what anyone else has.

Before eating, one of the girls or women will appear with a bowl, soap and a jug of hot water to wash your hands with. Food is eaten by hand from a communal bowl or plate. Although you may be presented with a plate and cutlery, it's best to try to eat the proper way. When eating, use only your right hand. *Ugali* is eaten by taking a small piece with your fingers and rolling it in the palm of your hand to make a small ball. The ball is then dipped in sauce and popped into your mouth. Don't worry about making a mess – your hosts will be most surprised if you don't.

Sexual harassment

Women, whether travelling alone or together, may come across occasional **persistent hasslers** but seldom much worse. Universal rules apply: if you suspect ulterior motives, turn down all offers and stonily refuse to converse, though you needn't fear expressing your anger if that's how you feel. You will be left alone – eventually. Really obnoxious individuals are usually on their own, fortunately. A useful trick if you're unmarried and travelling alone is to wear a "wedding" ring (silver ones feel safer than gold in terms of tempting robbery), though for this to work it would be helpful to take along a picture of a burly male friend à la Mike Tyson with a suitably husband-like message written on the back as "proof".

more likely than not does this for a living. Although there are no reliable figures for **HIV infection rates** on the islands, the disease's incidence is definitely on the increase, and it goes without saying that casual sex without a condom is a deadly gamble. Most **hotels** refuse to let unmarried couples share a room, and a good number insist on seeing a copy of a marriage certificate; passports should suffice if your surnames match.

Officially, **being gay** in Zanzibar can get you up to 25 years in the slammer (it's only 14 years on the mainland), although homosexuality is an accepted undercurrent on the coast. Be extremely careful whether you're with your partner, or are looking for one. Public displays of affection are guaranteed to offend or worse, though men holding hands is perfectly normal if it's part of a long greeting, or – rather amusingly – if you ask for directions and are being shown the way. Hotels will not let two men share a room, though two women sharing is usually fine. *Shoga* is a gay man; *msagaji* is a lesbian.

Travellers with disabilities

Zanzibar doesn't pose insurmountable problems for people in wheelchairs, and there are always willing hands to help you over hurdles. It's best to buy a through-ticket to Zanzibar, to avoid the obstacle courses and tiny taxis of Dar es Salaam and Nairobi, and forget about catching the ferry from the mainland, which is way too much hassle even for able people. If you're looking for an all-in tour, contact the tour operator Abercrombie & Kent, reviewed in the "Getting there" section at the start of this chapter.

Zanzibar **airport** is wheelchair friendly, not by design but because it's so basic – everything is at ground level. There are plenty of spacious minibus **taxis** outside, most doubling as vehicles for **spice tours**, and Unguja's main roads are mostly smooth asphalt. **Dolphin tours** are accessible too, as long as you don't mind being carried from the beach to the boat. **Jozani Forest** has a couple of boardwalks, parts of which can be used by wheelchairs.

Getting around **Stone Town** by wheelchair is easy, even without anyone to push you, as with the exception of Malawi and Creek roads in the north and east respectively, there are few vehicles to contend with (you have to use the actual roads outside the old town, as the pavements are pitted). Inside the labyrinthine old town, the only vehicles are occasional scooters, and there are no kerbs, though Pipalwadi Street in the south and a handful of others leading in from the north and east were in a bad state at the time of writing. Mizingani Road in the west is fine, as is all of Shangani and Vuga districts. Unfortunately, **rooms** in most of Stone Town's hotels are accessed via steep staircases, and there are no elevators, though a handful have ground-floor rooms, including the budget *Garden Lodge* and *Karibu Inn*, and the mid-range *Beit-al-Amaan*.

Almost all **beach hotels** have ground-level rooms, sometimes accessed via two or three steps. More important, if your body is sensitive to shocks, is road access, as most beach hotels worth staying at are some distance from the main asphalt roads. Those requiring the shortest drives along the connecting rough roads are Mtoni, north of Stone Town (0.5km), Paje on the east coast (there are hotels from 1km, and up to 3km from the asphalt road), Matemwe in the northeast (1–3km) and Kizimkazi in the south (0–1.5km). With a considerate driver, there's no reason why other beaches could not be considered too, excepting perhaps Nungwi and Kendwa which suffer from particularly rough access. **Pemba** is probably a less suitable destination, as the main reasons for going there are snorkelling and scuba diving, and the various ruins scattered over the island are along very rough roads. To get around on both Unguja and Pemba, use the large minibus taxis (of which there are a good number). These have plenty of space for wheelchairs, although drivers on the latter are a good deal more considerate than the ones on Unguja.

Contacts for travellers with disabilities

In the UK and Ireland

Holiday Care 2nd floor, Imperial Building, Victoria Rd, Horley, Surrey RH6 7PZ ☎0845/124 9971 or ☎0208/760 0072, ⓦwww.holidaycare.org.uk. Provides free lists of accessible accommodation abroad, and information on financial help for holidays.

Irish Wheelchair Association Blackheath Drive, Clontarf, Dublin 3 ☎01/818 6400, ⓦwww.iwa.ie. Useful information provided about travelling abroad with a wheelchair.

Tripscope The Vassall Centre, Gill Ave, Bristol BS16 2QQ ☎08457/585 641 or 0117/939 7782, ⓦwww.tripscope.org.uk. Registered charity providing a national telephone information service offering free advice on transport.

In the US and Canada

Access-Able ⓦwww.access-able.com. Useful website for travellers with disabilities.

Directions Unlimited 123 Green Lane, Bedford Hills, NY 10507 ☎1-800/533-5343 or 1-914/241-1700. Travel agency specializing in bookings for people with disabilities.

Mobility International USA 451 Broadway, Eugene, OR 97401 ☎1-541/343-1284, ⓦwww.miusa.org. Information and referral services, access guides, tours and exchange programmes.

SATH (Society for the Advancement of Travelers with Handicaps) 347 5th Ave, New York, NY 10016 ☎1-212/447-7284, ⓦwww.sath.org. Not-for-profit educational organization that has actively represented travellers with disabilities since 1976. Annual membership $45; $30 for students and seniors.

Twin Peaks Press PO Box 129, Vancouver, WA 98666-0129 ☎360/694-2462, ⓦwww.home.pacifier.com/~twinpeak. Publisher of the *Directory of Travel Agencies for the Disabled*, listing more than 370 agencies worldwide; *Travel for the Disabled*; and *Wheelchair Vagabond*, loaded with personal tips.

Wheels Up! ☎1-888/38-WHEELS, ⓦwww.wheelsup.com. Provides discounted airfare, tour and cruise prices for disabled travellers, and publishes a free monthly newsletter. Comprehensive website.

In Australia and New Zealand

ACROD (Australian Council for Rehabilitation of the Disabled) PO Box 60, Curtin ACT 2605; ☎02/6282 4333 (also TTY), ⓦwww.acrod.org.au. Provides lists of travel agencies and tour operators for people with disabilities.

Disabled Persons Assembly 4/173–175 Victoria St, Wellington, New Zealand ☎04/801 9100 (also TTY), ⓦwww.dpa.org.nz. Resource centre with lists of travel agencies and tour operators for people with disabilities.

Directory

Contraceptives Condoms are freely sold in pharmacies and supermarkets; a reliable local brand is Salama. Bring oral contraceptives with you.

Electricity Like Britain, Tanzania and Zanzibar use square three-pin plugs on 220–240V, though power surges and drop-offs widen the range considerably. If you're using sensitive electronic equipment, ensure that it or the transformer accepts voltages from 160V to 260V. All but the very cheapest hotel rooms tend to have sockets. Both Zanzibar and Dar are particularly afflicted by power cuts (blackouts). Things are worse at the end of particularly dry spells, when mainland reservoirs are too low to adequately power hydroelectric stations.

Laundry More expensive hotels have a laundry service, which can be very expensive if you've a lot to wash as prices are per item. In cheaper establishments, you can arrange things informally with the staff for a few thousand shillings.

Photography High-contrast equatorial sunlight plays tricks with exposure meters, so digital is the way to go – you can always retake shots that don't work. Popular belief equates the act of taking a picture of a person with stealing a piece of their soul, so always ask permission before doing so. It's also a bad idea to take pictures of anything that could be construed as strategic, including any military or police building, airports and harbours. Take spare batteries, and a spare high-capacity memory card, or films. To email your snaps, you'll need a USB-card reader to transfer the files in an Internet café.

Time Zanzibar is three hours ahead of Greenwich Mean Time, which means two hours ahead of Britain during the summer and three in winter; seven or eight hours ahead of US Eastern Standard Time; and 6.5–7.5 hours behind Australian time. Remember that the hours in "Swahili time" run from 6am to 6pm rather than noon to midnight, so that 7am and 7pm Western time equate to 1 o'clock in Swahili (*saa moja*), whilst midnight and midday are *saa sita* (six o'clock). It's not as confusing as it first sounds – just add or subtract six hours to work out Swahili time.

Tipping The average monthly salary is $50 (Tsh55,000). In local hotels, bars and restaurants, tipping is not the custom, but always appreciated. If you're staying in tourist-class establishments, staff may expect to be tipped: Tsh1000 wouldn't be out of place for portering a lot of luggage, but Tsh500 is adequate. For small services, Tsh200–500 is fine. Zanzibar's taxi drivers are accustomed to taking financial advantage of tourists in any case, so a tip is rarely needed.

Toilets All tourist-oriented hotels and restaurants have "Western"-style sit-down toilets. In cheaper places they may lack seats or paper and will need to be flushed with a bucket. Lowlier establishments have Asian-style squat toilets, often directly under the shower. They are mostly quite hygienic, and may also have flushing mechanisms. Locals rarely if ever use toilet paper, and there's a reason: in the tropical heat, rinsing your nether regions with water (using your left hand) is much cleaner than wiping with tissue, as long as you wash your hands properly afterwards. There's invariably a tap to hand, with a bucket for flushing and a plastic jug for rinsing. Toilet paper is sold in towns.

Guide

Guide

Dar es Salaam

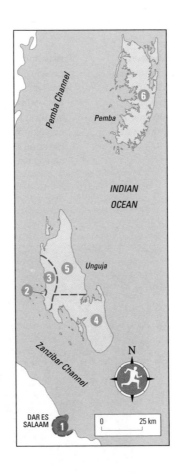

CHAPTER 1 # Highlights

✳ **Kariakoo Market** In the heart of the city's African area is one of the continent's busiest and brashest markets, which provides a welcome assault on the senses. See p.69

✳ **The National Museum** Every angle on Tanzanian culture and history, from Nutcracker Man and a prehistoric fish to wooden bicycles and xylophones. See p.70

✳ **Nightlife** With bars, nightclubs and dance halls galore, Dar is heaven for night owls, and also for carnivores – grilled meat is the traditional accompaniment to live music. See p.73

✳ **Arts and crafts** Dar's galleries, art centres and craft shops are shopping bliss, where you can buy anything from wire toys and contemporary paintings to life-sized Maasai warriors carved in wood. See p.75

△ Lutheran Church, Dar es Salaam

Dar es Salaam

Many visitors to Zanzibar arrive or depart from **DAR ES SALAAM**, Tanzania's erstwhile capital, as it's often cheaper to arrange transport over to Zanzibar here, than buying a through ticket from home. Starting life in 1862 as the site of Zanzibar's Sultan Majid's summer residence – the Bandur ul Salaam ("Palace of Peace") – Dar has grown to become East Africa's biggest city. Seventy percent of its four million inhabitants, many of them recent immigrants from the countryside, live in unplanned housing, often little more than slums. Their nickname for the city is **Bongo**, meaning "smart" or "clever", suggesting the skills required to survive in an urban expanse this size. Not surprisingly, visitors tend to spend as little time in the city as possible, but if you're on holiday for a couple of weeks, there's plenty to keep you busy, and the city's vibrant blend of traditional and contemporary cultures and communities provides an enjoyable and distinctly African contrast to Zanzibar.

Arrival, city transport, information and tours

Dar es Salaam International Airport lies 11km southwest of the city, a 25-minute drive along Nyerere Road. **International flights** land at Terminal 2, which has a bar and restaurant, and various foreign exchange bureaux (bad rates for travellers' cheques). Most **domestic flights**, including ones to and from Zanzibar, use Terminal 1, whose facilities are limited to a snack bar and charter airline offices. Taxis try to charge tourists upwards of Tsh12,000 from either terminal to the city centre; wilier travellers might pay Tsh8000. Daladalas to the city (Tsh200) run along the highway 500m from either terminal, though clambering aboard one with tons of luggage won't endear you to fellow passengers. The **ferry terminal**, where boats from Zanzibar dock, is on Sokoine Drive in the centre of town. It's perfectly safe to walk from there into the city by day, though you may be accompanied by "flycatchers" – hustlers.

City transport

Taxis can be found almost everywhere, and at night outside hotels, clubs, restaurants, bars, and at major road junctions. Licensed cabs are white, carry white number plates, and have a number painted on the side; others risk being pulled up by the police, at your inconvenience. Trips within the city shouldn't

Avoiding trouble

Dar es Salaam is a relatively **safe** city, but keep your wits about you if you've just landed and have yet to develop that worn-in appearance. The main hassle comes from irritating if harmless **flycatchers** – the mainland equivalent of Zanzibar's *papasi* (hustlers) – whose main line of business is touting wildlife safaris from disreputable companies. They hang around at the airport, the ferry port, the Askari Monument in the city centre, and outside the backpackers' hotels in Kisutu district. Some may also offer marijuana, or to change money – you'd need your head examining to accept either. As to **specific areas to avoid**, walking around by day should be safe wherever you are, as long as you're not visibly nervous or carrying valuables. At night it's always best to catch a taxi, though walking short distances along main streets in the central business district as far west as Kisutu should be fine, if you have nothing to get stolen – there are plenty of security guards. Lastly, be on your guard for **pickpockets** and **bag-snatchers** in Kariakoo's crowded market area, and at transport terminals.

cost more than Tsh2500, journeys to the inner suburbs (this includes most of the nightclubs) Tsh2500–4000, and Tsh4000–6000 to Msasani Peninsula north of the city. You'll pay more if you don't bargain.

Locals get around by **daladala** (shared minibus), which are invariably packed, noisy and uncomfortable, but surprisingly efficient and cheap, getting you almost anywhere for just Tsh200. The main central terminals ("stands") are **Posta** along Maktaba Street, and **Kariakoo** 3km to the west along Msimbazi Street.

Information and tours

Dar's **tourist office** (Mon–Fri 8am–4pm, Sat 8.30am–12.30pm; ☎022/213 1555, ✉ttb2@ud.co.tz) is on Samora Avenue, four blocks southwest of the Askari Monument. They have hotel price lists, a register of licensed safari operators, some brochures, and a free city map. A number of travel agents (see p.78) offer guided half-day **city tours** for $30–70 per person. Essentially car hire with an English-speaking guide, it's cheaper to negotiate a half-day fare with a taxi driver who speaks your language; Tsh25,000 should suffice, plus any entry fees.

Accommodation

Dar's **accommodation** covers all budgets and styles, and rates are cheaper than on Zanzibar. Between November and February, rooms in cheaper hotels and some mid-range places can become exceedingly hot and stuffy: get one with a balcony or air-conditioning.

Budget

Al-Uruba Hotel Mkunguni St, Kariakoo, 2km west of town ☎022/218 0133, ☎022/218 0135. In the populous area reserved by the British for Africans in colonial times, this Somali-run place is the city's best budget hotel and often full (book ahead), with friendly staff and small if cool en-suite rooms complete with cotton sheets, desk and chair, ceiling fan, window nets (some also have box nets), hot water, and even satellite TV. Busy restaurant downstairs. No alcohol. ❶

Holiday Hotel Jamhuri St, Kisutu, city centre ☎022/211 2246, ✉yasinmjuma@hotmail.com. A secure and decent backpackers' hotel with good double rooms, especially those with street-facing balconies. Some have bathrooms, but singles are tiny, stuffy and eminently avoidable. The reception is on the second floor. **❶**

Jambo Inn Libya St, Kisutu, city centre ☎022/211 4293, 🌐www.jambohotel.8m.com. Dar's most popular backpackers' haunt, but with very variable rooms, so ask to see a selection. Those at the front are noisy but their balconies are a boon. Internet café and overpriced restaurant downstairs (mediocre breakfast included). **❶–❷**

Safari Inn Off Libya St, Kisutu, city centre ☎022/211 9104, ✉safari-inn@lycos.com. Another backpackers' haunt, with small but bright, clean and airy en-suite rooms with big double beds, fans and nets. The bathrooms can be smelly and the welcome perfunctory. Internet café and cheap restaurant downstairs. Good breakfast included. **❶–❷**

🏃 **YWCA** Ghana Ave, city centre ☎022/212 2439, ✉ywca.tanzania@africaonline.co.tz. Recommended should the matriarchs take a shine to you, and if you don't mind the racket from the adjacent Posta daladala stand (5am–10pm). The rooms are a bit tatty but clean (and "en suite" may just mean a sink), but they have nets and fans, and there's a good cheap restaurant. The *askari* will let you in after the 11pm curfew. Reservations advisable. Paltry breakfast included. **❶**

Moderate

🏃 **The Courtyard** Ocean Rd, Upanga, 1.5km north of town ☎022/213 0130, ✉courtyard@raha.com. With its bougainvillea-festooned balconies, this three-storey hotel looks like part of New Orleans, rebuilt around a small swimming pool in, yes, a courtyard. The location isn't ideal, flanked by high-rise, low-cost housing, but service and standards are high. Standard rooms have a/c, phone, satellite TV, bathtub and minibar, but smell of bug spray (no nets); more expensive rooms are larger but otherwise identical. Amenities include the superb *Langi-Langi* restaurant, snack bar and bar, room service and travel desk. Breakfast included. **❻**

🏃 **Harbour View Suites** JM Mall, Samora Ave, city centre ☎022/212 4040, 🌐www .harbourview-suites.com. Large, modern, very good-value rooms at the top of a twelve-storey building, recommended particularly for the harbour views at the back (other rooms overlook the city). All have fully-equipped kitchens, huge satellite TVs and broadband sockets. Choose between four-poster nets or having your room sprayed. Rooms on the eleventh floor have balconies, whilst the executive suites have enough space for a harem. **❺**

🏃 **Q-Bar & Guest House** Off Haile Selassie Rd, Msasani Peninsula, 4.5km north of town ☎0744/282474, ✉qbar@hotmail.com. The main reason for staying here is for the lively if noisy nightlife downstairs. Its rooms are good value, with satellite TV, a/c, fridge and window nets; cheaper ones share bathrooms, and there's also a dorm ($12 per person). Breakfast included. **❹**

The Souk The Slipway shopping centre, Msasani Peninsula, 6.5km north of town ☎022/260 0893, 🌐www.slipway.net. Next to Msasani Bay, rooms have modern creature-comforts wrapped in classic Arabian styling, on three floors around a glass-covered atrium. The spacious rooms and apartments all have a/c and satellite TV, and The Slipway's upmarket bars and restaurants are within walking distance. **❺**

Expensive

Golden Tulip Touré Drive, Msasani Peninsula, 5km north of town ☎022/260 0288, 🌐www .goldentuliptanzania.com. This huge, over-the-top Arabian-style beach hotel is flogged as "a corporate hotel in resort surroundings", amply betraying its rather impersonal nature. The spacious standard rooms have balconies with sea views, and facilities include a huge swimming pool, poolside bar and grill, restaurant, Jacuzzi with sea view, fitness area, shopping mall and coffee shop. Breakfast included. **❼**

Kilimanjaro Kempinski Hotel Kivukoni Front, city centre ☎022/213 1111, 🌐www.kempinski -daressalaam.com. This 180-room 1960s monolith has been transformed into a classy five-star, with high standards and great harbour and sea views from its front rooms. All have a/c and pay TV. Facilities include two restaurants, three bars (one on the roof), a health spa, infinity swimming pool, and casino. **❼–❽**

Mövenpick Royal Palm Ohio St, city centre ☎022/211 2416, 🌐www.moevenpick-hotels.com.

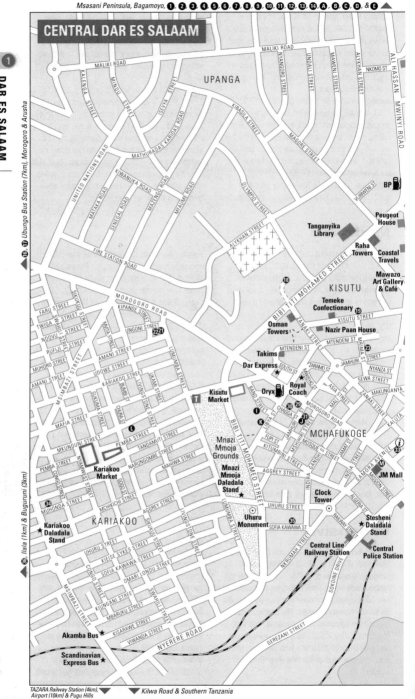

CENTRAL DAR ES SALAAM

UPANGA

KISUTU

MCHAFUKOGE

KARIAKOO

TAZARA Railway Station (4km),
Airport (10km) & Pugu Hills

Kilwa Road & Southern Tanzania

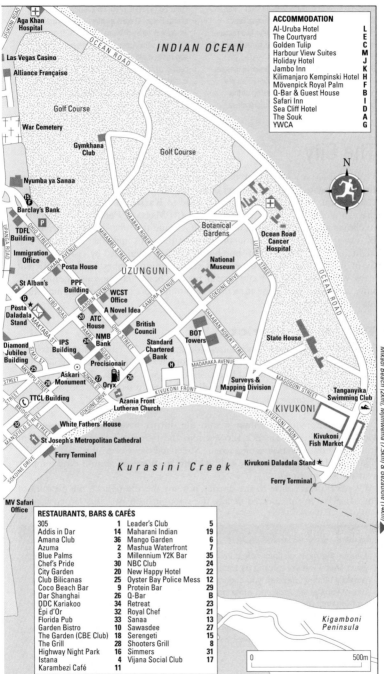

INDIAN OCEAN

Aga Khan Hospital

Las Vegas Casino

Alliance Française

OCEAN ROAD

Golf Course

War Cemetery

Gymkhana Club

Golf Course

Nyumba ya Sanaa

Barclay's Bank

TDFL Building

Immigration Office

Posta House

UZUNGUNI

St Alban's

PPF Building

WCST Office

A Novel Idea

Posta Daladala Stand

ATC House

NMB Bank

British Council

Standard Chartered Bank

BOT Towers

Diamond Jubilee Building

IPS Building

Precisionair

Askari Monument

Oryx

Azania Front Lutheran Church

TTCL Building

White Fathers' House

St Joseph's Metropolitan Cathedral

Ferry Terminal

MV Safari Office

Botanical Gardens

Ocean Road Cancer Hospital

National Museum

State House

Surveys & Mapping Division

KIVUKONI

Tanganyika Swimming Club

Kivukoni Fish Market

Kivukoni Daladala Stand ★

Ferry Terminal

Kurasini Creek

Mikadi Beach (2km), Mjimwema (7.5km) & Gezaulole (14km)

Kigamboni Peninsula

N

0   500m

ACCOMMODATION

Al-Uruba Hotel	L
The Courtyard	E
Golden Tulip	C
Harbour View Suites	M
Holiday Hotel	J
Jambo Inn	K
Kilimanjaro Kempinski Hotel	H
Mövenpick Royal Palm	F
Q-Bar & Guest House	B
Safari Inn	I
Sea Cliff Hotel	D
The Souk	A
YWCA	G

RESTAURANTS, BARS & CAFÉS

305	1	Leader's Club	5
Addis in Dar	14	Maharani Indian	19
Amana Club	36	Mango Garden	6
Azuma	2	Mashua Waterfront	7
Blue Palms	3	Millennium Y2K Bar	35
Chef's Pride	30	NBC Club	24
City Garden	20	New Happy Hotel	22
Club Bilicanas	25	Oyster Bay Police Mess	12
Coco Beach Bar	9	Protein Bar	29
Dar Shanghai	26	Q-Bar	B
DDC Kariakoo	34	Retreat	23
Épi d'Or	32	Royal Chef	21
Florida Pub	33	Sanaa	13
Garden Bistro	10	Sawasdee	27
The Garden (CBE Club)	18	Serengeti	15
The Grill	28	Shooters Grill	8
Highway Night Park	16	Simmers	31
Istana	4	Vijana Social Club	17
Karambezi Café	11		

Over 250 luxurious rooms with all mod-cons; rooms higher up at the back have sea views over a golf course. Facilities include two restaurants, swimming pool, sauna and gym. Breakfast included. ⑦–⑧

Sea Cliff Hotel Touré Drive, Msasani Peninsula, 7km north of town ℡022/260 0380, ⒲www .hotelseacliff.com. Perched on the tip of the peninsula, this 86-room hotel is a graceless,

thatched concrete block on the outside but very stylish inside. There's a choice of well-appointed en-suite doubles or twins, and for $20 more you get a sea view. Amenities include expensive bars and restaurants, a casino, bowling alley, shopping centre, gym and swimming pool. The downside is that there's no beach (it's on a cliff), and the almost entirely non-African clientele. Breakfast included. ⑥

The City

Dar es Salaam is a patchwork of influences, from the vibrant **Asian district** to the more sedate European quarter of **Uzunguni**, although to find any authentically African street life you'll have to head to **Kariakoo Market**, just west of the centre. A few kilometres north of Dar is **Msasani Peninsula**, the address of choice for diplomats, civil servants, NGOs and the otherwise rich, privileged or corrupt. The peninsula contains most of the city's upmarket restaurants and nightclubs, and a number of shoreline hotels too, often used by visitors coming to or from Zanzibar. In general it's the contrasting vibes of these different areas which provide the city's main interest beside languorous ocean views, since conventional tourist attractions are limited to a couple of museums and a number of crafts centres.

The Asian district

The western end of the city centre is occupied by the city's **Asian district**, a bustling quarter containing hundreds of shops, tea rooms, restaurants, goldsmiths and sweet shops, along with Hindu, Sikh, Jain and Muslim places of worship. This is the heart of historical **Uhindini**, the area reserved by the British for Indian coolies (indentured labourers) shipped in to help build the modern city.

The numerous communities within the district have retained strong individual characters. You're not allowed into the mosques unless you're Muslim (the main concentration is on Mosque Street and the streets off it), but both the Sikh and Hindu communities will be happy to show you around their temples: start on Kisutu Street.

There's no real centre to the district, nor any specific sights – the pleasure of the place lies in unexpected details: the wrought-iron swastikas (an auspicious

Dar's paan shops

One of the most distinctive features of Dar es Salaam's Asian area are the Indian *paan* shops, often doubling as tobacconists and corner shops. *Paan* is essentially a mildly narcotic dessert: you choose from a range of sweet spices, chopped nuts, bits of vegetable, syrup and white lime, which are then wrapped in a hot, sweet betel leaf (*mtambuu*), which is the mildly narcotic bit – it tastes as exotic as it sounds. *Paan* is chewed and sucked but not swallowed: pop the triangular parcel in your mouth and munch, then spit out the pith when you're finished. Good places to try it are Shehenai Paan House on Mrima Street, and Nazir Paan House at the west end of Kisutu Street.

symbol of prosperity and good fortune for Hindus, Buddhists and Jain) adorning the Hindu temples on **Kisutu Street**; men selling beautifully arranged flower petals outside them; the luridly coloured pyramids of Indian sweets; the *paan* shops; and the beautiful balconied houses on **Uhuru Street**, which is well worth heading to anyway for its colourful blaze of printed cloth *kitenge* panels, sold by shops and hawkers at its western end. In addition, don't miss **Kisutu Market** (daily 8am–5pm) on Bibi Titi Mohamed Street, an atmospheric if insalubrious little place selling fruit and vegetables, honey, beans and pulses, as well as baskets of squawking chickens, dried fish and some gorgeously pungent herbs.

Kariakoo

West of the Asian district, on the far side of the grassy Mnazi Mmoja Grounds, lies **Kariakoo**, the city centre's most African district. Kariakoo is made up of a dusty grid of streets, of which only some are surfaced, but whose mud-walled "Swahili houses" topped with corrugated-iron roofs have in recent years been giving way to mushrooming high-rises. Occupying much of the area set aside by the British for the city's African population, its name dates from World War I, when – after the expulsion of the Germans – thousands of Tanzanians were conscripted into the hated British **Carrier Corps** to serve as war porters. Their barracks were erected on a patch of ground that had been earmarked for a ceremonial park in honour of Kaiser Wilhelm II. After the war, Kariakoo was left to the African population. No amenities were provided, and even now many parts of the area still lack the most basic of facilities.

In spite of the poverty, Kariakoo exudes a solid sense of community that manages to combine both tribal and religious identities. In many ways, the district is a microcosm of the country, and its pan-Tanzanian nature has resulted in one of the most fascinating and headily colourful markets in Africa. **Kariakoo Market** (daily sunrise–sunset), whose bizarre roof resembles a forest of upturned black parasols, occupies the site of the former barracks. In the maze of shops and stalls surrounding it, you'll find everything from exotic fruits, vegetables, fish and freshly cooked meat, to aromatic spices, herbs, coffee, handicrafts, textiles, local brews (*pombe*), and children's toys made from wire and recycled tin cans. Old men sell medicinal herbs, potions and powders in little bottles salvaged from hospitals, as well as bundles of tree bark, dried lizards and seashells with curative properties. Elsewhere, great squawking bundles of trussed-up chickens create a clamour, whilst in other parts of the market you might be offered tart baobab seeds, snuff tobacco or dodgy imported electronics. What's most striking though, is the care with which everything is displayed, whether pieces of cloth rolled into tight cones and propped up on the ground, oranges and other fruits balanced atop one other in *fungas* (geometrical piles) or fresh flowers artistically inserted between mounds of coconuts. Visitors are welcome, of course, but take precautions against pickpockets, particularly in the packed streets south of the main building, where the second-hand clothes (*mitumba*) area gives you little more than elbow-room.

For a breather, join the locals at the famous **DDC Kariakoo Social Hall** on Muhonda Street. Tanzania's oldest African bar, it also serves up a wide range of tasty and dirt-cheap Tanzanian dishes, before – on Tuesdays, Thursdays and especially Sundays – turning into one of Dar's best-loved live music venues.

The Askari Monument, Kivukoni Front and the fish market

Tanzania's soldiers and members of the British Carrier Corps are commemorated by the **Askari Monument**, a bronze statue of a soldier at the roundabout between Samora Avenue, and Maktaba and Azikiwe streets in the city centre. Dar es Salaam's first buildings, erected during Sultan Majid's rule in the 1860s, faced the harbour along Kivukoni Front east of here. Though most have long since disappeared, a notable exception is the **White Fathers' House**, near the corner with Bridge Street, which served as the Sultan's harem until being put to holier uses by the Society of Missionaries of Africa, a Roman Catholic order founded by French Algerians in 1868, who began their first East African mission in Zanzibar in 1878.

Nearby, **St Joseph's Metropolitan Cathedral**, consecrated in 1897, is a major city landmark and a good place to experience Dar's vibrant church music (*kwaya*), best heard during Sunday Mass. The cathedral is notable for its twin confessionals facing the altar, one in Baroque style, the other Gothic. The squat, whitewashed **Azania Front Lutheran Church**, 200m to the east, is unmissable thanks to its fanciful tower, which looks like it should really be adorning a Rhineland castle. The *kwaya* here rivals that of St Joseph's.

Heading east along the bay, **Kivukoni Front** leads past a number of graceful German colonial buildings, most adorned with Indian-style wooden balconies, which are nowadays occupied by various government ministries and offices. At the eastern end of Kivukoni Front is the ferry (*mvuko*) terminal for Kigamboni and, almost opposite, **Kivukoni Fish Market** – not that you need directions to get there: the smell is unmistakable. Unsurprisingly, this is the best place in Dar – indeed probably the best along the entire coast – for seafood, with red snapper, kingfish, barracuda, squid, crabs, lobster and prawns all usually available if you get there early in the morning. Should you feel peckish, plenty of women are on hand working their magic over wide frying pans, or putting muscle into huge pots of *ugali* and cassava porridge.

The National Museum and Botanical Gardens

Tanzania's **National Museum** (daily 9.30am–6pm; $3, photography $10) on Shaaban Robert Street is rather smaller than you'd expect for a national showcase, but worth a visit since it briefly covers pretty much every aspect of Tanzanian culture and history, from prehistoric hominid fossils to colonialism and Independence. The exhibits of tribal culture are especially fascinating, and it's a pity no one has ever bothered to expand them, given that many of Tanzania's traditional cultures are now on the verge of disappearing.

The **Entrance Hall** is occupied by temporary exhibitions, often showcasing local artists, and a dusty Rolls Royce that was used by colonial governors and later President Nyerere. To the left of the entrance, the **Hall of Man** succinctly traces mankind's evolution with displays of stone tools, a cast of Ngorongoro's famous Laetoli footprints that showed that mankind's ancestors were walking upright long before anyone had imagined, and fossilized hominid skulls from Oldupai Gorge and elsewhere, including the one-and-three-quarter-million-year-old partial skull of *Australopithecus boisei*, whose impressive jaw led to him being dubbed "Nutcracker Man". Don't miss the hilarious letter from an irate newspaper reader in 1958, fuming about the "hideous" suggestion that man might have evolved from animals.

In the older building at the back of the grounds, the **Biology Hall** contains a large collection of seashells (including a truly enormous giant clam), corals, a couple of dull fish tanks, and – more interesting – an enormous pickled **coelacanth** caught in 2003. Until 1938, when a specimen was caught off South Africa, coelacanths were believed to have died out some 65 million years ago. Largely unchanged since their assumed genesis 350 million years ago, coelacanths are considered to be the closest living relative of the first fish that wandered ashore to become the ancestors of all us landlubbers.

The museum's real gems are in the adjacent **Ethnography Room**, its entrance marked by display cabinets containing grotesque clay figurines from the Pare and Sambaa tribes that were used in initiation ceremonies and to educate children. Things to look for include a strikingly beautiful beaded leather skirt from the Hadzabe hunter-gatherer tribe, brilliant fully functional wooden bicycles, and a number of musical instruments. There's a small **cafeteria** in one of the outbuildings selling sodas and cheap lunches.

The **Botanical Gardens** (daily sunrise–sunset; free), opposite the museum at the eastern end of Samora Avenue, date from German times and offer a shady oasis of peace and a wonderful escape from the city. The gardens are reasonably kept, and contain dozens of species of palm trees and primeval, fern-like cycads, as well as a raucous population of peacocks. If you're in luck, the explanatory leaflet (Tsh500) covering the plants and the garden's history may have been reprinted – ask at the gardener's office.

The Village Museum

Seven kilometres north of town along Ali Hassan Mwinyi Road, which turns into Bagamoyo Road, is the **Village Museum** (daily 9.30am–6pm; $4; catch a daladala marked "Mwenge" from Posta stand on Maktaba Street and get off at "Makumbusho"), founded in 1966 to preserve some of the architectural and material traditions of rural Tanzania. Spread out over the open-air site are nineteen **replica houses** built in the architectural styles of various tribes, each furnished with typical household items and utensils, and surrounded by small plots of local crops and animal pens. Although laudable, the aims of the museum became grimly ironic in the years following its establishment, when President Nyerere embarked on his economically disastrous policy of *Ujamaa*, in which the majority of rural Tanzanians were forcibly moved out of their villages to begin new lives as collective labourers in planned townships. By the time the experiment collapsed in the mid-1970s, the Tanzanian economy was in ruins. Traditional crafts and arts, such as carving, weaving and pottery, are demonstrated by resident "villagers", whilst a blacksmith explains the intricacies of his craft, which has existed in East Africa for at least two millennia. The finished products are sold in a shop that also stocks books and other souvenirs. There's a small café serving drinks and Tanzanian food, and afternoon performances of **traditional dance** (Tues–Sun 2–6pm; $4).

Eating

Dar es Salaam has no shortage of **places to eat**, though for traditional Swahili cuisine or seafood you'll find more choice and lower prices on Zanzibar. The one dish that's better on the mainland though is **nyama choma** (grilled meat), traditionally accompanied by grilled bananas (*ndizi*) or cornmeal porridge (*ugali*), with optional chilli sauce (*pilipili hoho*). *Nyama choma* is best sampled in the city's bars and live music venues (for which see p.74), where you order by weight.

Budget

The following are among the best of Dar's cheapies, where a full meal with soft drinks shouldn't cost more than Tsh5000.

Chef's Pride Chagga St, Kisutu, city centre. A busy and deservedly popular Tanzanian restaurant offering an embarrassment of choice, most of it freshly cooked, whether Zanzibari-style fish in coconut, biryani curry, tender roast chicken or pizza. It also dishes up fast-food favourites, snacks and great breakfast combos, with nothing much over Tsh3000. Daily until 11pm.

Dar Shanghai *Luther House Hostel*, Sokoine Drive, city centre. Tasty and affordable Chinese and Tanzanian food; also has good juices. Closed Sun lunch.

DDC Kariakoo Social Hall Muhonda St, Kariakoo, 3km west of town. Dar's longest-running bar and live music venue is also one of the best places for a really cheap eat, packing them in with metal platters of pilau, beans and stews for a mere Tsh600. Also has great *supu* for breakfast. Daily from 11am to late.

Épi d'Or Samora Ave, city centre. A friendly Lebanese bakery and café, perfect for breakfast or a light lunch. The Mediterranean influence shows in the wonderful fresh salads, snacks like *baba ghanouj* (aubergine and tahina purée) and panini. Coffee is the real thing, so are the juices, and they even bake croissants. No smoking or alcohol. Mon–Sat 7am–6pm.

Maharani Indian Kisutu St, Kisutu, city centre. Modest but highly recommended, with fresh and tasty food featuring a huge vegetarian choice, either à la carte (around Tsh2500) or in the famous lunchtime buffet, a bargain at Tsh3500 (Tsh4000 with meat). Daily until 9pm.

Retreat Mrima St, Kisutu, city centre. Don't let the stark cafeteria-like dining room put you off – this vegetarian place serves up seriously good South Indian food, plus a small selection of more average Chinese dishes, and lunchtime *thalis*. No smoking or alcohol. Tues–Sun until 9pm.

Royal Chef Lumumba St, Kariakoo, 1.5km west of town. Run by the same folks as *Chef's Pride*, and also highly recommended; this is one of the city's best cheap restaurants. The tasty food, both Tanzanian and Western, grills, meat, seafood or vegetarian, comes quickly and in huge portions, with an attractive streetside verandah to boot. Even the T-bone steaks and prawn dishes cost little more than Tsh3500. Daily until 11pm.

Simmers Jamhuri St, under *Holiday Hotel*, Kisutu, city centre. A friendly, locally-run place on two levels dishing up some of Kisutu's best food, whether liver stew, coconut fish and beef, or simple things like rice with beans and vegetables. Big portions, small prices. They also do good breakfasts. Daily for lunch, and dinner to 8pm.

Moderate

Expect to pay up to Tsh10,000 for a full meal at the following.

City Garden Corner of Garden Ave and Pamba Rd, city centre. The outdoor location is the main reason to eat here, with loads of seats under thatch, parasols and trees. The lunchtime buffets are good, and à la carte – including a range of fresh salads, seafood and pizza – is reasonably priced. Slow service, and no alcohol. Daily until 9pm.

The Grill Mkwepu St, city centre. A large and oddly plush place with attentive waiters, spotless table-cloths and icy a/c; there are also seats outside. The extensive menu majors on Indian, particularly Balti – lots of caraway and coriander – and you'll also find fajitas and enchiladas, Korean (Wed evenings), tandoor and teppinyaki, and a dozen ways of serving steak (Tsh9000 for 400g). The Tsh5000

lunchtime buffet is good value. Finish with a *shisha* water pipe. Open daily to around 10pm.

Istana Ali Hassan Mwinyi Rd, Mnananyamala, 5km north of town ☎ 022/276 1348. Welcoming and friendly place serving a small range of spicy Malaysian, Chinese and Indian dishes, most for under Tsh5000, with lots of vegetarian choice too. Meals are dished up on banana leaves if you like, and served at tables in garden huts – try the *nasi lemak* (steamed coconut rice) with *sambal ikan bilis* (anchovies, boiled eggs, fried peanuts and cucumber). Also has affordable buffets (around Tsh8000), with Malay (Mon), Chinese (Tues), seafood (Wed), satay (Thurs) and Indian (Sun). Evenings only.

Karambezi Café *Sea Cliff Hotel*, Touré Drive, Msasani Peninsula, 7km north of town. Beautifully located on the cliff edge with fine ocean views, the huge menu here centres around steaks, pizzas and other Mediterranean dishes. Open 24 hours.

Mashua Waterfront The Slipway shopping centre, Msasani Peninsula, 6.5km north of town. The location's the thing here, with lovely views over Msasani Bay – chow down on pizzas and grills, or just take a drink. Open daily until late.

Expensive

Unless otherwise stated, expect to part with upwards of Tsh15,000 for a full meal with drinks.

Addis in Dar Ursino St, off Bagamoyo Rd, Regent Estate, Mikocheni, 4.5km north of town. Even if you've eaten North Ethiopian food before, don't miss this place. The basic staple is *injera*, a huge soft pancake that you share with your partner, from which you tear bits off, to eat with a variety of highly spiced sauces and stews. Attention to detail is everything, from the traditional decor – even outside under the parasols – to the wafting incense. There's lots of choice for vegetarians; they also brew an excellent cup of coffee, and sell colourful Ethiopian art and beautiful silverwork. A little pricey, but thoroughly recommended. Catch a taxi. Closed Sun.

Azuma The Slipway shopping centre, Msasani Peninsula, 6.5km north of town. Authentic Japanese and Indonesian cuisine – the *sashimi* (raw fish) is superb. Lunchtime specials go for around Tsh8000. Closed all day Mon, and Sat & Sun evenings.

Sanaa *Golden Tulip Hotel*, Touré Drive, Msasani Peninsula, 5km north of town. Theme nights and expensive buffet lunches, including pasta (Wed), vegetarian (Thurs), steak plus live band (Fri), and a fun champagne brunch on Sunday, with plenty of activities for kids like face-painting and a bouncy castle – Tsh14,000 including use of pool.

Sawasdee *New Africa Hotel*, Azikiwe St, city centre. A large business-class hotel whose sublime 9th-floor rooftop restaurant (evenings only) offers beautiful harbour views and fabulous all-you-can-eat buffets (no more than Tsh15,000), currently: Thai seafood (Tues & Fri), Italian (Wed), Indian (Thurs) and barbecue (Sat). Thai dominates the à la carte menu at both places, everything characteristically aromatic and delicious, and there's a good wine list too. Ideal for a romantic tête-à-tête.

Serengeti *Mövenpick Royal Palm*, Ohio St, city centre. This plush hotel's main restaurant is great for splurging on pig-out buffets (upwards of Tsh15,000), including lavish breakfast spreads that you could hardly do justice to. Theme nights are the fishy "Neptune's Kingdom" on Thursday (includes lobster, crab claws, smoked sailfish and prawns), Italian (Mon), game meat (Tues), oriental (Wed), Indian (Fri), African (Sat) and South African "Cape Malay" (Sun).

Shooters Grill Kimweri Ave, Namanga, 4km north of town ☏ 0744/304733. Styled after a bush camp, with safari chairs, fake game trophies and plenty of wood and thatch, this is primarily for carnivores, and especially good for steaks (including a whopping 1kg T-bone). Live music Sun.

Drinking, nightlife and live music

Given its large Muslim population, Dar es Salaam isn't at first glance the most promising place for **bars and nightlife**. But head out into the suburbs to places like Kariakoo, Sinza, Ilala and Kinondoni, and you'll discover a wealth of **clubs** and **dance halls** brimming over with people dancing to live bands, or drowning their sorrows in any one of a thousand bars. If the local scene isn't to your liking, upmarket areas like Msasani Peninsula have more than their fair share of places too, as glitzy, brash or downright expensive as you like, though they also attract a lot of prostitutes on the prowl. Oddly enough, while bars and clubs popular with locals don't tend to change all that much, the more upmarket crowds are fickle with their favours, so you'd do well to check on a venue's popularity before heading out there. Taxis are the usual way of **getting**

around, even at the most unsociable hours, as all bars and clubs invariably have cabs waiting outside for customers.

Bars

See also the reviews of live music venues, most of which operate as bars when not hosting bands. In addition, all big hotels have bars, usually expensive and rather anodyne affairs screening sports on large screens, and with extensive snack and cocktail menus; the best of these is *Karambezi Café* at the *Sea Cliff Hotel*, with matchless ocean views.

City centre

Florida Pub Mansfield St, city centre. Near the ferry terminal, a very dark air-conditioned bar with haughty barmaids, pool tables, reasonably priced food and expensive drinks. Closed Sun.

The Garden (CBE Club) College of Business Education, Bibi Titi Mohamed St, city centre. Down-to-earth outdoor refuge for an afternoon (or evening) drink, with rickety tables under trees, *nyama choma*, and pool tables. Live music, especially rap, most Fridays.

Millennium Y2K Bar Sofia Kawawa St, Mchafukoge, city centre. Best of the bunch in this area, a friendly local bar with tables on a shaded street-front terrace and in a courtyard at the back. There's a pool table, cheerful Congolese music, full meals until 4pm, and snacks and *mishkaki* thereafter.

NBC Club Pamba Rd, city centre. A famous unmarked bar with two distinct sections, one inside with a TV, the other outside with a dartboard. Good soup, *nyama choma* and *ndizi*.

New Happy Hotel Ungoni St, Kariakoo, 1.5km west of town. The rooftop bar here is popular with locals, with views over part of the city, and a TV usually showing English football. The grilled goat meat is succulent, but beware of overcharging – pay as you order.

Protein Bar Jamhuri St, Kisutu, city centre. Barmaids alternating between boisterous and sulky, seasoned drunkards, the occasional tourist and attendant flycatchers all make for an eclectic – if usually agreeable – evening cocktail, when tables appear on the pavement.

Outside the centre

Some of Msasani Peninsula's restaurants – including the *Garden Bistro*, *Mashua Waterfront* and *Sweet Eazy* – also double as bars; see the restaurant reviews.

305 *Palm Beach Hotel*, Ali Hassan Mwinyi Rd, Upanga, 1.5km north of the city. A relaxing place to while away your time, with plenty of tables under shady trees and canvas at the front, though drinks attract a premium. Good food.

Coco Beach Bar Touré Drive, Msasani Peninsula, 4.5km north of the city. The most popular of Msasani's local joints, hardly surprisingly given its beachfront location (swimming possible). Beers are cheap by Msasani's standards, and a wide range of food is served. Pool tables, and a Sunday disco

from 4pm onwards (Tsh500).

Oyster Bay Police Mess Touré Drive, Msasani Peninsula, 5km north of the city. Astride a low ragstone headland, a huge if empty open-air bar in a nice bayside location.

Q-Bar Haile Selassie Rd, Msasani Peninsula, 4.5km north of the city. Popular with locals, expatriates, tourists and a welter of well-dressed prostitutes. Liveliest Wednesday and Friday when Roots Rockers band play. Also has good food, pool tables, sports on the TV, cocktails and shooters.

Nightclubs and live music

Dar's soubriquet of *bongo* ("clever") lent its name to Tanzania's latest musical fad, **Bongo Flava**, a vaguely defined casserole of rap, hip-hop and R&B that took East Africa by storm after the new millennium. Live performances are rare, and awkward to track down, so Bongo Flava – or whatever its latest incarnation will be called – is best sampled in the city's **nightclubs**. With entrance fees averaging Tsh5000, however, these are most popular with well-to-do Tanzanians, expatriates and tourists, and thus also with prospecting prostitutes. Things get really steamy after 10pm.

For a more local flavour, head out to any one of dozens of clubs, bars and **dance halls** around the suburbs, where dance bands ("jazz bands") – the oldest of which was founded in the 1960s – are still all the rage, and popular with all ages. Indeed, it would be well worth extending your stay to catch the legendary **OTTU Jazz Band** (also known as "Msondo", after their *mtindo* or dance style), or their great rivals, **DDC Mlimani Park Orchestra** ("Sikinde"). For something completely different, search out a **taarab orchestra**, the definitive musical expression of coastal Swahili culture. Dar's two big rivals are East African Melody and the Zanzibar Stars Modern Taarab. Most of Dar's live music venues are semi-open air, with a dance floor between the tables and the band. The atmosphere is invariably bright and easy-going, and you're likely to be the only non-Tanzanian there if you stay away from places on Msasani Peninsula. On Sundays, events start earlier (3–4pm as opposed to 8–9pm) and can have a more family-oriented feel. Entrance fees aren't normally more than Tsh3000, and may even be free.

Amana Club (aka *OTTU Social Club*) Uhuru St, Ilala, 5km west of town. A long-established social hall that's a superb place to be on Sunday, when home boys OTTU Jazz Band draw the masses, and the dancing goes on almost without stop until midnight. *Taarab* features on Wednesday night.

Blue Palms Garden Rd, Mikocheni, 6km north of town. Bright and cheerful bar, formerly *the* place with the monied crowd for a Saturday-night boogie until the *Garden Bistro* arrived. Currently more laid-back, though it still hosts the disco, and there's sometimes live music (Tues & Thurs; free). Food available. Closed Mon.

Club Bilicanas Simu St, city centre. Dar's foremost, brashest and most popular nightclub, with good lighting and sound, and a good number of prostitutes. Weekly events include the African Stars jazz band (Wed), discos (Thurs–Sat), rap, hip-hop and Bongo Flava (Sat), and a jam session on Sunday afternoon (4–8pm) followed by a disco with the latest Bongo Flava until the next morning.

DDC Kariakoo (aka *DDC Social Hall*) Muhonda St, Kariakoo, 3km west of town. This vast bar tucked under a vaulted roof is Dar's oldest, and home turf to the famous DDC Mlimani Park Orchestra (Sun). Tuesday features Zanzibar Stars Modern Taarab, and there's traditional *ngoma* music on Thursday.

Garden Bistro 498 Haile Selassie Rd, Msasani

Peninsula, 7km north of town. The same crowd as for *Q-Bar* on Friday piles into this place for the weekly disco on Saturday, with the prostitutes never lagging far behind. DJs on Friday.

Highway Night Park Morogoro Rd, 3km northwest of town. Dar's most exuberant 24hr dive, with live music some evenings (free entry) and dancers every night, including an acrobatic couple of polio victims on Sunday – amazing stuff. It gets packed at midnight when the music really gets going, and slowly fizzles out around 4am. Food is available here, at neighbouring kiosks and at basic restaurants in the area. The language barrier means that the prostitutes for which the place is infamous tend to leave tourists alone.

Leader's Club Tunisia Rd, Kinondoni, 2.5km north of town. A major venue favoured for big, one-off music-industry functions. It's also the home base of the TOT *taarab* orchestra (Sat), while the popular "Leader's Bonanza" bash on Sunday showcases a different band each week.

Mango Garden Mwinyijuma Rd, Kinondoni, 3km north of town. One of the best live venues, with FM Academia (Wed), Extra Bongo (Fri), African Stars (Sat) and Vijana Jazz (Sun).

Vijana Social Club Next to *Mango Garden*. Home turf to Vijana Jazz (Sun). Saturday features African Stars.

Shopping

Given the city's size and cosmopolitan nature, you can find pretty much anything you might need, either in the centre or in several modern shopping centres, most on the outskirts. The usual souvenirs you'll see elsewhere in Tanzania can also be found, and although the choice isn't as wide (or bewildering) as in Arusha, prices can be lower.

Souvenirs

Dar has a handful of excellent curio shops, a trio of contemporary art galleries and various arts centres. For the colourful **kitenge and kanga cloths** worn by women, the section of Uhuru Street between the clock tower and Bibi Titi Mohamed Street is excellent, with dozens of shops and vendors to choose from.

La Petite Galerie Oyster Bay Shopping Centre, Ghuba Rd, Msasani Peninsula, 4km north of town. Contemporary East African paintings and sculptures. Mon–Sat 10am–5.30pm, Sun 10am–4pm.

Mawazo Gallery & Art Café Next to the *YMCA*, Upanga Rd, city centre. A leading arts centre. Apart from semi-permanent exhibits (mainly sculptures), it stages temporary exhibitions and the odd concert. Light lunches and snacks available. Daily 10am–5.30pm (8.30pm on Wed).

.**Morogoro Stores** Haile Selassie Rd, Msasani Peninsula, 4.5km north of town. Famous for Tingatinga paintings (it was here that Eduardo Tingatinga first sold his work) but other handicrafts are also available, from canvases to crockery.

Mwenge Handicraft Centre Mandela Rd, Mwenge, 10km north of the city. Almost one hundred stalls, most of them selling identical Makonde woodcarvings, reproductions of studded Zanzibari chests, soapstone carvings from Kisii in Kenya, and Zambian malachite. Spend some time looking around and you'll turn up more unusual items, including traditional wooden stools, *bao* board games, Christian idols, masks, sisal baskets and bags, coconut shredders, batiks, cow bells, Makonde masks and paintings. Frequent daladalas to Mwenge terminal from Posta and Kariakoo, leaving you with a 600m walk. Daily 8am–6.30pm.

Nyumba ya Sanaa Ohio St, next to *Mövenpick Royal Palm*, city centre. The "House of Arts", also known as Nyerere Cultural Centre, is a unique handicrafts venue in which artists, most of them young, create and sell their work. Their output is generally of high quality and includes jewellery, textiles, pottery and ceramics, etchings, paintings, and the inevitable Makonde woodcarvings. Rather somnolent these days, you can still try your hand at painting, drawing, batik and etching. Traditional dances are performed most Fridays at 7.30pm (Tsh2000), and there's a small bar and modest restaurant for lunch. Shops Mon–Fri 8am–8pm, Sat & Sun 8am–4pm; workshops Mon–Fri 8am–3pm.

The Slipway shopping centre Msasani Peninsula, 6.5km north of town. Hosts an enjoyable handicrafts bazaar weekend daytimes, and has several art and craft shops, the best being Wasanii Art Centre (Mon–Fri 1–8pm, Sat 1–6pm), which holds month-long exhibitions of contemporary East African talent, often showcasing young (and hopefully up-coming) artists.

Tanzania Curio Shop Corner of Bridge and Mansfield streets, city centre. Attractively poky store selling a mixture of pure kitsch, malachite figurines, modern and antique Zanzibari silver (the dagger sheaths and heavy necklaces are especially attractive), coins and some beautiful reproduction Zanzibari chests. Closed Sat afternoon & Sun.

Listings

Airlines Air Tanzania, ATC House, corner of Ohio St and Garden Ave ☎022/211 7500, ⓦwww .airtanzania.com; British Airways, *Mövenpick Royal Palm*, Ohio St ☎022/211 3820, ⓦwww.ba.com; Coastal Aviation, Upanga Rd, facing Barclays ☎022/211 7959, ⓦwww.coastal.cc; EgyptAir, Matasalamat Mansions, corner of Samora Ave and Zanaki St ☎022/211 3333, ⓦwww.egyptair.com; Emirates, Haidery Plaza, corner of Upanga and Kisutu streets ☎022/211 6100, ⓦwww.emirates .com; Ethiopian Airlines, TDFL Building, Ohio St ☎022/211 7063, ⓦwww.flyethiopian.com; KLM / Kenya Airways, Peugeot House, corner of Bibi Titi Mohamed and Upanga streets ☎022/211 3336, ⓦwww.kenya-airways.com/ⓦwww.klm.com;

Precisionair, Pamba Rd ☎022/213 0800, ⓦwww .precisionairtz.com; South African Airways, Raha Towers, Bibi Titi Mohamed St ☎022/211 7044, ⓦwww.flysaa.com; Swiss, Lutheran Centre, Sokoine Drive ☎022/211 8870, ⓦwww.swiss .com; ZanAir, Airport Terminal 1 ☎022/284 3297, ⓦwww.zanaironline.com.

Banks and exchange Don't change money on the street. Good foreign exchange bureaux include Crown Forex, at the corner of India and Zanaki streets (Mon–Fri 9am–4.30pm, Sat 9am–12.30pm), and the one inside *Mövenpick Royal Palm* (Mon–Sat 8am–8pm, Sun 10am–1pm). Banks have better rates but take longer; the best are National Bureau de Change, Samora Ave, and NBC,

Moving on from Dar es Salaam

By ferry

Passenger ferries connect Dar with Stone Town (at least 7 daily) and Mkoani on Pemba (1–2 daily). All leave from **Dar es Salaam Ferry Terminal** in the centre of town on Sokoine Drive, behind the ferry ticket offices. Double-check fares and times before buying a ticket, and whether the $5 **port tax** is included. For an extra $5, most travel agents can buy the ticket for you. Advance bookings are not normally necessary, even during peak tourist season. Whichever boat you choose, be aware of **scams** connected with buying ferry tickets (see p.38), especially offers of resident rates to tourists.

You're almost certain to find daily sailings to **Stone Town** at 7.30am, 10.30am, noon, 4pm and sometimes also 2pm. Arrive an hour before departure. The most reliable boats are the MV *New Happy* ($20 including port tax; up to 4hr journey time), and the MV *Sea Express*, MV *Sea Star*, MV *Sea Bus* and MV *Sepideh* (all $35 in economy or $40 first-class, including port tax), taking 1.5–2.5hr. For **Pemba** (all via Stone Town), schedules change on an almost monthly basis. At the time of writing, the fastest was the MV *Sepideh* (Wed, Fri & Sun 7.30am; $50 in economy, $60 first-class, including port tax), arriving in Mkoani at 12.30pm. Cheaper ($30 economy, $35 first-class, including tax) but incredibly slow (the onward sailing from Stone Town is overnight, so overall journey times are around 18hr) are the MV *New Happy* to Mkoani, and either one of the MV *Aziza I*, MV *Aziza II* or MV *Mudathir* to Wete, all leaving Dar at noon on Friday, arriving at 6am on Saturday.

By plane

Dar es Salaam International Airport is 11km southwest of the city – allow an hour by road in case you get stuck in traffic. Most domestic **flights**, including ones to Zanzibar, take off from Terminal 1, though some Precisionair flights leave from Terminal 2 – check beforehand. A departure **tax** of $5 plus $1 safety tax is levied on domestic flights (taxes on international flights are included in the fare); bring cash for this, either dollars or shillings. You can book directly with the airline or via a travel agent – see "Listings". A taxi from the city centre should be no more than Tsh8000. Alternatively, catch a daladala from Uhuru Street at Mnazi Mmoja Grounds, next to Kariakoo, to P/Kajiungeni or Vingunguti.

The main airlines for the 20–25-minute hop to **Unguja** ("Zanzibar"), each with several flights a day, are Coastal Aviation, ZanAir and Precisionair, all operating light aircraft, and Air Tanzania, which uses a Boeing 737. For **Pemba**, the companies are ZanAir (twice a day; 1hr) and Coastal Aviation (once or twice a day; 1hr 30min).

corner of Azikiwe St and Sokoine Drive. NBC has a 24hr ATM for Visa/MasterCard (also at the airport). There are other ATMs at Barclays' TDFL Building (Ohio St) and The Slipway (Msasani Peninsula) branches, and at Standard Chartered's branches at NIC Life House, corner of Sokoine Drive and Ohio St; International House, corner of Garden Ave and Shaaban Robert St; and JM Mall, Samora Ave. Cash advances (up to $500 a week) on Visa, MasterCard, Delta and JCB cards can be made through Coastal Travels on Upanga Rd (Mon–Fri 9am–4pm, Sat 9am–noon). Advances on Amex cards are made through Rickshaw Travels at Peugeot House, Upanga Rd.

Bookstores Coffee-table books, novels, guide-books and maps can be bought at A Novel Idea (ⓦ www.anovelidea-africa.com), at The Slipway shopping centre on Msasani Peninsula (Mon–Sat 10am–7pm, Sun noon–6pm), and in town on Ohio St (daily 10am–7pm) next to *Steers*. There are second-hand bookstalls east of the Askari Monument on Samora Ave, Sokoine Drive and Pamba Rd.

Courier services DHL ⓣ 022/286 1000; their most useful branch is in Peugeot House (ⓣ 022/211 3171) at the corner of Bibi Titi Mohamed and Upanga streets, near *Mövenpick Royal Palm*.

Embassies and consulates Canada, 38 Mirambo St, city centre ⓣ 022/211 2831; Ireland, 353 Touré Drive, Msasani Peninsula, 4km north of town

☎022/260 2355; Italy, 316 Lugalo Rd, Upanga, 1.5km north of town ☎022/211 5935; UK, Umoja House, corner Mirambo St and Garden Ave, city centre ☎022/211 0101; US, 25 Msasani Rd, off Old Bagamoyo Rd, 4km north of town ☎022/266 8001.

Hospitals and clinics Best for emergencies is the modern Aga Khan Hospital, Ocean Rd, Upanga, 1km north of town ☎022/211 5151. Recommended clinics, both on Msasani Peninsula, are Nordic Clinic, Valhalla Estate ☎0741/325569 (24hr) or 022/260 1650, ⊛www.nordic.or.tz; and the Dutch-run IST Clinic, International School of Tanganyika Campus, Ruvu St, Masaki ☎0744/783393 (24hr) or 022/260 1307.

Internet Dar has hundreds of Internet cafés, so you should be able to find one within a block or two of wherever you are. Rates average Tsh500 an hour. Be wary of banking or using credit cards online as computers are often infested with malware.

Post The main office is on Maktaba St in the centre. There's a branch at Sokoine Drive near Mkwepu St.

Supermarkets Dar's supermarkets stock an expensive selection of mainly imported goods. The most central are ShopRite (Mon–Fri 9am–6pm, Sat 10am–3pm) at JM Mall, Samora Ave and Imalaseko (Mon–Fri 9am–7pm, Sat 9.30am–4pm, Sun 10am–4pm) in Pamba House, on the corner of Garden Ave and Pamba Rd.

Telephones There are card phones throughout the city in shopping centres, and outside post offices; cards can be bought at nearby kiosks. The main TTCL office is on Bridge St, off Samora Ave (Mon–Fri 7.45am–midnight, Sat & Sun 8.30am–midnight). The cheapest way of calling internationally is the Net2Phone Internet service offered by some Internet cafés, including Millennium on Jamhuri St in Kisutu (Mon–Sat 9am–9pm; around Tsh200 per minute).

Travel agents Coastal Travels, Upanga Rd, facing Barclays ☎022/211 7959, ⊛www.coastal.cc; Easy Travel & Tours, Raha Towers, Bibi Titi Mohamed St, corner with Maktaba St ☎022/212 1747, ⊛www.easytravel-tanzania.com; Takims Holidays Tours & Safaris, Mtendeni St, Kisutu ☎022/211 0346, ⊛www.takimsholidays.com.

② Stone Town

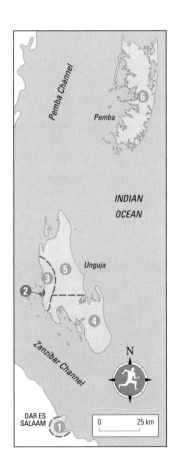

CHAPTER 2 # Highlights

✳ **Emerson & Green** One of Africa's most magical hotels: a wonderful blend of classic Swahili style and romantic modern imagination, set in a fine nineteenth-century mansion. **See p.92**

✳ **National Museum** Occupying the waterfront House of Wonders is Tanzania's best museum, its informative and well-presented displays covering every aspect of Zanzibari history, life, customs and beliefs. **See p.97**

✳ **Central Stone Town** Africa meets the Orient in the most atmospheric town south of the Sahara. **See p.104**

✳ **The slave cells** In the basement of the Anglican Mission's former hospital, two tiny cells where slaves were kept before market day provide a poignant reminder of the inhumanity of the slave trade. **See p.104**

✳ **Eating out** Not for Stone Town mainland Tanzania's chips-with-everything menus. Instead, enjoy some of East Africa's finest dining experiences at the many restaurants which make full use of the islands' rich spices and abundant seafood. **See p.109**

✳ **Forodhani Gardens** Stone Town's nightly waterfront street food market, with a choice of chow that would spoil a sultan. **See p.110**

△ Dhow, Stone Town waterfront

Stone Town

This is the finest place I have known in all of Africa...
An illusive place where nothing is as it seems. I am mesmerised...

David Livingstone, 1866

ocated on Unguja's west coast, **STONE TOWN** is the cultural and historical heart of Zanzibar, and probably the most fascinating and atmospheric African city south of the Sahara. Known locally as *Mji Mkongwe* (Old Town), Stone Town in many ways resembles the medinas of North Africa and the Arabian Peninsula, with its magical labyrinth of narrow, twisting streets, bustling bazaars and grand Arab mansions. In spite of the neglect which followed Tanzania's independence, the town's original **layout** and fabric remain virtually intact, making it easily the finest and most extensive example of the Swahili trading settlements that dot the islands and coastline of East Africa. Most of the town was built in the nineteenth century at the height of the monsoon-driven dhow trade, when Zanzibar was the most important commercial centre in the western Indian Ocean, acting as a conduit for all manner of goods shipped in from the mainland, most notoriously ivory and slaves. The pitiful cells under the last slave market can still be seen, as can two former palaces (now museums), an early eighteenth-century Omani fortress, two cathedrals and some Persian-style baths, along with a wealth of less important but no less impressive buildings.

Above all, Stone Town is a **city of contrasts**. The essence of the city is its cosmopolitan nature, its ability to absorb and blend outside influences, and the fusion of cultures can be read in the faces of its inhabitants: African, Indian, Arabian, European, and every possible combination in between. Nowadays, hydrofoils bob up and down beside the fishing dhows in the harbour, and there are Internet cafés in glorious old mansions with crumbling facades. Women in black *buibui* veils chat on mobile phones, with kids dressed in baseball caps in tow; noisy scooters mingle with hand carts, and hotels now flaunt satellite TV and air-conditioning as well as traditional *semadari* four-poster beds. Yet somehow everything, even the tourists, seems to fit. In the words of UNESCO's citation, which declared it a World Heritage Site in December 2000, the town is "an outstanding material manifestation of cultural fusion and harmonization". It would be churlish not to agree.

Some history

In spite of its centuries-old aura, Stone Town is a relatively young place, and most of its buildings date only from the last 150 years or so. Although the **Portuguese** established a small trading post at Shangani promontory in 1503, Stone Town's history only really starts after their expulsion by **Omani Arabs**. Fearing counterattack by the Portuguese, and also from rival Mazrui Arabs based in Mombasa,

Technically, the name **Zanzibar** applies to the entire archipelago, including Unguja and Pemba islands, although rather confusingly, **Unguja** is also known as **Zanzibar Island**. To add to the conundrum, the capital of Unguja, **Zanzibar Town**, is often referred to as **Stone Town** (as we have done) – although properly speaking this name refers only to the older sections of Zanzibar Town, rather than to the entire city. And to top it all, locals now consider the western part of Ng'ambo – which for Stone Town's inhabitants was literally "the other side" – as part of Stone Town, even though, historically, it was built of mud.

the Omanis quickly established their presence in Zanzibar and in what eventually became Stone Town; their fort, largely unaltered today, was completed in 1701. The foundation of the town itself is generally considered to date from the reign of an indigenous ruler (a *Mwinyi Mkuu*, literally "Great Proprietor") named Hasan, who cleared away the peninsula's scrub some time after 1728. During Hasan's time Stone Town was a peninsula, separated from the bulk of Unguja by Darajani Creek, which ran along what is now Creek Road.

It wasn't until the start of the nineteenth century, however, that the town began to grow up around the fort. The first **stone buildings** were constructed during the reign of the Omani sultan, Seyyid Saïd, who in 1832 shifted his capital from Muscat to Stone Town. Helped along by the establishment of clove plantations that had been introduced from Madagascar in 1818, Zanzibar quickly grew rich and the old mud houses were replaced with multistorey constructions made of coral stone quarried from nearby islands. This period coincided with the rising importance of the **slave trade**, which at its height saw the transportation of sixty thousand slaves annually from the mainland to Zanzibar, from where they found ready markets in Arabia, India and French Indian Ocean possessions. The sultan received a tax on every sale, and as the town expanded his revenues multiplied, as did his palaces.

The **building boom** lasted almost sixty years and was responsible for most of what we see today. But behind the waterfront facade of palaces all was not so grand. David Livingstone, passing through in 1865–66 before starting his final journey, noted that the town "might be called 'Stinkibar' rather than Zanzibar" due to the stench from "two square miles of exposed sea-beach, which is the general depository of the filth of the town" – a far cry from the celebrated scent of cloves that sailors could allegedly smell from far out at sea. Similarly, the English physician Dr James Christie (who arrived in 1869 at the start of a devastating **cholera epidemic** that claimed ten thousand lives in Stone Town alone) described the town as "a closely-packed, reeking suffocation of dirt-caked stone and coral-lime houses, whose open drains, abundant night-soil and busy vermin help erase any image of oriental glamour".

The end of the epidemic, in 1870, coincided with the accession of **Sultan Barghash**, who must have felt particularly ill-starred when, only two years into his reign, a violent cyclone swept across the island, devastating his fleet and decimating the clove plantations on which much of his revenue depended. The **slave trade** too was increasingly being hindered by British warships, and was banned in 1873, effectively marking the end of Zanzibar's economic independence. Nonetheless, Stone Town continued to grow and the sultan embarked on the construction of several monumental palaces and civic buildings.

When the **British Protectorate** over Zanzibar was imposed in 1890, the development of Stone Town was more or less complete; an 1892 map of its labyrinthine network of streets would still be useful today. As part of their efforts to clean up the city, the British introduced the **Indian crow**, an aggressive scavenger that was intended to keep rodent populations at bay. Unfortunately, the crows also pushed numerous native bird species towards extinction, and now they threaten several important bird havens on mainland Tanzania. But the main changes were outside Stone Town: the reclamation of Darajani Creek to the east, the conversion of the open area south of the town into the leafy European residential quarter of Vuga, and the filling out of the administrative district at Shangani. The waterfront gained an involuntary facelift after a **British bombardment** in 1896, undertaken to ensure that their choice of sultan took power. The bombardment, known as the shortest war in history (see p.97 & p.223), lasted all of 45 minutes, destroyed two palaces and was sufficient to elicit the prompt surrender of the usurper. British influence in Stone Town itself,

△ Children sitting on cannon, Stone Town

however, was negligible other than encouraging its gradual sanitization. By the 1920s a more romantic vision of Zanzibar had begun to replace the images of filth, squalor and slavery that epitomized the nineteenth century.

The **1964 Revolution** was the single most important event in modern-day Stone Town's history. In one night of terror, some twelve thousand Indians and Arabs were massacred by a ragtag army of revolutionaries, prompting the mass exodus of all but one percent of Stone Town's non-African population. The new government, steeped in the socialist ideology of the Eastern Bloc (witness the regimented housing blocks in Ng'ambo, built by East German "friendship brigades"), had neither the money nor the political inclination to concern itself with Stone Town's upkeep. Tenants of the palaces and merchants' houses that had been converted into low-cost state housing could not hope to keep the lavish buildings in any decent state of repair, and so the old town was left to crumble into the advanced state of decay and disrepair in which it languishes today.

The **economic liberalization** ushered in by Tanzanian President Mwinyi's election in 1985 finally brought hope to Stone Town. The Zanzibar Stone Town Conservation Unit was set up the same year, and by the early 1990s several projects had got off the ground with funding from the Aga Khan Trust for Culture. In 1994, Stone Town was declared a Conservation Area, and it's hoped that the recent addition of Stone Town to UNESCO's World Heritage list will attract further funding to help restore the town to its original magnificence.

Arrival, information, city transport and tours

Most people arrive in Stone Town **by plane** or **by ferry** from either Dar es Salaam or Pemba. Information on leaving Stone Town is given on p.122.

Zanzibar International Airport – known by the delightful Kiswahili phrase *Uwanja wa Ndege*, the Stadium of Birds – is 7km south of Stone Town. There are several foreign exchange bureaux in the arrivals hall; rates are decent and they also change travellers' cheques. Daladalas on the #505 route start from the north end of the traffic island outside the airport, and charge Tsh300 to the terminus on Creek Road. Taxi drivers will lie shamelessly about their fares, and might even angle for $20 (roughly Tsh20,000) at first. A fair price would be $5, so bargain hard. Alternatively, upmarket hotels, tour operators and travel agents can pick you up if arranged in advance: you'll pay $15–20 for a vehicle seating six or seven.

The **ferry port** is in the harbour at the north end of Stone Town. Depending on the political climate in semi-autonomous Zanzibar, passengers arriving from Dar es Salaam may be expected to visit the immigration and customs offices before leaving the port, a farcical procedure given that Tanzanian visas are valid for Zanzibar. It's best just to walk past, unless there's some kind of barrier (there isn't normally) and it's obvious that some kind of paperwork is needed. Taxi drivers hang around for new arrivals: using a taxi to find a hotel on your first day is recommended, if only to avoid the clouds of commission-hunting *papasi* (hustlers who target tourists). If you're walking, the easiest way to a hotel is to stay on one of the main roads flanking Stone Town for as long as possible before diving into the labyrinth.

The main stands for **daladalas** (the local term for them is *gari ya abiria*) are along Creek Road in Darajani, opposite and alongside the Central Market. Coming from Unguja Ukuu in the south, or from Chwaka, Pongwe or Uroa in the northeast, you'll be dropped short at Mwembe Ladu, east of town, from where there are frequent onward daladalas to Darajani. There are few if any hustlers at Darajani, as hardly any tourists travel by daladala, and finding a taxi is easy.

Information

The Zanzibar Tourist Corporation (℡024/223 8630, ✉ztc@zanzinet.com) has two **tourist offices**, neither of which are particularly useful or impartial: there's one at the port (Mon–Fri 8am–4pm, Sat 9am–1pm; no phone), and the other is at the top of Creek Road (Mon–Fri 7.30am–5pm; ℡0747/482356 or 0747/438851). For **specialized queries**, contact the Stone Town Conservation & Development Authority, between the House of Wonders and Palace Museum on Mizingani Road (Mon–Fri 8am–3.30pm; ℡024/223 0046, ✉stonetown@zanzinet.com), or the Community-Based Rehabilitation Programme in the Old Customs House, also on Mizingani Road (same hours; ℡024/223 6489, ✉cboffice@akcsz.org).

For **maps and printed material**, seek out a bookshop (see p.121). The best maps of Stone Town are insets in Giovanni Tombazzi's hand-painted *New Map of Zanzibar (Unguja Island)*, and in harms-ic-verlag's *Zanzibar*; other maps are woefully inaccurate. Printed practical information is limited to the quarterly *Recommended in Zanzibar*, a free glossy listings booklet that includes some interesting articles as well as tide tables helpful for timing trips to the beach, and the similar *The Swahili Coast* magazine. They're available at the tourist office in the port and various hotels, restaurants and tour operators around town.

City transport and tours

The best way of getting around Stone Town is **on foot**. Distances are relatively short, and in any case most of the streets are too narrow for cars (though not for scooters – be prepared to leap out of the way, particularly along Kenyatta Road). Still, if you're feeling lazy in the midday heat or need a ride back at night, there are plenty of **taxis** around. The main stands are at the Central Market (also known as Darajani Market); the north end of Kenyatta Road; Vuga Road near the old Majestic Cinema; the south end of Kaunda Road; Forodhani Gardens; and outside the ferry port, as well as outside the busier night-time venues. Drivers are happy to escort you on foot to your hotel inside Stone Town for an additional tip. A ride across town currently costs Tsh2000 (Tsh2500–4000 at night).

All of Stone Town's **tour operators** (see p.129) offer half-day guided walks through the town – a good way to get your bearings – going to all the major

Safety and *papasi*

Although incidents of tourists being robbed are on the increase, you're most unlikely to run into trouble in Stone Town, which remains one of Africa's safest cities. Nonetheless, unless you're in a large group, you should be wary of **walking at night** in badly lit areas, particularly along the shore (the section between Kelele Square and Suicide Alley, and Suicide Alley itself, has a reputation for "undesirables"), near the Big Tree on Mizingani Road, north of the port (a favoured haunt for alcoholics), and along Creek Road. Similarly, the town's **beaches** are unsafe after dark. Walking inside the old, maze-like part of town is actually quite safe, not that it feels like that if lost at night. Lastly, don't walk around Stone Town between 6pm and 8pm during **Ramadan**, when the streets clear as people descend on the mosques and then their homes for dinner, leaving plenty of room for the less scrupulous to target unsuspecting tourists.

The local "beach boys", known as **papasi** (meaning a tick), can be genuinely useful, knowledgeable and even fun to have around, but most are quick-talking hustlers out to get commission from hotels, restaurants, shops and even bars, and some are just thieves. It's best to decline their advances politely but firmly. See p.129 for reliable tour operators.

sights, and costing $15–35 per person. Alternatively, your hotel should be able to fix you up with a reliable guide for much less. For something different, Kawa Tours offer a couple of unusual walking tours for Tsh10,000 per person as well as the standard trips: the more unusual ones include cultural tournées to the Michenzani housing estate in Ng'ambo, and "Stone Town at Night", which includes a short introduction to the art of drumming. They have an office just inside the entrance of the Old Dispensary on Mizingani Road (daily 9am–4pm; ☎024/223 3105).

Accommodation

There's a huge range of **hotels** to choose from in and around Stone Town, fitting all tastes and pockets – though (as throughout Zanzibar) it's almost impossible to find a double room for much under $20. Only a few officially drop their rates in low season, but **bargaining** is possible – and in fact expected – at all the cheaper places, particularly during the rains (March–May). During this time, note that rooms can be extremely damp, with mildew on bedroom walls and towels that never dry, so to avoid fungal infections take especial care with your personal hygiene. Unless noted otherwise, room rates include **breakfast** – sometimes served on a rooftop terrace. **Credit cards** are accepted in all of the expensive options, but not normally in the other ones listed; exceptions are noted.

The advantage of staying in the labyrinthine old part of town is that prices are cheaper and you'll be in the thick of things, though actually finding your hotel can be a challenge at first, and be aware that most hotels are at least five minutes from the nearest drivable road. Many rooms come equipped with traditional

Zanzibari **semadari beds**: indestructible four-poster affairs often inlaid with painted panels, and draped with voluminous **mosquito nets**. Always check nets for size and holes, as Zanzibar has a lot of mosquitoes and malaria is easily caught. Box nets hung from a rectangular frame are far preferable to round nets, which your limbs are more likely to come into contact with during sleep, but check also whether box nets reach the ground all around the bed, and if not, whether it's possible to tuck it in around the mattress – the island's mosquitoes are experts in finding even the smallest aperture.

Budget

Annex Malindi Lodge Between *Warere Town-house* and *Bandari Lodge*, Malindi ☏024/223 0676. A budget option near the port with twelve rooms in a rambling old house shared with the owner's charming family. Second-floor rooms are best, arranged around a sunny courtyard where breakfast is served, and are good value if a little tatty. The hotel arranges trips and vehicle rental but you'll have to haggle. **②**

Bandari Lodge 100m north of the port gate, Malindi ☏024/223 7969. One of Malindi's better budget choices, and especially cheap for singles. The nine high-ceilinged rooms, all with bathrooms except for one double, are in better condition than those in nearby *Annex Malindi Lodge*, and are fresh and clean, all with *semadari* beds and box nets. Guests have use of a kitchen, but breakfast is not included. **②**

Bwawani Hotel North of Gulioni Rd between the ocean and a saltwater swamp, Funguni ☏0747/486487. An ugly concrete hulk built by the government in 1972, with 108 suites accessed off dark hospitalish corridors. Thankfully it's not all bad: the north-facing rooms (forget the decrepit south-facing ones) have balconies and distant glimpses of the ocean, tiled floors, clean bathrooms, phones, TVs and a/c. Facilities include the adjacent *Komba Discotheque*, a basic restaurant and bar (closes 9pm), and a swimming pool. **②**

Flamingo Guest House Mkunazini St, Kibokoni ☏024/223 2850, ✉flamingoguesthouse@yahoo .com. One of the cheapest, with six good if simple rooms around a small courtyard with a fountain. All rooms have box nets and fans; $4 more gets you a private bathroom with Western-style toilets, and another $4 gets you a triple. Breakfast is served on the roof. **①**

Florida Guest House Vuga Rd, Vuga ☏024/223 3136, ✆024/223 1828. Also very cheap, with eight clean rooms, mostly en suite. There's also a suite for two or three people, with two beds, satellite TV, a fridge and a spotless modern bathroom. Breakfast not included. **①**

Garden Lodge South of Stone Town on Kaunda Rd ☏024/223 3298, ✉gardenlodge@zanlink.com.

Good budget accommodation and friendly staff. Its eighteen rooms, including triples, are all en suite and equipped with *semadari* beds and cotton sheets, box nets and ceiling fans. The ground-floor rooms are cheaper, and have bathtubs but no hot water; the cooler but more expensive rooms on the two floors above have bigger beds and do have hot water, but showers only, and they smell of air "freshener". The better ones have street-facing balconies, there's a TV lounge, and food is available – you can eat on the roof. **②**

The Haven Guest House Between Vuga Rd and Sokomuhogo St, Vuga ☏024/223 5677. A reasonable first-night choice ($10 per person) but nothing special, and the idle men hanging around outside can become irritating. The rooms have nets and fans but share bathrooms; they also have triples. **①**

🏃 **Jambo Guest House** Signposted west off Mkunazini St, Mkunazini ☏024/223 3779 or 0747/415948, ✉jamboguest@hotmail.com. Popular with backpackers, with a friendly feel and cheap rates. The nine rooms (some triple, six with a/c) have shared bathrooms, and are large and clean if rather spartan, with ceiling fans and box nets. The management can help arrange reliable budget tours, bicycles and motorbikes. Internet access is available for guests (Tsh1000/hr) and there's satellite TV in the lounge. No food other than breakfast, but the jungly *Green Garden Restaurant* is opposite (closed April & May). **①**

Karibu Inn Off Forodhani St, Forodhani ☏024/223 3058, ✉karibuinn@zanzinet.com. Partly renovated but still a little shabby, this is still a decent – and clean – budget choice, and enjoys a good location close to the sea front. It has almost twenty en-suite rooms, scattered over four half-storeys, some on the ground floor. All beds have cotton sheets, round if adequately sized mosquito nets and fans, and some of the doubles and triples (just $10 more) also have a/c. There are also three dorms ($10 per person), each with a/c and bathroom, and two of them with fridges. **②**

Hotel Kiponda & Restaurant Behind the Palace Museum on Nyumba ya Moto St, Kiponda ☏024/223 3052 or 0747/411653,

FUNGUNI

Dhow Harbour

Tanzania Postal Bank

MBUYUNI

Bharmal Building

MALINDI

Fish Market

Police

Cine Afrique (closed)

Mbara Mosque

Old Dispensary

KIPONDA

Harbour & Ferry Fort

INDIAN OCEAN

"Big Tree"

Old Customs House

KOKONI

Ally Keys

Nungwi Daladala Stand

DARAJANI

Stone Town Conservation & Development Authority

Shiva Shakti Hindu Temple

HURUMZI

Hurumzi House

Palace Museum

House of Wonders (National Museum)

Forodhani Gardens

Gatehouse

Ngome Kongwe (Omani Fort)

FORODHANI

NBC Bank

Orphanage

Former British Consulate

Mambo Msiige

ACCOMMODATION

Africa House Hotel	aa
Annex Malindi Lodge	C
Baghani House Hotel	Z
Bandari Lodge	B
Beit-al-Amaan	S
Beyt al Chai	iii
Bwawani Hotel	F
Chavda Hotel	W
Clove Hotel	N
Coco de Mer Hotel	Q
Dhow Palace Hotel	Y
Emerson & Green	M
Flamingo Guest House	gg
Florida Guest House	hh
Garden Lodge	ii
The Haven Guest House	ff
Hotel International	R
Jambo Guest House	cc
Karibu Inn	P
Hotel Kiponda & Restaurant	A
Malindi Guest House	G
Malindi Lodge	ee
Manch Lodge	D
Hotel Marine	V
Mazson's Hotel	H
Mzuri Guest House	K
Narrow Street Hotel	J
Pyramid Hotel	X
Riverman Hotel	I
Safari Lodge	U
Shangani Hotel	bb
St. Monica's Guest House	O
Tembo House Hotel	dd
Vuga Hotel	E
Warere Townhouse	T
Zanzibar Serena Inn	

RESTAURANTS

Archipelago Café & Restaurant	5
Bahari Restaurant	O
China Plate	7
Dhow Palace Hotel	Y
Dolphin Restaurant	15
The ETC Plaza	17
Fisherman Restaurant	12
Hotel Kiponda & Restaurant	L
Indiano Restaurant & Bar	D
Kidude Café & Restaurant	8
Kisimani Restaurant	W
La Fenice	18
Le Spices Rendez-Vous (New Maharaja Restaurant)	21
Mercury's	2
Monsoon Restaurant	4
Mukhy's Café	1
Nyumbani Restaurant	22
Old Fort Restaurant	10
Pagoda Chinese Restaurant	20
Passing Show Hotel	3
Radha Food House	9
Sambusa Two Tables	23
Sunrise Restaurant & Bar	16
Sweet Eazy Restaurant & Lounge	6
Tower Top Restaurant	M
Tradewinds Restaurant	aa
Wings	13
Zanzibar Serena Inn	T

N

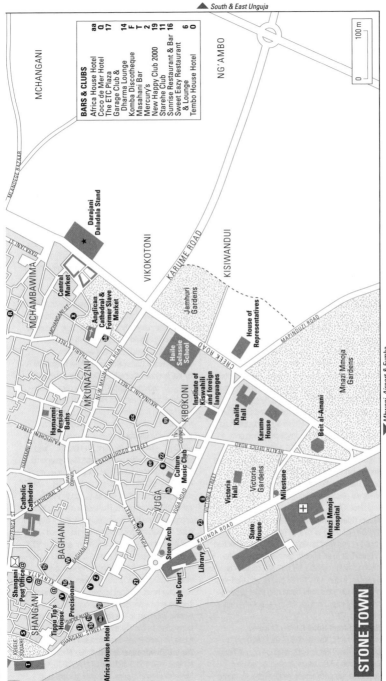

STONE TOWN

2

BARS & CLUBS
Africa House Hotel	aa
Coco de Mer Hotel	0
The ETC Plaza	17
Garage Club &	
Dharma Lounge	14
Komba Discotheque	F
Masahani Bar	T
Mercury's	2
New Happy Club 2000	19
Starehe Club	11
Sunrise Restaurant & Bar	16
Sweet Eazy Restaurant	
& Lounge	6
Tembo House Hotel	0

89

Ⓔ hotelkiponda@email.com. Quiet and comfortable, this well-kept former mansion has fourteen rooms, including some triples. The walls are unusually thick, so the interior stays cool even in mid-summer. Rooms vary in size and price, the cheapest ones little more than cells sharing bathrooms, the larger and more expensive ones with day beds and private facilities. Most have box nets, all have ceiling fans, and the renovated bathrooms have clean Western-style toilets complete with seats and paper. An average breakfast is served on the roof. Credit cards accepted. ❷–❸

Malindi Guest House 200m north of the port, Malindi ☎ 024/223 0165, Ⓔ malindi@zanzinet.com. One of the best of Stone Town's budget houses, enjoying a friendly ambience, helpful service, and wonderful decor. The rooms are excellent, all with nets, fans and safes, and some with bathrooms; the only minor niggle is that some beds might be too short for tall people. The manager can help arrange reliable tours with no mark-up on prices, and the rooftop (where breakfast is served) has good views over the harbour. ❷

Malindi Lodge Funguni Rd, Malindi ☎ 024/223 2359, Ⓔ info@sunsetbungalows.com. An attractive budget option near the port, its entrance prettily adorned with brass plates. The nine rooms, including one triple, are in good condition, all with nets and a/c. Bathrooms, whether shared or private, have Western-style toilets and reliable hot water. The hotel makes up for the lack of a rooftop terrace with a common balcony on both floors. ❶

Manch Lodge Between Vuga Rd and Sokomuhogo St, two doors up from *Haven Guest House*, Vuga ☎ 024/223 1918, Ⓔ moddybest@yahoo.com. A large, good-value hotel ($10 per person), with twenty rooms including three with bathrooms and some with three or four beds, all with nets and fans. The tiled Western-style toilets are clean, and there's a pleasant balcony with recliners on the first floor. ❶

Mzuri Guest House Malawi Rd, Malindi ☎ 024/223 0463 or 0741/774261. Handily placed near the port, and feeling like a down-at-heel bed & breakfast in an English seaside town, this has eleven smallish rooms, all with a/c, round mosquito nets, fan, fridge, satellite TV, phone, and well-kept private bathrooms with hot water, toilet paper and soap. Well appointed for the price, but still rather mundane. ❶

Narrow Street Hotel Narrow St, corner with Kokoni St, Kokoni ☎ 024/223 2620 or 0747/411842, Ⓔ narrow22@yahoo.com. A favourite with budget travellers, though it's nothing special at the price and is getting tatty. Its mixed

bunch of rooms (six doubles or twins and two triples) are en suite and have *semadari* beds, fans and phones; $5 more gets you a/c. It's better value if you haggle. ❷

Pyramid Hotel Kokoni St, Kokoni ☎ 024/223 3000, Ⓔ pyramidhotel@yahoo.com. A long-standing and good-value backpacker's favourite, boasting a TV lounge, rooftop terrace for its excellent Zanzibari breakfast, laundry service and really friendly and knowledgeable staff. The eleven rooms (one with bathroom), all recently renovated, have two *semadari* beds with crisp cotton sheets, box nets, fans and high ceilings, and some have balconies. Steep staircases. ❷

Riverman Hotel East of Tharia St, Mchambawima ☎ 024/223 3188, Ⓔ rivermanhotel@yahoo.com. This three-storey place just north of the Anglican Cathedral is good value ($10 per person) if you don't mind sharing bathrooms. All rooms, including some triples, have tiled floors, small fans, box nets, and table and chair. Luggage storage is free, there's a safe for valuables, and a pleasant courtyard for dining. ❶

Safari Lodge Malindi St, near Kokoni St ☎ 024/223 6523, Ⓔ asc@raha.com. Clean, well-equipped rooms with *semadari* beds and box nets, private bathrooms (hot water), a/c, fans and cable TV, the only spoiler being the harsh fluorescent strip-lighting which robs it of any charm. ❷

St. Monica's Guest House Off New Mkunazini Rd by the Anglican Cathedral, Mkunazini ☎ 024/223 0773, Ⓔ monicaszanzibar@hotmail.com. Run by the Anglican Church, this basic but cheap and clean hostel has seen better days but can't be matched for chilling historical atmosphere (and the lingering ghosts of slaves), as one of its two buildings – formerly the mission hospital – was constructed directly on top of the slave market's infamous underground cells. All fourteen rooms have fans, and one has a/c – they can get a little musty, something that seems to add to the historical weight of the place. The rooms over the slave chamber share a wooden verandah. Has a plain but good restaurant (generally for breakfast and lunch) and a small gift shop. No alcohol or smoking. ❷

Vuga Hotel Pipalwadi St, Vuga ☎ 024/223 3613, Ⓔ vugahotel2001@yahoo.com. Appealing two-storey Swahili-style house in a less-than-appealing neighbourhood, centred around a sunny courtyard. The ten rooms are generally good, though ones lacking windows to the street are extremely stuffy. Depending on the room and your bargaining skills, it can be good value. Breakfast not included. ❷

Warere Townhouse Behind *Annex Malindi Lodge*, Malindi ☎ 024/223 3835 or 0747/478550, Ⓦ www.wareretownhouse.com. A simple, decent and welcoming option, with ten smallish rooms on three floors, all with fans and traditional *semadari* beds, and most with private bathrooms, a/c, cable TV and a minibar. The best rooms are at the front with balconies, and there's a rooftop terrace for breakfast. ②

Moderate

STONE TOWN | Accommodation

Baghani House Hotel Signposted east off Kenyatta Rd, just after the *Dhow Palace Hotel*, Baghani ⊕024/223 5654, ⓔbaghani@zanzinet.com. An attractive choice in a big old house handsomely furnished with antiques, masks and archive photographs. The hotel is popular with families (and often full in high season), and its eight clean, high-ceilinged rooms – singles or doubles – have private bathrooms (some with bathtubs), cable TV, minibar, fans and box nets. Credit cards accepted. ④

Beit-al-Amaan Victoria St, Vuga ⊕0747/414364 or 0747/411362, ⓦwww .houseofpeace.com. Run by the same people as the *Monsoon Restaurant*, this "House of Peace" occupies a converted two-storey town house. It's the business both in terms of comfort and (authentic) Zanzibari style, and for the pocket, with its six large rooms offering the best value in Zanzibar. As such, they should be booked well in advance. The rooms and common areas are decorated with colourful and pleasing Swahili artwork, seashells, old Persian carpets and all sorts of antiques. The beds are, predictably enough, big old *semadari* four-posters fitted with box nets; all but the huge downstairs room have private bathrooms, and there's a kitchen on top should Stone Town's market inspire you. ③–④

Chavda Hotel Baghani St, Baghani ⊕024/223 2115 or 0745/363738, ⓔchavdahotel@zanlink .com. A lovely, well-maintained former Indian merchant's mansion adorned with its original imported Indian fittings, plenty of reproduction furniture, and Chinese vases that were all the rage in the nineteenth century. The sixteen rooms, arranged on three floors, are all en suite (doubles have bathtubs) with *semadari* four-posters, safes, satellite TV, a/c, minibar, and a clutter of furniture. The more expensive twin-bed rooms have balconies. There's a good restaurant, the *Kisimani*, upstairs (particularly good breakfasts), and free airport pick-up. Credit cards accepted. ⑤

Clove Hotel Hurumzi St, behind the House of Wonders ⊕0747/484567, ⓦwww .zanzibarhotel.nl. Run by a very helpful and welcoming Dutch lady who formerly made hats in Amsterdam, this wonderfully located and laid-back hotel contains eight unfussy but very comfortable rooms, the better ones higher up, all with fans,

fridges and Western-style bathrooms. There's a lovely roof terrace with a sea view and lovely sunsets, and drinks available; the hearty breakfast is also taken there. Closed May. ③

Coco de Mer Hotel Off Forodhani St, Forodhani ⊕024/223 0852, ⓔcocodemer_znz@yahoo.com. An unexciting but friendly mid-range choice with thirteen cramped rooms (including some triples), all with large *semadari* beds and box nets, fans, reproduction antiques and well-kept bathrooms with hot water. There's also a nice semi-open-air restaurant on the first floor overlooking the street (main courses around Tsh3500–5000), and a ground-floor bar open to all. ④

Dhow Palace Hotel Signposted east off Kenyatta Rd, Shangani ⊕024/223 3012, ⓦwww .tembohotel.com. This beautiful and tranquil Omani mansion from the 1870s is one of Stone Town's plusher offerings, and preserves much of its original Arabian flair. Service is smart and efficient, and the 28 spacious rooms (including some triples) are good value, with bathrooms featuring blue-tiled sunken baths, and bedrooms a/c, phone, cable TV, minibar, big *semadari* four-posters or brass beds, box nets, Persian rugs and a smattering of antiques. The better rooms and suites have balconies, and amenities include a swimming pool in the main courtyard (you can also use the one at *Tembo House Hotel*), an attractive rooftop restaurant with panoramic views (à la carte works out cheaper than taking half- or full-board), and room service. No alcohol. Credit cards accepted. Closed April & May. ⑤–⑥

Hotel International Just south of Kiponda St, Mchambawima ⊕024/223 3182, ⓔhotelinter@zanlink.com. This four-storey former palace, restored to resemble a giant cuckoo clock, is an attractive option. The twenty rooms are arranged around a big atrium and have bathrooms, box nets, a/c, cable TV, phone, hair dryer, fridge and plenty of windows. Six rooms also have balconies (same price), one with a distant sea view. There are a few tables and chairs on a rooftop gazebo giving great views over the town, but no restaurant (or alcohol). Has a foreign exchange bureau. ④

Hotel Marine Corner of Mizingani and Malawi roads facing the port entrance, Malindi ⊕0747/411102 or 0747/496615, ⓔhotelmarine @africaonline.co.tz. The 24 en-suite rooms,

91

arranged around an airy atrium dominated by a wooden staircase, have large cable TVs, minibar, phone, a/c and small but mighty fans, wall-to-wall carpet, and hot water. Triple rooms are available for $10 more. There's the *Indiano Restaurant & Bar* at the side by the street, and a pool table. ❸

Mazson's Hotel Kenyatta Rd, Shangani ☎024/223 3694. Occupying a none-too-gracefully expanded nineteenth-century building, this large place could do with some sprucing up though its rooms are comfortable in a functional way, each with noisy a/c, cable TV and phone, but no nets (rooms smell of bug spray). There's little difference between

standard, deluxe and premium rooms other than size, though the latter are enjoyable marvels of kitsch. Rooms at the front share wide balconies, and there's a restaurant but no alcohol. ❺

Shangani Hotel Kenyatta Rd, opposite Shangani post office, Shangani ☎024/223 3688 or 0747/411703, ✉shanganihotel@hotmail .com. Hidden behind an impressive reception that resembles a nineteenth-century gentlemen's club, complete with pool table, is a charmless and very tatty modern hotel, though to be fair, a long-delayed renovation is now imminent. There's a rooftop restaurant and coffee shop. Credit cards accepted. ❸–❹

Expensive

Africa House Hotel Suicide Alley, Shangani ☎0747/432340, 🌐www.theafricahouse-zanzibar .com. Formerly the English Club, this grand colonial shoreline building contains fifteen elegantly furnished en-suite rooms, all with a/c, cable TV, phone and fridge (hidden in the furniture), and the better ones with ocean views. The claimed "regal" ambience expresses itself through plentiful antiques, Persian carpets, old photographs, gilded mirrors, and golden tassels and brocade adorning the heavy green drapes hung around the four-poster beds. Facilities include room service, a good library, travel shop and gift shop, two restaurants, and its famous terrace bar, ever popular at sunset. Rates halve April–June. Airport transfer included. ❻–❽

Beyt al Chai (aka *Zanzibar Stone Town Inn*) Kelele Square ☎0747/444111 or 0747/413996, 🌐www .stonetowninn.com. One for the luvvies: six small-ish wooden-floored rooms occupying a gorgeous nineteenth-century three-storey building, stylishly decked out with silk and organza draperies and comfy antiques, though it's all rather basic for the price, even if the more expensive "Sultan" rooms have bathtubs in the bedroom. All have a/c and bathrooms, and the two on the top have sea views over Kelele Square. ❻–❽

Emerson & Green 236 Hurumzi St ☎0747/423266 or 0747/438020, 🌐www .emerson-green.com. Set in Tharia Topan's magnificent Hurumzi House (p.106), this is East Africa's most atmospheric hotel, an utterly delightful and bewitchingly beautiful place offering heaven on earth for incurable romantics, and – a rarity on Zanzibar – very reasonable rates for what's effectively a self-indulgent foray into the semi-mythical world of *The Arabian Nights*. Style is everything: an assured reinterpretation of classic Zanzibari (Afro-Arabian-Indian) themes – heavy

carved teak doors, Omani bronzes, stained glass, opulent drapes, Persian rugs, Venetian Murano chandeliers, heavy roof beams of Burmese teak, and lots of fittingly camp touches courtesy of its American owners, Emerson Skeens and Tom Green. Each of its sixteen rooms (accessed by steep staircases, so not suitable for wheelchairs) has its own quirky character, from the "Ballroom", dominated by a giant chandelier, and the "North" and "South" rooms with open-air bathtubs shielded from the street by wooden latticework screens, to the "Keep", "Pavilion" and "Tour" suites which have open-sided, turret-top gazebos fitted with day beds. Most rooms have unobtrusive a/c and fans, and there are no TVs or phones. There's the famous *Tower Top Restaurant* on the roof, and *Kidude Restaurant* next door. Closed mid-April to end May. Needless to say, book well in advance. ❻–❽

Tembo House Hotel Shangani St, Shangani ☎024/223 3005, 🌐www.tembohotel.com. Built in the 1830s to house the American Embassy, and later serving as a merchant's house, in the 1980s this became what is still a very busy package-tour hotel, thankfully not completely overshadowed by the uninspiring wing that was added in 1994. Whilst it's not as stylish as other sea-front options, and service is famously shoddy (verging on the disagreeable), the beach-front location and lovely swimming pool are undeniable draws. The rooms are fine: filled with oriental and Zanzibari antiques, they're mostly spacious and fitted with all mod-cons. Get one with an ocean view or, better still, an ocean-facing balcony to justify the expense. There's the shoreline *Bahari Restaurant* (no alcohol) with tables under Indian almond trees, and a rooftop terrace for sunbathing. ❺–❻

Zanzibar Serena Inn Kelele Square, Shangani ☎024/223 3587, 🌐www.serenahotels.com. Located at the westernmost tip of Stone Town, this occupies the former Cable & Wireless Telegraph House and the adjacent Chinese Doctor's House. In tune with other Serena hotels, service is friendly and faultless, standards are at international five-star levels, and the rooms – all sea-facing – come with all mod-cons. However, the buildings' restoration was perhaps a tad overzealous as they lack both authenticity and intimacy, and whilst there are plenty of amenities, including several bars and restaurants, a beauty salon, and a large outdoor swimming pool by the shore, it's impossible to justify the price unless you get discounted rates as part of a package. ⑨

The Town

Stone Town divides into several distinct sections, centred on the grandiose **waterfront**, whose monumental buildings run south from the port to the Forodhani Gardens. To the south is **Shangani Point**, the site of an early fishing village and later the city's principal European quarter. East of here is the leafy residential and administrative suburb of **Vuga**, founded by the Europeans. Heading inland from the waterfront brings you to the most atmospheric of the city's districts, **central Stone Town**, a bewildering, souk-like labyrinth of narrow streets and alleyways, flanked with crumbling mansions and mosques. On its east side, the labyrinth is bounded by Creek Road, beyond which is **Ng'ambo**, a packed and tumbledown area where the majority of Zanzibar Town's inhabitants now live.

Along the waterfront

The **waterfront** is Stone Town's showpiece, a glorious strip of monumental yet delicate architecture through which the nineteenth-century sultanate expressed its wealth and power. The bulk of the buildings you see today were erected by **Sultan Barghash**, whose reign (1870–88) coincided with the end of the slave trade and, not unrelatedly, the eventual loss of the Busaïdi dynasty's independence two years after his death, when Zanzibar was declared a British Protectorate. The approach by ferry from Dar es Salaam, or any trip to the islands off Stone Town, gives you the best view over the wide waterfront panorama, starting with the port to the north, and Zanzibar's most beautiful building, the Old Dispensary, then south along Mizingani Road past the Palace Museum and the jewel-box House of Wonders with its clock tower, now the National Museum, to the squat bulk of the Omani Fort and the grassy Forodhani Gardens.

The sights covered in this section can easily be browsed in an hour, but to spend any time inside either of the museums, or bargain-hunting in the Omani Fort's souvenir shops, you should plan for a good half-day at least. Although you'll see kids swimming off the **beach** in Stone Town, the water is very polluted, especially during the rains; the nearest clean beaches are north of Bububu (p.140), and around the islands off Stone Town (p.132).

The port and fish market

Zanzibar Port was built on land reclaimed by the British in 1925; the waterfront had previously continued along Mizingani Road. The northern continuation of Mizingani Road, past Malawi Road in **Malindi area**, takes you to a **fish market** which is every bit as pungent as you might fear. This area is dodgy after dark however, so take care. The **dhow harbour** is accessed from the northern end of the road, and is nowadays mainly used as a fishing wharf; mornings are the best time to visit. There are only few of the large commercial *jahazi* dhows left nowadays; your best chance of seeing them is during the *kaskazi* monsoon season between December and March.

△ Stone Town street

The Old Dispensary

About 200m south of the port entrance, on your left at the junction with Malindi Road, is the **Old Dispensary** (also known as the Ithna'asheri Dispensary or Nasser Nurmahomed Charitable Dispensary), a grand four-storey building which, in spite of the disused customs sheds opposite robbing it of its waterfront location and views, is one of Stone Town's finest and most beautiful landmarks.

The sumptuousness of the dispensary's design and decoration is reminiscent of British colonial architecture in India – no coincidence really, given that it was constructed by craftsmen brought in especially from India by the dispensary's founder, **Sir Tharia Topan**. An Ismaili businessman, Topan was one of the wealthiest men in Zanzibar at the end of the nineteenth century, much of his wealth having accrued from his multiple functions as head of customs, financial adviser to the sultan, and banker for the most infamous of slave traders, Tippu Tip (see p.103 and the "Zanzibar and the Slave Trade" colour insert). Perhaps to atone for his relationship with the latter, Topan's charity financed the building of the dispensary, as well as a nondenominational school, the first in Zanzibar.

Originally called the "Tharia Topan Jubilee Hospital", the **foundation stone** was laid with a golden trowel by Topan himself in 1887 to mark Queen Victoria's Golden Jubilee. Unfortunately, Topan died in India in 1891 without ever seeing the building complete. Work continued with funding from his widow, and the final stages of its construction were overseen by the British engineer Frederick Portage in 1894. In 1900, the building was bought for use as a charitable dispensary. The Dispensary itself occupied the ground floor, and the first and second floors – whose galleries overlook a U-shaped courtyard – were converted into apartments for the use of the doctor and his family.

Following the 1964 Revolution, the building – like most of Stone Town's grand buildings – was abandoned by its occupants. Under government ownership, the building fell into a grave state of disrepair and seemed close to collapse until the Aga Khan Trust for Culture leased the building from the government in 1990. Following an ambitious restoration programme, the Old Dispensary formally reopened in 1996, beautifully and sensitively returned to its former glory. Unfortunately, with most of its rooms now occupied by offices and the rest empty, the place still seems to be searching for its purpose in life. There's no entry charge, and visitors are encouraged to look around (daily 9am–5pm, sometimes open later).

The "Big Tree"

Some 100m beyond the Old Dispensary, opposite *Mercury's* restaurant, is the **"Big Tree"** – a gigantic Indian banyan that spreads its crown over the junction between Jamatini and Mizingani roads. The tree was planted by Sultan Khalifa bin Haroub in 1911 and has grown so large that it is now home to a family of vervet monkeys. The ample shade offered by its boughs and aerial roots has long been a favourite place for dhow builders. Although these are not so much in evidence today, it's still a good place to enquire about day-trips to the islands off Stone Town, in those bobbing, orange canvas-topped boats moored a short distance away (see also "Tour companies" on p.129).

The Old Customs House

Continuing along the sea front, beyond the Big Tree, the big building on your left just after *Seaview Restaurant* is the **Old Customs House**. Rather oppressive from the outside and unprettified within, it's nonetheless quite a beautiful construction, one that manages, in between its thick walls and pillars, to retain a remarkable levity. It's fitting, then, that its top floor is occupied by that most ethereal of activities, music-making. The **Dhow Countries Music Academy** (Mon–Fri 9am–7pm, Sat 9am–5pm; ☎0747/416529, ⓦwww .zanzibarmusic.org) welcomes visitors, whether you're there just to have a look, buy CDs (they stock dozens of Zanzibari recordings, mostly $16–18), or enquire about their **courses**. These range from 45-minute lessons for tuition in dance, *oud* (lute), *qanun* (zither), *ngoma* (drums), *zumari* (reed pipe), *tarumbeta* (trumpet), *kodian* (accordion) or violin (all $5 per lesson), to whole semesters over several months costing a very reasonable Tsh10,000 a month plus Tsh5000 registration.

Palace Museum

Further on, the large, whitewashed, three-storey building facing the ocean is the **Palace Museum** (Mon–Fri 9am–6pm, Sat & Sun 9am–3pm; Ramadan daily 8am–2.30pm; Tsh3000 or $3). Apart from the distinctly Arabic-style architecture, the main draw is the chance to see inside the former sultan's palace, with the furniture and other possessions he left behind when his family fled the Revolution, including a very tasteful Formica wardrobe.

The present building, constructed in the late 1890s, is the second to have occupied the site. The first palace, the **Beit al-Sahel** (House of the Coast), was built between 1827 and 1834 by Seyyid Saïd as his official town residence, but was completely destroyed, along with the Beit al-Hukm (House of Government) behind it, by the British bombardment of 1896. The Beit al-Sahel was used by the sultan for entertaining visitors with *taarab* music and concubines. When **David Livingstone** passed by in 1865, the traditionally hedonistic welcome was put aside and the doctor's conservative tastes catered to with fruit syrups and a band playing British tunes.

The new building, erected shortly after, served for a time – at the sultan's invitation – as the residence of General Lloyd Mathews, who had arrived in Zanzibar in 1877 at the age of 27 to organize and command a European-style army for Sultan Barghash. The palace subsequently became the sultanate's official residence in 1911, when Seyyid Ali abdicated in favour of Sultan Khalifa bin Haroub, and remained so until the Revolution, when the sultan escaped on his yacht to Dar es Salaam and thence into exile in England. After 1964, the building – renamed the Peoples' Palace – was used for government cabinet meetings and gatherings of the Revolutionary Council, during which time it was stripped of most of its internal fittings (which presumably now beautify the houses of former politicians). The palace was converted to its present use as a museum in 1994, but is still used for *Idd Barazas*, opulent banquets held at the end of Ramadan.

The bulk of the museum's collection comprises the furniture and fittings that survived the Revolution, a selection as eclectic as the tastes of the sultans who lived here. The **lower floors** are dominated by a wealth of ebony furniture, gilt Indian chairs, Chinese recliners, formal portraits and boxed international trade treaties and other documents, whilst the **top floor** gives way to the surprisingly proletarian taste of the last sultan, Jamshid bin Abdullah, including a Formica wardrobe captioned "A style much favoured in the Fifties". The real **highlight**, though, is the room re-created from the memoirs of Princess Salme (see p.139), a daughter of Seyyid Saïd, whose elopement in 1866 with a German merchant caused such a scandal that she was effectively ostracized by her family until the end of her life. Also interesting are a pair of rooms that belonged to two of Sultan Khalifa's wives, one furnished in staid British Victorian style, the other with a more flamboyant Indian touch. Most exhibits are self-explanatory and well labelled, although official guides offer their services at the entrance. Their English may not be all that good, but they know their stuff. The service is free, but a Tsh1000–2000 tip is expected.

The **graveyard** in the Palace's untended garden houses the mortal remains of sultans Khaled, Barghash and Khalifa, as well as the unfinished tomb of Seyyid Saïd. The area is closed to visitors, though an extra tip might facilitate access.

The House of Wonders – Beit al-Ajaib

With its balconies, colonnaded facade and large clocktower, the next major building along the waterfront – the Beit al-Ajaib or **House of Wonders**, which houses the **Zanzibar National Museum of History and Culture** (daily: July–March 9am–6pm; April–June 9am–5.30pm; Tsh3000 or $3) – is Zanzibar's most distinctive and emblematic landmark. It occupies the site of a seventeenth-century palace that belonged to a certain Queen Fatuma binti Hasan. After the expulsion of the Portuguese by Oman, the Queen – who had remained loyal to the Europeans – was sent into a ten-year exile in Muscat. The present building, a ceremonial and administrative palace completed in 1883, was the culmination of Sultan Barghash's extravagant building spree. Its statistics amply justify its name: it was the tallest building in East Africa at the time (and remains the tallest in Stone Town); it was the first to have running water and electric lighting (installed in 1906 as a sweetener by an American company in return for the contract to construct the Bububu railway); and it was also the first to have an electric lift (long since broken). However, a legend that thousands of slaves are buried under the House of Wonders' foundations to ensure their strength appears to be nonsense, given that the last slave market closed in 1873, and that by 1883, when construction was in progress, British influence in all official matters was pervasive.

The House of Wonders joined two other palaces in the sultanate's Stone Town complex, the Beit al-Sahel and the Beit al-Hukm, which were subsequently connected by elevated suspension bridges so that the sultan, his family and ministers would not have to mingle with the masses down below. The entrance to the building is guarded by two sixteenth-century bronze **Portuguese cannons**, captured by the Persians at the siege of Hormuz in 1622 and brought to Zanzibar during the reign of Seyyid Saïd. One of them bears an embossed Portuguese coat of arms: an armillary sphere (a globe encircled with bands) that was introduced by Dom Manuel I (1495–1521). One of the cannons dates from his reign, the other from his son's, Dom João III (1521–57). Both guns also bear Persian inscriptions.

The cannons didn't much help the Portuguese at Hormuz, but they do appear to have worked magic in protecting the House of Wonders during the 45-minute **British bombardment** of the waterfront on August 27, 1896, when both the Beit al-Sahel and Beit al-Hukm were reduced to rubble, and a lighthouse that had been constructed in front of the House of Wonders was so badly damaged that it had to be pulled down. The House of Wonders itself escaped the bombardment virtually intact, and even the crystal chandeliers in its salon remained in place. The decision was made, nonetheless, to reconstruct the front facade, which was fitted with a new tower containing the old lighthouse clock – note that this **clock** tells the time according to the Swahili system: to get Western time, add or subtract six hours. The palace was subsequently used as a residence by sultans Seyyid Hamud (1896–1902) and Seyyid Ali bin Hamud (1902–11) before being converted into government offices and use as an Ideological College of Politics in the 1970s.

Stylistically, the building is something of a jumble, perhaps owing part of its strange appearance to the fact that a British marine engineer had a hand in its design. The cast-iron pillars that support the surrounding tiers of balconies are really far too thin for the building's grandiose proportions, centred around a huge-roofed atrium. This is dominated by a sewn *Jahazi la Mtepe* **dhow** named *Shungwaya*. Last built for real in the 1930s, this is a replica, reconstructed in Zanzibar under the supervision of craftsmen from Kenya's Lamu Archipelago over 2003–4. Modern myth has it that iron nails were traditionally not used in boat construction for fear of the magnetic effects of the ocean floor. The accompanying displays chronicle the work, efforts to preserve the other traditional forms of boat-building and seafaring in East Africa, navigation, and the evolution of the monsoon-driven dhow trade. In a side room is a smashed up 1950s **Zephyr** automobile, once driven by President Karume – Tanzanian driving skills obviously being much the same back then.

The museum's **other displays** – all worth taking time to see properly – occupy two more floors of the building, the rooms accessed from broad galleries indoors and from balconies outside. The heavy ornamental doors, and their gilded Qur'anic inscriptions, are ostentatious statements of the vast wealth of the Zanzibari sultanate, most of it gleaned from the slave trade. The exhibits are exceptionally well presented, with good photographs and detailed information in both Kiswahili and English, and cover most aspects of Zanzibari life, culture and history. Some highlights are a whole room dedicated to *kangas* (the colourful cloth wraps worn by women); Dr David Livingstone's medicine chest; bicycle lamps that run on coconut oil; an exceptionally thoughtful display on traditional Swahili music; several rooms on Zanzibari food and cooking; and a fascinating section dedicated to **traditional healing**, which includes a *pini* (charm) containing herbs and, so it is said, a dog's nose – just the thing to help exorcise evil spirits, though sadly the famous bottle containing a genie that's also part of the collection appears to have been spirited away.

Ngome Kongwe (the Omani Fort)

Just southwest of the House of Wonders, **Ngome Kongwe**, or the Omani Fort (daily 9am–8pm or later; free entry except evenings when performances are held), comprises four heavy coral ragstone walls with squat cylindrical towers and castellated defences, and makes for a calm and hustler-free place to sit for an hour or two.

The fort dates back to the years following the expulsion of the Portuguese by the **Omanis** in 1698. The victorious Omanis quickly set about defending their gains, completing the fort in 1701. Its **walls** incorporate the last remnants of two hundred years of Portuguese presence on the island: the foundations of a chapel (erected 1598–1612) and an adjoining merchant's house which were incorporated into the wall of an early fortification which was, in turn, incorporated into the fort. The garrison was modest, however, with only fifty soldiers billeted there in 1710. Other than deterring a Mazrui attack in 1754 and putting down "civil disturbances" in 1784, the fort saw little action and for much of the nineteenth century **Zanzibari control** over the western Indian Ocean was so complete that the defence of Stone Town wasn't seen as a priority. During this time the fort served as a jail and the venue for public executions, which were held outside the east wall. The fort's use as a prison, and the inclusion of the old Portuguese chapel in its walls, might explain the curious transformation of the Portuguese word for church (*igreja*) into the Kiswahili word for prison (*gereza*).

In the **twentieth century** the fort saw a variety of different uses, first as a market, then as a customs house, and in the 1920s as a depot and shunting yard for the Bububu railway (p.141), which was routed directly into the courtyard through the main entrance. In 1949 the courtyard found a new vocation as the Zanzibar Ladies' Tennis Club. After an inevitable period of neglect following the Revolution, the fort was restored in 1994 and now functions as the **Zanzibar Cultural Centre**, containing various craft shops, an open-air amphitheatre that hosts live music concerts several evenings a week (announced on a sign outside the fort), a couple of tour companies, the *Old Fort Restaurant* (p.111), and – in the gate house – the office for the Festival of the Dhow Countries (p.117).

Forodhani Gardens

The formal **Forodhani Gardens**, formerly the Jamituri Gardens, were the original site of the two cannons now outside the House of Wonders, part of a battery of guns which gave their name (*mizingani* means cannons) to Mizingani Road. The name *forodhani* – meaning a ship's cargo or a reloading place – alludes to the **slave trade**, when slaves would be landed here before being taken to the market further south in what's now Kelele Square. The site was occupied by customs sheds until 1935, when the Jubilee Gardens were laid out in honour of King George V's Silver Jubilee. The following year, coinciding with the Silver Jubilee of Zanzibar's Sultan Khalifa bin Haroub, the central bandstand, fountain, seats, and the small and currently derelict pier were added. The "ornamental arch" facing the pier is a bland concrete affair, erected in 1956 for the arrival of the Queen of England's sister, Princess Margaret – though, as it turned out, she eventually landed elsewhere.

The gardens are a pleasant, shady place to relax under the midday sun, and there are a handful of curio stalls and Maasai waiting to have their pictures taken (for a fee), but Forodhani really comes alive after sunset when it hosts the best **street food market** in East Africa (see p.110). If you're around in January, ask about the **dhow races**, usually involving *ngalawa* outriggers, which sail from Forodhani to Prison Island and back.

Shangani and Vuga

From the southeastern corner of Forodhani Gardens a footbridge leads to the Zanzibar Orphanage, previously an English Club and Indian School. The road passes under the Orphanage to emerge in **Shangani**. This, the westernmost point of Stone Town, occupies Ras Shangani, a triangular promontory flanked by a narrow beach that was originally the site of a small fishing village, of which no trace remains. Shangani was where, in the mid-nineteenth century, Seyyid Saïd gave Europeans land for building their embassies, consulates and religious missions. Towards the end of the century, when the Europeans became the dominant force on Zanzibar, the area naturally became the nucleus of their new administration, whilst the area to its south, Vuga, was developed into a residential and diplomatic district, its wide boulevards and open green spaces providing a soothing contrast to the claustrophobic hustle and bustle of Stone Town itself. Nowadays, Shangani is where you'll find most of the upmarket hotels, restaurants and bars, and – of course – a good many *papasi* too.

Zanzibar and the "Dark Continent"

For much of the nineteenth century, Zanzibar's sultanate controlled East Africa's major slave and ivory caravan routes, which connected a string of Indian Ocean ports such as Bagamoyo and Kilwa to the slave-hunting grounds of Africa's Great Lakes, over 1000km inland. As such, Zanzibar became the logical starting point for a number of European and American **expeditions** into the "Dark Continent.

At first, the rationale behind the expeditions had been little more than curiosity, but by the mid-nineteenth century, more pragmatic reasons had come to the fore: commerce, evangelism and conquest. The first of note were the German missionaries **Ludwig Krapf** and **Johannes Rebmann**, who in 1846 left Zanzibar for the mainland with the intention of converting coastal tribes to Christianity. Though they met with little success, Rebmann became the first European to see **Mount Kilimanjaro**, and Krapf the first to see Mount Kenya. However, their reports of snow-capped mountains close to the Equator were ridiculed by folks back home.

Together with the maps being drawn of the area, the reports prompted some to ponder the age-old question of the **source of the Nile**, whose location had bamboozled geographers since Herodotus, the "Father of History", had wrongly stated that West Africa's Niger was a branch of the Nile. The interest in resolving the riddle was no mere academic exercise: whoever controlled the Nile could control its floods, and would therefore control Egypt.

The first serious expedition was conducted by two British soldiers, **Richard Francis Burton** and **John Hanning Speke**, who in 1857 set off from Zanzibar to "discover" Lake Tanganyika. The impetuous Burton believed the lake to be the Nile's source, but Speke thought better. Leaving behind a grumbling and sickly Burton, Speke headed south, having been told of Lake Victoria by an Arab slave-trader. As soon as he set eyes on the shore in August 1858, Speke was convinced that the millennial quest was finally over. In time-honoured fashion, few back home believed him, so to verify his theory Speke set off once more from Zanzibar in 1860, this time accompanied by the Scottish explorer **James Augustus Grant**. After circling half the lake in a clockwise direction, they sailed down the Nile all the way to Cairo. "The Nile is settled," cabled Speke from Khartoum. Indeed it was.

Livingstone …

In the Victorian imagination, however, it was not Speke but two other explorers who came to be indelibly associated with Africa's exploration, and with each other.

Dr David Livingstone, an introspective Scottish missionary, had been exploring Africa since the 1840s, having crossed the Kalahari Desert, "discovered" Mosi oa Tunya – the "Smoke that Thunders" – which he dutifully rechristened the Victoria Falls, and became the second European to see **Lake Nyasa**. For all this, Livingstone's lasting fame came from his graphic and impassioned tirades against the horrors of the Zanzibari-controlled **slave trade**, particularly the massacre of hundreds of market women in the Congo by Arab slavers: "Shot after shot continued to be fired on the helpless and perishing. Some of the long line of heads disappeared quietly; while other poor creatures threw their arms high, as if appealing to the great Father above, and sank." Livingstone's words obliged the British Government to blockade Zanzibar, forcing a reluctant Sultan Barghash to close Stone Town's slave market, thus hastening the end of the slave trade – and ultimately of slavery – in East Africa.

After a brief sojourn in Britain, Livingstone sailed for Zanzibar in 1866, having been commissioned by the Royal Geographical Society to explore the country between Lake Nyasa and Lake Tanganyika. So began the five-year odyssey that was to end with his famous "Doctor Livingstone, I presume?" encounter with Stanley at Ujiji. Stanley headed back to the coast and worldwide acclaim, whilst Livingstone stayed behind, eventually succumbing to dysentery at Chitambo in Zambia, where he died in 1873. It was not his last journey – his African servants **James Chuma** and **Abdullah Susi** buried the doctor's heart at the spot where he died, then embalmed his body, wrapped it in calico, encased it in a bark cylinder, sewed this in turn into a sailcloth, and tarred it shut. Thus wrapped, they carried the body back to Bagamoyo – an epic eleven-month, three-thousand-kilometre journey. From Bagamoyo the body was transferred to Zanzibar and thence to London, where Livingstone was buried as a national hero at Westminster Abbey on April 18, 1874.

... and Stanley

Among Livingstone's pallbearers was **Henry Morton Stanley**. Twenty-eight years Livingstone's junior, at the age of 17 Stanley took work on a ship from Liverpool to New Orleans. Always the self-assured self-publicist, eleven years later he was working as the **New York Herald**'s scoop journalist when the paper's eccentric manager, James Gordon Bennett (he of "Gordon Bennett!" fame), commissioned him to cover the inauguration of the Suez Canal and then find Livingstone, who had been "missing" for five years. Arriving in Zanzibar, he borrowed a top hat from the American consul to pay a visit to Sultan Barghash, who issued him with letters of recommendation. In keeping with Stanley's larger-than-life character, the expedition set off with 192 men and six tonnes of stores, including glass beads, reams of American cloth, coral and china for trading, and two silver goblets and a bottle of champagne for the day he met Livingstone.

Exactly 236 days later, 76 pounds lighter, and having buried eighteen porters and guards, his two European companions, both his horses, all 27 donkeys and his watchdog, Stanley arrived in **Ujiji** on the shore of Lake Tanganyika, having heard that an elderly white man was there. The date was November 10, 1871. "I would have run to him," wrote Stanley, "only I was a coward in the presence of such a mob – would have embraced him, but that I did not know how he would receive me; so I did what moral cowardice and false pride suggested was the best thing – walked deliberately to him, took off my hat, and said: 'Doctor Livingstone, I presume?'"

Following his successful encounter, Stanley abandoned journalism and dedicated himself to exploring Africa, which he subsequently recounted in a series of derring-do books bragging about his adventures. Receiving a commission to find the southernmost source of the Nile, Stanley returned to Zanzibar in September 1874, this time for an epic 999-day journey across the breadth of Africa following the Lualaba and Congo rivers to the Atlantic, which he reached on August 12, 1877. His third and fourth trips, from 1879 to 1884, were commissioned by King Léopold II of Belgium and laid the foundations of the **Congo Free State** (subsequently the Belgian Congo) by establishing settlements, constructing roads and "negotiating" over 450 dubious land deals with local leaders, effectively robbing them of their territory and laying the ground for one of the most glaring examples of European misrule ever witnessed. Stanley's summation of Livingstone: "He is not an angel, but he approaches to that being as near as the nature of a living man will allow."

The former British and American consulates

Passing through the tunnel under the Orphanage continue straight to the junction of Kenyatta Road and Shangani Street. The building facing you on your right was the **British Consulate** from 1841 to 1874, during which time it housed various nineteenth-century explorers. The building is now home to the Zanzibar State Trading Corporation (ZSTC) and cannot be visited. More or less behind it, on Shangani Street, the **Tembo House Hotel** on your right occupies what used to be the American Embassy, constructed in 1834.

Shangani Post Office

Taking a left up Kenyatta Road (be wary of traffic), the impressive colonnaded green and white building on your left beyond the junction with Gizenga Street is **Shangani Post Office**, which served as Zanzibar's main post office from its inauguration in 1906 until the end of the sultanate – it's now a branch office. This is one of several buildings in and around Stone Town designed by **J.H. Sinclair**. Trained in classical architecture, Sinclair came to Zanzibar in the wake of the British bombardment of 1896 as a young administrator, and gradually worked his way up the ranks to become British Resident (Britain's "advisor" to the sultan; effectively Zanzibar's political governor) between 1922 and 1924. His early work is characterized by an easy blend of Islamic forms and Classic detail, but over time his style, dubbed "Saracenic", became increasingly detached from European tradition, so much so that his contemporaries joked about him having "gone native".

Other notable structures by Sinclair include the State House, High Court, Central Market, Bharmal Building, and Beit al-Amani – formerly the Peace Memorial Museum.

Kelele Square

A hundred metres beyond *Tembo House Hotel*, Shangani Street widens into the leafy **Kelele Square**. Though it's now one of Stone Town's most peaceful areas, its name – which means "shouting", "noisy" or "tumultuous" – hints at its terrible past, when the square was used as Zanzibar's main **slave market**, before this shifted to Mkunazini in the late 1860s (p.104). At the height of the slave trade in the 1830s, an estimated sixty thousand slaves passed through the market every year.

The first building on your right is **Mambo Msiige** (not open to visitors), meaning the "Inimitable Thing", its name apparently deriving from the extravagance of the construction, for which thousands of eggs were used to strengthen the mortar. The building's structure was also reinforced with the bodies of slaves, who were entombed alive in the walls during its construction – a common enough practice at the height of the slave trade.

Mambo Msiige was erected between 1847 and 1850 by a prominent Arab merchant, and later served as the town's first post office and the headquarters of the Universities' Mission to Central Africa (1864–74) – a sombre irony given that they had come to Africa to eradicate the slave trade. **Sir John Kirk**, an abolitionist luminary, lived in the house from 1874 to 1887 in his capacity as the British consul general, and the explorer **Henry Morton Stanley** spent time here too: the room at the top, quite visibly not part of the original structure, is said to have been built especially for his use. After 1913 the building became a European hospital, and presently houses a number of government departments, though there are long-standing plans to convert it into a Museum of Exploration.

The **Zanzibar Serena Inn** next door occupies two buildings restored in the 1990s for use as part of the Aga Khan's luxury *Serena* hotel chain. The main building (you can get inside as long as you don't look too scruffy) was the Cable & Wireless Building, which was connected via Bawe Island to Aden (Yemen) by telegraphic cable. A room on the first floor next to *The Terrace Restaurant* contains phones and relays from the period. The smaller adjacent building was built in 1918 and is popularly known as the Chinese Doctor's House.

Tippu Tip's House

The riches to be had from the slave trade are perhaps best understood (with a little imagination, admittedly) by visiting **Tippu Tip's House** along the poetically named Suicide Alley, south of Kelele Square. Tippu Tip was, in the latter half of the nineteenth century, the richest and most powerful slave-trader in East Africa. Many a European explorer curried his favour to obtain safe passage on the mainland, as his influence – and fear of his name – spread along the caravan routes into eastern Congo. Although the home of the infamous slave trader (see the "Zanzibar and the Slave Trade" colour insert) is now in an advanced state of decay, its door is one of Stone Town's most elaborate, and it also boasts a set of black and white marble steps. The house is currently occupied by various local families, evidently undaunted by the popular belief that the house is haunted by the spirits of slaves. A polite enquiry may elicit an invitation to have a look around; a tip (no pun intended) would be appreciated.

Africa House Hotel

Continuing down Suicide Alley, past the infamous *New Happy Club* (see p.116), you come to a small square dominated by the **Africa House Hotel**, a grand old building to your right with a heavy carved door studded with brass spikes. The building was erected in 1888 as the exclusive English Club (the oldest such establishment in East Africa), though in time membership was opened to Americans and other Europeans. It provided members with a taste of Old Albion: gin and tonics on the terrace, a library, wood-panelled committee rooms, billiard halls, and powder rooms for the ladies. Social activities included cricket, golf, hockey and tennis on land reclaimed at Mnazi Mmoja after World War I, and a New Year fancy-dress ball, which attracted sizeable crowds of excited locals to witness this amusing manifestation of *wazungu* culture.

After the 1964 Revolution, the building was predictably neglected, and has only recently been restored as a luxury hotel. The club remains famous for its ocean-facing terrace bar, built above garages added on between the wars for its members' motorcars. Nowadays, anyone is welcome to have a look around, and a sunset drink on the outdoor terrace is one of the highlights of a stay in Stone Town.

The High Court

Suicide Alley runs into Kenyatta Road (watch out for traffic here), which opens into a small roundabout at the junction with Vuga and Kaunda roads. The **High Court** (Korti Kuu) on the right (1904–8) is another of J. H. Sinclair's syncretic creations, and perhaps the most successful. The domed tower was apparently originally fitted with a golden ring so that the Archangel Gabriel could carry the structure up to heaven on the day of reckoning, although quite why heaven would need a courthouse remains a mystery. Another mystery is the forlorn Neoclassical Doric stone arch standing in the triangular garden opposite, whose provenance no one seems to know for sure.

Victoria Hall and Gardens, and the State House

Some 100m further along Kaunda Road on the left are **Victoria Hall and Gardens**, once used by Sultan Barghash's harem, and presented to the town in 1887 on the occasion of Queen Victoria's Golden Jubilee. The hall itself, locked at the time of writing, was built over the harem baths and functioned as Zanzibar's Legislative Council Chamber from 1926 until the Revolution, and was restored in 1996 to house the all-too-necessary Zanzibar Sewerage and Sanitation Project. The gardens contain some graves of the Barwani family of Omani Arabs, and many exotic plant species like tea, cocoa and coffee, planted by the British Consul General, Sir John Kirk. The south end of the hall and gardens is marked by an octagonal marble **milestone**, showing London as 8064 miles away – the distance by ship after the Suez Canal was opened in 1869. The marble came from the ruins of Sultan Barghash's Chukwani Palace south of town, destroyed by fire in 1899.

Set back from Kaunda Road opposite the Victoria Gardens is the **State House**, another of Sinclair's works, which originally housed the British Resident. The building is now home to the President's Office and is out of bounds. Photography of any part of the building is forbidden.

Central Stone Town

Away from the waterfront, Stone Town is a labyrinth of narrow, twisting streets, dotted with faded mansions and mosques, and crisscrossed by serpentine alleyways that unexpectedly open out onto semi-ruined squares alive with food vendors, hawkers and, at night, crowds of people enjoying coffee on the stone *barazas*. Getting lost is unavoidable – and part of the pleasure. If you really get stuck, any local will show you the way, or just keep walking along the busiest street and you'll emerge onto one of the main roads that bounds the old town. Safety is not a problem by day, though you should take care at night since parts of the town lack streetlights; although still rare, muggings and other incidents involving tourists are becoming more frequent. For more information on safety in Stone Town, see the box on p.86.

Stone Town's **main sights** are the Hamamni Persian Baths, the turn-of-the-century Catholic Cathedral of Saint Joseph, and the Anglican Cathedral Church of Christ which occupies the site of Africa's last slave market, the cells of which can be visited. The **main commercial areas**, containing a clutter of shops and stalls in the manner of an Arab souk or bazaar, are along and off Hurumzi and Gizenga streets and in Changa Bazaar – most easily accessed from behind the Omani Fort or House of Wonders – where you'll find dozens of antique dealers, craft shops, fabric and jewellery stores. The main streets running north to south – Sokomuhogo and Tharia/Mkunazini – are less hectic and have fewer souvenir shops, so provide a more leisurely introduction to life in the old town.

The slave market and Anglican Cathedral

On the eastern edge of Stone Town, the Anglican Cathedral occupies the site of Africa's last **slave market**, closed in 1873 by a reluctant Sultan Barghash under pressure from the British. Stone Town's original slave market had been at Kelele Square in Shangani, but it's here in Mkunazini, where the market shifted in the 1860s, that the appalling cruelty of the trade hits home. Next to the cathedral, in the basement of the former mission hospital (now part of *St. Monica's Guest House*), are the **slave chambers**: tiny, dingy cells that each housed up to 75 people until market day. Conditions were squalid in the extreme: the cells are so small that most people couldn't stand upright; the only furnishings were a pit in the centre and a low platform around the sides; and there were no windows. One of the cells is now lit by artificial light; the other has been left unlit save for two slits at one end that hardly make a dent in the gloom. The cells are visited as part of a **guided tour** run by the church (daily 9am–6pm; Tsh2000), which also includes the cathedral.

The juxtaposition of the cells with the imposing **Anglican Cathedral Church of Christ** might appear grimly ironic but, in the spirit of Christian evangelism, replacing the inhumanity of the slave trade with the salvation of God made perfect sense. Named after Canterbury Cathedral, its foundation stone was laid on Christmas Day 1873, the year the market closed, on land donated by a wealthy Indian merchant named Jairam Senji. The project was funded by the Oxford-based Universities' Mission in Central Africa, and construction proceeded under the supervision of **Bishop Edward Steere**, third Anglican bishop of Zanzibar. Steere, who had been pivotal in securing the mission's support, was a tireless individual, whose other achievements included the compilation of the first English–Kiswahili dictionary and the first Kiswahili translation of the Bible. Steere himself conducted the first service, on Christmas Day, 1877. The cathedral's design follows a basilican plan, blending the Perpendicular neo-Gothic form then popular in Victorian England with Arabic details. The unusual barrel-vaulted roof was completed in 1879, and the spire was added in 1890. The clock in the cathedral's steeple was donated by Sultan Barghash on condition that the spire's height did not exceed the House of Wonders, which remains Stone Town's tallest building. A stark and pensive modern **sculpture** (by Clara Sornas) in the cathedral courtyard shows five bleak figures placed in a rectangular pit and shackled together with a chain brought from Bagamoyo, the most notorious of the mainland slave-trading ports – a devastatingly poignant memorial to the horrors of the slave trade.

The cathedral's **interior** also abounds with reminders of the trade. A red circle in the floor beside the altar marks the position of a post to which slaves were tied and whipped to show their strength and resilience before being sold, while behind the altar is the grave of Bishop Steere. The small crucifix on a pillar beside the chancel is said to have been fashioned from a branch of the tree under which David Livingstone's heart was buried. Livingstone is also remembered in a stained-glass window, as are British sailors who died on anti-slaving patrols in the western Indian Ocean. The cathedral organ, made by Henry Willis & Co. of Ipswich, England, can be heard during Sunday services (weekly in Kiswahili, monthly in English), together with joyous gospel singing.

Hamamni Persian Baths

The contrast between the misery of the slave market and the slave-financed luxuries of the **Hamamni Persian Baths** (daily 10am–4pm, ask for the caretaker across the road to let you in; Tsh2000 including a short guided tour – tip expected; guidebook Tsh2000), 250m to the west, can come as something of a shock. Commissioned in the early 1870s by Sultan Barghash, the Hamamni baths (from the Arabic word for baths, *hammam*) were designed in the Persian style by the architect Hadj Gulam Husein and opened to the public, with the proceeds going to a charitable trust (*wakf*) managed by the sultan, in much the same way that the admission fee you now pay goes to the Zanzibar Orphanage.

△ Hamamni Persian Baths

The baths are quite small and their design is surprisingly plain; the only decoration of note is the red-brick pattern above the lime stucco rendering outside, topped by a crenellated parapet. The baths ceased functioning in the 1920s, and despite partial restoration in 1978, remain bone dry. The guided **tour** isn't up to much, but the baths are a good place to head for in the midday heat, the dry air, thick walls and stone floors providing a welcome respite from the sweltering heat outside.

The Catholic Cathedral of Saint Joseph

The twin towers of the **Catholic Cathedral of Saint Joseph** can be seen from pretty much every rooftop balcony in Stone Town, but the cathedral isn't all that easy to locate on foot. The best way is to start on Kenyatta Road and head down Gizenga Street, where a right turn down Cathedral Street brings you to it. Although the site lacks the historical significance of the Anglican Cathedral, the Catholic Church was equally involved in the struggle against the slave trade, its main memorial being the Freedom Village for slaves in Bagamoyo in mainland Tanzania.

The cathedral's foundation stone was laid in July 1896, and the first Mass was celebrated on Christmas Day, 1898, two years before completion. The design is loosely based on the Romano-Byzantine cathedral of Notre Dame de la Garde in Marseilles, while the interior is painted with badly deteriorated frescoes depicting scenes from the Old Testament. Masses are held regularly and are the best time to visit, when an organist accompanies the choir. At other times, when the main entrance is usually closed, you might gain access through a small passageway leading through the convent at the back of Shangani Post Office.

Hurumzi House

Running a short distance west to east from behind the House of Wonders is **Hurumzi Street**, one of Stone Town's best places for rummaging around souvenir and antique shops. Near the end on the right, an unassuming sign marks the entrance to the beautifully restored and opulent **Hurumzi House**, now Stone Town's best hotel, *Emerson & Green* (see p.92). The house was constructed by the wealthy Ismaili businessman Tharia Topan (also responsible for the Old Dispensary; see p.95) to serve as both the sultanate's customs house and his private residence. Topan's good relations with Sultan Barghash allowed him to make it the second-highest building in Stone Town, after the House of Wonders. Its name comes from its use by the British after 1883 to buy the freedom of slaves, to ease the pain of Arab slave-owners after the abolition of slavery; *hurumzi* means "free men" (literally "those shown mercy"). The conversion into the present hotel has been gloriously done, and it's well worth looking around even if you've no intention of staying here; the rooftop restaurant is also the best place to see the colourful tower of the Shiva Shakti Hindu Temple across the road.

A few metres west of Hurumzi House, along an alley heading north, hang **spider webs** belonging to some of the biggest arachnids you're ever likely to see. That no one has brushed them away is explained by an Islamic tradition (*hadith*) which recounts that the Prophet Muhammad once took refuge from his enemies in a cave and was saved by a spider that swiftly spun its web across the cave entrance; the Prophet's enemies saw the unbroken web and went on their way. Christian traditions relate a similar story about the Holy Family's flight to Egypt when escaping Herod's soldiers.

Mnara Mosque

Most of Stone Town's 51 **mosques** are surprisingly restrained and unobtrusive affairs, certainly compared to the ostentation of the waterfront palaces, but then few if any of the sultans were much given to religious contemplation. Indeed, you won't even notice the majority of the mosques unless you walk past their entrances and glimpse their simple prayer halls (strictly no photography). There are few embellishments, and only four have minarets, one of which is the Sunni community's curious **Mnara Mosque** (or Malindi Mosque), near the northern tip of Stone Town, its strange minaret (*mnara*) one of only three conical minarets in East Africa (the other two are on the Kenyan coast) and decorated with a double chevron pattern which is best seen from Malawi Road. The mosque is probably Stone Town's oldest, the minaret most likely predating the first mention of the mosque in 1831, when it was rebuilt by Mohammad Abdul Qadir al-Mansabi, whose remains are buried in front of the *mihrab* prayer niche. Non-Muslims aren't allowed inside.

Creek Road and eastwards

The whole area running up the east side of Stone Town along the fume-filled dual carriageway of **Creek Road** (also known, inaccurately, as Darajani Road) was, until the twentieth century, a saltwater creek. Its name, Darajani, came from the first bridge (*darajani*) to be erected across the creek in 1838 during the reign of Seyyid Saïd. The creek separated Stone Town from the mud-and-thatch district of Ng'ambo to the east, which remains much more African in feel than the oriental alleyways and grand buildings of Stone Town. Officially Creek Road is now Benjamin Mkapa Road, after the Tanzanian president, but his unpopularity in Zanzibar means it's still universally known by its old name.

The British reclaimed the southernmost portion of the creek in 1915 to make way for the English Club's playing fields; this broad and grassy area is now municipal land, known as **Mnazi Mmoja** ("one coconut tree"), as indeed there is. The derelict cricket pavilion still stands here – just – in the southeast corner. At the end of Ramadan, the park serves as the main focus for the Idd al-Fitr celebrations, attracting thousands of people over the four-day holiday. At other times it's used for football matches. It wasn't until 1957 that the rest of the creek – by then a filthy and foul-smelling swamp – was drained, leaving only a small reed-filled marsh between Gulioni Road and the *Bwawani Hotel*.

At the south end of Creek Road stands the **Beit al-Amani** (House of Peace), which was until recently a museum (the collection is now in the House of Wonders). It's unclear what the building's next use is going to be, but it's worth the walk for its external architecture: a squat but elegant octagonal construction topped by a Byzantine-style dome. It was the last of J. H. Sinclair's creations, and opened in 1925 on the anniversary of the 1918 armistice as the Peace Memorial Museum. It's the most Islamic of Sinclair's works, dubbed "Sinclair's mosque" by detractors and the "House of Ghosts" by locals, for whom the concept of a museum was a strange novelty.

Central Market

Zanzibar's lively and colourful **Central Market**, also called Darajani Market, lies just outside Stone Town, about halfway up Creek Road. Liveliest in the morning from 9am onwards, the market and streets around it have pretty much everything you might need, from meat and fish, cacophonous bundles of trussed-up chickens, and seasonal fruit and vegetables (and some exotic fruits like apples) to herbs and spices, radios, TVs and mobile phones, bicycles, shoes and sandals, swaths of brightly patterned cloth and – years after the fad subsided elsewhere – Teletubbies.

The main building, a long tin-roofed affair flanking Creek Road, opened in 1904 as the **Seyyidieh (or Estella) Market** and was probably the second of J. H. Sinclair's constructions after the Bharmal Building. Actually little more than a glorified shed, it houses the meat and fish sections, the smell of which announces the market's presence from a fair distance.

More enjoyable for sensitive souls is the **fruit and vegetable area** in the enclosure behind the main building. Though the mythical scent of cloves and spices is absent (most are nowadays sold in sealed plastic bags), the fruit and vegetables are presented with care, arranged according to shape, with anything round – oranges, mangoes, passion fruit – usually in a unit of five called a *fumba* (meaning heap), while less spherical fruits come ready-wrapped in palm-frond baskets.

Be careful around the market area **after dark**: with its lack of streetlights and many dark corners, it's prime territory for muggers.

Bharmal Building

Constructed around 1900, the **Bharmal Building** – towards the top of Creek Road on the left – is the earliest and most European of Sinclair's buildings (the comparison with his last work, the Peace Memorial Museum, which bears nary a wisp of his classical training, is startling). Stylistically somewhere between an Arab palace and English manor house, the Bharmal Building is not Sinclair's best creation, though the profusion of plaster mouldings hints at the Orientalist direction his work was to take, and one should bear in mind that when built it would have been facing the creek rather than a fume-filled highway. Previously the office of the British Provincial Commissioner, the building currently houses the offices of Zanzibar Municipal Council.

The Blue Mosque and Livingstone House

Reaching the north of Creek Road, a left turn takes you down Malawi Road to the roundabout by the port entrance, while a right skirts the reed-filled salt-water swamp between Gulioni Road and the *Bwawani Hotel* – the only remnant of Darajani Creek. Some 700m along Gulioni Road is a modern mosque built out over a small artificial lake, which goes by the name of the **Blue Mosque**. A left here, which leads to the service entrance of the *Bwawani Hotel*, takes you past patches of mangroves and tidal mudflats where **dhows** are still built or repaired. The occasional spice tour stops here, but the area is largely ignored, and the workers should be happy to show you round if they're not too busy.

Back on Gulioni Road, the old two-storey house on the opposite side of the road, now almost surrounded by new apartment blocks, is the fine two-storey **Livingstone House**. Now the headquarters of the Zanzibar Tourist Corporation, it was built in 1860 by Sultan Majid and saw use as a rest house for various European explorers and missionaries, most famously David Livingstone, who spent time here in 1865–66. The proximity of the swamp presumably inspired the good doctor to come up with his "Stinkibar" epithet.

Ng'ambo

Beyond Livingstone House, a right turn down along a broad dual carriageway (you can also get there along Karume Road from Creek Road) brings you into the poorer but vastly more populous half of Zanzibar Town known as **Ng'ambo**. The name is a throwback to the days when Stone Town was still a peninsula, bounded to the east by Darajani Creek. As Stone Town filled up, its poorer inhabitants, most of them African, were forced to decamp to the main island opposite, which the Arab elite patronizingly referred to as *ng'ambo*, "the other side".

The centrepiece of this unloved new town, which is actually now 130 years old, is **Michenzani**, 600m along Karume Road. Its pretty name ("tangerine trees") spectacularly fails to disguise Tanzania's most dismal experiment in socialist urban housing. Flanking each of the four roads radiating from a vast roundabout are the kind of grey, numbered and deeply neglected multistorey blocks of flats one would expect to see in Stalinist Russia. No surprise, then, to learn that their design and construction was supervised by East German engineers in the late 1960s and early 1970s, during Tanzania's economically disastrous experiment with African socialism, *Ujamaa*. Nonetheless, the housing blocks – and the ramshackle slums around them – do provide an abrupt and perhaps welcome return to reality for those who have become jaded with the tourist-trap some consider Zanzibar to have become.

The best way to get a real feel for how "the other side" lives is on a **cultural walking tour** (Tsh10,000 per person) organized by Kawa Tours; see p.86.

Eating

Stone Town is Tanzania's culinary apotheosis, offering an embarrassment of choice when it comes to **eating out**, from the glorious nightly food market in the Forodhani Gardens and some very good local restaurants, to dozens of sophisticated or romantic establishments, including several right by the shore (great sunsets), and others on rooftops within the old town for good views over the city and, if the view isn't blocked by other buildings, the Zanzibar Channel beyond. Menus generally feature traditional **Zanzibari cuisine**, combining subtle use of the island's spices and coconuts with seafood including prawns, crab, octopus and lobster, while more conservative tastes are catered for with pasta, pizza, Indian and Chinese dishes, and even burgers and chips.

Apart from the Forodhani Gardens, the market on **Creek Road** and the daladala stand opposite are also handy for street food, especially in the morning for cups of scalding *uji* (eleusine) porridge, and *supu*, a savoury broth containing pieces of meat, chicken, vegetables or fish. Another good spot is the **Big Tree** on Mizingani Road, where there's usually someone selling *mishkaki* skewers of grilled goat meat, and another with a sugarcane press for juice. In the evenings, the west end of **Malawi Road** near the port is popular with passengers catching night ferries. For something more traditional, it's well worth seeking out one of the **coffee barazas** inside the old town, where the beans are roasted, ground and brewed on the stone benches (*barazas*) that line the streets: a tiny cup of piping Arabica costs a negligible Tsh20–50. One of the liveliest *barazas* is in Sokomuhogo Square, at the corner of Sokomuhogo, Cathedral and Baghani streets. Its popular name, **Jaws Corner**, derives from the film once shown on its TV; locals still spend the evening glued to the screen, usually featuring pirated movies more often than not bizarrely dubbed or subtitled into Chinese. Televisions are usually also set up about halfway along Baghani Street, and along New Mkunazini Road just west of Mkunazini Street. "TV Corner", at the bottom of Mkunazini Street near Vuga Road, is another likely spot. Some *barazas* also serve spiced tea called *zamzam*, named after a sacred well in Mecca.

The Forodhani Gardens

For all its refined restaurants, the best place for eating out in Stone Town, indeed in the whole of Zanzibar, is at the open-air street food market held in the waterfront **Forodhani Gardens** after sunset, which combines a magical twilight atmosphere with a variety and quality of food to put many a five-star hotel to shame, though check seafood carefully before ordering in low season, when it's not always as fresh as it should be. It's also one of the cheapest places to eat, where a couple of thousand shillings will leave you well and truly stuffed. That said, don't necessarily believe starting prices: it's that ever-endearing Zanzibari habit of asking a "special price, my friend" of tourists.

Every evening, seven dozen *baba lisha* ("feeding men") set up trestle tables, charcoal stoves (*jikos*), gas lanterns and home-made *kibatari* oil-lamps and prepare the food. The **choice** is regal, ranging from grilled or stewed seafood caught that morning and sauced with local spices, to goat meat served with a superb home-made chilli sauce (*pilipili hoho*) and, more rarely but deliciously, tamarind sauce. The market is also a great place to try "Zanzibari pizzas" (*mantabali*), actually chapatis stuffed with egg, vegetables or whatever takes the cook's fancy, and resembling fat spring rolls. Other **snacks** worth sampling include spiced *naan* bread and *andazi* doughnuts, grilled cassava (*muhogo*), fried potato and meat or vegetable balls (*katlesi* or *kachori*), samosas (*sambusa*) filled with meat or vegetables and salads. You can even get grilled bananas topped with melted chocolate.

Drinks are abundant too, with sodas, freshly pressed seasonal juices (including sugar cane, wrung noisily out of hand-operated iron presses), gently spiced *zamzam* tea, Turkish coffee, coconut milk (*dafu*) and – at the start of the year – delightfully tangy tamarind juice (*mkwaju*) all available.

Unfortunately, eating out during **Ramadan** can be quite expensive, as the government bans restaurants not attached to hotels from opening during the day. There are some exceptions, though the cloth screens with which the proceedings are often covered lend a furtive aspect to dining at that time; the restaurants reviewed below remain open during Ramadan unless otherwise indicated.

Budget

The following restaurants are among the cheapest in Stone Town, most of them aimed as much at locals as tourists. Unless you're splurging on prawns or lobster, a full meal with soft drinks shouldn't cost more than Tsh5000.

Dolphin Restaurant Halfway along Kenyatta Rd, Shangani. An attractive place with a mangrove pole (*boriti*) ceiling, turtle shells on the walls, and a noisy African grey parrot. The speciality is grilled red snapper with coconut sauce, though the daily specials are worth tasting – things like crab claws, *biriani* or *pilau*, octopus, or green lentils with fish – and are good value at Tsh3500 including a starter, even if portions aren't overly generous. You can sample a half lobster for Tsh7000. Finish your meal with a *shisha* water pipe. Daily 9am–9.30pm; closed Ramadan daytimes.

Mukhy's Café Malawi Rd, near Malindi Bureau de Change, Malindi. Something between a grocery and a fast-food place, this has just two tables inside and a few more on the pavement, and is very basic, but is good for trying typical Tanzanian snacks, particularly *kababu* (meat balls), egg "chops", and what they call "cutlets", being a boiled egg or minced mutton wrapped in a thick ball of mashed potato. The oily *sambusas* are the only sour note. No alcohol. Daily 7am–10pm; closed Ramadan.

Old Fort Restaurant Ngome Kongwe (Omani Fort), Forodhani St. A relaxed place for lunch, with two menus: a rather humdrum printed one for fish *pilau*, vegetable curry, chicken *ugali* and 1970s favourites like prawn cocktails and beef stroganoff (mostly around Tsh3000), and rather more interesting daily specials chalked up on a blackboard for things like grilled prawns (Tsh6000) and seafood platters (Tsh8500). Also has snacks, milkshakes,

coffee, and booze from the attached bar. Daily 9am–1pm; closed Ramadan daytimes.

Passing Show Hotel Malawi Rd, Malindi. This looks like a typical local restaurant, with dirty floors, metal-legged furniture and TVs in the corner, and so it is, but the ruckus of diners that make it difficult to find a table at lunchtime also says something about the food: that it's excellent, cheap, and comes in huge portions. The *pilau*, *biriani* and stews are particularly good, including fish or cashew nuts in coconut sauce, and chicken – you pay more for the tougher but tastier free-range variety than for bland battery-farm broilers. Nothing much over Tsh2000. No alcohol. Daily 6am–10pm; closed Ramadan.

Radha Food House Off Forodhani St beside *Karibu Inn*, Forodhani. A vegetarian Indian restaurant famed for its *thali* (Tsh5000), and also offering tasty samosas, spring rolls, lentil or chickpea cakes, and perfumed sweets for dessert. There's a small but well-stocked bar too. Daily 9am–10pm.

Sunrise Restaurant & Bar Kenyatta Rd, Shangani. A local *hoteli* aiming at the tourist trade and which, apart from its awful toilets, comes recommended. The food, a mixture of local and international, is well priced, with most dishes under Tsh3000. You can also eat on its sunny street-side terrace, or in a courtyard at the back. Daily 10am–11pm.

Wings Shangani St, opposite *Tembo House Hotel*, Shangani. US-style fast food, for those going cold turkey. No alcohol. Daily until 8pm.

Moderate

With Tsh5000–10,000 to spend on a main course and perhaps a starter, most of Zanzibar's manifold delights lie within reach (lobster being the expensive exception), and there are some truly fabulous restaurants to choose from.

Archipelago Café & Restaurant Off Forodhani St, south end of Forodhani Gardens. On an open-sided first-floor terrace with expansive ocean views, it's not just the location

that's fresh but what they conjure up in the kitchen. The menu is an attractive blend of Swahili, more typically African, and international dishes (including pizza), all very reasonably priced at Tsh6000 or under for generous portions: try the spicy *pilau*, the excellent kingfish with chilli and mango sauce, or red snapper simmered in orange. They also do great breakfasts (and divine cakes), plus cappuccino, espresso, and Arabian-style cardamom-laced coffee. No alcohol. Daily 8am–11pm; closed Ramadan daytimes, and April & May.

Bahari Restaurant *Tembo House Hotel*, Shangani St. The menu here flirts briefly with most cuisines (the smoked sailfish is always good), and is pretty affordable, with a four-course set menu costing just Tsh10,000. Service can be very slow, however, and there's no alcohol, but it is Stone Town's only proper beach restaurant, and you can also use the swimming pool. Daily 8am–10pm; closed Ramadan daytimes.

China Plate Forodhani St, at the south end of the tunnel, Forodhani. On the open-sided second floor, this nonetheless gets uncomfortably hot at the start of the year despite the ceiling fans, but is worth bearing for genuine Chinese cooking. The menu provides the habitual head-scratching selection: the seafood is good, of course (upwards of Tsh7000 including rice or noodles), and there are also a number of tofu dishes. Starters and soups are all very cheap (under Tsh2000), and they also make fresh fruit and vegetable juices. Daily noon–2.30pm & 6–9.30pm.

Dhow Palace Hotel Signposted east off Kenyatta Rd, Shangani ⊛ www.tembohotel.com. An attractive rooftop restaurant with panoramic views and a small but affordable menu (Tsh6000–7000 for most main courses), including octopus and fish in coconut sauce, and some European dishes. Free escort to and from your hotel at night. No alcohol. Daily noon–3pm & 6–9pm; closed Ramadan daytimes.

🏃 **The ETC Plaza** Corner of Suicide Alley and Shangani St, Shangani. A congenial and comfortable bar and restaurant on three floors, the top floor being open-air with views over the ocean, and with good music. Good by day or at night, when candles add to the atmosphere. The food's not half bad either (most dishes costing under Tsh7000), whether moussaka, sandwiches, or seafood: the bouillabaisse is highly recommended as a starter, followed by a seafood casserole simmered in creamy coconut sauce, or crab *pilipili* with ginger, fresh basil and pepper. They also do milkshakes, and freshly brewed coffee served from brass samovars. Daily noon–late; closed mid-April to mid-June.

Indiano Restaurant & Bar *Hotel Marine*, corner of Mizingani and Malawi roads facing the port entrance, Malindi. Good Indian food is on offer here as long as their *tandoor* oven is fired up; otherwise

meals risk being microwaved. The oven-baked *ajwain tikka* chicken marinated with cashew nuts and served with lemon rice is worth trying (Tsh6000), as is the Goan fish curry (Tsh4500) with mustard, garlic, ginger and onion gravy. Main courses with rice average Tsh7000–8000. Good selection of drinks. Daily noon–3pm & 6.30pm–late.

Kidude Café & Restaurant Beside *Emerson & Green*, Hurumzi St, Hurumzi. Named after Zanzibar's much-loved nonagenarian *taarab* singer and suitably kitted out in neo-Arabian style, this cosy, air-conditioned place is open for drinks, cakes and snacks and throughout the day, and for light Mediterranean-style lunches and more substantial à la carte dinners, though prices are rather hiked up. Daily 11am–10pm; closed mid-April to end May.

Hotel Kiponda & Restaurant Behind the Palace Museum on Nyumba ya Moto St, Kiponda. Perched at the top of the hotel with a fine view through between the houses, the daily specials can be enticing, such as chicken in tamarind and ginger, though at other times the something-with-chips style isn't so hot. Evening à la carte is good, though, and there's nothing much over Tsh5000. No alcohol. Daily 7–10am, 11am–3pm & 6–9pm; closed Ramadan daytimes.

Kisimani Restaurant *Chavda Hotel*, Baghani St, Baghani. One of the better rooftop restaurants, with marble-topped tables, antique chairs, carved wooden latticework, and good views over the city and of sunsets. The tempting menu covers the lot, from typically Zanzibari seafood dishes, Indian and Chinese (all very good) to not so exciting European fare. Mains average Tsh7000. There's also a bar. Snacks and drinks throughout the day, full meals 1–3pm & 4–11pm; closed Ramadan daytimes.

🏃 **Mercury's** North end of Mizingani Rd near the Big Tree. Named after the rock star, this stylish yet informal bar and restaurant has a beautiful oceanside setting to recommend it, especially the sunset (there are plenty of tables on wooden decking over the beach), and the good food. The fun menu covers both classic Zanzibari dishes and international favourites, and includes plenty of fresh salads and pasta, excellent pizzas, seafood seasoned nicely with saffron, chilli, ginger and garlic, and an ample "Seafood Extravaganza", where Tsh18,000 gets you grilled lobster, fish, squid, prawns, octopus and crab, served with roast potatoes and salad. Desserts are hearty: chocolate cake, mango crumble or sticky almond *halua* goo, or finish with a *shisha* pipe. Count on Tsh10,000–15,000 for a full meal excluding drinks, or Tsh6000–8000 for most mains. There's live

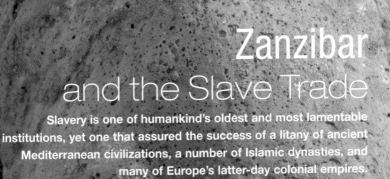

Zanzibar
and the Slave Trade

Slavery is one of humankind's oldest and most lamentable institutions, yet one that assured the success of a litany of ancient Mediterranean civilizations, a number of Islamic dynasties, and many of Europe's latter-day colonial empires.

Slaves in the hold, East African slave ship

The slave trade in East Africa and Zanzibar

In the nineteenth century, the East African slave trade – controlled by Zanzibar – also funded the construction of most of Stone Town. Although slavery had existed in East Africa since ancient times, trade in slaves was slight, and it was only with the conquest of East Africa by **Omani Arabs** in the 1600s that the trade began to eclipse the traditional importance of gold, ivory and spices in commerce. Fuelled by spiralling demand for cheap plantation labour in newly-established **European colonies** around the Indian Ocean and beyond (in some cases as far away as Brazil), the Omanis began developing and exploiting a number of trade routes on the African mainland, some of which penetrated over a thousand kilometres to Africa's great lakes – Nyanza (Victoria), Nyasa (Malawi) and Tanganyika.

Convoy of slaves, 1889

Lay down my heart

Tanzania's mainland dhow port of Bagamoyo, which in the nineteenth century was at the end of the 1200km-long caravan route from Lake Tanganyika, took its name from the words of a slavers' song, in which *bwaga moyo* meant "put down my heart" – a metaphor for a place where the burdens of a tiring voyage could finally be abandoned.

Be happy, my soul, let go all worries
soon the place of your yearnings is reached
the town of palms, Bagamoyo...

For captives, however, *bwaga moyo* was cruelly ironic; to "put down one's heart" would have meant to abandon any lingering hopes of escape.

Tippu Tip

The most infamous of East Africa's slave traders was Hamed bin Muhammed al-Murjebi, better known as **Tippu Tip** – a bird with characteristic blinking eyes – on account of a pronounced facial twitch.

The second half of the nineteenth century was a time of great change in the African interior. Old tribal alliances were breaking down and young upstarts were busy carving out their own chiefdoms. Using this chaotic climate to his advantage, Tippu Tip's combination of ruthlessness and financial sense enabled him to become one of the richest and most influential slave traders in East Africa. By the late 1860s, he was leading slave caravans of more than four thousand men, and over the years became king-maker among many of the chiefdoms the caravan routes passed through, including Upper Congo, of which he was *de facto* ruler. Stanley, whom he accompanied down the Congo River in 1876, considered Tippu Tip "the most remarkable man ... among the Arabs, Waswahili and the half-castes in Africa".

By the end of the 1880s, however, European ascendancy had put an end to the slave trade. With his trading options now limited, Tippu Tip called it a day and returned to Zanzibar, where he lived out his retirement as a wealthy and respected member of Swahili society, his pension assured by seven plantations and at least ten thousand personal slaves.

Stone Town, Slave Town

By 1811, the British sea captain Thomas Smee estimated that three-quarters of Stone Town's population – then around twelve thousand – were enslaved, of whom some six to ten thousand were transported annually to the Omani capital, Muscat. The riches to be made from the slave trade were immense, and in 1841 prompted the Omani Sultan, **Seyyid Saïd**, to take the unprecedented step of shifting his capital to Zanzibar. The move heralded the start of a three-decade-long **golden age**, during which time most of Stone Town's palaces and mansions you can see today were built. The heights of these riches were matched only by the depths of the trade's cruelty, no less brutal or inhumane than the trans-Atlantic trade's infamous "floating coffins".

Memorial statues, Stone Town

The foundations and pillars of several buildings in Stone Town, including Mambo Msiige, are said to contain the bodies of slaves who were entombed alive, supposedly ensuring the building's strength. Stone Town's original slave market was **Kelele Square**, whose name means "shouting", or "tumultuous". In the 1860s, the market was shifted to the far side of Stone Town, away from the prying eyes of British anti-slaving patrols. The dingy **underground cells** where slaves were kept before market day can be visited, and together with the poignant modern sculptures outside provide a harrowing reminder of mankind's often extraordinary inhumanity.

The market's closure in 1873 pushed the trade underground, quite literally. At **Mangapwani**, a man-made cavern was excavated from the coral-stone shore, in which slaves being loaded or offloaded from dhows were hidden. Even today, with its entrance wide open to the sky, it's a singularly claustrophobic place.

The long road to abolition

From the first hesitant British moves against slavery in the 1820s (with the signing of the Moresby Treaty), it took almost a century for slavery in East Africa to be abolished completely. Indeed, for the first forty years or so, British involvement "against" the trade seemed more directed toward keeping out their French competitors. It was only with the publication of David Livingstone's tirades against the horrors he had witnessed in Central Africa that public opinion back in Europe was ignited, and forced more concerted action. This culminated in 1873 with the official abolition of the slave trade in Zanzibar by a reluctant Sultan Barghash, though most forms of slavery itself were only outlawed in 1897, and domestic slavery continued until 1917 – a scandalous concession by the new British rulers to appease Zanzibar's wealthy elite. Overall, the nineteenth century saw over a million lives traded in Stone Town alone. Countless more perished, uncounted, on the arduous treks from their homes to the coast.

Slave-related sites in Zanzibar

➤ **David Livingstone p.100** – celebrated missionary-cum-explorer whose vivid descriptions of the abuses of the slave trade pricked Victorian Britain's conscience, and finally pushed his government into action.

➤ **Hurumzi House p.106** – now a beautiful hotel, this was where the British bought slaves their freedom at the end of the nineteenth century.

➤ **Kelele Square p.102** – site of Stone Town's first slave market, and of Mambo Msiige, in whose walls slaves are said to have been buried alive.

➤ **Mangapwani slave chamber p.142** – a claustrophobic man-made cave on Unguja's northwestern shore, used by slavers after abolition to hide their cargoes from the prying eyes of the British Navy's anti-slavery patrols.

➤ **Mbweni Mission p.137** – a former refuge for ransomed slave women and their children.

➤ **Stone Town's slave market and cells p.104** – the town's second slave market, which witnessed the heights of the slave trade's wealth and depths of depravity, is now occupied by the Anglican Cathedral; adjacent underground cells provide a harrowing reminder of the trade's cruelty.

➤ **Tippu Tip's House p.103** – nineteenth-century home of East Africa's most successful, powerful and notorious slave trader.

Slave caves, Mangapwani

Freddie Mercury

Farok Bulsara, better known as **Freddie Mercury**, the flamboyant lead singer of the glam-rock group Queen, was born in Stone Town on September 5, 1946, to a family of wealthy Zoroastrian Parsee immigrants from India. Various **houses** around Shangani claim that Freddie lived there. If you're into tracing his roots, *Mercury*'s restaurant on Mizingani Road is the place to start – they're nuts about him.

At the age of nine, Farok was sent to boarding school in India, and never returned to Zanzibar. He ended up studying graphics at Ealing College in London, where in 1970 he formed Queen and adopted his stage persona. Somewhat ironically, given that the Bulsaras fled Zanzibar in the aftermath of the bloody 1964 Revolution, Queen's song *Bohemian Rhapsody* – which contains the phrase "Bismillah [in the name of God], will you let him go?" – was embraced by Zanzibari secessionists campaigning for independence from the mainland.

Freddie Mercury died on November 24, 1991, a day after making public his battle with AIDS.

kidumbak music on Friday from 7pm, more tourist-oriented melodies on Saturday (from 8pm), and – ineluctably – good odds on hearing *Bohemian Rhapsody* and Freddie's other hits at other times (see box above). Pizzas and drinks all day, other meals 12.30–3pm & 7–10pm; closed Ramadan daytimes.

Monsoon Restaurant Forodhani Gardens ☎0747/410410. From the folks who brought you *Beit-al-Amaan* hotel comes one of Zanzibar's most atmospheric restaurants (with good food too), where meals are served in a pillared dining room with cushions on woven rugs replacing seats, though if you wish you could sit outside instead under a thick canopy of palm trees and bougainvillea, as long as it's not Ramadan. The light lunches (under Tsh5000) are refreshing, featuring dishes like hummus, guacamole and falafel, and whilst the short main menu concentrates on seafood (most dishes around Tsh6000, grilled half-lobster with tamarind sauce for Tsh14,000; four-course set menus under Tsh12,000), there's plenty for other tastes too, such as tasty vegetarian grilled and stuffed aubergine. All meals are accompanied by side dishes and condiments you won't find elsewhere, such as pumpkin cooked in creamy coconut, mange tout in peanut sauce, home-made mango chutney, and there's a good South African wine list. Reservations are advisable, especially for Wednesday and Saturday evenings when the atmosphere is completed with live *taarab* or *kidumbak* music (7.30–10pm). Daily 10am–midnight.

Nyumbani Restaurant Off Sokomuhogo St, facing *Haven Guest House*, Vuga ☎0744/378026 or 0747/413622, ℮amirbatikstudio@yahoo.com. A private home belonging to an artist and his wife that doubles as a restaurant in the evenings. The $7 set menu, all traditional Swahili, is guaranteed to fill you up and tickle your taste buds. Book ahead; deposit required. Mon–Sat evenings only.

Pagoda Chinese Restaurant Suicide Alley, facing *Africa House Hotel*, Shangani ☎024/223 4688. Family-run Chinese place with average food and moderate prices, and a good lunchtime special for under Tsh4000. No pork. Daily 11.30am–2.30pm & 6–11pm.

Sambusa Two Tables Victoria St, just off Kaunda Rd, Vuga ☎024/223 1979 or 0747/416601. Highly recommended family-run place situated on the first-floor verandah of a private house. The traditional Zanzibari food just keeps on coming (samosas, fishcakes, marinated aubergine, and superb octopus), and costs around Tsh10,000. Phone or pass by beforehand to let them know you're coming. No alcohol. Open for lunch and dinner; closed Ramadan daytimes.

Tradewinds Restaurant *Africa House Hotel*, Suicide Alley, Shangani. On the second floor above the famous sunset terrace bar, the dining room here is rather dreary (and afflicted with horrible muzak) but you can always sit on the wooden sea-facing balcony. Seafood is the predictable speciality, including a great spicy seafood soup (Tsh5000), good marinades and grills (best for dinner; platter for Tsh12,500), and Zanzibar's classic fish or octopus with coconut sauce combos (Tsh7000–8000). Desserts could do with a bit more inspiration however. Three courses, excluding drinks, easily tops Tsh15,000–20,000, though just pasta or pizza won't be more than Tsh6000. Daily 7.30am–10pm.

Expensive

Over Tsh10,000 for a "basic" (fish or octopus) main course is not uncommon at Stone Town's posher places, where full three- or four-course meals with a few drinks may lighten your pocket by anything up to Tsh50,000. It's worth enquiring whether someone's opened another **dhow restaurant**.

Shisha water pipes

A number of Zanzibari restaurants offer diners an aromatic **water pipe** (*mfereji* in Kiswahili) with which to finish their meals. Also called narghile, hookah or hubble-bubble, a **shisha** consists of a glass bottle half filled with water, through which smoke from fruit-flavoured tobacco is drawn along a flexible tube encased in embroidery or beadwork. *Shishas* are wonderfully ornate and decorative instruments, with bold brass heads and fanciful, rather femininely shaped blown-glass water jars incised, inlaid or colourfully painted with floral arabesques, sprays and geometric motifs. In the nineteenth century, when pipes were all the rage with Zanzibar's aristocracy, *shishas* provided a pleasurable means of relaxing for an hour or two in good company, no doubt helped along by a strong dose of nicotine, and were also objects of considerable social importance. Offering to share one with a guest was a treasured mark of trust and friendship, and withholding the honour was an insult – one which led to a diplomatic spat between France and the Ottoman Empire in the 1840s.

By the twentieth century, the water pipe had outlived its time: the hectic pace of modern life favoured **cigarettes** over the more leisurely *shisha*, and it's only in the last decade that its popularity has returned, both in a Muslim world that is increasingly looking back to its roots, and in fashionable cafés around the globe for whom neo-Orientalist chic and decadent, ostentatious style are once more back in vogue.

The *shisha's* origins in medieval India are decidedly more proletarian, having been invented to soften the harsh edge of **marijuana** smoke: in those times, an immature coconut served as the container, the liquid being the coconut's own milk. From India it was but a short hop to Persia, where, come the introduction of tobacco from the Americas in the 1600s, the humble coconut became the ornate *objet d'art* we know today.

The secret of the *shisha's* sweet taste and fragrance is the sticky plug of **special tobacco**, called *mkate wa tumbako*, the best hailing from Egypt, Iran and Turkey. Unlike cigarette tobacco, *shisha* tobacco is dark, fresh and strong, for which reason it used to be washed with pomegranate juice or rose water before being compacted. Nowadays, it's blended with glycerin and fruit pulp or flavoured molasses, particularly apple, though you'll also find apricot and peach, banana, liquorice, mint, cherry, grape, melon, pineapple, vanilla, and even pistachio or strawberry. The better restaurants have a menu to choose from.

Smoking a shisha

Preparing and **smoking a shisha** is an art in itself. The tobacco plug is placed in the shallow perforated dish at the top of the pipe. Traditionally, slow-burning charcoal is placed around the edges (never in the centre), though nowadays you may well find the waiter covering the tobacco with aluminium foil to apply a "self-lighting" charcoal briquette on top. Smoking is a social occasion, and even heavy puffers will be hard pressed to finish a whole pipe by themselves. Take it slow: a plug can last over an hour. While smoking, there are several points of **etiquette** to observe: keep it on the ground; don't use it to light cigarettes (a big faux-pas); and place the tube back on the table when you're done rather than handing it to the next person. Whether you inhale deeply or keep the smoke in your mouth is up to you, but do be aware that whilst there's little or no tar in the smoke, it is loaded with nicotine and carbon monoxide.

There have been several in the past; the last one regrettably caught fire and sank. All offered two-hour sunset cruises, either with drinks and snacks, or a full-on meal, and charged $25 to $40 per person. The folks at *Sweet Eazy Restaurant & Lounge* should know the latest, as the dhows set sail from the landing beside it.

Fisherman Restaurant Shangani St, opposite *Tembo House Hotel*, Shangani. A long-established French *bistrot*-style restaurant majoring on seafood prepared in a variety of styles. It's a little pricey but the food is always fresh, and the welcome warm and unpretentious. Apart from seafood, there's pasta, meat and poultry dishes. Daily 9am–10pm; closed April & May.

La Fenice Shangani St, one block north of *Africa House Hotel*, Shangani. Italian restaurants can usually be relied on for style, and this one's no exception. The menu is thoroughly refined, with the full raft of Italian and French Riviera aperitifs (pastis, martinis), first starters including fried avocado, then pasta (Tsh5000–6000) as a second starter, and some inspired main courses such as crab *alla Veneziano*, dorado cooked with saffron, courgettes and balsamic vinegar, or lobster flambée (Tsh23,000). It's not hard to succumb to their ice creams as well, hot chocolate dressing optional. And of course the coffee is *perfetta*, as is the wine list. Daily 10am–10.30pm.

Le Spices Rendez-Vous (New Maharaja Restaurant) Kenyatta Rd, Vuga. Set in an attractive terracotta-tiled interior, this friendly upmarket abode is justly famed for superb north Indian cuisine (it has an embarrassment of choice for vegetarians), and it also has a good range of French à la carte for less adventurous tastes. Pricey but big portions, and there's live entertainment Tuesday evenings. Tues–Sun 11.30am–3pm & 6.30–11pm.

Sweet Eazy Restaurant & Lounge Kenyatta Rd, close to NBC bank, Forodhani. Sadly lacking sea views, this nonetheless comes highly recommended, offering a mouth-watering selection of outstandingly good and totally authentic Thai and African cooking that makes particularly effective use of Zanzibar's wealth of ingredients. A few examples are the tamarind casserole, featuring prawns and crab, fish and squid, cooked in coconut milk flavoured with tamarind, green pepper, tomato, onion and garlic; the classic Thai spicy prawn soup, with lemongrass stems, mushrooms, tomatoes, lime, coriander, spring onions and chilli; and an inspired take on lobster, cooked with red curry, sweet basil, lime and lemongrass (Tsh23,000). Then there's the

dubiously named "Bangkok Action": no Ping-Pong balls in sight though, it's actually *teppinyaki*-style cook at your own table (Tsh8500). All very light and eminently suited to the climate, the only heaviness other than the puddings being the menu itself, sandwiched between two ridiculously oversized wooden boards that must be the bane of the poor waitresses. Well-stocked bar, and good list of French and South African wines (upwards of Tsh16,000). Live music Friday nights except April & May. Daily 11am–late.

Tower Top Restaurant *Emerson & Green*, 236 Hurumzi St, Hurumzi ☏ 0747/423266 or 0747/438020, ⊛ www.emerson-green.com. Effortless sophistication and inspirational views from the roof of the second-highest building in Stone Town, dinner here is as good an excuse as any to have a poke around East Africa's most atmospheric hotel, before you settle down, minus shoes, on the giant pillows and Persian rugs to watch the sunset, cocktail in hand. The six-course menu changes daily and offers something for everyone (including vegetarians). The cost, excluding drinks, is $25 Monday–Thursday, and $30 otherwise, when live music completes the mood (traditional African *ngoma* on Friday, *kidumbak* on Saturday, and *taarab* on Sunday). Reservations required. Dinner only; closed mid-April to end May.

Zanzibar Serena Inn Kelele Square, Shangani. This five-star hotel contains two restaurants, the elegant *Baharia*, and the outdoor *The Terrace* on top, though you can also eat by the swimming pool; book ahead or arrive early for tables with ocean views. The various menus are designed to pamper, and feature French *haute cuisine* blended with Swahili flavours and clever use of spices; for example deep-fried crab claws coated with mustard seeds and served on a tomato and saffron *coulée*. It's also a good place for grilled lobster (Tsh28,000), glazed with garlic, lime and butter, whilst if you really want to break the bank, Tsh42,000 gets you a four-course dinner. Most main courses cost Tsh15,000–18,000. In addition to the restaurants, there's also a coffee shop with a limited but well-balanced and attractive choice of light meals, including smoked sailfish. Daily for lunch and dinner.

Drinking and nightlife

Tourism has brought with it a small but growing number of **bars and night-clubs**, which sit somewhat uncomfortably in what's still very much a Muslim town – part of the reason why police have a whimsical habit of bringing an abrupt end to proceedings after midnight (if that should happen, just be polite and go home). Apart from *Africa House Hotel*, the longest-established drinking holes are a number of very local dives on the outskirts of Stone Town that cater primarily for mainland Tanzanians: recommended among these (take a taxi to find them) are *Kwa Kimti* and *Sai Bar*. Places geared more towards tourists are reviewed below.

Africa House Hotel Suicide Alley, Shangani. For decades this has been the favoured haunt of expats, tourists and mainlanders, drawn to its first-floor terrace *Sunset Bar* to watch the sun slip behind the ocean, just to the south of the silhouetted East Usambara Mountains. There's a good range of drinks, including a fine South African wine list and particularly imaginative cocktails (Tsh4000–6000), many incorporating Konyagi, Tanzania's home-grown papaya gin. There's also a good snack menu (pasta and pizza for Tsh3500–5000, and an all-day breakfast), whilst darts, a pool table and *shisha* pipes are available (Tsh2000), and there's the *Pirate Cove* nightclub in the basement with state-of-the-art lighting and strobes. Be careful walking in the surrounding area after dark. Daily 10am–10pm.

Coco de Mer Hotel Off Forodhani St, Forodhani. A nicely stylish and quiet bar at street level (no outdoor tables, though). Daily 10am–midnight except March–June (4pm–midnight), and during Ramadan, when it opens after sunset.

The ETC Plaza Corner of Suicide Alley and Shangani St, Shangani. One of the most appealing bars in the city (and with superb food; see p.112), with three levels, the best on top with nice ocean views. The staff are friendly, the mood is chilled out, there's good music (and impromptu jam sessions), and milkshakes and juices are also available along with cocktails (Tsh4000). Daily noon–late; closed mid-April to mid-June.

Garage Club & Dharma Lounge Shangani St, Shangani. Two interconnected places: the very mellow *Dharma Lounge* at the front, which is an upmarket bar that doesn't admit prostitutes, and the club at the back (Tsh2000 entry), which does. The latter is currently Stone Town's leading disco, with plenty of strobes and spinning mirrored globes, and a lively mixture of music ranging from modern *taarab* to rave and Bongo Flava. Daily 9pm–3am.

Komba Discotheque *Bwawani Hotel*, Funguni. Stone Town's oldest disco and popular with locals, with a large swimming pool beside it. No smoking. Tues–Sun 9pm–3am; closed Ramadan.

Masahani Bar *Zanzibar Serena Inn*, Kelele Square, Shangani. A sophisticated Arabic ambience with lots of period decor, and food and drinks available throughout the day, plus tea and cakes. Daily 11am–midnight.

Mercury's North end of Mizingani Rd near the Big Tree. Along with *Africa House Hotel*, this enjoys the best sea views, and is especially blissful for sunset. It can get really busy at night, particularly on Friday when there's live *kidumbak* (often Makame Fakis; 7–11pm), and on Saturday, when there's another live band (8pm–midnight). The bar's well stocked, with a ton of cocktails (try the "Zanzibarbarian": tropical juice, Bacardi, Malibu and clove syrup), pizzas are available all day, and they have *shisha* water pipes (Tsh3000). Daily 8.30am–late; closed Ramadan daytimes.

New Happy Club 2000 Suicide Alley. A very local dive that's chock-full of prostitutes and a startling array of lowlife. Good as an antidote to the excesses of tourism but otherwise probably best avoided (as Suicide Alley should be at night unless you're in a large group). Daily noon–late; closed Ramadan daytimes.

Starehe Club Shangani St, Shangani. Formerly the European Yacht Club, this is now an unpretentious outdoor bar accessed through a curio shop, with a terrace overlooking the beach and harbour, albeit through a chickenwire fence. Drinks and food are cheap, though the blackboard menu is hopelessly out of touch with the kitchen's actual contents; you're usually limited to chicken with chips or *ugali* (Tsh1500), or *nyama choma* (grilled meat). Weekends are good for music: *kidumbak* on Friday, reggae on Saturday (both from 9pm), and – sometimes in high season – a live band on Sunday from 4pm. Daily 8am–midnight.

Sunrise Restaurant & Bar Kenyatta Rd, Shangani. Another cheap place with coolish beers and sodas, some tables in a courtyard at the back, and others at the front. Daily 10am–11pm.

Sweet Eazy Restaurant & Lounge Kenyatta Rd, close to NBC bank. A nicely chilled out bar (and superb restaurant; see p.115) popular with well-to-do Zanzibaris, expats and tourists. There are no sea views, unfortunately, but you can sit outside under palm trees, and it's very cosy inside. Also plays great retro rock (Velvet Underground, The Doors, Hendrix), and – except in April and May – hosts the rather more touristy Coconut Band on Fridays from 10pm (free entry). Daily 11am–late.

Tembo House Hotel Shangani St, Shangani. Soft drinks only, but with a lovely beachfront location, and use of its swimming pool for Tsh3000. Open all day; closed Ramadan daytimes.

Live music

Stone Town's **live music scene**, although vibrant, can be difficult to find as a lot of bands only play for weddings and other social functions, with few venues for more public performances. Still, with a little patience and probably a lot of asking around, you should be able to track down a few events. Apart from groups mentioned below, do ask about performances by Nadi Ikhwan Safaa (also called Malindi Taarab), which celebrated its centenary in 2005. See also the bar reviews for *Mercury's*, *Starehe Club* and *Sweet Eazy Restaurant & Lounge*.

Annual festivals in Stone Town

"The greatest cultural festival in East Africa" claims the brochure, and that's no exaggeration. Established in 1997, the **Festival of the Dhow Countries** (formerly the Zanzibar International Film Festival) is a firm fixture on the African cultural calendar, and provides as good a reason as any to try to get to Zanzibar in the first half of July. No longer restricted to cinema, the festival has been growing steadily, featuring dozens of groups of musicians from all over Africa, the Arabian Peninsula, the Near East and Indian Ocean, almost as many films and art exhibitions, together with acrobats, film and video workshops, special activities for women and young people, award ceremonies, and an innovative mobile wide-screen cinema that brings the magic of cinema to outlying villages on Unguja and Pemba. No mean feat considering the traditional foot-dragging, pocket-lining nature of Zanzibari bureaucracy. The **music** menu is especially alluring, having in recent years featured rare and beautiful sounds from Sufi dervishes, Egyptian Nubian drummers, an Ethiopian circus, and sacred Islamic praise songs from Gujarat. The main **venues** are the Forodhani Gardens and Ngome Kongwe (the Omani Fort) for film, music and dance, the House of Wonders for exhibitions and children's activities, and the Old Dispensary. For information and exact dates, contact ZIFF, Ngome Kongwe (in the gate house), PO Box 3032, Zanzibar ☏0747/411499, ⓦ www.ziff.or.tz.

Since 2004, a welcome addition to the music scene has been the **Sauti za Busara** (Sounds of Wisdom) festival, held over four nights in February, its scope ranging from *taarab*, rap and hip-hop to big-name bands from Zimbabwe and Mozambique, but especially from Tanzania. For more information, contact the Dhow Countries Music Academy (p.96), or Busara Promotions, PO Box 3635, Zanzibar ☏024/223 2423 or 0747/428478, ⓔ busara@zanlink.com.

Culture Music Club Vuga Rd, next to *Florida Guest House*, Vuga. Headquarters of one of Zanzibar's best-loved *taarab* orchestras, who practice here and occasionally put on concerts.

Dhow Countries Music Academy Old Customs House, Mizingani Rd. If anyone knows about upcoming events, it'll be this lot. Their various student orchestras also give performances.

Haile Selassie School Creek Rd, opposite Jamhuri Gardens. Unlikely as it sounds, this school is a good place to catch performances of *taarab*.

Khalifa Hall Ben Bella School, corner of Creek and Vuga roads. Another school that likes hosting *taarab*.

Ngome Kongwe (Omani Fort) Forodhani St. The open-air amphitheatre here hosts "A Night at the Fort" two or three times a week (7–10pm), being rather flaky interpretations of traditional dances from around Tanzania. Entry costs $5, or $10 including a sometimes mediocre barbecue. A sign outside the fort announces the next performance.

Police Mess Off the road going to the airport. The Police Band, performing a lively brand of the jazz or dance music so popular in Dar es Salaam, perform here Friday and Saturday nights. Take a taxi.

Shopping

Stone Town is a veritable Aladdin's Cave for souvenirs, with hundreds of shops containing a huge variety of handicrafts, Arabian and Indian antiques and local products. Prices can be reasonable if you're into bargaining, and competition makes it easy to play one shop's prices off against another's.

Local items to look out for include all manner of **jewellery**, modern and antique **silverwork**, and wooden **Zanzibari chests** with hammered brass hasps, staples and straps, and secret compartments. More portable are henna, incense, soaps and even bubble bath. Also typically Zanzibari are woven **palm-leaf items** like mats (*mkeka*) and baskets (*mkoba*), the latter often containing a selection of spices. Unfortunately, the **spices** for which Zanzibar is famous usually come powdered and pre-packaged, and are nothing you can't buy back home. Rather better are **aromatic oils**, which use coconut oil as a neutral base. **Clothing** – and **fabrics** – are another speciality: these include colourful cotton *kangas* (see p.239) bearing Kiswahili proverbs for women, the heavier sheets without proverbs called *kitenge*, and more simple woven *kikois* with fringed edges worn by men, together with their intricately embroidered *kofia* caps.

The biggest concentration of souvenir and craft shops is along **Gizenga Street** (especially behind the Omani Fort and House of Wonders) and its continuation **Changa Bazaar**. **Hurumzi Street**, which runs parallel to Changa Bazaar, is also good and has several henna "tattoo" parlours and chest-makers. **Kiponda Street**, east of Changa Bazaar, has more antique shops and places specializing in silverwork, while **Tharia Street** and its continuation **Mkunazini Street** is where most of the gold jewellers are. Unless otherwise noted, the shops below

What not to buy

It's illegal, both in Tanzania and internationally, to buy or export items made of **ivory**, **coral**, **turtle shell**, unlicensed **animal skins** and **furs**. Trade in several species of **seashell** is also illegal, especially larger species such as tritons, and in any case their collection has dire consequences for the marine environment. Please don't buy any of these products.

Throughout Unguja and the Tanzanian mainland you'll come across abstract wood carvings and paintings inspired by the **Makonde**, one of Tanzania's and Mozambique's largest and most heterogeneous tribes. The birth of the Makonde woodcarving tradition is entwined with the mythical origin of the people themselves:

In the beginning, there was a male creature who lived alone in the bush, unbathed and unshorn. The creature lived alone for a long time, but one day felt very lonely. Taking a piece of wood from a tree, he carved a female figure and placed it upright in the sun by his dwelling. Night fell. When the sun rose in the morning, the figure miraculously came to life as a beautiful woman, who of course became his wife. They conceived a child, but it died three days later. "Let us move from the river to a higher place where the reeds grow," suggested the woman. This they did, and again she conceived, but again the child survived only three days.

"Let us move higher still, to where the thick bush grows," the woman said. And again they moved, and a third time a child was conceived, this one surviving to become the first true ancestor of the Makonde.

The myth alludes to the Makonde's movement away from low-lying and frequently flooded areas of northern Mozambique. As a result of this, they became isolated from other tribes and developed an exceptionally strong sense of identity. They remain one of very few Bantu-speaking people in East Africa still to reckon descent flows from mother to daughter rather than from father to son, and motherhood is considered a quasi-sacred state of being. Indeed, such is the female domination of Makonde society that men travelling alone still carry a carved female figure to give them protection.

Nowadays, Makonde carvings are much more abstract, in keeping with the tastes of tourists and collectors. Their best-known works are the "tree of life" or "people pole" carvings in the **Ujamaa style**: intricately carved columns of interlocking human figures representing unity, continuity, and communal strength or power – *dimoongo* in the Makonde language. *Ujamaa* has many meanings – brotherhood, cooperation, family and togetherness – and was a byword in post-Independence Tanzanian politics. The central figure is invariably a mother surrounded by clinging children, supporting (literally and symbolically) later generations. Lively and full of movement, rhythm and balance, these are the works that justly brought the Makonde their fame. Lesser-known styles include the naturalistic **Binadamu style**, which represents traditional modes of life: old men smoking pipes, women fetching water, and so on, and the later, much more abstract **Sheitani style**, depicting folkloric spirits in distorted, often fantastically grotesque forms.

This latter style finds its most exuberant expression in **Tingatinga paintings** – vibrantly colourful tableaux of cartoon-like animals and figures daubed in bicycle paint, made and sold virtually everywhere. The style takes its name from Eduardo Saidi Tingatinga, born in the 1930s to a rural Makonde family, who moved to Dar es Salaam when he was 16. He worked on building sites, and in his spare time made paintings and signboards for shops. In the mid-1960s, he began selling his paintings, but was literally cut down in his prime in 1972, when police mistook him for a criminal and shot him dead. His tribal heritage is echoed in his use of *sheitani* ("spirit") imagery. Modern Tingatinga paintings are invariably geared to tourists, depicting safari animals, baobab trees, Kilimanjaro and rural scenes, and, lately, abstract renditions of Maasai warriors dancing in a row. The tourist themes are no reason to dismiss them, as they make singularly cheerful and attractive souvenirs, whether or not they're copied by the hundred. Prices are generally very reasonable, and a large A3-sized painting shouldn't cost more than Tsh15,000, depending on your bargaining skills.

tend to be open from Monday to Saturday between 9am and noon, and 2pm
to 6pm, and on Sunday from 9am to 1pm.

Abeid Curio Shop Cathedral St, opposite the
Catholic Cathedral. One of several antique shops
between the Cathedral and Sokomuhogo St (Jaws
Corner), good for things like Zanzibari chests,
silverwork, clocks and British colonial kitsch.

Capital Art Studio Kenyatta Rd. Established
in 1930, this sells a huge selection of archive
black-and-white photos (both on display and in
boxes you can rifle through), covering pretty much
every aspect of Zanzibari life and history. Mon–Sat
9am–12.30pm & 3–6pm, Sun 9am–12.30pm.

Forodhani Gardens Best in the evening when
the food market is held and there are a dozen or
so stalls selling mainly Makonde woodcarvings,
together with cheap wooden and beaded jewellery in the style of the Maasai, who are among the
stall-holders.

Kanga Bazaar Mchangani St, behind Central
Market, off Creek Rd. The whole street here is
stuffed with shops and stalls selling *kangas*,
kitenges and *kikois*, in a glorious feast for
the eyes.

Kibiriti Gallery Boutique Gizenga St. Kibiriti
makes and sells hand-painted batiks that are also
sold at Hurumzi souvenir shop next to *Emerson
& Green*. The stock is limited and expensive, but
lovely.

Lookmanji Arts & Antiques Off Forodhani St,
next to *Archipelago Café & Restaurant*. A large
selection covering most bases, especially good for
woodcarvings, masks and batiks.

Memories of Zanzibar Kenyatta Rd, opposite
Shangani Post Office. A huge souvenir shop: choose
from reproduction maps, banana-leaf collages,
batiks, rugs, some very luxurious and expensive
Indian fabrics, masks (some more authentic-look-
ing than others) and loads of jewellery. There's also
a good selection of coffee-table books, and CDs of
Zanzibari music. Daily 9am–6pm, closed weekends
from March to May.

Ngome Kongwe (Omani Fort) Forodhani St.
A very calm place to browse for an hour or two,
with a handful of souvenir shops, a gold jewel-
ler, and the exceptional "Art Gallery" (Mon–Fri
8am–7.30pm, Sat & Sun 8am–9pm) in the west
tower on the far side of the grassy quadrangle for
quality paintings, batiks and tie-dye. There's also a
bar and restaurant.

Zanzibar Curio Shop Changa Bazaar. A glorified
junk shop, packed to the rafters with fascinating
stuff from old marine compasses and Omani astro-
labes to gramophones and novelty tin models from
British times. One of the best places to get an idea
of the opulence and decadence enjoyed by Zanzibar's wealthy before the 1964 Revolution. Mon–Sat
9am–6pm, Sun 9am–1pm.

The Zanzibar Gallery Mercury House, Kenyatta
Rd at the corner with Gizenga St. Zanzibar's best
curio shop, selling everything from clothes to
pickles, lovely reproductions of ancient maps,
Indian fabrics, masks, studded wooden chests, *bao*
games and scented toiletries. Best of all, it's also
the best bookshop on the isles, with a huge selection of Africana, novels, and some gorgeous works
on Zanzibar published by the gallery's owner and
renowned photographer, Javed Jafferji. Mon–Sat
9am–7pm, Sun 9am–2pm, shorter hours from
March to May.

Zanzibar Secrets Kenyatta Rd at the top end
of Shangani St. Not all that much choice here
but extremely stylish, and a must for homemak-
ers. Currently popular are weirdly fluid Moroccan
leather lampshades, and fabulously warm and
colourful fabrics. Massage oils, flavoured teas,
reproduction masks and candles are also stocked.
Mon–Sat 9am–8pm, Sun 8.30am–2pm.

Listings

Air charters Reliable companies include Precisionair and ZanAir; see "Airlines" for both. Expect
to pay around $3 per kilometre for a 5-seater
Cessna 206.

Airlines Air Excel, in Arusha on the mainland
℡ 024/254 8429, © reservations@airexcelonline
.com; Air Tanzania, beside *Wings* restaurant off
Shangani St ℡ 024/223 0297, ⊛ www.airtanzania
.com; Coastal Aviation, Kelele Square, Shangani
℡ 024/223 9664, ⊛ www.coastal.cc; Emirates,
south of Gulioni Rd – head east from the top of
Creek Rd and it's on the next dual carriageway on
the right ℡ 024/223 4956, ⊛ www.emirates.com;
Precisionair, *Mazson's Hotel*, Kenyatta Rd, Shangani
℡ 024/223 4521, ⊛ www.precisionairtz.com;
ZanAir, off Malawi Rd behind *Passing Show Hotel*

☎024/223 3670, ⊛www.zanair.com. See also "Travel agents", most of whom deal with airlines.

Bicycle rental Most cheap hotels can fix you up with a bicycle for $5 a day. If you want to arrange things yourself, Maharouky Bicycle Hire, Creek Rd just north of the market, has plenty. You may be asked for a deposit, of anything up to $50; get a receipt.

Books and maps Zanzibar's best bookshop is The Zanzibar Gallery, Kenyatta Rd, and there's also a good if slightly more expensive choice at Memories of Zanzibar on the same road; both are reviewed opposite.

Car and motorbike rental A normal saloon suffices for most of Unguja's roads, but if you plan on driving extensively along the coast (sandy roads), 4WD might be better. Prices with unlimited mileage but excluding fuel average $50/day for a saloon, $70–80 for 4WD. Add $10–20 a day for the services of a driver. Arranging things informally with a taxi driver can work out marginally cheaper. Unlike car rental on the mainland, there's no, or very limited, excess liability in Zanzibar, meaning you're largely covered in case of an accident, but do read the small print. For motorbikes (*pikipiki*), first read the advice in Basics (pp.36–37). The main place is Ally Keys in Darajani (see the map on pp.88–89; ☎0747/411797, ⊜allykeys768@yahoo .com), where $25/day gets you a 250cc motorbike, helmet and full insurance.

Embassies and consulates The nearest are in Dar es Salaam; see p.77.

Hospitals and medical centres The main hospital is the poorly equipped government-run Mnazi Mmoja Hospital, Kaunda Rd ☎024/223 1071, 024/223 1072 or 024/223 1073. Much better are Afya Medical Centre, between Kenyatta Rd and Baghani St ☎024/223 1228, and Zanzibar Medical Group, Kenyatta Rd near Vuga Rd ☎024/223 3134.

Internet There are lots of Internet cafés around town, charging a standard Tsh1000/hr. Easiest to find are those on Kenyatta Rd: Cross Road Internet Café opposite *Sunrise Restaurant & Bar* (Mon–Sat 9am–8pm, Sun 10am–8pm); the large but unfriendly Shangani Internet Café a short distance north (daily 9am–9pm); and Two Shot Internet, beside Malkia Minimarket on Forodhani St (daily 9am–11pm).

Language courses The highly respected Institute of Kiswahili and Foreign Languages (Taasisi ya Kiswahili na Lugha za Kigeni), Vuga Rd, Vuga (☎024/223 1964 or 024/223 3337) is the main place for tuition, charging $5/hr. The usual course is a one-week, 20hr affair; cheaper deals are available for longer courses, and there's the possibility of arranging accommodation too. Try also KIU,

based at the *Salvation Army Hostel* in Dar es Salaam (☎022/285 1509, ⊛www.swahilicourses .com), who offer a two-week, four-hour-a-day course in Zanzibar for $120.

Library The library occupies the former *Zanzibar Gazette* office, Kaunda Rd next to High Court (Mon–Fri 9am–6pm, Sat 9am–2pm).

Money NBC bank, Forodhani St (Mon–Fri 8.30am–4pm, Sat 8.30am–1pm), takes ages but has the best rates, minimal commission, and also a 24hr ATM for international Visa, MasterCard and Delta. Barclays Bank, ZSTC Building, Gulioni Rd, also has a machine. Rates at forex bureaux are bad, hotel forexes even more so, but service is much quicker: try Malindi Bureau de Change, Malawi Rd (Mon–Sat 8am–4pm, Sun 8am–3pm), one of the few to also change travellers' cheques. There are other places on Kenyatta Rd near NBC bank. Credit cards (MasterCard, Visa, Delta and JCB) can be used for cash withdrawals at Coastal Travels, next to *Zanzibar Serena Inn* on Kelele Square (Mon–Sat 9am–2pm & 3–5pm); the maximum is $500 a week. Western Union money transfers can be picked up at the Tanzania Postal Bank on Gulioni Rd (Mon–Fri 8.30am–4pm, Sat 8.30am–noon).

Pharmacies Keriy's Pharmacy, Shangani St opposite *Tembo House Hotel* ☎0748/445454 (daily 9am–9pm, closed 4–8pm during Ramadan); Fahud Pharmacy, Creek Rd, Darajani ☎024/223 5669 (daily 8am–midnight).

Photography Develop and print films at home, as quality on Zanzibar is poor, despite modern equipment, and there are no slide-film processing facilities at all. Film can be bought at several shops at the north end of Kenyatta Rd; check storage conditions and expiry dates.

Police Stone Town's police station is at the corner of Malawi and Creek roads in Malindi ☎024/223 0771 or 024/223 0772; for driving permits (if you're hiring a taxi for outside town, or are driving with a national, not international licence), the office is inside *Bwawani Hotel*.

Post, couriers and freight Shangani Post Office, Kenyatta Rd, has a not entirely reliable poste restante service (ensure letters are addressed "Shangani Post Office, Kenyatta Rd, Shangani"). For sending parcels home couriers are the only reliable method: DHL, Kelele Square ☎024/223 8281; EMS, Shangani Post Office, Kenyatta Rd ☎024/223 0889.

Snorkelling equipment For buying, there's an unnamed shop on Shangani St, under *Africa House Hotel*. For rental, any tour operator or boat owner will fix you up.

Supermarkets and groceries The main supermarket is Shamsuddin, off Creek Rd behind

Daladalas

All Unguja's **daladalas** (*gari ya abiria*) start in or around Stone Town, and operate during daylight hours only, usually 7.30am–5pm. The routes are numbered according to no logic whatsoever, but thankfully vehicles are also marked with their destinations. Details are given throughout this book. The main daladala terminals (*stands*) in and around Stone Town are: **Darajani**, opposite Central Market on Creek Road; "**Nungwi stand**", also on Creek Road a short distance north of the Central Market; **Mwembe Ladu**, 2km east along Gulioni Road; and **Mwana Kwerekwe**, 5km southeast on the road towards the east coast. Frequent daladalas connect the latter two with Darajani, especially #510 marked "M/Kwerekwe". A list of the most useful daladala, and the terminals they depart from in Stone Town, follows

Unguja's daladalas

#101 Mkokotoni – Nungwi stand

#102 Bumbwini – Darajani

#112 Kitope – Nungwi stand

#116 Nungwi – Nungwi stand

#117 Kiwengwa – Nungwi stand

#118 Matemwe – Nungwi stand

#119 Muwanda – Nungwi stand

#121 Donge – Darajani

#203 Mwakaje – Darajani

#206 Chwaka – some from Darajani, most from Mwembe Ladu

#209 Pongwe – Mwembe Ladu

#214 Uroa – Mwembe Ladu

#225 Mwera Pongwe – Darajani

#308 Unguja Ukuu – Mwembe Ladu or Mwana Kwerekwe

#309 Jambiani – Darajani or Mwana Kwerekwe

#310 Makunduchi – Darajani or Mwana Kwerekwe

#324 Bwejuu – Darajani

#326 Kizimkazi – Darajani and Mwana Kwerekwe

#336 Kibondeni – Darajani and Mwana Kwerekwe

#501 M/Kidatu – Darajani

#502 Bububu – Darajani

#504 Fuoni – Darajani and Mwana Kwerekwe

#505 Airport (Uwanja wa Ndege; marked "U/Ndege") – Darajani

#507 Kiembe Samaki (marked "K/Samaki"; for Unguja Ukuu) – Darajani

#508 Tomondo – Darajani

#510 Mwana Kwerekwe (marked "M/Kwerekwe") – Darajani

#511 Kidichi Spice (marked "K/Spice") – Darajani

#517 Kwarara – Mwana Kwerekwe

Central Market (Mon–Sat 9am–8pm, Sun 9am–2pm; closed Fri noon–2.30pm; closed Fri noon–2.30pm; Malkia Minimarket, with less choice, is at the south end of the tunnel in Forodhani (Mon–Sat 10am–10pm; closed 3–7pm during Ramadan). There's an unnamed supermarket on Gizenga St, one block from the post office. For fresh bread, pastries and cakes, go to Dolly's Patisserie, Kilosa House, Kenyatta Rd, in Shangani

Minibuses

An easy way of getting to the east coast (Paje, Jambiani or Bwejuu), or to Nungwi in the north, is on one of the daily tourist **"beach transfer" minibuses**, which are more comfortable than daladalas and will deposit you directly outside your hotel. Most tour operators and budget hotels in Stone Town can fix you up with a seat. The ride costs Tsh3000–5000 depending on the season and who you talk to, or more if you can't be bothered to bargain or if the minibus leaves almost empty. Be clear where you want to go, otherwise the driver will take you to a hotel that pays him the best commission. It's best to pay when you arrive, though giving a small advance for fuel is fine. Upmarket hotels and travel agents run a similar service but milk their captive audience by charging $50–100 for a four-to-six-seat vehicle (and sometimes per person). **Hiring a taxi** works out cheaper (starting price $40–50) and gives you the chance of sharing the cost with other beach-goers. If you choose this approach, you'll also have to buy a permit for driving outside Stone Town: it costs Tsh2500, and can be bought without fuss at a police-run office inside *Bwawani Hotel*.

Flights

To get to the **airport**, catch daladala #505 (marked "U/Ndege"; Tsh300) from Darajani, or use a taxi: it should cost no more than Tsh5000, though of course they'll try for more. Departure taxes, paid in cash, apply if not included on your ticket: $6 or Tsh6000 including safety levy on flights within Tanzania, or $25 plus $8 safety levy on international flights. Airlines are listed on p.120.

Ferries

Ticket offices for most **ferry companies** (for Dar es Salaam and Pemba) are inside the port, and tend to be open all day until 6pm, though tickets for night ferries can be bought until departure time. Buying a ticket inside the port can be a pain, as you'll probably be trailed by commission-hunting *papasi*. Few travel agents will book tickets for you if this is the case, so ensure it's you and not the *papasi* who does the talking when buying. Fares for tourists ("non-residents") are priced in dollars; you can pay the shilling equivalent, but the exchange rate is bad. The fare should include a $5 port tax. Don't try to get the cheaper "resident" fares, or you'll run into trouble with the ticket inspector and will have to pay the full whack plus a bribe or fine to smooth things over. Boats and schedules for **Dar es Salaam** change frequently, but there are at least seven daily sailings, including the overnight MV *Flying Horse*, leaving at 10pm to arrive at 6am. The most reliable boats are the MV *New Happy* ($20 including port tax), and the MV *Sea Express*, MV *Sea Star*, MV *Sea Bus* and MV *Sepideh* (all $35 in economy or $40 first-class, including port tax), all taking two to three hours. For **Pemba**, by far the quickest ferry is the MV *Sepideh* (Wed, Fri & Sun; $40 second-class, $50 first), taking under three hours to reach Mkoani. At the time of writing, all other ferries were overnight, leaving at 8pm or 10pm to arrive at 6am ($30 first-class, $25 second, $20 in third): the MV *Serengeti* on Tuesday, Thursday and Saturday; the government-run MV *Mapinduzi* or MV *Maendeleo* on Thursday; the MV *New Happy* on Friday; and the MV *Aziza I, II* or MV *Mudathir*, also on Friday (their office is 100m south of the port on Mizingani Road). The MV *Mudathir* or *Aziza* continues on to **Tanga** on the mainland; the MV *New Happy* may also cover this route.

(daily 8am–8pm). Alcohol is sold in various shops along Kenyatta Rd.
Swimming pools Nicest of the lot is the beachside pool at *Tembo House Hotel* (Tsh3000). *Dhow* *Palace Hotel* charges the same, whilst *Bwawani Hotel* asks a very reasonable Tsh1000 for use of their huge pool with swim-up bar and sun loungers.

Telephones The cheapest way to call abroad is through the Internet: Shangani Internet Café, Kenyatta Rd (daily 9am–9pm) charges Tsh500/minute to terrestrial lines and Tsh1500/minute to mobile phones; although line quality isn't up to much, at a quarter of the price of normal calls you can't complain. For normal international calls, expect to pay over $2 a minute: try Zantel, Kaunda Rd beside the High Court (Mon–Fri 8am–5pm, Sat 8am–1pm), or *Dolphin Restaurant*, Kenyatta Rd (daily 9am–9.30pm; closed Ramadan daytimes). More practical, but not always reliable, is to use a card-operated phone outside Shangani Post Office; cards, sold inside, cost Tsh5000 or Tsh10,000.

Travel agents Coastal Travels, Kelele Square, Shangani ☎024/223 9664, ⓦwww.coastal.cc; Easy Travel & Tours, Malawi Rd opposite *Hotel Marine* ☎024/223 5372, ⓦwww.easytravel-tanzania.com; Tabasam Tours and Travel, Kenyatta Rd facing *Dolphin Restaurant* ☎024/223 0322, ⓦwww.tabasamzanzibar.com; ZanTours, off Malawi Rd behind *Passing Show Hotel*, Malindi ☎024/223 3670 or 024/223 3768, ⓦwww.zanair.com. All can arrange wildlife safaris on the mainland.

3

Around Stone Town

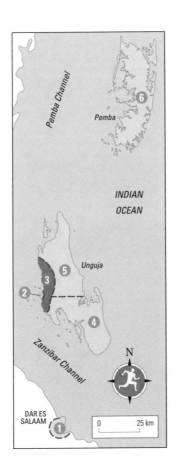

125

CHAPTER 3 # Highlights

* **Spice tours** See, touch, smell and taste Zanzibar's famous spices, followed by a slap-up meal. **See p.129**

* **Changuu Island** Perfect for messing about on boats, snorkelling, and petting giant tortoises, who are relatives of the dinosaurs. **See p.133**

* **Chumbe Island Coral Park** Zanzibar's best snor-kelling reefs, perfect as a day-long excursion or for longer stays at the island's ecologically sound lodge. **See p.134**

* **Mangapwani** This claustrophobic man-made cave where slaves were hidden from the sight of prowling British Navy cruisers provides a shocking reminder of the inhumanity of the slave trade. **See p.142**

△ Mbweni ruins

Around Stone Town

There's a wealth of possible day-trips from Stone Town, all of them arrangeable through tour operators – an option worth considering as the mark-up isn't always that much more than the cost of arranging things yourself, and of course it's much less hassle.

The half-day **spice tours** are virtually obligatory, and include a visit to **Kidichi Persian Baths**, and sometimes also to the creepy slave chambers at **Mangapwani** (which can also be visited by daladala). Other possibilities include a half-day **dolphin safari** involving a ride down to Kizimkazi on the southwest coast (see p.150) and a boat trip in search of resident dolphin pods. This trip can also be combined with a walk through **Jozani Forest**, a sooth-ing and highly recommended experience that gets you eye to eye with a colony of endangered red colobus monkeys.

Also recommended is a half- or full-day boat trip to **Changuu (Prison) Island**, during which you can snorkel and feed a colony of giant tortoises, and **Chumbe Island Coral Park** for some of the world's most stunning snorkelling reefs, virtu-ally untouched coral rag forest, and a gem of a lodge. Other islands that could conceivably be combined with a trip to Prison Island are **Chapwani**, which has a lovely beach and a lodge, and **Bawe Island**, with another good beach and snorkelling. **Scuba diving** is possible around all the islands with the exception of Chumbe.

Apart from the islands off Stone Town, the best clean **beaches** close to Stone Town are Fuji Beach near Bububu, 8km to the north, and Mbweni, 7km to the south.

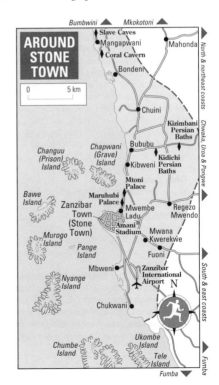

Organized tours

There are close to one hundred **tour operators** in and around Stone Town, most of them offering a standard selection of excursions at pretty standard prices. At the budget level you'll almost certainly be sharing the trip with up to eight other tourists, and may be travelling by daladala or minibus. For private trips in an air-conditioned Land Rover or Land Cruiser, expect to pay three times more than the prices quoted in our reviews. Unfortunately, a lot of companies are unreliable and quote ludicrously inflated "starting prices"; if this happens, look elsewhere. Similarly, ignore approaches by *papasi*. For a more flexible tour, you can **rent a car** (preferably with a driver; see p.121). Most hotels can fix you up with a reliable guide; make sure they speak your language and have an ID card issued by the Commission for Tourism.

Diving and snorkelling off Stone Town

For an introduction to scuba diving and snorkelling in Zanzibar, see p.46.

The waters off southwest Unguja aren't Zanzibar's cleanest and, with underwater visibility averaging a humble 10m, experienced **scuba-divers** don't have all that much to look forward to other than wreck dives. However, the sheltered nature of the area's reefs do make them suitable for novices. **Snorkelling** trips to most of the islands described in this chapter can be arranged through Stone Town's tour operators, or through the two dive centres reviewed below; both charge $20 per person (minimum two) for a trip to two reefs, including Bawe Island, Prison Island and the Panga sandbank.

Murogo Reef is the highlight, its dramatic pinnacles and gullies filled with colourful hard corals and some soft growths which attract a wide variety and quantity of fish. **Boribo Reef**, further south, is good for large pelagics. The shallower reef east of **Bawe Island** has brain corals and, a little deeper, gorgonian sea fans; sand sharks and blue-spotted stingrays may also be seen here. **Pange Reef** surrounds a sandbank handy for sunbathing. Another favourite is **Turtles Den**, which lives up to its name thanks to its turtle-friendly barrel sponges. The most interesting **wrecks** are the *Great Northern* at Fungu Reef (see p.134), and – for history buffs only, given the poor visibility – the remains of HMS *Glasgow*. A present from Britain to Sultan Barghash, it was sunk in 1896 by the Royal Navy during their 45-minute bombardment of Stone Town and, in 1912, was dynamited and the resulting pieces dumped into deeper water.

Dive centres

Stone Town has two PADI-accredited dive centres, both open daily until around 6.30pm.

Bahari Divers Forodhani St, just south of the tunnel ☏0748/254786, ⓦwww.zanzibar-diving.com. A small, friendly and flexible outfit. A four-day Open Water course costs $320, Advanced Open Water $250, and Dive Master $650. Two dives with lunch cost $75. Night and wreck dives possible. They also have a centre in Wete on Pemba Island.

One Ocean (The Zanzibar Dive Centre) Kenyatta Rd, beside *Sweet Eazy Restaurant & Lounge* ☏024/223 8374, ⓦwww.zanzibaroneocean.com. Highly experienced and knowledgeable outfit offering the full range of PADI courses (same prices as Bahari Divers), plus instructor training and underwater camera hire. Night and wreck dives possible, and novices can learn the ropes in a swimming pool. They also have dive centres at Dongwe in the east, and at Kiwengwa and Matemwe in the northeast.

Wildlife safaris on the Tanzanian mainland, whilst offered by a number of Zanzibari tour operators, are invariably much cheaper if arranged in Dar es Salaam, where you'll also have more choice. The main destinations are the coastal **Saadani National Park**, for an unusual "beach and bush" experience together with boat tours along mangrove-lined estuaries in search of hippos, crocodiles and birds, and **Selous Game Reserve** in southern Tanzania, which also offers boat trips (along the Rufiji), heart-stopping walking encounters with big game, and extremely plush if expensive accommodation.

Tour companies

The less reputable **tour companies** are in the habit of quoting ludicrously inflated "starting prices"; if this happens, look elsewhere. Similarly, ignore approaches by *papasi* and stick to the companies reviewed below who should be reliable. As ever, feedback from fellow travellers is the best source of up-to-date advice. Apart from dedicated tour operators, budget **hotels** can also arrange trips; be careful though, as some deal with dodgy companies and also aren't averse to overcharging. A reliable exception is *Jambo Guest House*. **Prices** below are per person. Where two prices are given (eg $15/35), the first is for a person in a group of four, the second in a couple. Discounts are available for larger groups. Most tour company offices are open daily until sunset.

Blue Dolphins Tours & Safaris East end of Changa Bazaar ☏ 0747/424858, ⊛ www .bluedolphinstours.com. A new company useful for arranging cultural day-trips to Tumbatu Island (otherwise almost impossible to access), where you can visit ancient ruins and meet fishermen, farmers and local families ($40/60, excluding food and drinks). No beach lounging, given Tumbatu's Islamic ethics. A combined trip to Jozani Forest and Zala Park costs $25/30.

Eco+Culture Tours Hurumzi St, facing *Kidude Restaurant*, Hurumzi ☏ 024/223 0366 or 0747/410873, ⊛ www.ecoculture-zanzibar.org. A recommended company that promotes

Spice tours

From humble beginnings a couple of decades ago, when a taxi driver had the idea of taking backpackers into the lush centre of Unguja to teach them a thing or two about the herbs and spices for which the isles are famous, the half-day **spice tour** has grown into Zanzibar's most popular excursion.

The trips centre on a **guided walk** around a spice farm (*shamba*) where you're shown herbs and spices, fruits and other crops, and are given fascinating descriptions of their uses, with plenty of opportunities for smelling and tasting. For a list of some of the herbs and spices, and their **medicinal uses**, see pp.130–131; Zanzibar's fruits, with their Kiswahili names, are listed on p.262. Things to look out for include the "lipstick tree", whose pods produce a vibrant red dye; the "iodine tree", whose clear sap is used as an antiseptic; a "soap bush", whose berries lather like soap; and a species of wild cucumber which, when cooked with coconut milk, makes a shampoo for treating dandruff.

Lunch, which follows the tour, is generally included in the price and features *pilau* rice and vegetables seasoned with the herbs and spices you'll have seen growing, washed down with spiced tea or fresh coconut milk.

All **tours** leave in the morning (9.30am at the latest), and return around 2pm unless the tour includes Mangapwani. The guides know their stuff, even on the cheaper tours, though with the latter make sure you have a responsible driver. **Additional options** can include a visit to Kidichi Persian Baths and the slave cave at Mangapwani, and some trips also include the Maruhubi ruins and Livingstone's House, neither of which are particularly interesting. The tours finish with a stop at one of the roadside kiosks selling packaged spices, essential oils and tourist trinkets.

The quest for **spices**, and desire to circumvent the Arab monopoly over the western end of the Silk Road, was a primary motivation behind Europe's dogged persistence in its seaborne **voyages of discovery**, which culminated – in 1498 – with Vasco da Gama's opening of the sea route to India. Long before then, however, Zanzibar had traded spices with Arabia, India, and even with China and the Far East, but it was the **Omanis** – who succeeded the Portuguese – who found that Zanzibar's hot and humid climate was just perfect for the cultivation of spices.

Herbs, spices and their uses

Many herbs and spices have medicinal properties. While in a natural state they are quite safe to use, **essential oils** (*mafuta*) should only be used externally and in moderation. Aromatherapy oils, blended with coconut oil, are softer.

Cardamom (*hiliki*) Pods bearing small sticky seeds from a perennial bush of the ginger family. Smelling like disinfectant, the seeds aid digestion and freshen breath if chewed, are stimulating and, it is said, are an aphrodisiac. The scent lends itself well to Zanzibar's classic *pilau* rice, and to flavour coffee. Superstition means you should only use an odd number of pods.

Chilli (*pilipili hoho*) Introduced from the Americas by the Portuguese, chillis are part of the nightshade family. Their active alkaloid, *capsaicin*, speeds up the metabolism, inhibits cholesterol deposits, is a powerful antioxidant, and gives a short-lived "high". Applied externally it relieves aches and pains.

Cinnamon (*mdalasini*) According to Herodotus, cinnamon "quills" came from the land of Bacchus, where great birds used the sticks to build nests on inaccessible cliffs. The Arabians, he said, used to cut up their dead animals and scatter the flesh nearby; the birds would seize the pieces and fly with them up to their nests which, unable to support the additional weight, would come crashing down. Nice try, but in fact cinnamon is the peeled inner bark of a Sri Lankan species of laurel. Zanzibaris use it to treat tuberculosis, and – as an oil – as an antiseptic mouthwash or to treat fungal infections. It's also useful against lice, warts and stings. Eaten, it eases nausea and hypertension, and is a cold cure if taken in tea.

Cloves (*karafu*) Cloves – originally from Indonesia's Molucca Islands – are the sun-dried flower buds of an evergreen tree from the myrtle family. Their name comes from the Latin for nail. The pungent but pleasant smell derives from a high concentration of *eugenol*, an essential oil used medicinally as local anaesthetic (highly effective against toothaches), in perfumes and, of course, in cooking. Cloves also have antiseptic and analgesic properties: inhaled with steam, they ease respiratory problems, and sucking cloves reduces alcoholic cravings.

Coriander (*gilgilani*) The seeds and leaves of a feathery annual herb of the parsley family, native to the Mediterranean but used throughout the Old World since at least 5000 BC. An infusion of seeds held in the mouth relieves toothache, and also works against indigestion and migraine. The oil (*coriandrol*) is good for easing cramps.

Cumin (*uzile*) The seeds of a low annual plant originally from the Middle East, chewed or eaten to aid digestion and relieve diarrhoea.

Eucalyptus (*mkaratusi*) The aromatic oil from the leaf glands of this omnipresent tree relieves headaches and fevers, and, inhaled with steam, soothes colds and respiratory problems.

Ginger (*tangawizi*) Aromatic and pungent rhizome (rootlike stem) of a perennial plant originally from Southeast Asia, which saw widespread use in China from where it spread to East Africa two thousand years ago. Its propagation is simple, requiring nothing more than planting a stem. Powdered or fresh, ginger is used to treat flatulence and abdominal cramps, and its anti-emetic properties are ideal for the morning after (makes you less likely to vomit). It's perhaps best savoured as *chai tangawizi* in ginger-laced tea.

Jasmine (*yasmini or asumini*) The short-lived flowers of the jasmine tree are as delicate as they are fragrant. Picked when still closed, jasmine flowers find all sorts of decorative use, from being scattered on a bride-to-be's bed as an aphrodisiac, to being strung into necklaces, waist bands and in a *kikuba* posy worn by women during celebrations. The following morning they're dried and ground into a fine powder called *tibu*. This is dusted on shrouds before burial, and – when mixed with olive oil and rose water – is used as a massage balm to smooth skin, ease tension and do away with depression.

Lemongrass (*mchaichai*) A gorgeously aromatic grass used as a morning pick-me-up infusion. It's good for fevers and jaundice, and in Zanzibar is associated with ancestors, as it was planted on top of graves. The steam-distilled oil, *citronella*, is used in medicines, soap, perfume, and in cooking, particularly with coconut milk. It also finds local use as a mosquito repellent.

Nutmeg (*kungu manga*) Nutmeg – like cloves, native to the Moluccas – is one of Zanzibar's weirdest-looking spices. The familiar hard nut is the stone at the heart of a tree's apple-like fruit. Under the flesh is a shiny, black, veined nut covered in a thin bright orange filigree called mace (*aril*). The hallucinogenic properties of both nutmeg and mace are well known, and used as such by Zanzibari women in an infusion or as an oil applied to the eyes. Don't overdose: half a nut ground and drunk with milk or water will get you smashed for at least 24 hours.

Peppercorns (*pilipili manga*) Traded for at least three thousand years, peppercorns are the berries of a shrubby climbing vine native to India's Malabar Coast. Black pepper is the dried unripe berries, which are in fact green; white pepper is picked when the berries begin to ripen – they're blanched in boiling water and their outer covering is rubbed off. In Zanzibar, don't miss trying a bunch of pickled green peppercorns – eye-watering but with a more subtle flavour than either white or black. Pepper's alkaloid, *piperine*, stimulates saliva and gastric juices, helps blood flow, and reduces flatulence, fevers, headaches and diarrhoea. It also eases urinary infections and asthma.

Sesame (*gigiri*) Possibly originating in East Africa, sesame seeds are from an annual plant cultivated since ancient times. Its main use is in cooking, particularly desserts. The oily seeds treat constipation, and are effective against anaemia and tinnitus.

Sweet basil (*mrehani*) A stimulating annual herb of the mint family, originally from India and Iran, with antidepressant properties. The purple leaves ease digestive and nervous disorders, and, applied topically as a paste, coax out insect stings. The oil relieves headaches and fevers and may be an insect repellent. Zanzibaris drink it as tea.

Turmeric (*manjano*) Used in cooking for its vibrant yellow colour, turmeric powder is made from the ground rhizome of a ginger-like plant. It's an anti-oxidant and anti-inflammatory, aids metabolisation of fats, thins the blood and eases gall bladder and liver problems. Zanzibaris use a pomade of turmeric and lime juice to treat sores.

Vanilla (*vanila*) The pods of this tropical climbing orchid, often seen up in palm trees, are anything but plain. Originating in the Americas where it featured in *xocoatl* (a chocolate beverage), the fruit is a fleshy but scentless pod measuring up to some 20cm long; its amazing aroma emerges after four or five months of curing and sun-drying. Its name derives from an archaic Latin term for sheath or vagina, a reference to the flower's elongated shape which is pollinated artificially with a wooden needle. Vanilla is an aphrodisiac.

ecological and cultural tours, along with more standard options. Their wide "menu" includes a spice tour with a medicine man ($20/30 including a superb lunch), day-trips to Nungwi ($35/50 including lunch), Jambiani village ($30/45 including lunch) and Unguja Ukuu ($40/60), and – in planning – a cave tour.

Madeira Tours & Safaris Facing *Baghani Hotel*, Baghani ☎024/223 0406 or 0747/415107, ⓦ www.madeirazanzibar.com. Efficient, responsible, and with a wide range of options: spice tour ($30/40), a half-day Prison Island trip ($25/35), Jozani ($40/50), dolphins ($50/70 excluding lunch), a trip combining a spice farm visit, Mangapwani and Nungwi beach ($55/65), and a full day's fishing with locals off Mkokotoni ($80/100).

Mitu's Spice Tour Off Malawi Rd, Malindi ☎024/223 4636 or 0747/418098. Self-proclaimed inventor of the spice-tour industry, former taxi driver Mr Mitu has now retired, but his sons continue to offer reliable and entertaining tours shared with others at a standard $10 per person for over six hours, including Kidichi and Mangapwani. The same for just a couple costs $70 per person.

Sama Tours Gizenga St, behind the House of Wonders ☎024/223 3543 or 0747/430385, ⓦ www.samatours.com. Noted for the unhurried nature of its trips, the standard options include a spice tour ($25/45), Jozani ($20/35) and a full-day Prison Island excursion ($20/35). Other trips include a full day on the east coast ($20/35), a three-hour dhow cruise ($20/40) and one-day cultural tours of Jambiani or Nungwi ($20/45). A full-day combining dolphin-spotting with a trip to Jozani Forest goes for $41/71 including lunch and fees.

Tabasam Tours and Travel Kenyatta Rd, facing *Dolphin Restaurant* ☎024/223 0322, ⓦ www.tabasamzanzibar.com. Calm, unhurried and professional, the choice including half-day spice tours ($21/25 with lunch), a day-long dhow and snorkelling trip combining Prison Island, Bawe Island and Chapwani Island ($46/56 with lunch), and a full day with snorkelling at Chumbe Island ($75 including lunch). They also offer a good-value combined spice and city tour for $30/36.

Three Legs Tours Shangani St, opposite *Starehe Club* ☎0747/431892. A friendly cooperative run by polio victims, whose trips – uniquely – can also be made by *tuktuk*, a diminutive motorized rickshaw. Office open weekdays only.

Tropical Tours & Safaris Kenyatta Rd ☎0747/413454 or 0747/411121, ⓔ tropicalts@hotmail.com. Cheap and reliable: spice tours ($15/25), Prison Island ($20/25), Jozani Forest or Dunga Palace and the east coast (both $25 per person in a couple), and dolphins ($25 per person). They can also book ferry tickets.

ZanTours Off Malawi Rd, behind *Passing Show Hotel*, Malindi ☎024/223 3670 or 024/223 3768, ⓦ www.zantours.com. An expensive if thoroughly reliable company offering a variety of unusual trips, including full days on Chumbe Island (around $100), live-aboard diving, and flying safaris to Selous Game Reserve on the mainland. Their standard trips include spice tours ($25), Prison Island ($30), and a combined dolphin safari and Jozani Forest excursion for $50–80.

Islands off Stone Town

A number of small islands within a few kilometres of Stone Town can be visited as day-trips, and provide ideal refuges from the frenetic atmosphere of the town and its hustlers. **Prison Island**, the most popular destination, combines the attractions of snorkelling on a shallow reef with the chance to pet giant tortoises. The largest island, **Bawe Island**, is infrequently visited and usually combined with Prison Island, but also has good snorkelling. There are also a couple of privately owned islands: the incomparable **Chumbe Island**, in the heart of a protected marine area, boasts one of the world's most beautiful snorkelling reefs and virtually untouched coral rag forest, and is home to the rare Ader's duiker and coconut crab; and **Chapwani Island**, with its small and intimate lodge, lovely beaches and dikdik antelopes.

Changuu Island (Prison Island)

A trip to **Changuu Island**, a narrow kilometre-long strip 5km northwest of Stone Town, is a popular, enjoyable and cheap way of getting out of town. There's a beautiful beach, good snorkelling on the shallow fringing reef, a nineteenth-century ruin, patches of coral rag forest, and the giant tortoises (*changuu*) from which the island gets its Kiswahili name.

Once used as a transit camp for slaves, the island's English name comes from a **prison** that never was. Following the abolition of the slave trade, the British built what was supposed to be a prison, but which only saw use as a yellow-fever quarantine camp. The crumbling cells and ruins of the hospital boiler-house can still be seen, while the courtyard is nowadays inhabited by a colony of showy peacocks. A narrow trail behind the ruins leads into a patch of forest, home to a herd of diminutive **suni antelope** – spotting them isn't too difficult as long as you tread softly. The forest is also good for **birdlife**; look for the intricately woven sock-like nests of weavers hanging from the trees.

The fenced enclosure behind the restaurant contains a colony of **giant tortoises**, some of them the descendants of four tortoises from Aldabra Atoll in the Seychelles, which were presented to the British Regent in 1919. They breed from January to May; the male copulatory organ is in the tail. At over two hundred kilograms in weight, the biggest – aged anything up to 100 years – are second in size only to Galapagos tortoises, and like their cousins are real dinosaurs, having evolved some 180 million years ago. By 1997, **theft** had reduced the population to just seven. The colony was subsequently restocked, but between 1998 and 2004 another eighty tortoises – almost half the population – disappeared. Tsh500 buys you a bowl of spinach and some quality bonding time, but watch out for sharp beaks, and don't sit on them as some tourists like to do – they're hot enough as it is already.

Practicalities

A **lodge** with 25 cottages is currently being built on the island (Stone Town's tour operators will know the score). In the meantime, **day-trips** are the only way of seeing the place, either as a half- or full-day excursion from Stone Town. The boat ride, from the landing next to *Sweet Eazy Restaurant & Lounge*, takes 30–45 minutes. Hotels and tour operators can arrange things for you, but you can also arrange things directly with the boatmen; the ride itself shouldn't cost more than Tsh5000 for the return trip. More expensive are the smart modern boats, with sunscreens usually adorned with advertising; apart from these there's little difference in the quality of service on offer. An entrance fee of $4 (or shilling equivalent; not included in tour rates) is paid at a small shack near the landing on the island. Snorkelling gear can be rented in Stone Town or on the island if not included in the cost; count on Tsh2000. Most people bring **picnics**, but food and drinks are available at a **restaurant** facing the beach where the boats arrive (meals from Tsh3500).

Bawe Island

Lying 6km west of Stone Town, **Bawe** is the largest of the islands near Stone Town and is popular with scuba-divers. Uninhabited for want of fresh water, the island acquired modest fame in the 1880s when it served as a base for East Africa's first underwater telegraphic cable. The cable ship, the *Great Northern*, arrived in Zanzibar in 1882 and eventually laid 1950 nautical miles of cable between Aden (Yemen) and Mozambique via Zanzibar. The ship's wreck lies off Fungu Reef.

Practicalities

The easiest way of **getting to Bawe** is to combine the trip with a visit to Prison Island; most tour operators can arrange this. The more interesting way of getting here is to rent a boat at the dhow harbour (turn right 50m inside Stone Town's harbour entrance). The journey takes thirty to ninety minutes depending on the seaworthiness of your conveyance. There are no facilities whatsoever on Bawe, so if you plan on snorkelling, eating or drinking, bring everything you'll need with you from Stone Town.

Chumbe Island Coral Park

Chumbe Island Coral Park, 6km off Chukwani south of Stone Town, was Tanzania's first marine protected area, and encloses one of the richest and finest coral gardens in the world, as well as rare coral rag forest. The island's name aptly encapsulates the notion of a rich ecosystem as a living entity: it means a creature, or a being.

Coral growth and diversity along the shallow **reef** is among the highest in East Africa, and marine life diversity is astonishing, with more than two hundred

△ Snorkelling off Chumbe Island

species of stone corals and around ninety percent of all East African fish species, over four hundred in all. Needless to say, **snorkelling** is superb (scuba diving is prohibited), and several snorkelling trails with "floating underwater information modules" have been established. Marine life includes parrotfish (the ones that peck at the coral), lobsters, giant groupers, Moorish idols, lionfish, angelfish, butterfly fish and triggerfish. Rarer are large blue-spotted stingrays, dolphins, and a couple of batfish who like following snorkellers. There's also a resident hawksbill turtle, and Oscar, a large cave-dwelling potato grouper.

But it's not just marine life that makes Chumbe special. Most of the island is covered with pristine **coral rag forest**, which contains a surprisingly rich variety of flora and fauna given the lack of permanent groundwater. The survival of the forest is largely due to the absence of humans on the island, settlement having been limited to temporary fishermen's camps and the keeper of the lighthouse (which was built in 1904 and fitted with its present gaslight in 1926; its 132 steps can be climbed). The forest, which can be explored along a number of **nature trails** that have been carefully laid without breaking the forest canopy, is one of the last natural habitats of the rare coconut crab and endangered Ader's duiker, reintroduced in 1997 after being wiped out by hunters in the 1950s. The species exists only on Zanzibar and in Kenya's Arabuko-Sokoke Forest. It's also possible to walk around the island at low tide; you'll see **mangroves**, and be able to poke around intertidal rock pools for crabs, starfish and shellfish. Over on the bleak and rocky eastern side of the island, look out for petrified corals and fossilized giant clams, the latter an estimated 15,000 years old.

Little of this would have survived were it not for the efforts of conservationists. The Zanzibar Channel is one of the most over-fished areas in East Africa, particularly by local boatmen providing the raw material for foreign factory ships moored in international waters. A spirited campaign led to the closure of Chumbe's western reefs to fishing and commercial exploitation in 1992, and in 1994 the government formally opened the Chumbe Reef Sanctuary. For its pains, the project has been rewarded with a string of prestigious international awards. The island and its reefs are explored either in the company of one of the park's rangers (a friendly and informative bunch of former fishermen), or by using laminated route plans and leaflets. If you have $200 per person to spare, the superb and truly eco-friendly **lodge** offers a memorable investment. All profits are channelled back into conservation and environmental education. There's no beach, but with so much other natural beauty around you'll hardly miss it.

Practicalities

You can visit the island on a day-trip, or by staying at its intimate and justifiably pricey lodge (all profits go into conservation or educational activities). The **boat** leaves from the beach at *Mbweni Ruins Hotel* (see p.137), 7km south of Stone Town, every day at 10am, taking thirty to forty minutes for the nine-kilometre crossing. The transfer is free for overnight guests; day-trippers pay $75, which includes entry fee, lunch (on a beautiful sea-view terrace) and activities. It's best to **reserve in advance**, as day-trips may not be allowed if the lodge is full (Chumbe Island Coral Park ☎024/223 1040 or 0747/413582, Ⓦ www.chumbeisland.com).

Accommodation at ⚓ *Chumbe Island Eco-Lodge* (closed mid-April to mid-June; full board ❾) is in seven romantic split-level *bandas* overlooking the ocean, with casuarina poles for walls and palm fronds for roofs. All have a large living room, handmade furniture and hammock. The "ecotourism" tag is more than just an advertising gimmick: rainwater is filtered and stored under the floors,

The coconut crab

The **coconut crab** (*Birgus latro*; also known as the robber crab and nicknamed "the rhino of the invertebrates") is the world's largest land crab, reaching 60cm–1m in length and weighing three to four kilograms. Originating in Polynesia, it appears to have made its way to the western Indian Ocean by being carried along by ocean currents while in its plankton stage, or was introduced by early sailors as a source of food.

The crabs are crimson or bluish black in colour, and their unusual **name** comes from their amazing ability to climb trees, a skill popularly believed to be for wrenching off coconuts. True or not, they do climb trees and certainly feed on fallen coconuts, as well as on hermit crabs, to which they are related. The main differences between the two species, other than size and an aptitude for arboreal gymnastics, is that the coconut crab sheds its shell and is nocturnal. By day, you might see them hiding in rocky crevices on the coral cliffs or burrowed in the roots of palm trees; at night, they emerge to forage for fruit and coconuts, which can be stored in their burrows.

Coconut crabs have long been considered a delicacy and aphrodisiac throughout the Indian Ocean, and so have been hunted to the point of extinction. On Zanzibar, the crabs were also used as bait in fish traps – their struggles attracted fish – though the crabs drowned after two days in water. Other factors contributing to their decline are unnatural predators such as rats (introduced when the lighthouse was built in 1904, but eradicated in 1997), pigs (introduced by the Portuguese) and monkeys. In Tanzania, the species is limited to Chumbe and Chapwani islands off Stone Town, Misali Island off Pemba, and Mbudya Island north of Dar es Salaam.

hot water and electricity are provided by solar power, ventilation is achieved naturally with cleverly designed roofs, and toilets create no waste. There are no TVs or phones and, apart from the activities on the island, entertainment is limited to watching the palm trees sway in the breeze. Meals, taken on an inspiring seaview terrace, are a mixture of Zanzibari, Arabic, Indian and African cuisine, with good options for vegetarians too. The price includes transfer from Mbweni, entry fees, soft drinks, walks and snorkelling. Rates may be cheaper if booked through a reputable travel agent in Stone Town.

Chapwani Island (Grave Island)

Like Chumbe, **Chapwani Island** – 3km due north of Stone Town (rather too close for any desert island make-believe) – is privately owned, and you're only allowed to land if you buy a meal or are spending a night in the lodge, both of which require reservations. The island is tiny, measuring barely 600m long by 60m wide, with a beautiful sandy beach on one side and a series of coral inlets dotted with tidal swimming pools on the other. Though it lacks the quantity and quality of Chumbe's reefs and terrestrial flora and fauna, Chapwani still has plenty to make it a pleasant hideaway, including dikdik antelopes, a colony of fruit bats, hermit and coconut crabs, interesting birdlife, and good swimming and snorkelling at all tides. There's also the **cemetery**, established in 1879, from which the island draws its English name. Among the untended tombs here are those of sailors from the HMS *Pegasus*, which was sunk by the German cruiser *Königsberg* at the start of World War I. It took the British almost a year to locate and finally destroy the cruiser, which had sought refuge in the Rufiji River delta, south of Dar es Salaam.

The fifteen-minute boat ride from Stone Town costs $15 per person each way if arranged through **Chapwani Island Lodge** (☎024/223 3360 or 0747/322102, ⓦ www.chapwaniisland.com; closed April & May; full board ❾), which has five thatched cottages with two large guest rooms apiece on the south side of the island, each with its own secluded area of beach and a sea-facing terrace. The large bedrooms are pretty simple, but cheerfully kitted out with African prints and antiques, and also have generator-powered ceiling fans and solar-heated water. The beachside **restaurant** conjures up Italian-inspired dishes with a touch of oriental and African cuisine, and is particularly strong on seafood. **Activities** include sundowners on the beach (with the twinkling lights of Stone Town to the south), canoeing, snorkelling, and boat trips to Changuu or Bawe islands.

Mbweni

On the coast 7km south of Stone Town, **MBWENI** is a popular day-trip with locals and visitors alike, thanks to its botanical gardens, the poignant ruins of a nineteenth-century Christian mission and freed slave colony, and an excellent restaurant at the *Mbweni Ruins Hotel*, which alone provides reason enough to come here.

The hotel is set amidst the ruins of a nineteenth-century **Anglican mission**. Formerly a plantation, the seven-acre site was purchased in 1871 by the Oxford-based Universities' Mission to Central Africa. Four years later, under Bishop Steere, a colony of freed slaves was established. The ruins of the chapel and St Mary's School date from this time – the school was used by girls freed from captured slave dhows, and by daughters of freed slaves. Caroline Thackeray, the school's first headmistress and cousin of novelist William Makepeace Thackeray, is buried in the graveyard of St John's Church nearby. The church, in the late English Gothic style, was built in 1882. In 1920 the school and buildings were sold to the Bank of India, under whose ownership they fell into ruin. Services are held at St John's Church every Sunday at 9am.

Aptly complementing the ruins are the glorious cascaded **botanical gardens** founded by the Scottish physician, **Sir John Kirk**, during his lengthy stint as Britain's first Consul General. A botanist by profession (in which capacity he had accompanied Livingstone up the Zambezi), Kirk was the main authority on East African flora, and introduced many of the 650 species found in the garden, including sausage trees, Madagascan periwinkle, devil's backbone and over 150 palms. Many of the plants are labelled, and there's a nature trail which you can walk on your own (the hotel has bird, plant and butterfly lists) or accompanied by a guide from the hotel.

For more information about the Mbweni mission, see Flo Liebst's book *Zanzibar, History of the Ruins at Mbweni*, available at the hotel.

Practicalities

There's no problem walking or cycling the 7km from Stone Town, but it's far easier to catch a taxi – Tsh7000 would be good going. Alternatively, catch a #505 daladala from Darajani (for the airport) and get off at Mazizini police station next to the signposted junction for Mbweni. Follow the Mbweni road and turn right again after 800m. The ruins and the hotel are 900m along.

Accommodation is at the *Mbweni Ruins Hotel* (☎024/223 5478, ⓦ www .mbweni.com; breakfast included ❼–❽), a peaceful and cosy place beside the ocean with thirteen spacious suites, including the "Baobab Suite" with a rooftop terrace. All have air-conditioning, sea- and garden-facing verandahs, and are furnished in traditional style with four-poster beds and oriental rugs, but are rather plain for the price. The narrow beach isn't Zanzibar's best either, as there are plenty of mangroves and the sand is coarse, but this at least attracts a rich variety of birdlife. Facilities include a freshwater swimming pool overlooking the sea, a beach bar, natural-health centre, and an excellent clifftop restaurant (around Tsh10,000 for lunch, upwards of Tsh15,000 for dinner) where you might be joined by bushbabies. Barbecues are sometimes held in the ruins, or on a dhow, and trips to Changuu, Bawe and Chumbe islands can be arranged.

North of Stone Town

Attractions north of Stone Town include a couple of **ruined palaces** at Maruhubi and Mtoni, and **Persian baths** at Kidichi, all of which can be visited as part of a spice tour (see box on p.129). Some tours also include **Mangapwani**, about 20km north of town, which apart from a lovely beach, has a natural cave and a man-made cavern that was used for holding slaves. All these places can be visited under your own steam. There's also a good beach near Bububu at **Fuji Beach**.

Maruhubi

Just off the road to Bububu, 3km north of Stone Town amidst mango and coconut trees, are the ruins of **Maruhubi Palace**, built by Sultan Barghash in 1882 to house his harem of 99 concubines and one wife. Dark legends tell of the former being killed if they did not satisfy the sultan's wishes, and of others being put to death after having fulfilled the carnal desires of visiting dignitaries. The largely wooden palace, one of the most beautiful of its time (there's a photo in the House of Wonders), was gutted by fire in 1899 and the marble from its Persian-style bath house was subsequently stolen, leaving only the foundations of the bath house, an overgrown collection of coral stone pillars and a small aqueduct that carried water from a nearby spring to cisterns, which are overgrown with lilies. To get here, walk or catch one of the frequent #502 Bububu daladalas from Darajani. Access is free.

Mtoni Palace

About 2km beyond Maruhubi is the bustling village of **Mtoni** and the ruins of **Mtoni Palace**. Built by Seyyid Saïd between 1828 and 1832 as his first official residence, the palace at one time housed the sultan's three wives, 42 children and hundreds of concubines. The main building had two floors with elegant balconies, and other buildings included baths, a mosque and an unusual conical tower that served both as a meeting place and a place for meditation, while the gardens contained a menagerie of wildlife, including ostriches, flamingos and gazelles.

Like Maruhubi, much of Mtoni Palace was destroyed by fire, in 1914, leaving only the mosque intact. The advent of World War I saw the mosque converted into a warehouse, and it was later destroyed when the present oil depots were constructed. Nowadays nothing more than a few walls and collapsing roofs remain, and the ruins would be unremarkable were it not for their association with **Princess Salme** (see box below), daughter of one of Seyyid Saïd's

Princess Salme

Princess Sayyida Salme bint Saïd bin Sultan was born on August 30, 1844, to the Sultan of Oman, Seyyid Saïd, and a concubine (sarari) named Jilfidan. Although Salme's early childhood, much of which was spent at Mtoni, was by her own account idyllic, her adult life was to be much more turbulent.

Sultan Saïd died when Salme was 12, beginning a period of rivalry which ended with the creation of the separate sultanates of Zanzibar and Oman. In the former, Salme's brother **Barghash** unsuccessfully attempted to usurp the throne from his half-brother Majid. In 1859, Salme's mother died in a cholera epidemic, and Salme went to live with her half-sister, Khole, with whom she played a minor role in Barghash's second and equally doomed attempt to seize power. For her part in the plot, Salme spent several years in internal exile before making peace with Majid – something that permanently soured her relations with Barghash.

Salme returned to Stone Town in 1866, where she lived next door to, and began an affair with her future husband, a German merchant named **Rudolph Heinrich Ruete**. Heinrich's Christianity meant that problems were inevitable and when, in the same year, Salme became pregnant, Heinrich realized the danger and made arrangements to smuggle her out of Zanzibar aboard the German vessel Mathilde. Although this attempt at escape was foiled at the last moment, Salme, aided by Dr John Kirk and his wife, succeeded in boarding HMS Highflyer on August 24 and fled to Aden.

The couple's child was born in December, and when Heinrich arrived on May 30, 1867, Salme converted to Christianity, was baptized as Emily, and married her lover – all on the same morning. In the afternoon, they set sail for Hamburg. Although their first child died young, Salme and Heinrich went on to have three more children before Heinrich was killed in a tram accident in 1870. Following the death of her husband, Salme spent much of her time campaigning for the restitution of the "rights" she had forfeited by converting to Christianity, but her family remained deaf to her entreaties.

Finally, in 1885, the **German government** sent her to Zanzibar aboard the Adler, escorted by five warships, the idea being to use her as a pawn in obtaining Zanzibar as a German protectorate. The attempt backfired: Sultan Barghash was outraged by his sister's presence and refused to see her. When Barghash died in March 1888, Salme hoped for a change of heart from his successor, Seyyid Khalifa bin Saïd, and once more returned to Zanzibar, only to be shunned again. She spent ten days on the island before leaving for the last time in October 1888. The rest of her life was one of restless travel and writing, in the latter expressing what were, for her time, visionary ideals about health care, literacy, education, and cross-cultural understanding. When Salme died of pneumonia in 1924, the dress she had been wearing during her elopement, and a bag of sand taken from the beach at Mtoni, were found among her possessions.

The Palace Museum in Stone Town has an entire room dedicated to the errant princess. For **further information**, see the website of the Sayyida Salme Foundation, ⓦ www.sayyidasalmefoundation.org.

concubines, whose elopement with a German merchant caused a colossal scandal. In her autobiography, *Memoirs of an Arabian Princess*, she beautifully describes the opulence of palace life at Mtoni in the 1850s and 1860s, where she was born and spent her early childhood.

Practicalities

The remains of the **palace** can be seen off the path that goes beside the oil depot to the beach; route #502 daladalas from Darajani (for Bububu) pass by the junction. **Accommodation** is at ⚓ *Mtoni Marine Centre* (☎024/225 0140, ⒲www.mtoni.com; breakfast included ❷–❻), a laid-back and welcoming hotel which caters for all budgets, set in palm-tree-studded lawns with good views of Chapwani Island and Stone Town over the ocean. All rooms have air-conditioning and private bathrooms. The best are in the two-storey "Palm Court", and are spacious, elegant, and have sea views from verandahs, balconies, and even from the bathtubs of the four rooms on top. Not as good are the "Club Rooms", which overlook the gardens and lack privacy. The "Standard Rooms" at the back near the road are considerably more basic but very cheap, whilst bungalows have kitchens, lounges and up to three bedrooms. Amenities include a swimming pool, recliners and parasols on the sandy beach, aromatherapy overlooking the ocean, a kids' playground, dhow cruises and other day-trips, and – reason enough for coming to Mtoni – good **restaurants**. The stylish *Mtoni Marine Restaurant* is famed for its fusion of local and international styles, seafood being the predictable speciality. It has tables right on the beach, and is particularly romantic at night, what with your toes in the sand, candles on the tables and the stars above (reservations recommended; ☎024/225 0140). There's live music most nights, including *taarab* (and a barbecue) on Tuesday for Tsh10,000. The more casual *Mcheza Bar & Bistro* has wood-fired pizzas, chargrills, burgers, cocktails and sports on TV (meals around Tsh4000–6000), whilst *Zan Sushi Bar* on the beach excels at sushi and sashimi (raw fish, including lobster).

Bububu

The first clean beach north of Stone Town is at **Bububu**, a densely populated area 10km north of the city beyond a none-too-attractive industrial suburb. There's a reasonable range of cheapish guest houses and one exceptionally atmospheric upmarket option, but if it's a beach holiday you're after you'd be better off elsewhere, where the beaches are nicer and there's a wider choice of accommodation.

Practicalities

Route #502 **daladalas** to Bububu run every few minutes throughout the day from Stone Town's Darajani terminal on Creek Road. **Fuji Beach** is 300m off the main road down a track from Bububu police station, and takes its name from *Fuji Beach Bar*, which was set up here a couple of decades ago by a Japanese expatriate. He's long gone, but the bar, which also serves cheap meals, still exists and remains popular with locals and day-trippers from Stone Town, and hosts a beach disco on Saturday and Sunday nights until midnight. Don't leave items unattended on the beach: there have been thefts in the past.

There are two good **hotels**, facing each other off the main road from the police station. The most atmospheric is *Salome's Garden* (☎024/225 0050,

Bububu may have inherited its name from the sound of a nearby spring or, it is said, from the whistle of Africa's first train, when a two-foot-gauge track was laid from Stone Town to Sultan Barghash's summer palace at Chukwani, south of the city, in the 1880s. The railway saw little use, however, and was pulled up after the sultan's death. Between 1905 and 1909 a second line – the Bububu Light Railway – was constructed by an American company, Arnold Cheney & Co. It consisted of seven miles of three-foot gauge and connected Stone Town's Omani Fort with Sultan Ali bin Hamoud's clove plantation at Bububu. The railway quickly became infamous, as a government official recounted in 1911:

"The whole width [of the railway] is blacked, while the engines, which belch forth clouds of smoke and sparks into the front upper storey windows, cover the goods in the shops below, not to speak of the passengers, with large black smuts. Funeral processions are interrupted, old women are killed, houses and crops are set on fire ... and no redress can be obtained."

Thankfully for locals, the advent of the motorcar scuppered plans for the railway's extension to Mkokotoni, and the track was finally abandoned in 1927.

Ⓦ www.salomes-garden.com; ❻), a restored nineteenth-century country house just behind Fuji Beach. The orchards, gardens and ruins are enclosed by a tall wall, giving the place an enchanting Alice-in-Wonderland feel. The building itself, with four large, high-ceilinged bedrooms stylishly furnished with original antiques, was built by Seyyid Saïd and is claimed to have been the last place that Princess Salme slept before her elopement and escape. In July and August, you can only rent the whole house ($800 for up to ten guests). Rates include full house staff, including a cook. Facing *Salome's Garden* is *Imani Beach Villa* (Ⓣ 024/225 0050, Ⓦ www.imani.it; ❺), an Italian-run mini-resort set in a garden with lots of whitewash and *makuti* thatch. The restaurant in the small, enclosed garden is good for seafood (try the barracuda *carpaccio* or kingfish ravioli) and Swahili dishes, and a full range of excursions is offered.

Kidichi and Kizimbani Persian baths

Included in most spice tours is a visit to the **Kidichi Persian Baths** (daily 8am–4pm; Tsh1000, though the guide will expect a tip), 2.5km east of Bububu, which have survived in remarkably good condition. They once formed part of a palace built in 1850 by Seyyid Saïd for the use of his second wife, a grand-daughter of the Shah of Persia named Binte Irich Mirza and also known as Sheherazade, who apparently was fond of hunting. The baths' ornamental stucco decorations depicting lotus flowers, peacocks, cloves, coconut palms and dates were made by Persian Zoroastrians, as Muslims were forbidden by the Qur'an from depicting Allah's worldly creations.

Daladalas (#511, marked "K/Spice") run directly to the baths from Stone Town's Darajani (Creek Rd) terminal, or catch a #502 to Bububu and walk the remaining 2.5km east; the baths are on the right side of the road. About 2.5km further east, at **Kizimbani**, is another set of baths, less elaborate and in a more ruinous state, also dating from Seyyid Saïd's reign. His estate at Kizimbani was where, in 1818, clove trees were first planted in Zanzibar. At its height, the estate is said to have contained three hundred thousand of them.

Mangapwani

Some 25km north of Stone Town is **Mangapwani** village, with a lovely stretch of clean beach and a couple of caves in the coral ragstone facing the sea. The name means "Arabian Shore", possibly alluding to one of the caves, a man-made chamber used for hiding slaves after the trade with Oman was outlawed in 1845. The cave saw even more use after the rest of the slave trade was abolished in 1873, when black-market prices took off (the trade only finally stopped after the Abushiri War of 1888–89, which gave Germany total control over the mainland coast). The dank and claustrophobic **slave chamber** is one of the most shocking of Zanzibar's sights and, like the underground cells beside Stone Town's last slave market, conveys the full horror and misery of the East African trade. It consists of two rectangular cells hewn out of the soft coral rock, accessed along a deep and narrow passage and sealed by a heavy door, which was originally covered with coral ragstone, all of which served to hide slaves from the prying eyes of British Navy cruisers on anti-slavery patrols. For the slaves, being shut up here would have been a terrifying experience, as no light – and not much air – could penetrate from the outside.

Two kilometres south is a **coral cavern**, this one natural and larger than the slave chamber, and of interest for its spiritual importance to locals. The cavern, which contains a pool of fresh water, was discovered in the early 1800s by a plantation slave-boy when one of the goats he was herding fell into the void. Like other caves in Zanzibar and on the mainland, it contains offerings to ancestors left by locals seeking their intercession in mortal affairs – a good example of the syncretic nature of Zanzibari Islam, which blends orthodox teachings with popular beliefs.

Practicalities

Mangapwani can be visited as part of a spice tour if the entire group agrees, though operators can be reluctant given the bad state of the road and the extra distance involved. It can also be incorporated into one of the north coast day-trips offered by many tour operators, which include a spice tour and Nungwi beach.

To reach Mangapwani by **public transport**, catch a #102 ("Bumbwini") daladala from Darajani terminal (Creek Rd) in Stone Town. Some daladalas turn left off the main road into the village and continue towards the coast, which is preferable if you don't fancy walking too much. If you're dropped on the main road, which is more likely, walk northwest through Mangapwani village. The turning for the **coral cavern** is 600m along on the left – it lies 1km south of there along a narrow track. For the **slave chamber**, ignore the turning and continue on to the coast. Just before the coast (roughly 1.5km from the main road, or 1km beyond the coral cavern turning), the road veers north – the slave chamber is 500m further on.

If you're taking lunch at the *Mangapwani Serena Beach Club* you can catch their complimentary shuttle bus from Stone Town: it leaves from outside the *Zanzibar Serena Inn* at 8.30am and 11.30am, and returns at 4pm or 5pm. The club's **restaurant**, halfway between the two caves, blends high style and service with a relaxed atmosphere, beautiful location and view, and a private beach. The food is pricey but worth every shilling: the catch of the day, or a mixed seafood salad, costs Tsh10,000, whilst a regal seafood grill will set you back Tsh24,000. It's open daily for lunch, and for dinner by reservation through the *Zanzibar Serena Inn* in Stone Town (pp.92–93). The club has a **water-sports** centre for snorkelling, canoeing and catamaran sailing. There's no accommodation.

Southern Unguja

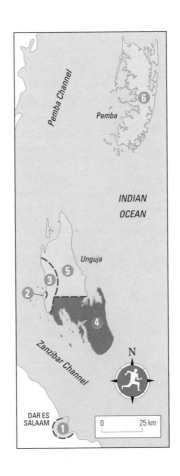

CHAPTER 4

Highlights

✳ **Jozani Forest** Ideal for escaping the heat, this soothingly cool and shady forest contains troops of endangered red colobus monkeys, and its adjacent mangroves are worth a visit too. **See p.147**

✳ **Dolphin tours** The fishermen of Kizimkazi have developed a veritable dolphin-spotting industry in the protected waters of Menai Bay Conservation Area; another source of pride is one of Africa's oldest mosques. **See p.150**

✳ **Eating** With fresh seafood within swimming distance, eating out can be a real pleasure, with many restaurants excelling in the art of Swahili cuisine, and a good number offering great Italian dishes too. **See p.152, p.159, p.161, p.164 & p.165**

✳ **Mwaka Kogwa Festival** Every July, the sleepy fishing community of Makunduchi gets together for a four-day shindig in celebration of the Persian New Year. **See p.154**

✳ **Beaches** Wide and sandy, southeast Unguja's beaches should be all you've dreamed of, and most of the hotels aren't half bad either, often combining romance with very competitive prices. **See p.157, p.159, p.161 & p.166**

△ *Ngalawa* outrigger, Jambiani

Southern Unguja

Beaches, romantic hotels and superb restaurants, snorkelling and scuba diving, an ancient mosque, primeval forest, mangroves, monkeys, and boat tours in search of dolphins – **southern Unguja** has it all. And, despite also having more than its fair share of hotels, most of the south retains a very local and untrammeled kind of feeling, where you're as likely to share the beach with fishermen and women harvesting seaweed as you are with fellow tourists.

If it's a beach you're after, the southeast coast is best, with five main locations to choose from. From south to north, these are **Jambiani** and **Paje**, both with pleasingly village-like ambiences, and the former also offering a cultural

Mangapwani, ▲ Bububu & Northern Unguja ▲ Northern Unguja ▲ Uroa & Pongwe

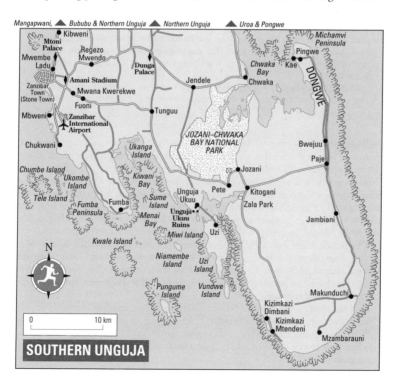

SOUTHERN UNGUJA

For an introduction to scuba diving and snorkelling in Zanzibar, see p.46.

The entire east coast is fringed by a long barrier reef, whose soft corals make any dive particularly photogenic. The shallow and sheltered coral gardens inside the lagoon offer ideal conditions for **novices**, whilst the deeper and exposed drop-offs outside the barrier attract more **experienced divers** (but can only be attempted in calm weather). Visibility is best between November and January, when 40m is common. It can drop to around 10m from July to September, but plankton blooms at that time, attracting big pelagic species, including giant groupers. The best time for **dolphins** is from October to March, whilst humpback and sperm **whales** on their southward migration might be seen (or, more likely, just heard) in September and October.

As the name suggests, **Turtle Garden**, off Paje, is good for turtles; the barrel sponges so beloved of them also attract giant eels, trigger fish and puffers, whilst the sandy bottom is populated by guitar sharks, eagle rays and stingrays. For exquisite corals (brain, tabletop and lettuce formations dominate), **Unicorn (Jambiani) Reef** is hard to beat. Another recommended site is the clear and calm **Stingray Alley**, also off Jambiani, where you may witness shoals containing literally hundreds of blue-spotted stingrays.

Dive centres

The following dive centres are PADI-accredited; check others out thoroughly before diving with them.

Rising Sun Dive Centre Breezes Beach Club, Dongwe ⓣ0747/415049, ⓦwww .risingsun-zanzibar.com. Highly experienced and knowledgeable, also about sites off Kizimkazi. They're well-equipped and have solid safety standards (and small groups), and offer one of Zanzibar's most exhaustive Open Water courses, with four pool dives and six in the ocean when just four or five in all is the norm elsewhere. They teach up to Instructor level. For experienced divers, exploration dives to uncharted reefs are possible by prior arrangement, as are night dives and trips to Mnemba Atoll.

Scuba Do Fumba Beach Lodge, Fumba Peninsula ⓦwww.scuba-do-zanzibar.com. Branch of the well-regarded Kendwa-based dive centre in the north; see p.183.

village tour; a string of modest bungalow-style mini-resorts at **Bwejuu**, some of whose restaurants are seriously good; **Dongwe**, further north along Michamvi Peninsula, which risks turning into package-tour hell but for the time being is still recommended; and, at the very top of the peninsula, the tiny fishing village of **Kae**, with next to no facilities but a beach to wow the most jaded of eyes. All these beaches are wide and sandy, though at low tide the ocean recedes considerably so you'll only be able to swim in two roughly six-hour "shifts" each day.

The south coast has a far smaller choice of beaches and hotels, the best being bungalow resorts at **Fumba Peninsula** (expensive) and **Unguja Ukuu** (affordable), close to the ruins of an ancient town. But for most visitors, the chance of spotting or even swimming with **dolphins**, on boat trips from **Kizimkazi** village, is the reason for coming here; the village is also home to what's arguably sub-Saharan Africa's oldest mosque. Another excellent excursion is to **Jozani Forest**, Unguja's last sizeable patch of primeval ground-water forest, where walks give good odds on seeing otherwise endangered red colobus monkeys, and a host of fascinating wildlife in nearby mangroves.

Jozani Forest and around

Whether you're heading to or coming back from Kizimkazi or Unguja's southeast beaches, you won't want to miss the magnificent and soothing **Jozani Forest**, the largest remaining patch of the indigenous ground-water forest that once covered all of Unguja. Protected by an NGO since 1995, Jozani is now at the heart of Zanzibar's first national park, which also comprises equally important mangroves and intertidal zones. For a closer look at the forest's creepy-crawly denizens such as snakes and chameleons, any trip to Jozani or Kizimkazi can easily be combined with a visit to **Zala Park**, established by a local teacher for enlightening his charges.

Jozani–Chwaka Bay National Park

Lying 38km southeast of Stone Town, just north of the road to the beaches and Kizimkazi, is **Jozani Forest**, now part of fifty-square-kilometre

---

Baobab trees

Zanzibar's giant **baobab trees** always surprise visitors to the island. Known in Kiswahili as *mbuyu* (plural *mibuyu*), to botanists as *Adansonia digitata*, and popularly as the calabash tree, the baobab is one of Africa's most striking natural features. With its massive, smooth silver-grey trunk and thick, crooked branches, it's the grotesque and otherworldly appearance of the trees that impresses more than anything. The trunk's circumference grows to ten metres after only a *century*, and by the time the tree reaches old age, it may be several times more. Most live to at least six hundred years, and carbon dating suggests that the oldest can reach an astonishing three thousand years.

Needless to say, the baobab is supremely adapted to **semi-arid habitats** (which in Zanzibar means the coast itself), its range stretching right across Africa and eastwards to Australia, where it's known as the bottle tree. One of its secrets is its fibrous and extremely porous wood which rots easily, leaving a huge cavity in the trunk that fills with water during the rains. The immense **water-carrying capacity** of the trunks – anything up to a thousand litres – enables the tree to survive long spells of drought. For this reason alone, the baobab has long been useful to humans, and the Kamba tribe of Kenya, who migrated north from Kilimanjaro five centuries ago, say in their legends that they moved in search of the life-giving baobabs: the Ukambani Hills, where they settled, are full of them.

The baobab has myriad other uses too. The calabash-like seed pods form handy water containers and bailers; the seeds and fruit pulp ("monkey bread") are rich in protein and vitamin C and make an invigorating drink; young leaves have medicinal uses; and the bark, when pounded, yields good fibre.

The tree's shape has given rise to several **legends**. Some say that baobabs used to be in the habit of walking around the countryside on their roots, until one day God got tired of their endless peregrinations and resolved to keep them forever rooted to the soil, replanting them upside-down. In Zanzibar, a pair of baobab saplings were traditionally planted at either end of the grave of an important person, which in time grew together to form one tree, enclosing the tomb within their roots in which the spirit of the deceased would dwell.

Jozani–Chwaka Bay National Park, the island's first terrestrial nature reserve (daily 7.30am–5pm; $8). The forest is home to a variety of wildlife once common all over the island, including Sykes' (blue) monkeys, red colobus monkeys, bush pigs, diminutive Ader's duiker and suni antelopes, elephant shrews, chameleons and lots of birds. There are several **nature trails**, ranging from an easy hour's stroll to a half-day hike. Route descriptions are given in a leaflet available at the gate, though taking an official **guide** is recommended (no fee but tip expected), and obligatory if you want to see monkeys inside the forest – those outside the gate can easily be spotted on your own.

Apart from the forest, the park contains several other types of interconnected habitats, including swamp forest, evergreen thickets, mangroves and salt-tolerant grassland. These environments can be seen along the **Pete–Jozani Mangrove Boardwalk**, which loops through coral thicket vegetation, mangrove forest and across a creek in the north of Pete Inlet. The walk starts in a car park under a large tamarind tree, 1km south of the forest gate, and finishes nearby. An informative leaflet containing a sketch map is available for free from the forest entrance gate; the boardwalk entrance fee is covered by the ticket for Jozani. Typical thicket **fauna** includes snakes, lizards, mongooses, Ader's duikers and the nocturnal civet cat. Birdlife is also good, ranging from purple-banded and olive sunbirds to kingfishers and blue-cheeked bee-eaters.

Practicalities

Jozani is usually visited as part of an organized day-trip to see Kizimkazi's dolphins, but the forest can easily be visited by **public transport**: daladalas (Tsh700) from Stone Town's Darajani terminal on Creek Road to Bwejuu (#324), Jambiani (#309) and – most frequently – Makunduchi (#310), drive

Red colobus monkeys

Jozani is best known for its large and characterful population of **Kirk's red colobus monkeys**. The species is endemic to Unguja, as it has been isolated from other red colobus populations on the Tanzanian mainland for at least ten thousand years, during which time it has evolved different coat patterns, food habits and calls.

A decade or so ago, the monkeys were considered to be on the road to extinction, but the protection of the forest in the 1990s appears to have reversed the trend. Their current population is estimated at around 2500 in and around Jozani, accounting for one third of their total number. The local population is steadily increasing, perhaps not so much because of conservation but through the continued destruction of their natural habit elsewhere.

The monkeys are known locally as *kima punju* – poison monkeys – as it was believed that dogs who ate them would lose their fur, and trees and crops would die if the monkeys fed off them. The name may also come from their inability to digest sugars from ripe fruit: however, their four-chambered stomachs can tackle unripe and potentially toxic fruit with ease, helped along by their habit of eating charcoal.

Two troops of thirty to fifty individuals are frequently seen, one inside the forest (usually flashes of red accompanied by the crashing of branches) and another that frequents a patch of open woodland just outside the gate. The latter are habituated and completely unfazed by human presence, making them incredibly photogenic. However, for your own and their **safety**, do not approach closer than three metres, avoid eye contact and noise, and do not feed or otherwise interact with the monkeys. Also, it's not advisable to visit Jozani if you're ill: monkeys are susceptible to infectious human diseases and have little resistance.

past the gate throughout the day, the last back to Stone Town passing at around sunset, though it'd be wise to get to the road by 5pm just in case. Alternatively, taxi or car rental from Stone Town costs around $40 for half a day.

The best **time to visit** Jozani is early morning or late afternoon, when there are fewer visitors and the wildlife is at its most active. The evening light is superb for photographing the troop of red colobus monkeys near the gate, whilst the morning light is deliciously soothing.

There's an **information centre** at the gate, a snack bar, and a community-run gift shop that stocks CDs, postcards and woven baskets (the biggest costing $14) made from dried and bleached palm fronds called *ukindi*. Barely 100m away, just outside the park boundary, is the locally run ✈ *Jozani Tutani* **restaurant** (daily 8am–4pm), surrounded by trees and coconut palms, and the songs of birds and cicadas. Its meals are tasty and cheap, and include fried octopus (Tsh2500), garlic prawns (Tsh5000) and an excellent seafood pizza (Tsh3000). They also do good juices, and sell sodas and beer.

Zala Park

As a complement to Jozani, you could pay a visit to **Zala Park** (Zanzibar Land Animals Park; daily 8.30am–5.30pm; Tsh3000 including guided tour), 5.5km south of Jozani along the Kizimkazi road at Muungoni. Founded by a school teacher in 1994 for educational purposes, this is basically a small family-run zoo housing reptiles and amphibians that gives you the chance to see chameleons and snakes at close quarters. Organized trips to Kizimkazi may stop by on the way back. You can also get there from Stone Town's Darajani terminal (Creek Rd) on a #326 daladala.

The south coast

For most visitors, Unguja's **south coast** means only one thing: dolphin tours. Visits to resident pods off the fishing village of **Kizimkazi** are Zanzibar's most popular excursion after spice tours, and the opportunity of swimming with them exerts an irresistible allure. There are serious concerns about the impact of this popularity on the dolphins themselves, however. Should Kizimkazi's tourist circus turn you off, a fine alternative way of seeing dolphins – and virtually no other tourists – is from the north side of Menai Bay, either from **Unguja Ukuu** or **Fumba Peninsula**. The latter also has a scuba-diving centre, and both have remote hotels recommended for their beaches. The 420-square-kilometre **Menai Bay Conservation Area**, which covers most of the water, coastline and islands between Fumba in the west and Kizimkazi in the east, was created in 1997 as a "Gift to the Earth". East of Kizimkazi lies **Makunduchi**, a sleepy fishing community that comes alive once a year for the vibrant Mwaka Kogwa festival.

Kizimkazi

At the south end of Unguja, 53km from Stone Town, is the pretty fishing village of **KIZIMKAZI**, known to tourists for its **dolphin tours**, and to historians as the one of the oldest continuously inhabited settlements on Zanzibar, one that had also served as capital for Zanzibar's traditional rulers, the Wawinyi Wakuu, at various times before the Omani conquest in the eighteenth century.

The village actually comprises two places: **Kizimkazi Dimbani**, which contains East Africa's oldest standing mosque and is where most dolphin tours depart from; and **Kizimkazi Mkunguni** (sometimes called Kizimkazi Mtendeni), 3km to the south, which has a fledgling hotel strip, and a couple of ancient **baobab trees**, the oldest and biggest of which is thought to be over 600 years old, and was used as a transmissions mast during World War II when communications gear was strapped to its crown.

The **beaches** at both places are beautiful, and swimmers are likely to share the water with easily amused local children; be wary of stepping on sea urchins, however. Kizimkazi and Pungume Island also offer excellent but largely unexplored **diving**. See the box on scuba-diving on p.146.

Arrival and accommodation

Most tourists come to Kizimkazi on a dolphin tour (see below), but it's easy to get there by **public transport**: catch a #326 daladala from Stone Town's Darajani terminal on Creek Road. Few people stay **overnight**, but if you do you'll have the chance to get out on the water the next morning before the crowds arrive. Kizimkazi Dimbani is the more beautiful of the two villages, with a lovely sheltered bay in which dozens of outrigger canoes are moored, but there's only one hotel. All of the following include breakfast.

Kizidi Restaurant & Bungalows Kizimkazi Dimbani ☎0747/417053. On the northern headland flanking the bay, this is the best of Kizimkazi's options, thanks to glorious views from each of its five rooms (large and clean; one has three beds). There's also a bar and a huge, expensive restaurant that gets packed with day-trippers for lunch. In the evening, you're likely to have the place to yourself. ❸

Kizimkazi Coral Reef Village Kizimkazi Mkunguni, 500m south of the baobabs beside an ugly cottage resort ☎0747/479615 or 024/223 1214, ✉mkazi_coreevi@yahoo.com. Six cramped but clean rooms in three *bandas* at the back of a large beachside plot (no views from the rooms),

all with a/c, fan, box nets and Western-style bathrooms with hot water. There's a good restaurant, *Pomboo's Grill*, and the staff are particularly friendly. ❸

Kizimkazi Dolphin View Cottage Kizimkazi Mkunguni, 1.5km south of the baobabs ☎0747/434959. A somewhat down-at-heel place with several cottages on a low cliff (the water comes right up at high tide), whose staff seem surprised to have visitors. Its double rooms, all en suite, are large and breezy, and $15 more gets you a sea view. Singles can be shared by couples. Its bar and restaurant have waned in popularity with day-trippers. ❷–❸

Dolphin tours

The waters off Kizimkazi are home to several pods of bottlenose and Indo-Pacific humpback **dolphins**, which are the main reason tourists come here. For many, the chance to swim with them is the experience of a lifetime; the odds of sighting dolphins on any given day are claimed to be eighty percent (calm days are best, as rough seas force the dolphins into deeper water), but whether you want to "play and swim" – as the brochures and tour companies wax lyrically – is really up to your sensibilities. For some visitors, the experience

Dolphin-tour practicalities

Buying a place on a **prearranged dolphin safari** in Stone Town, or from most south-east coast beach hotels, is the easiest way to go about things. Prices quoted generally exclude lunch (anything from Tsh1500 to Tsh25,000 depending on where and what you eat), and a $3 conservation-area entry fee, paid before boarding the boat. Some trips include snorkelling on an extensive reef fringing **Pungume Island**, 13km offshore. Note that most of the boats are shared between companies no matter what you're paying; the only real differences with more expensive excursions is that group sizes are smaller, road transport is by Land Cruiser rather than minibus, and the boats are fibreglass rather than wood. If combined with Jozani Forest, an extra $8 to cover the forest entry fee is charged; any extra payment over this is really just a gratuity.

 Arranging things yourself in Kizimkazi has the disadvantage of having to contend with some offensively pushy touts, but the advantage of costing considerably less than an organized tour (especially if you travel by daladala), and – by staying overnight in Kizimkazi – being able to sail off early in the morning before the masses arrive. The main cost is boat rental, generally Tsh35,000–40,000 per boat for around two hours. To that, add Tsh3000–5000 per person for snorkelling equipment, and $3 (Tsh3000) per person for the conservation-area fee, which your boatman will collect for you. To avoid hassle with the touts, it's best to arrange things through a hotel or restaurant: *Cabs Restaurant*, *Kizimkazi Coral Reef Village* and *Kizidi Restaurant & Bungalows* are all reliable. Whatever you arrange, ensure the boat has adequate shade.

comes depressingly close to Disneyland, with dozens of noisy boats crowding and hounding the dolphins on a daily basis, the tourists encouraged to leap into the water just as pods are passing by. The potentially detrimental effects of this regular disturbance are the subject of on-going research, so think twice before taking part in the melee. If you do decide to go, try and adhere to the following **guidelines**: encourage your skipper not to chase the pods; if you enter the water, do so away from the dolphins and with as little disturbance as possible; when in the water, stay close to the boat; avoid sudden movements; allow the dolphins to come to you and do not under any pretext attempt to touch them.

Dimbani Mosque

Kizimkazi's other claim to fame – and usually included in dolphin tours – is **Dimbani Mosque**, on the main road 100m back from the bay at Kizimkazi Dimbani. Founded in the year 500 of the Islamic Hegira calendar (1107 AD), it is East Africa's oldest standing mosque, and direct proof of the Persian migration which led to the establishment of the Shirazi civilization and people, and, ultimately, of the Swahili themselves. From the outside, the mosque – which is still in use – doesn't look too different from any other building in Dimbani: it has the same rusty corrugated metal roof, and there's little other than a roadside plaque to indicate its importance. Indeed, most of the mosque was completely rebuilt in 1770, but the atmosphere inside could hardly be more different, having retained the simple but graceful form and style typical of twelfth-century Persian mosques. In the north wall – the only part that definitively dates from the twelfth century – is an ornate *mihrab* prayer niche indicating the direction to Mecca. To its left, a florid Kufic inscription carved in coral ragstone contains verses from the Qur'an and commemorates the mosque's establishment. The inscription to the right of the *mihrab* is in Arabic, and records the eighteenth-century rebuilding.

Admission to non-Muslims is prohibited during prayer times, and to women at all times. Visitors should remove their shoes and cover up bare limbs before entering, ask permission before taking photographs, speak quietly, and leave a donation in the box provided.

The **graves** outside the mosque, one with a headstone resembling a toadstool, another with a curious checkerboard engraving, include those of – in the words of the signpost – "pious single-handed Sheikh Ali Omar, one-legged Sayyid Abdalla Saïd bin Sharif, Mwana bint Mmadi and her son Mfaume Ali Omar the Guard of the Town Drum". With luck, this drum – which would have been used on ceremonial occasions as a symbol of kingly authority – should be on display in the House of Wonders in Stone Town in the near future.

Miza Miza Cave

Some trips to Kizimkazi also include a visit to **Miza Miza Cave** (or Kizimkazi Cavern) on the shore. The cave contains a freshwater pool and a vaguely human-shaped stone, and has a taboo associated with it stating that one should not call out the name of a person inside the cave. The story goes that once upon a time a local chief had two wives who quarrelled incessantly. One day they both went to the cave to fetch water. The elder wife filled her calabash and emerged from the cave while the younger one, who was called Miza, was still inside. The elder wife called Miza by name, which echoed inside the cave, whereupon the unfortunate Miza was turned into stone.

Another legend connected to the cave recalls the founder of Kizimkazi, said to be a king named Kizi, who twice called upon Allah to protect the town's inhabitants from invaders. The first time, a swarm of bees saw them off; the second, the population took refuge in the cave, whose entrance miraculously sealed itself up until the invaders had passed by.

Eating and drinking

Kizimkazi's popularity with day-trippers means there's plenty of choice for **eating out**. With the exception of *Jichane Restaurant* the following places remain open during Ramadan.

Cabs Restaurant & Dolphin Safaris Kizimkazi Dimbani. An enticing menu, with seafood a speciality: try the seashell meat with potatoes, spices and ginger. Most fish dishes are very good value at Tsh4000. Evening barbecues are held whenever there are enough punters.

Jichane Restaurant Kizimkazi Mkunguni, near the big baobab. The only really local place, with basic meals for Tsh1500 (at least that's what locals pay). If you want something other than rice with fish or chicken – prawns or lobster, for example – ask what's available in the morning.

Kizidi Restaurant & Bungalows Kizimkazi Dimbani. Larger, more sophisticated but considerably more expensive than *Cabs* across the beach, this nonetheless gets packed for lunch (evenings are a complete contrast). Meals start at Tsh7000, though at that price the pasta and omelettes are very poor value.

Better are prawns at Tsh10,000 and lobster for Tsh15,000. A seafood platter will relieve you of Tsh25,000.

Kizimkazi Dolphin View Cottage Kizimkazi Mkunguni, 1.5km south of the baobabs. No fixed menu, just what you arrange with the cook. Standard dishes (chicken or fish with chips or rice) cost Tsh3000–4000, spaghetti ("supergatte") is just Tsh2500, and fancier things like prawns and octopus Tsh5000.

Pomboo's Restaurant Kizimkazi Mkunguni, 500m south of the baobabs at *Kizimkazi Coral Reef Village*. A good wide menu, most of it available as they tend to be busy with day-trippers at lunchtimes, and with a lovely beach-front location in which to enjoy it. Grilled or marinated fish of the day goes for Tsh5000, grilled calamari with tamarind sauce is Tsh6000, and the seafood grill is good value at Tsh10,000.

Unguja Ukuu

Just under thirty kilometres southeast of Stone Town, the fishing village of **Unguja Ukuu** is more used to archeologists than it is to tourists, thanks to the **ruins** of an ancient town at the neck of Ras Kitoe peninsula, 1km beyond the village. Nowadays little more than rubble, nothing much is known about the place other than it was probably one of the first settlements on Zanzibar: excavations have unearthed **sixth-century** Sasanian pottery from pre-Islamic Persia, and a gold dinar dated 798 AD, that was minted during the reign of Harun bin Rashid, the anti-hero of *The Thousand and One Nights*. In later years, Unguja Ukuu – "Great Unguja" – served as the island's main port, and briefly also as capital of the island under the Hadimu tribe. The rapacious **Portuguese** captain Ruy Lourenço Ravasco put an end to the town by sacking it in 1503, after which the Hadimu moved their capital inland to Dunga.

To get to Unguja Ukuu, catch one of the frequent #308 **daladalas** (Tsh1000) from Mwembe Ladu or Mwana Kwerekwe, both just outside Stone Town (frequent daladalas to either from Darajani terminal). If you're staying overnight the bungalows can pick you up for $30 per vehicle each way. **Accommodation** is available at Menai Bay Beach Bungalows (℡0747/411753, www.menaibaybungalows.com; half-board ❺), recommended not so much for its rooms (which are pretty basic but fine) but for the matchless location in a palm grove on the edge of a gorgeous west-facing, crescent-shaped beach. The rooms, two in each of five large bungalows, have bathrooms and verandahs for sunsets. Sunsets are also rather wonderful from the romantic **restaurant** nestled under a giant baobab tree – you can also eat at a table on the beach. They do a good rendition of Zanzibar's classic coconut-crusted fish with mango chutney, and vegetarian options are available. The other big attraction is a wide variety of half- and full-day **tours**, organized in conjunction with Stone Town's Eco+Culture Tours (see p.129). Apart from the usual itineraries, these include boat trips to mangrove forests and islands, a trip across the causeway to **Uzi Island**, and – for dolphins – a **sailing excursion** to the uninhabited islands of Miwi, Niamembe or Kwale in Menai Bay, themselves perfect for snorkelling, sunbathing on delightful beaches, and eyeballing the denizens of intertidal rock pools. If arranged through Eco+Culture Tours in Stone Town, the latter trip costs $60 per person in a couple including a seafood barbecue, whilst an additional $10 per person gets you a canoe excursion through mangroves, and a visit to a cave.

Fumba Peninsula

The northwestern side of Menai Bay is bounded by **Fumba Peninsula**, the tip of which lies barely 18km south of Stone Town. Surprisingly, given the beautiful beaches, tourism has largely passed it by, though a new upmarket **beach hotel** may be a sign of things to come. This is the *Fumba Beach Lodge* (℡0747/860504, www.fumbabeachlodge.com; half-board ❾), which boasts an impressive two kilometres of coastline containing three sandy coves. There are 26 rooms, so it's not as exclusive as the price might warrant, and the style is an odd blend of clean Scandinavian lines and Swahili style. All have sea views, and the suites have rooftop terraces. Amenities include a cliff-top swimming pool, a bar built into an old dhow, and a branch of Kendwa's well-regarded Scuba Do **dive centre** (see p.146 & p.183) for the full range of PADI courses.

Excursions are run through Adventure Afloat (℡0747/423162, ⓦwww .safariblue.net if you want to arrange things yourself from Stone Town), whose speciality is an enjoyable day's sail from Fumba to **Kwale Island**, for dolphin-watching, mucking about on *ngalawa* outriggers, and lazing on or snorkelling around sandbanks, complete with a delicious seafood lunch. This costs $43 per person from Fumba, more if you start in Stone Town. Like Scuba Do, Adventure Afloat is safety-conscious, and carries all the requisite equipment. To **get to Fumba**, the hotel charges $50 per minibus from Stone Town (one way). Daladalas aren't too frequent: ask at Darajani stand on Creek Road.

Makunduchi

Despite its proximity to Kizimkazi and Jambiani, the nebulous settlement of **MAKUNDUCHI**, in the far southeast of Unguja, hardly receives any visitors, and though the beach is as beautiful as any other on the island, its last hotel closed years ago – a good thing too, given the negative effect that most tourist hotels have on local culture and the environment.

Most of Makunduchi's inhabitants survive on fishing and seaweed farming, colourful piles of which you'll find laid out to dry all over the place. The

The Mwaka Kogwa festival

One of the most extraordinary of Zanzibar's celebrations, not so much for the music as for the theatre that surrounds it, is the celebration of the Persian New Year in the third or fourth week of July. Called **Mwaka Kogwa**, the four-day festival – introduced by Zoroastrian immigrants from Shiraz in Persia over a millennium ago – is at its most exuberant in Makunduchi. Although the dates no longer coincide with the Persian new year, or **Nairuz**, they do coincide with the end of the harvest that follows the long rains, and as such have kept all their original spiritual significance. The **rituals** that take place on the first day are intended to cleanse the old year and to bless the new.

The proceedings begin with houses being swept clean, and a **ritual bath** in the sea (*mwaka kogwa* literally means "washing the year"). By mid-morning, most of Makunduchi's inhabitants have descended on the centre of town, where a medicine man (*mganga*) erects a **thatched hut** while accompanied by singing women. A group of elders enter the hut, upon which the *mganga* sets it alight. The men wait until the last moment before making good their "escape", giving a fine opportunity to the more theatrically inclined. The smoke that issues at this moment indicates the direction in which the fortunes of the following year will blow: it's perhaps no coincidence that the Kiswahili word for the year's end, *kibunzi*, also means a divining board. The burning of the hut is followed by the settling of old grievances in the form of **mock fights** between two groups of men, one from the north of Makunduchi, the other from the south, who flail each other with sticks or banana stems while spurred on by raucous insults and jokes from the ever-vocal women.

The rituals complete, the following three days consist of **feasting**, dancing to *taarab* and drumming, and even drinking (behind cloth screens, so as not to offend the more religiously orthodox). Throughout this time women are dressed in their finest *kangas*, and young girls in the frilly Edwardian-style frocks so typical of Africa. All wear lots of kohl around their eyes, vibrant lipstick and garishly painted cheeks, and have their hands and feet painted with arabesque henna "tattoos". Outsiders are welcome to join the celebrations; in fact, it's considered bad luck to be without at least one guest over this period, so you might also be invited to stay with locals.

settlement is for the most part modern, with a few large blocks of Soviet-style flats, a post office and bank (usually closed) and a police station. But despite the socialist veneer of modernity, Makunduchi remains a very traditional sort of place, something best seen during the exhilarating **Mwaka Kogwa festival** in July (see box opposite).

The 69-kilometre asphalt road from Stone Town is covered by #310 **dala-dalas** from Darajani (Creek Rd) terminal throughout the day. There's **no accommodation**, but there are a couple of simple **restaurants** on the main road where the daladalas drop you, and a diminutive fish market 2km to the west. The **beach** is at the end of the road at Kigaeni; snorkelling and fishing excursions can be arranged with local fishermen, but bring your own equipment as there's no guarantee of finding stuff in Makunduchi.

The southeast coast

Unguja's **southeast coast** is a major tourist destination, its magnificent white sandy **beaches** lined for the most part with swaying coconut palm and casuarina trees. Despite the attention of sun-worshippers, the coast retains a much more local, isolated and meditative feel than the north and northeast coasts – Unguja's other big beach areas – and with the exception of a handful of expensive resorts at Dongwe on Michamvi Peninsula, tourist development remains low-key. There are no tall buildings, nor many walls to keep locals out, and in fact in most places you'll be sharing the beach with women collecting seaweed, fishermen hunting for squid and octopus with spears, and children invariably delighted to kick a football around with you.

The main beaches are at Paje, Bwejuu and Jambiani, the most beautiful at **Paje** village, at the end of the asphalt road from Stone Town. Strung out a few kilometres to the north, **Bwejuu** has a wider choice of accommodation, and some seriously good restaurants. The longest of the beaches is at **Jambiani**, which starts 5km south of Paje and whose sands roll on for another 5km. Small affordable hotels are scattered all along, and Jambiani is also home to a cultural **village tour**, providing a welcome glimpse of local life. North of Bwejuu is a scatter of large beach resorts at **Dongwe**, but for those who really want to get away from it all, **Kae**, at the top of the peninsula facing Chwaka Bay, has just three very modest guest houses.

At **low tide** on all southeast-coast beaches, the ocean recedes for hundreds of metres; if you're just coming for a day and want to be sure of swimming, consult the tide tables published in the free listings magazine, *The Swahili Coast* (available at Stone Town's better hotels and restaurants). The entire coast is protected by a fringing **coral reef**, so the calm conditions inside the shallow lagoon make for safe paddling for small children, and superb **snorkelling**, which can be arranged almost everywhere. **Scuba diving** is also memorable, both inside and – for more experienced divers – outside the barrier reef. Most hotels offer **excursions** similar to those run from Stone Town (see p.128): spice tours are more expensive though ($25–35 per person), trips to Jozani Forest are cheaper, and the cost of dolphin safaris are pretty much the same. **Bicycles** can be rented at most hotels.

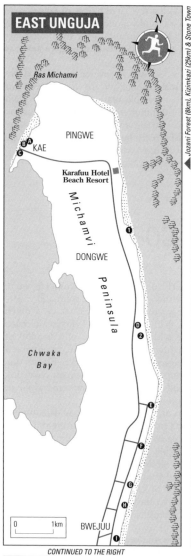

EAST UNGUJA

SOUTHERN UNGUJA | The southeast coast

EATING & DRINKING

Andy's Karibuni Romantic Garden	**F**
Bellevue Bungalows & Restaurant	**J**
Blue Sea Restaurant & Bungalow	**A**
Bwejuu Dere Guest House	**K**
The Door	**2**
East Coast Visitor's Inn	**Y**
Evergreen Bungalows	**I**
First & Last Bar & Restaurant	**3**
Gomani Guest House	**8**
Jamal's Restaurant	**4**
Kae Beach Bungalows	**C**
Karibu Restaurant	**7**
Kim's Restaurant	**5**
Kimte Beach Inn	**aa**
Kinazi Upepo Hotel	**T**
Mount Zion Long Beach Bungalows	**V**
Mustapha's Nest	**M**
Paje Beach Bungalows	**S**
Paje by Night	**R**
Paje Ndame Village	**P**
Pakachi Beach Hotel	**U**
Palm Beach Inn	**L**
Paradise Beach Bungalows	**O**
Pingo Restaurant	**6**
Ras Michamvi Sea View Restaurant	**B**
Red Monkey Bungalows	**cc**
Rocky Restaurant	**1**
Sau-Inn Hotel	**X**
Seven Seas Bungalows	**N**
Shehe Bungalows	**Z**
Sunrise Hotel & Restaurant	**G**

Jozani Forest (8km), Kizimkazi (25km) & Stone Town

BWEJUU

PAJE

INDIAN OCEAN

JAMBIANI

Jambiani School

Mande's Gift Shop

Abu's Son Store

Post Office & Minimarket

Makunduchi (rough road: 9km) ▼

Ras Michamvi

PINGWE

KAE

Karafuu Hotel Beach Resort

Michamvi

DONGWE

Peninsula

Chwaka Bay

BWEJUU

0   1km

ACCOMMODATION

Andy's Karibuni Romantic Garden	**F**	Kae Beach Bungalows	**C**	Paradise Beach Bungalows	**O**
Arabian Nights Hotel	**Q**	Kimte Beach Inn	**bb**	Ras Michamvi Sea View Restaurant	**B**
Bellevue Bungalows & Restaurant	**J**	Kinazi Upepo Hotel	**T**	Red Monkey Bungalows	**cc**
Blue Oyster Hotel	**W**	Mount Zion Long Beach Bungalows	**V**	Robinson's Place	**H**
Blue Sea Restaurant & Bungalow	**A**	Mustapha's Nest	**M**	Sau-Inn Hotel	**Y**
Breezes Beach Club	**E**	Oasis Beach Inn	**X**	Seven Seas Bungalows	**N**
Bwejuu Dere Guest House	**K**	Paje Beach Bungalows	**S**	Shehe Bungalows	**aa**
East Coast Visitor's Inn	**Z**	Paje by Night	**R**	Sunrise Hotel & Restaurant	**G**
Evergreen Bungalows	**I**	Paje Ndame Village	**P**		
Hotel Sultan Palace	**D**	Pakachi Beach Hotel	**U**		
		Palm Beach Inn	**L**		

Jambiani

The long stretch of beach at **JAMBIANI**, 5–10km south of Paje, possesses a wild, windy and fascinating beauty. The fringing reef lies several kilometres out, and the intervening area is a mix of sandbanks, coral reefs and shallow water, which at low tide can turn up a surprising variety of marine life. The people of Jambiani have long been involved in **fishing**, and at times dozens of *ngalawa* fishing boats are moored together just off shore, while in the evenings there's the joyous spectacle of young boys racing after their handmade model dhows, painstakingly made from sandals or bits of wood with plastic bags for sails. It's the community feeling of Jambiani that makes it special, something worth exploring further through its highly recommended **local cultural tourism programme**, which offers visits to traditional herbalists, seaweed farms and a sacred local cave. The name "Jambiani" comes from the Arabic word *jambiya*, meaning a dagger with a broad curved blade, an example of which was reputedly found on the beach by early settlers.

Walking north or south of Jambiani beach, you'll see strange rock mounds at the water line. Called *viali* or *vyayo*, these contain **coconut husks** (*makumbi*), which are buried for three to six months for softening (the saltwater deters rot), then beaten to separate the fibre, which is used to make rope (coir).

Practicalities

The "beach transfer" tourist **minibuses** (see p.123) take about ninety minutes to cover the 56km from Stone Town, and shouldn't charge more than Tsh4000. **Daladalas** – #309 from Stone Town – are infrequent and unpredictable; enquire the day before at Darajani terminal on Creek Road for departure times, and be prepared to head out to Mwana Kwerekwe terminal 5km southeast of the city, where you may have more choice. The daladalas take two to three hours, and leave no later than 3pm. **Returning** to Stone Town, the first heads off at 6am, and the last at 3pm. If you're **driving** from Makunduchi, be prepared for a slow progress across the very bumpy road (at least an hour).

The post office and minimarket (daily 6am–10pm) on the main road opposite *Karibu Restaurant* rents out **bicycles**, as does Abu's Son Store, also on the main road. There's no official **money-changing** facility, so get this sorted in Stone Town before arriving. **Internet access** is possible at the *East Coast Visitor's Inn*.

When choosing a room, note that **hotels** on the northern part of the beach are pretty isolated from most of the bars and restaurants. All the following are shown on the map opposite; distances given below refer to the distance from Jambiani School. **Breakfast** is included in room rates unless otherwise noted.

Seaweed farming

One of Zanzibar's biggest foreign-exchange earners these days is **seaweed** (*mwani*), of which over ten thousand tons are exported annually to ready markets in the Far East. Seaweed cultivation was introduced to southeastern Unguja almost two decades ago as an income-generating project for local women, for whom it has brought a measure of financial independence in what is still a very male-dominated society. The seaweed is "planted" by tying it to ropes that are then staked in rows in the shallow intertidal zone of the lagoons, before being harvested and dried for a week, when it turns beautiful shades of russet, purple, green, mustard and blue.

Accommodation

Blue Oyster Hotel 800m north ☎024/224 0163, ⓦwww.zanzibar.de. An architecturally clumsy two-storey affair, but good value nonetheless, with friendly, efficient service and ten clean rooms, five with private bathroom (the others are considerably cheaper). They can also arrange cheap and reliable excursions, and there's a restaurant and bar on the ocean-facing terrace. ❷–❸

East Coast Visitor's Inn 900m south ☎024/224 0150, ⓦwww.visitorsinn-zanzibar.com. An affordable, functional set-up offering fifteen en-suite bungalows (most with sea views) around a parking area, and ten en-suite rooms in a guest house set back from the beach. The rooms are well kept and there's a large open-sided restaurant and bar offering reasonable if unexciting food, Internet access and various activities. Rooms ❷, bungalows ❸

Kimte Beach Inn 3.2km south ☎0747/430992 or 024/224 0212, Ⓔkimte@lycos.com. Rasta-run place with Zanzibar's best beach bar, seven en-suite rooms, a dormitory ($10 per person), and a basic but fun *banda* raised on tall stilts beside the bar. Dhow trips and snorkelling can be arranged (from $7 per person including boat ride). ❷

🏃 **Mount Zion Long Beach Bungalows** 3.8km north, halfway between Jambiani and Paje ☎0747/439034 or 0747/439001, ⓦwww .mountzion-zanzibar.com. Another friendly Rasta place, with four good, simple cottages (eight rooms) on top of a grassy headland with partial sea views, and uniquely designed thatched *bandas*

on the gorgeous beach below (beds, nets and electric light; shared bathrooms) in the form of two pyramids, one on top of the other – very cool. As might be expected, the bar is very good, as is the food (fresh fish, also vegetarian), and the whole atmosphere is imbued with a very relaxing vibe. ❸, half-board ❹

Oasis Beach Inn 200m north ☎0747/469217. Locally run hotel with lovely beach-front views from its six front rooms, and with more rooms at the side. Also has a good beach bar and restaurant. ❸

Pakachi Beach Hotel 4km north, just north of the *Mount Zion* ☎024/224 0001 or 0747/423331, ⓦwww.pakachi.com. Three rooms and a large family house ($100) on the land side of the road, all en suite and with *semadari* beds. There's a bar and restaurant on a low headland on the other side of the road beside the beach. Run by young Rastafarians, the reggae-fuelled atmosphere is suitably laid-back. They also have fishing equipment, canoes, and an *ngalawa* for snorkelling ($10 per person including equipment). ❸

Red Monkey Bungalows 3.8km south ☎024/224 0207 or 0747/419635, Ⓔstandard@zitec.org. On a small, breezy beach plot at the forgotten south end of the beach, this place has seven rooms with private bathrooms in individual bungalows, and a standard restaurant. ❷

Sau-Inn Hotel 600m south ☎024/224 0205 or 0747/457782, ⓦwww.sauinn.net. This

Jambiani Cultural Village Tour

Zanzibar's first cultural tourism programme, the **Jambiani Cultural Village Tour**, is part of a wider effort to establish small-scale community-run development projects. The village tour offers a highly recommended half-day diversion exploring aspects of local life and culture, something that is lamentably lacking in so many other tourist areas in East Africa. Part of the $10 fee goes into a village development fund to finance primary healthcare, a children's nursery and various educational projects.

The **tour** itself is guided by the local coordinator, Kassim Mande, who fills you in on Jambiani's history before taking you round a subsistence farm, to a *mganga* (herbalist) to learn the medicinal uses of various herbs and plants, and on to a seaweed farm. There's also the option – which needs to be arranged in advance – of visiting a sacred limestone cave (*kumbi*), which may have been used to hide slaves after the abolition of the slave trade in the late 1800s; it's a four-hour walk there and back. The exact itinerary is flexible and is determined by your interests. The project's Jambiani **office** is at Mande's Gift Shop (☎0747/469118; open most days, no fixed times) on the main road. They also offer a selection of other tours across Unguja, and the shop stocks a small selection of curios, including spices and essential oils. For further information and reservations for day-trips from Stone Town ($30–45 per person depending on group size), contact Eco+Culture Tours (see p.129).

medium-sized resort is the only place with a swimming pool (Tsh5000 for day guests), and also the only place in southern Unguja where you're likely to get bothered by *papasi* (beach boys). The forty rooms in thatched cottages have a/c, satellite TV and spotless bathrooms, and most overlook the pool. Facilities include a bar and restaurant, and Internet access. ❻

Shehe Bungalows 2.8km south ☎024/223 3949 or 0747/418386, ✉shehebungalows@hotmail.com. This place has a great view from its first-floor bar and restaurant. The rooms, in a row of cottages facing the ocean on both sides of the main building, are fine and have bathrooms. Good value. Breakfast not included. ❷

Eating and drinking

There are a lot of **restaurants** to choose from, and not just in the hotels, so prices are keen by Zanzibari standards. All the following are shown on the map on p.156; distances given below refer to the distance from Jambiani School.

East Coast Visitor's Inn 900m south. Reasonable value if you choose carefully, with some mouth-watering dishes like banana fritters, marinated prawns in coconut sauce, and a large number of crab and jumbo prawn dishes for Tsh5000–6000. They also do milkshakes.

Gomani Guest House 3.5km south, by the mobile phone mast. A good range of cheap and filling dishes, with fish of the day for Tsh2500 and grilled lobster in lemon butter for Tsh8000. There's a great view of the ocean from the headland. Order an hour in advance. No alcohol.

Karibu Restaurant 1.9km south ☎024/223 3545. Fast becoming a Jambiani institution, everything here is literally home-cooked, as the restaurant is in a family home. The food – all local Swahili dishes – is good as well as cheap. Drop by a good few hours before you dine to discuss what you'd like to eat.

🏃 **Kim's Restaurant** 1km north, near *Blue Oyster Hotel*. One of a growing number of locally run places aimed at tourists, this one decorated with shells and with particularly good – and cheap – food, from snacks and starters (fish cakes, succulent fried octopus, garlic soup; all Tsh1000–2000) to the classic coconut-crusted fish with mango chutney, baby octopus grilled with ginger and chilli (both Tsh3500), or baby lobster in coconut sauce (Tsh8000).

🏃 **Kimte Beach Inn** 3.2km south. Zanzibar's most chilled-out beach bar (Rastafarians know a thing or two about this), very well stocked including single malts and cocktails (Tsh3500), and with excellent music – from reggae and The Doors to danceable club sounds, plus evening campfires

and even swings at the bar itself. Meals are well priced at around Tsh4500–5500, with pizzas costing a little less.

Mount Zion Long Beach Bungalows 3.8km north. Romantic candlelit dinners, nice music, the sound of the waves ... The food's not half bad either, particularly anything fishy. There are vegetarian options too, and they'll jump through hoops to try to please. Well priced at around Tsh5000.

Pakachi Beach Hotel 4km north, halfway between Jambiani and Paje. Mellow Rasta place on a low headland by the beach. Good music and a wide choice of food, including pizzas and pasta (Tsh4500–5500); weekend evenings feature a Swahili three-course buffet for $15.

Pingo Restaurant 700m south, just off the beach between *East Coast Visitor's Inn* and *Sau-Inn Hotel*. Simple, open-sided bar and restaurant with a choice of snacks and tasty seafood (around Tsh3000). Leisurely service but generous portions.

Red Monkey Bungalows 3.8km south. A pretty standard menu with most mains costing Tsh3000–4000, including octopus. A fresh seafood platter or small lobster goes for Tsh12,000.

Sau-Inn Hotel 600m south. A breezy restaurant and bar with a sea view and a choice of seafood, European/American or Zanzibari, ranging from Tsh4000–5000, and there are occasional "Swahili Night" buffets for Tsh8000.

Shehe Bungalows 2.8km south. The first-floor open-front bar enjoys a fantastic view over the beach and lagoon. The limited choice of dishes should be ordered well in advance, and range from average to excellent depending on who's cooking.

Paje

The friendly fishing village of **PAJE**, 51km east of Stone Town at the end of the asphalt road, is the easiest place on the southeast coast to get to by public transport.

The village is a nondescript shamble of houses, but also one of the more tranquil and characterful places on the island. Its white sandy **beach** is also gorgeous, backed by postcard-perfect swaying palms and, more often than not, with that heart-lifting shade of turquoise in the water. In common with Jambiani, it's also refreshing to share the beach with locals, including some of Paje's five hundred female seaweed farmers, and fishermen cycling to work. The proximity of the village makes some holiday-makers feel awkward about donning swimming costumes, but the locals are a tolerant lot and, so long as you don't go topless or canoodle in public, there's no problem (off the beach, please do cover up – some hotels provide *kangas* or *kitenges* for this). At low tide, the sea can recede by up to a kilometre, so **swimming** is restricted to two six-hour periods each day.

Practicalities

Coming from Stone Town, either buy a seat on a "beach transfer" **minibus** (see p.123; no more than Tsh4000), or catch a #324 **daladala** for Bwejuu from Darajani terminal on Creek Road (Tsh1000). These leave roughly hourly between 9am and 2pm. **Leaving** Paje, the first daladala passes through around 6.30am, the last no later than 4.30pm.

Accommodation

Some of Paje's **hotels** are decidedly average, but with such a nice beach, frankly who cares. Most are clustered together at the south end of the village and the majority offer massages and those perennial favourites, hair plaiting and henna tattoos. The following hotels are marked on the map on p.156; all include breakfast in their rates.

Arabian Nights Hotel On the beach at the south end of Paje ☏ 024/224 0190, ⊛ www .pajedivecentre.com/arabiannights. Two rooms in each of four very closely spaced modern bunga- lows, somewhat Scandinavian in style, with big floor-to-ceiling windows, bathtubs and verandahs, but little privacy given the cramped layout; $10 more gets you a sea view. The indoor restaurant is similarly functional, but overall it's fine for the price. Facilities include 24hr Internet access, snorkelling, water-skiing and use of kayaks. ❺
Kinazi Upepo Hotel On the beach at the south end of Paje ☏ 0748/655038, ⊛ www.kinaziupepo .com. Locally run, this has eight bungalows set in a coconut grove containing very ordinary rooms (some with round mosquito nets rather than square). Much better, albeit more basic (bed, net, and that's about it) are five cute coconut wood and *makuti* thatch *bandas* on stilts (shared bathrooms) which, unlike the bungalows, have good sea views. For triple rooms, add $10. There's also a character- ful beach bar and good restaurant. ❷–❸
Paje Beach Bungalows On the beach at the south end of Paje ☏ 0747/461917 or 0747/497876, ⊛ www.pajebeachbungalows.com. Basic but adequate, this is a cluster of closely spaced modern bungalows plus an architecturally infelicitous two-storey house, all with steep

thatched roofs. Twenty rooms in all, the better ones – for $10 more – with sea views. The restau- rant/bar is on the beach, flanked by day-beds and thatched parasols. ❸–❹
🏃 **Paje by Night** Behind *Kitete Beach Bunga- lows* ☏ 0747/460710, ⊛ www.pajebynight .net. An excellent bar and sublime restaurant are the main attractions here, together with a friendly, funky and laid-back atmosphere and Italian-style hospitality – all of which makes it easy to ignore the lack of beach or sea views (the beach is 100m away). There are 24 simple but well-kept rooms in colourfully painted rows, some with a/c; rates depend on how big they are and whether there's hot water. There's also a couple of quirky two-floor "jungle bungalows" likely to pit parents against their kids about who's going to sleep upstairs; these also have rooftop terraces. Fishing trips with locals can be arranged, as can massages and henna body-painting. Also has a nice craft shop, and hammocks slung all over the place. Closed May. ❹
Paje Ndame Village On the beach 2km north of Paje village ☏ 0747/865501, ⊛ www.ndame.info. A small resort set back in a grove of coconut palms; its 24 guest rooms (not all with sea views) are small and not terribly inspiring, but they're comfortable enough. There's also a bar, gift shop, coconut-rope loungers

and parasols on the beach, a good Italian/Swahili seafood restaurant, and expensive snorkelling trips (Tsh10,000 per person including boat ride). ❸

🏃 **Paradise Beach Bungalows** On the beach 3.5km north of Paje village ☎024/223 1387 or 0747/414129, 🌐www.geocities.jp/paradis-ebeachbungalows. A friendly, peaceful and likeable place snuggled into a grove of coconut palms, this is one of the southeast coast's nicest hotels if you can do without electricity, and is famed for its exquisite and affordable food. Its ten Swahili-styled bedrooms, all en suite (seven with sea views) are large and comfortable, and there are three stand-alone cottages at the back with covered roof terraces. Facilities include a bar, a good library, cultural tours and dhow trips (Tsh5000), and courses in cooking and Kiswahili. Bicycles and snorkelling equipment available. ❷–❸

Eating and drinking

Most of Paje's **bars** and **restaurants** are in its hotels.

Kinazi Upepo Hotel On the beach at the south end of Paje. Right on the beach, this has an airy and friendly bar and restaurant (with hammocks and beach loungers too), open throughout the day for drinks and snacks, including fresh juices, smoothies, milkshakes, ice cream and real coffee. The lunchtime menu is the usual blend of Swahili, European and seafood; evening meals vary, but always include fresh seafood, something spicy, and a vegetarian option. Around Tsh5000.

Paje Beach Bungalows On the beach at the south end of Paje. Not the most rousing menu, and the lovely sea view is sadly through glass windows (to avoid monsoon winds), but prices are cheaper than most: fish or octopus (or burgers, for that matter) costing just Tsh3500, and prawns from Tsh4000. Alcohol is limited to beer.

🏃 **Paje by Night** Behind *Kitete Beach Bungalows*. Zanzibar's best bar, with good music, laid-back vibes and good company. Uniquely, it's also open 24 hours. The food (10am–10pm) is well up there too, and many ingredients are home-grown: the wood-fired pizzas (Tsh5000–6000) please even Italians, the lasagne is excellent, and where else could you sample homemade ravioli stuffed with fish and almonds? It's also very good value at Tsh7000 or under for most dishes, with a three-course Swahili dinner costing Tsh10,000–15,000. There's always a vegetarian option, and the wines (mainly South African and Spanish) are cheap for Zanzibar, at Tsh15,000–20,000 a bottle.

Paje Ndame Village On the beach 2km north of Paje village. Reasonably priced Italian and Swahili dishes, including octopus and potato salad with basil and garlic (Tsh4500), pasta with crab sauce (Tsh6000), mixed fish grills (Tsh10,500) and grilled prawns with spinach (Tsh9000). Shoots itself in the foot with instant coffee.

🏃 **Paradise Beach Bungalows** On the beach 3.5km north of Paje village ☎024/223 1387 or 0747/414129. An unusual and successful mix of Swahili and Japanese cuisine, and excellent value at Tsh4000–5500 for a three-course lunch or dinner (the menu changes daily). The Japanese cuisine is especially recommended, whether classic sushi and sashimi (raw kingfish, squid and tuna; both Tsh12,000), or chicken teriyaki seasoned with ... Coca-Cola! (Tsh7000). There's also a small bar, and – for that extra thrill – a table in a tree house. Book ahead if you're not staying overnight.

Bwejuu

Five kilometres north of Paje is the even smaller village of **BWEJUU**. The beach north of here is highly rated, as you can tell from the string of bungalow hotels that back it. As at Paje, the tide heads out a low way, so there's no swimming at low tide unless you're up for a long hike across coral flats and tidal pools (beware of getting caught out by an incoming tide). There are, however, some excellent **snorkelling** spots within walking distance. Most hotels have **bicycles** for their guests, either free or for a nominal sum.

Practicalities

Bwejuu is covered by roughly hourly #324 **daladalas** from Stone Town's Darajani terminal on Creek Road, the first leaving at around 9am, the last at 2pm. The ride takes just over an hour, and costs Tsh1000. "Beach transfer"

Henna

Along with hair braiding, a long-standing favourite with female tourists is having a **tattoo**. Not a real tattoo, of course, just a painting using the pounded or powdered sun-dried leaves of the henna shrub, called *mhina* in Kiswahili (*Lawsonia inermis* in Latin). When steeped in water and mixed with lemon juice to make a fine paste, henna reacts with the keratin present in skin, hair and nails to form a greenish brown or even red stain that lasts several weeks before fading entirely. The plant is indigenous to northeastern Africa, India and the Middle East, and was extensively used as a cosmetic in ancient Egypt, even in the adornment of mummies. The henna painting tradition was introduced to Zanzibar by Arab merchants sailing the monsoon, for whom the plant and its pigment symbolized health and purity, beauty, prosperity and happiness, and – more practically – toughened the skin against the rigours of Arabia's desert climate. It subsequently became an integral part of Swahili culture and folklore.

The **designs**, applied to palms, fingers and fingernails, ankles and soles, are invariably complex and beautifully florid arabesque filigrees, sometimes accentuated with dots of a natural black dye. Each design has a name or purpose, and may even contain meanings concealed in the abstract design itself. Henna's **application** is a time-consuming process requiring skill and patience: it can take up to six hours a day for three days, as older layers of pigment are overlaid with fresh henna to deepen the colour. As such, henna is not "everyday wear", but reserved for special occasions: communal festivals such as **Idd al-Fitr** at the end of Ramadan and **Maulidi**, the celebration of the Prophet Muhammad's birthday; family events such as the birth of a child (when henna powder is also sprinkled on the newborn's head), a male child's circumcision, when a girl reaches puberty, or for a wedding. For the latter, some traditions dictate that the couple's names be hidden in the bride's henna designs, and that only when the groom finds his name can the marriage be consummated ...

minibuses (Tsh4000–5000; see p.123) also go to Bwejuu. **Leaving** Bwejuu, the first daladala (coming from Kae) passes through at around 6am, and the last leaves Bwejuu at 4pm.

Accommodation

There's a huge choice of **accommodation**, mostly small bungalow "resorts", and most are reasonably priced. Breakfast is usually included in room rates. Distances given below assume *Bwejuu Dere Guest House* to be the centre of the village. See map on p.156.

Andy's Karibuni Romantic Garden On the beach 3km north of the village ☎0748/430942, ⓦwww .eastzanzibar.com. Run by a charming Hungarian woman, this simple, laid-back place on a sandy beachside plot has seven bungalows (all with showers and Western-style toilets) sleeping two to seven people each. The food, cooked to order, is exquisite. Stay away if you don't like big dogs, even soppy and friendly ones. ➍

Bellevue Bungalows & Restaurant 500m north of the village ☎0747/465271, ⓦwww.geocities .com/bellevue_zan. A friendly, locally owned place on a hill on the land side of the road, with good views and the beach just a minute away. The four rooms in two bungalows come with private bathrooms, big heavy beds and nets. There's excellent food too (half-board is an extra $5 for two people), and activities on offer including sailing trips by *ngalawa*. ➋

Bwejuu Dere Guest House Village centre ☎0747/434607. Four lacklustre but cheap guest houses in one, two of them (#1 and #2) on the beach. The small rooms are cleanish and share bathrooms, but only worth it if you're on a strict budget ($10 per person; hence its popularity with backpackers). ➊

Evergreen Bungalows On the beach 800m north of the village ☎024/224 0273 or 0748/408953, ⓦwww.evergreen-bungalows.com. The beach-front plot is the best thing here, though the seven recently renovated thatched bungalows (ten rooms) are good value, and there's also a cheaper but very basic first-floor *banda* with a verandah, accessed up very steep steps. They offer a wide variety of trips (run by themselves), including mangrove tours by boat ($12–18 per person) or by bicycle ($8), and a village tour ($5). Food available. ❷–❸

Mustapha's Nest 700m south of the village on the west side of the road ℡ 024/224 0069, 🌐 www .fatflatfish.co.uk/mustaphas. A long-established and very welcoming place run by local Rasta Mustapha and his family. Accommodation is in several coral-walled thatched-roof *bandas* set in beautiful gardens, and the bar is as good a place as any to learn African drumming. ❷

Palm Beach Inn On the beach 200m south of the village ℡ 024/224 0221 or 0747/411155, 🄴 mahfudh28@hotmail.com. An intimate clutter of buildings beside the beach, well run and with good service, but rather pricey. Rooms have a/c, fridge, hot showers and *semadari* beds, and there's a large bar, painfully expensive restaurant, and inexpensive excursions, including free village trips and an excursion to a seaweed farm. ❺

🏃 **Robinson's Place** On the beach 1.3km north of the village ℡ 0747/413479 or 0748/595572, 🌐 www.robinsonsplace.net. A small, whimsical and highly recommended place run by a Zanzibari–European couple, where the lack of electricity is billed as an attraction (lighting is by kerosene lamps). There are only five rooms (so book well ahead), all equally eclectic in design, though the best is at the top of a two-storey Robinson Crusoe-style house by the beach. There's also the "main house" at the back, with a huge en-suite room decorated with lots of trinkets. Other rooms share clean bathrooms. Meals, drinks and siestas are taken in a cool beach "banda", a circular architectural take on the traditional Swahili coffee *barazas* (the benches that line buildings) complete with stained cement and soft, adobe-like forms. Meals are limited to a sumptuous breakfast and dinner (guests only; around Tsh7000). ❸

Seven Seas Bungalows On the beach 600m south of the village ℡ 0747/481767. A peaceful, cheap and very friendly Tanzanian-run place on a lovely scrubby beach (a refreshing change from the water-guzzling lawns common elsewhere), with just seven rooms in four bungalows, each with fan, Western-style toilet and shower. There's also a good restaurant and friendly bar. ❶

Sunrise Hotel & Restaurant On the beach 2km north of the village ℡ 024/224 0170, 🌐 www .sunrise-zanzibar.com. A cheerfully offbeat choice run by a charming Belgian, with a friendly, unfussy atmosphere, recommended restaurant, swimming

△ Women farming seaweed, Bwejuu

pool (with sun loungers), and even a dovecote. The en-suite "garden" rooms at the back are dark and not particularly good value; for an extra $15, much better to get a room in one of the thatched, beach-facing bungalows (two rooms in each), for more privacy and sea views. The usual range of tours can be arranged, and Internet access is available. ❺

Eating and drinking

Most of Bwejuu's **restaurants** are attached to hotels, and some are outstandingly good. For your own supplies, try Mbochwe Minimarket on the main road south of *Palm Beach Inn*.

Andy's Karibuni Romantic Garden On the beach 3km north of the village. Superb Hungarian cooking plus Zanzibar delights in a laid-back venue. The speciality is *lecso*, a Hungarian stew with onion, tomato, chili, garlic and spices. Full meals around Tsh5000.

Bellevue Bungalows & Restaurant 500m north of the village. Another good place for home cooking, with good seafood (full meals around Tsh5000, including succulent fish and crab) and freshly roasted coffee (natural, spiced or laced with ginger). Meals take up to two hours to arrive.

Bwejuu Dere Guest House Village centre. Fairly average but cheap restaurant (fish Tsh3500, prawns Tsh6000), plus a more attractive beer garden behind the main building with mainland favourites like grilled goat meat (*nyama choma*) with bananas (*ndizi*). Closed Ramadan.

Evergreen Bungalows On the beach 800m north of the village. Eat by the beach, or take a drink on a swing. There's a good broad range of food; lunches cost around Tsh5000, whilst something more substantial for dinner, for example grilled tuna with tamarind sauce or garlic prawns, averages Tsh6500–8500.

First and Last Bar & Restaurant 400m north on the west side of the road. Functions mainly as a local bar, which is liveliest on Friday and Saturday nights; cheap basic food whenever they have a chef.

Jamal's Restaurant 200m south of the village, opposite *Palm Beach Inn*. A not-so-cheap local place capitalizing on the tourist trade. Seafood dishes cost around Tsh3000, chicken up to Tsh4000, and they also do old favourites like spaghetti. Alcohol limited to beer. Closed daytime during Ramadan.

Mustapha's Nest 700m south of the village on the west side of the road. A great option for drinks or meals, with lunch (Tsh3000) and candlelit dinners (Tsh4000) featuring fresh seafood (fabulous octopus). Mellow jam sessions some nights.

Palm Beach Inn On the beach 200m south of the village. Overpriced for standard dishes (for example fish at Tsh8000), but worth trying for its less common offerings, such as fried gazelle (Tsh10,000) or whole fried duck (Tsh18,000). Also has a friendly bar, and you may catch traditional dancers in the evening.

Seven Seas Bungalows On the beach 600m south of the village. This is Bwejuu's main local bar, a pleasantly cheerful sort of place. There's good simple food (Tsh3500–4000; full meals around Tsh8000), and snacks, too.

Sunrise Hotel & Restaurant On the beach 2km north of the village. Quirky surroundings to suit an attractively quirky menu, covering seafood plus unusual treats like gazpacho, puffed crab pancakes and fish soup with rouille and croutons, plus – make room – superb desserts such as fried banana in pancake with melted chocolate, and an acclaimed Belgian chocolate mousse whose fame has spread far and wide (the owner being Belgian, it's a matter of national pride). There are also good vegetarian options, such as okra with black mustard seeds, coriander, cumin and tomato. Prices are reasonable, with most mains courses costing Tsh7000–9000, and there's a good choice of cocktails and South African wines ($22–26 a bottle).

Dongwe

As you head up Michamvi Peninsula north of Bwejuu, the last of the bungalows give way to **Dongwe**. Sparsely populated, dusty and rather dull when seen from land, the beautiful sandy beaches that lie hidden behind the walls and thickets (these gradually disappearing as more and more plots are sold to hoteliers) have attracted an ever-increasing number of wilfully expensive **beach hotels** to the shore, most of them dealing mainly with pre-booked package tours. If you have the money (count on at least $300–400 a day for two), and are happy forgoing local authenticity for pampered service and mod-cons, these hotels may be worth considering, though none are anything like intimate, and are poor value compared to similarly priced places elsewhere. As at Bwejuu, the ocean recedes into the far distance at low tide; the sheltered lagoon is fine for children.

Practicalities

The only daladala that runs along the peninsula leaves Kae, at its northern tip, early in the morning, and returns in the afternoon. So, without a car, the only practical way of getting around is by **bicycle**: most hotels in Bwejuu, Paje and Jambiani can fix one up for a few thousand shillings a day.

Accommodation

The following are marked on the map on p.156.

Breezes Beach Club ☎0747/415049, Ⓦwww.breezes-zanzibar.com. A large and somewhat impersonal upmarket beach resort behind a forbidding wall, whose hidden costs (including charges for water sports and sea views) can come as a nasty surprise. Still, the seventy rooms – in bland two-storey blocks – have all mod-cons, and there are tons of amenities, including a huge swimming pool, a thalassotherapy (saltwater) health spa, fitness centre, floodlit tennis court, several restaurants and bars, evening entertainment, Internet access, the thoroughly recommended Rising Sun Dive Centre (see box on p.146)

and other water sports, and a great beach. Half-board. ❼–❽

Hotel Sultan Palace ☎024/224 0173, Ⓦwww.sultanzanzibar.com. Overlooking a narrow beach, this is small for a "palace", but standards of service and its architecture are suitably sultanic, and the fifteen idiosyncratically designed rooms are spacious and have everything you'd expect for the price (though only eight have sea views). Meals – mainly Swahili and Mediterranean – can be taken on the beach or on one of several secluded terraces in the main building. Closed April & May. Full-board. ❾

Eating and drinking

For upmarket dining, try the hotels. Cheaper, more atmospheric, intimate, unpretentious and tasty **restaurants** are listed below, and make the journey to Dongwe well worthwhile. If you're not staying in Dongwe, access without your own vehicle is by bicycle, as daladala times aren't useful.

The Door Just south of *Hotel Sultan Palace*, Dongwe ☎0747/414962 or 0748/374930, Ⓔthedoor_zanzibar@hotmail.com. Named after the channel in the barrier reef opposite, this is a classy but informal clifftop restaurant run by a Swahili–Italian couple, who pride themselves on attracting clients and staff from the big hotels hereabouts. The excellent cooking is both sophisticated and very affordable, making you wonder how on earth the hotel restaurants can justify their prices. The menu – which changes daily (there's always a vegetarian option) – is a blend of Italian classics and seafood, punctuated by inventive Swahili-inspired touches such as spiced sauces or lemongrass tea. Grilled fish of the day is a bargain at Tsh6000, as is the grilled lobster in ginger and garlic (Tsh12,000). The grilled seafood buffet, in high season only, costs $25. Apart from food, there's also a beach down a long and particularly steep flight of steps, and good snorkelling within swimming distance: locals

rent masks and snorkels for Tsh3000, and they can also fix you up with a *ngalawa* outrigger for around Tsh15,000 per boat for two or three hours. Open lunchtimes until 4pm; dinner by reservation only.

Rocky Restaurant Kijiweni Beach, 2km south of *Karafuu Hotel Beach Resort*, Dongwe ☎0747/435191. Sitting on a small, breezy coral outcrop about 3m above sea level (at high tide you wade out to it), this is one of Zanzibar's nicest locations, and is well priced. They have a small but enticing menu (order a few hours ahead): rice with grilled fish, squid or octopus (all extremely fresh; Tsh4000). For prawns or lobster, it's best to order the day before, though they may be willing to swim out to the fishermen on the reef to collect your order. They don't usually have alcoholic drinks (and their sodas are warm), but they're willing to see what's available in the village; it's probably best to bring your own though. Order at least two hours in advance. Closed Ramadan lunchtimes.

Kae

The road at the top of Michamvi Peninsula becomes diabolically rocky as it heads 2km west towards the village of **Pingwe**, the entrance to which is marked by a grove of coconut palms. There's nothing to see there, and the handful (literally) of tourists who come here generally continue on to the beach at the tiny fishermen's settlement of **KAE** (also known as Pingwe), 1km further on, 13km beyond Bwejuu. As long as your idea of a perfect beach isn't of the sanitized, seaweed-cleaned, cocktail-on-a-sunbed-and-disco-in-the-evening variety, this is, well, the perfect **beach**: powdery white sand, leaning coconut palms, beautiful shades of blue, turquoise and green in the water, scuttling ghost crabs, irregular grids of staves for collecting seaweed, dozens of wooden *ngalawa* outriggers moored offshore, hardly any other beach-goers, nor *papasi* trying to sell their grandmas, and – for now – silence. Of course, it's probably only a matter of time before the developers move in and trash the magic by prettifying the place with lawns, tall walls and higher prices, so enjoy it while you can.

Practicalities

Public transport is limited to just one daladala a day. It leaves Kae at 5am, and heads back from Stone Town's Darajani terminal on Creek Road at 3.45pm. Confusingly, the vehicle is marked "Bwejuu" (#324), so in Stone Town ask for the one for Pingwe. The ride costs Tsh1000 and takes two to three hours. Given the timing, the daladala is useless for day-trips; if you're coming from Bwejuu, Paje or Jambiani, rent a bicycle; most hotels can fix you up with one for a few thousand shillings. Incidentally, the **ferry** from Kae to Chwaka that's still marked on some maps has never existed, though you may find octopus fishermen willing to take you at high tide, when they set off for Chwaka's fish market. There are no fixed prices for the thirty-minute crossing, and anyone not fluent in Kiswahili pays far above local rates – Tsh4000 per person would be good going.

There are just three **guest houses**:

Blue Sea Restaurant & Bungalow 200m north of *Kae Beach Bungalows* ☎0747/464398. Two single-room bungalows and one double, set back from the beach in a palm grove with no direct sea views. ❸

Kae Beach Bungalows At the end of the road beside the beach ☎0747/475299 or 0747/487723, ⓦ www.kaebeachbungalows.com. In a beautiful location, this has just three en-suite bungalows, not really with views as they're side-on, and whilst they're basic, they're airy and perfectly comfortable, and also come with a day-bed and solar-powered lights (there are also day-beds on the beach). The restaurant, which does have views, takes two hours to deliver, and you should pre-order for coolish beers and

sodas. Rice with fish or Kae's speciality, octopus, costs Tsh5000. With a bit of patience, they can arrange various boat trips, including cruises around mangroves, or snorkelling (Tsh30,000 per *ngalawa* for a few hours, plus Tsh3000 per person for snorkelling equipment). Breakfast included. ❷

Ras Michamvi Sea View Restaurant 150m north of *Kae Beach Bungalows* (no phone). The beach here is a total heart-stopper, with sand so soft you could rub a baby's bottom with it. There are just three rooms around a courtyard in the manner of mainland guest houses – all pretty basic, the rooms with twin beds, box nets, modern bathrooms and nothing much else. Breakfast included, and meals available (count on at least an hour). ❸

Northern Unguja

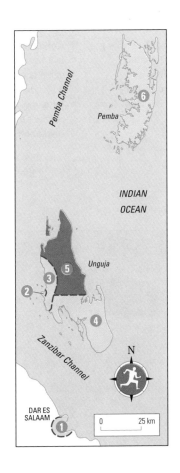

CHAPTER 5 # Highlights

* **Mnemba Atoll** The wide, shallow reefs surrounding the heart-shaped Mnemba Island are perfect for snorkelling or scuba diving, whatever your level of experience. See p.171 & p.180

* **Pongwe** A diminutive fishing village whose sandy coves are as close as Zanzibar gets to picture-postcard paradise. See p.177

* **Nungwi** Zanzibar's liveliest beach destination, and among the more enticing too, with heaps of seafood restaurants, bars and activities, including a natural tidal aquarium filled with turtles. See p.181

* **Kendwa** A quieter alternative to Nungwi, with good-value accommodation and a wonderful beach, perfect for sampling *dolce far niente* – the sweetness of doing nothing. See p.188

△ Aerial view of Mnemba Island

5

Northern Unguja

The beaches of **northern Unguja**, particularly at Ras Nungwi at the very tip of the island, were the first to be discovered by foreign beach bums, when – back in the bell-bottomed Seventies – a handful of hippy escapees started calling at Zanzibar on their cosmic journey to Kathmandu. Not without reason: even today, with the bulk of Zanzibar's hundred thousand annual tourists sunning themselves in the north, hotel development has been surprisingly modest and unobtrusive (the exception being Kiwengwa in the northeast), and by and large the place still lives up to the old hippy mantra of "peace and love", a refrain you'll still hear a fair amount nowadays from local Rastafarians.

The north-coast beaches of **Nungwi** and **Kendwa** are the ones to head for if you value youthful vibes, bars and restaurants. Generally more sedate and upmarket are the modest beach resorts strung along the northeast coast. Rounding the cape, **Matemwe** is the first of these, and generally favoured by upmarket travellers. Most of its hotels are on a cliff edge, though the beach goes on for miles. South of here are **Pwani Mchangani** and **Kiwengwa**, the latter overrun by enormous and often noisy all-inclusive package-holiday resorts popular with Italians. Completely different are the sandy coves at Pongwe, which contain Zanzibar's nicest beaches and just two modest hotels. **Uroa** and **Chwaka**, further south, are just as quiet.

At all of these places you can arrange a variety of **activities**, including snorkelling, sometimes scuba diving or sunset dhow cruises, and – at the bigger hotels – a range of noisier water sports. As for culture, the only site worth visiting is **Dunga Palace** on the road to Chwaka. There are a few other ruins closer to Nungwi, and on the island of **Tumbatu**, although this should only be visited if you have a genuine interest in the Swahili. Still, if you've seen some of the historical sights around Stone Town, that's probably enough – once you get your toes in the powdery white sand, you'll be most unlikely to want to leave.

The northeast coast

As you approach Unguja's **northeast** coast, the vegetation becomes scrubbier, with coconut palms, baobabs and thorny thickets replacing the lush spice

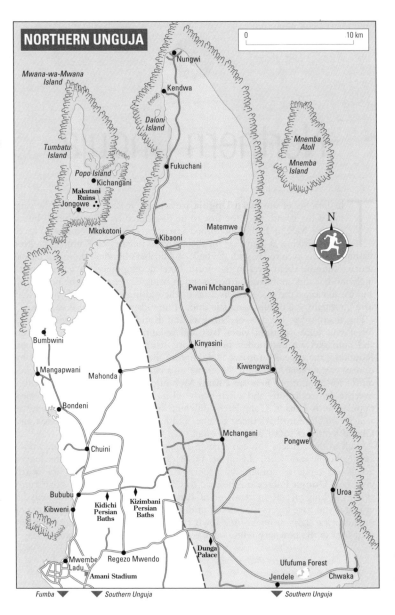

plantations of the interior, before giving way to a broad swath of fine white sand backed by a line of waving palm trees and the turquoise expanse of the Indian Ocean.

Following the **abolition** of the East African slave trade by a reluctant Sultan Barghash in 1873, a number of places along the remote northeast coast of Unguja – especially Chwaka Bay, Uroa and Pongwe – saw use as il'legal

slaving ports, continuing the trade with the Seychelles and French Indian Ocean possessions until the beginning of the twentieth century. Much of the northeast still retains an attractively isolated feel, in spite of Stone Town being just two hours' drive away, and – with the exception of Kiwengwa – sees

Diving off Unguja's northeast coast

For an introduction to scuba diving and snorkelling in Zanzibar, see p.46.

At the centre of Zanzibar's dive scene is **Mnemba Atoll**, a shallow reef enclosing the heart-shaped Mnemba Island and surrounded by steep drop-offs. Sometimes dismissed for its modest underwater visibility (20m on average, dropping to 10m or less in July and August), the atoll is nonetheless a divers' paradise, both on account of the variety of **corals** and associated fish life, and for reasonable odds on sighting turtles, dolphins and other big species. There's also a slim but ever-tantalizing possibility of seeing or hearing **whales** between September and October. Dive sites on the barrier reef further north are described on p.182. **Visibility** is at its best in January but sea conditions are calmest in late October and November, when you're less likely to have problems with swells.

The wide depth range of **Kichwani Reef** (from 3m to beyond sport-diving limits), on the south side of the atoll, suits all levels of divers and snorkellers. Dolphins are often seen from the boat, evidently attracted by the huge diversity and abundance of fish, often in large schools, including one-eyed jacks, sweetlips, big-eyes and five-lined snappers. Running west from Kichwani, **Aquarium Reef** (16–22m) has a wide range of corals, both soft and hard, inhabited by all sorts of colourful species including Moorish idols, whilst sponges attract hawksbill and green turtles, the whole lot arousing the appetite of white- and black-tipped reef sharks. The reef is suitable for novices but is best tackled as a two-tank dive combined with another reef. Also on the south side and suitable for novices is **Wattabomi Reef** (10–25m), dominated by brain and plate corals. It's a great place for chancing upon green turtles; other biggies that may put in an appearance include peppered moray eels, dolphins and, most likely, blue-spotted ribbontail rays. The lovely **Coral Garden** (from 6m to below sport-diving limits) in the west is one of the best dives for corals, with a wide and beautiful variety, including large fans. Given the depth amplitude, there's plenty of variety in fish life too, from octopus and eels (garden and snow flake) to swarms of reef fish, rays, turtles and, lower down, circling barracuda and occasional black-tipped reef sharks. For advanced divers (in perfect conditions only), **The Big Wall** on the atoll's eastern side is a deep, near-vertical coral face pitted with small caves: an incredible drift dive with plenty of game fish (rays, tuna) and, frequently enough, reef sharks, though reported sightings of gigantic whale sharks are as rare as the animals are extraordinary – the best odds are in September or October.

Dive centres

The following are recommended PADI-accredited **dive centres** in Matemwe. Rising Sun Dive Centre in Bwejuu (see p.146) also covers Mnemba, as do all outfits based in Kendwa and Nungwi on the north coast; see p.183.

One Ocean (The Zanzibar Dive Centre) *Matemwe Beach Village*, Matemwe ☏0747/417250; *Bluebay Beach Resort*, Kiwengwa ☏024/224 0241; *Ocean Paradise Resort*, Pwani Mchangani ☏0747/439990, ⓦwww.zanzibaroneocean.com. Highly experienced and knowledgeable, with centres throughout Unguja – read the review on p.180.

Zanzibar Beach Hotel & Resort Matemwe ☏0747/417782, ⓦwww .zanzibarbeachresort.com. Costly but experienced and strong on safety, offering thorough training for PADI courses up to Dive Master (training dives are done in the hotel's pool).

very few tourists. The main **beaches**, from south to north, are Chwaka, Uroa, Pongwe, Kiwengwa and Pwani Mchangani, and Matemwe. The sprawling expanse of sand at Matemwe and the sheltered coves at Pongwe are especially beautiful, whilst for a really local feel Chwaka and Uroa are recommended. All these places have accommodation. Whilst the choice isn't huge, there's enough to suit all tastes and pockets. You might want to avoid Kiwengwa though, where a number of huge all-inclusive package resorts have blighted one of the most beautiful stretches of beach on Unguja, and embittered locals.

All the northeastern beaches can be adorned by pungent **seaweed** between December and February – "an unwanted Christmas present" in the words of one hotelier – though most hotels clear their beaches regularly, heedless of any knock-on effects on the ecosystem. Be aware that at **low tide** the ocean recedes considerably, so swimming isn't possible all the time. A host of **activities** is offered by most of the larger hotels to complement the beach lounging, including reef walks, sailing and water sports, while **snorkelling** gear can be rented locally and is superb in the shallow intertidal waters. **Scuba-divers** will find their nirvana on the northeast coast, especially off Mnemba Atoll, though you'll need a measure of luck regarding sea conditions and seasons.

Daladalas serve all these places, but for getting around there's nothing better than hiring a bicycle and heading off along the beach, which serves as a highway for locals. Bikes are also ideal for getting to the ruins of **Dunga Palace**, the last seat of the traditional rulers of Zanzibar (the Wawinyi Wakuu), and to **Ufufuma Forest**.

Stone Town to Chwaka

There are a couple of places worth visiting along the road from Stone Town to Chwaka: the ruins of **Dunga Palace**, and the delightful **Ufufuma Forest**, which, like Jozani, gives visitors the chance of spotting red colobus monkeys.

Dunga Palace

Nineteen kilometres east of Stone Town lie the ruins of **Dunga Palace**, a pleasant stop on the way to or from the coast. Apart from its sense of history, the site offers views over much of the island, and the overgrown garden is an attraction in itself, with some beautiful Indian almond trees (*mkungu*). Unlike Unguja's other palaces, which were built during the Omani sultanate, Dunga was the last seat of the traditional rulers of Unguja, the **Wawinyi Wakuu** (singular: *Mwinyi Mkuu*). Oral tradition links the Wawinyi Wakuu to Shirazi settlers from Persia who arrived over a thousand years ago, and with whom Unguja's original inhabitants intermarried to create the Hadimu tribe. The ruling dynasty's family name of al-Alawi, however, suggests roots in the Filal district of Saudi Arabia, where Morocco's present-day royal family (the Alaoui) also originated.

The **palace** was built early in the nineteenth century by Hassan bin Ahmad al-Alawi, whose rule coincided with the gradual usurpation of his power by Zanzibar's Omani sultan, Seyyid Saïd in Stone Town, who demanded tribute from him in return for "protection". Nonetheless, Al-Alawi retained the right to dispense justice over and collect taxes from his African subjects, and despite the curtailing of his powers remained far from impoverished, as can be seen at Dunga. The **palace**, built around a central courtyard, originally had two storeys

△ Dunga Palace ruins

and a rooftop garden, and its windows were fitted with stained glass, now exhibited in the House of Wonders.

Excavations in the 1920s turned up drums and horns – traditional emblems of power along the Swahili coast. The excavations also revealed a well half filled with human skeletons, possibly the victims of an archaic belief that mixing blood with mortar would ensure the solidity of a building's foundations. Dunga's victims may have been killed when the palace was fortified under the rule of Muhammad bin Ahmad al-Alawi (1845–65). The Mwinyi Mkuu remained important enough to justify the clearing of the road from Stone Town to Dunga during the reign of Sultan Majid (1857–70) so that the Sultan's stage-coach – a gift from Queen Victoria to Seyyid Saïd – could pass through.

Muhammad bin Ahmad al-Alawi died in 1865 at the age of 80 and was succeeded by his son, Ahmad bin Muhammad al-Alawi. Ahmad was jailed by Sultan Barghash in 1871, allegedly for tyranny, and died of smallpox two years later without leaving an heir, marking the end of the dynasty. The palace was demolished in 1910, and the ruins you see now – low walls, archways, stone staircases and some pillars – are mostly the product of a 1994 reconstruction.

Access by **public transport** is easy, with relatively frequent daladalas to Chwaka (#206 from Stone Town's Darajani terminal on Creek Road) passing by throughout the day. Daladalas to Uroa (#214) from Mwembe Ladu, 2km east of Stone Town, also pass by.

Ufufuma Forest

Five kilometres west of Chwaka is the locally managed **Ufufuma Forest**, harbouring a small population of red colobus monkeys (see p.148), dikdiks, impala and a rich variety of birdlife. There are also a number of sacred caves that are used by locals – along with ancestral spirits, they're also home to colonies of bats. The forest is run by EPUJE (Environmental Protection of Ufufuma/Jendele), whom you should contact before coming to be sure of finding someone there. Write to PO Box 1861, Zanzibar, or contact Mustafa Makame (✉himauje@yahoo.com), Hussein Ame Njuma (☎0747/423255), or a tour company in Stone Town (see p.129). The $6 entry fee includes a guided walk, seasonal fruits and other refreshments.

The forests near Chwaka provided the last evidence for the existence of the **Zanzibar leopard**. Once used by Zanzibari witchdoctors in ceremonies, this nocturnal animal was last seen in the 1970s, and since prints, droppings and a suspected den were discovered near Chwaka in 1994, no trace has been found, leading to the sad conclusion that the Zanzibar leopard is now extinct. The blame would appear to lie at the door of the beach-hotel developers, whose wholesale clearance of thickets and coastal forest have decimated the leopard's natural habitat.

Chwaka

The northeast coast's largest settlement is **CHWAKA**, a fishing village on the west shore of the wide mangrove-fringed Chwaka Bay. The village receives few visitors, which means that you're likely to be the only tourist here – and the centre of attention for dozens of excitable kids. Apart from men and women out on the shallow sandbanks and exposed reefs collecting shellfish and octopus, the beach is largely deserted. Although swimming is impossible at low tide, this is the best time to see the waders and other birds that feed on the plentiful shellfish hidden just beneath the sands. Sunrise over Michamvi Peninsula on the other side of the bay is always special, and there are few if any mosquitoes thanks to a sturdy sea breeze.

Apart from the beach and the bay, the open-air **market** at the end of the road on the shore is another attraction. A quiet place for much of the day, it becomes lively at high tide and in late afternoon, when the fishermen pull up in their

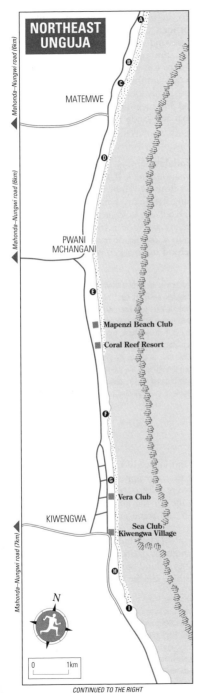

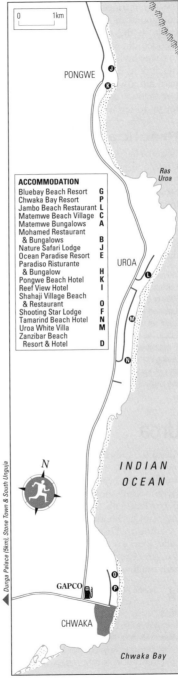

ngalawa outriggers to sell the day's catch. To the north of the market, beside a compound of holiday homes, is a cluster of men weaving wicker lobster pots, while to the south of the market, 100m beyond an enormous baobab tree, wooden dhows continue to be made using traditional methods.

A worthwhile **excursion** from Chwaka is to the mangrove forests that line much of its bay, combined with a boat trip through the twisting maze of channels and a walk to inspect local wildlife, especially crabs. *Shahaji Village Beach* (see below) can arrange day-trips for around $40 including a *ngalawa* outrigger for up to seven people; otherwise, hire a boat and guide at the fish market.

Practicalities

Chwaka lies 32km east of Stone Town. **Daladalas** on route #206 go straight to Chwaka from Stone Town's Darajani terminal on Creek Road, roughly hourly from 6am to 6pm. Daladalas to Uroa (#214 from Mwembe Ladu, 2km east of Stone Town) turn north at the GAPCO filling station just before Chwaka, leaving you with a kilometre or two to walk. Details on boats across Chwaka Bay from Kae, at the tip of Michamvi Peninsula, are given on p.166.

Chwaka has just two **hotels**. There are also a couple of basic *mgahawas* (tea houses serving simple meals) in the area behind the market; you'll need to ask directions, as they lack signs.

Chwaka Bay Resort 500m north of the market; fork left after 200m or follow the beach ☎ 024/224 0289 or 0747/423293, ✉ chwaka@zanlink.com. A modest and often deserted Swedish–Tanzanian resort set on a broad plot with access to a lovely beach. The best of the thirty rooms are at the front in five double-storey buildings; a little cheaper but lacking sea views are bungalows on a raised area set well back from the shore. All have a/c or fans and terraces or balconies. Facilities are limited to a bar, a cavernous restaurant and a swimming pool. Breakfast included. ❹

Shahaji Village Beach & Restaurant Formerly *Raha Beach*, 500m beyond *Chwaka Bay Hotel* (no phone). Two very basic rooms in two bungalows, with attached shower (cold water) and clean squat toilets, but no electricity. The views across the bay from the terraces are the main draw. Food needs to be ordered well in advance and can be bland. Haggle to avoid inflated room rates. ❷

Uroa

About 9km north of Chwaka is the spread-out village of **UROA**. The welcoming cries of "Jambo" from excited toddlers are more appealing than the village itself, but the beach, albeit bleak and windswept at times, is certainly refreshing. Despite some modest hotel developments, life for the villagers continues as it always has, with fishing, seaweed collection and some cultivation comprising the main livelihoods.

Getting to Uroa, catch one of the hourly #214 **daladalas** from Mwembe Ladu, 2km east of Stone Town (there are frequent daladalas to there from the Darajani/Creek Road terminal); the last leaves around 6pm. Several **hotels** – all with restaurants – are spread along the coastline; see the map on p.175.

Jambo Beach Restaurant 500m north of Uroa village ☎ 0747/460446. A really friendly, locally run place on a lovely stretch of beach, with seven basic but beautiful twin-bed *bandas* with sandy floors, made entirely from natural materials like banana thatch and coir rope (shared bathrooms only), plus one en-suite bungalow. There's also a good beach restaurant (most meals around Tsh4500, pasta is cheaper at Tsh3000), snorkelling equipment is available (Tsh2000; not fins), and sailing trips can be arranged (Tsh15,000–20,000 per *ngalawa* outrigger). Evenings see occasional performances of traditional music. Breakfast included. ❶–❷

The Uroa coin hoard

In 1943 a young boy, sent by his father to dig up roots between two baobab trees in Uroa, unearthed one of the most astonishing **treasure troves** ever found in East Africa. It contained no less than 3204 coins, most of them minted in fifteenth-century Kilwa Kisiwani on the mainland, which at that time was the wealthiest and most powerful city-state in East Africa.

The hoard at Uroa was most likely buried in 1503 to avoid the rapacious attentions of the Portuguese captain **Ruy Lourenço Ravasco**, who had sacked the Unguja's capital at Unguja Ukuu. According to the Portuguese chronicler João de Barros, Ravasco was "bombarded and attacked with arrows" by local inhabitants, who refused him food or tribute. In reply, Ravasco spent two months seizing shipping between Zanzibar and the mainland – some twenty boats in all. Local merchants learned to circumvent Ravasco's attacks by landing on the east shore of Zanzibar, so Ravasco sailed to the area between Uroa and Chwaka. After beating off an attack by boats, a landing party was sent to Chwaka Bay. According to Barros, resistance was quashed with a single salvo from a Portuguese cannon that killed 35 defenders, including a son of the Mwinyi Mkuu. The Mwinyi Mkuu sued for peace, which was granted in exchange for thirty sheep and a yearly tribute of one hundred *meticais* in gold.

Tamarind Beach Hotel 1.5km south of Uroa village ☎0747/411191 or 024/223 7154, ⓦwww .tamarind.nu. An informal and good-value if slightly tatty resort-style hotel, with fourteen clean rooms (all with private bathroom) in attractive stone cottages, each with a small roof terrace. The gardens adjoin the beach, and there's a breezy bar and restaurant. Snorkelling and boat trips available. Breakfast included. ❹

Uroa White Villa In the centre close to Uroa Primary Health Care Unit; follow the signs ☎0741/326874, ⓦuroawhitevilla.net. A modern, German-run place on the beach with comfortable, spotless accommodation (mostly en suite). The restaurant does good Swahili dishes (mains Tsh4500–7000) – the *pilau* with fresh tuna is especially tasty – and also sells alcohol. Boat trips and snorkelling can be arranged, and there are discounts on rooms if booked ahead. ❺

Pongwe

The tiny fishing village of **PONGWE** lies at the end of the fifteen-kilometre stretch of road from Chwaka, and 46km from Stone Town. There's nothing much to it, but the beach – a handful of small sheltered coves with unbelievably clear water and lots of swaying palm trees – is the stuff of dreams.

Getting here by **daladala** (#209 from Mwembe Ladu just east of Stone Town) can be awkward, as it doesn't run every day, so enquire the day before, and be prepared to head out to Mwembe Ladu, 2km east of Darajani (frequent daladalas), in case the driver decides to start there. Don't confuse Pongwe with Mwera Pongwe (#225 daladala), which is a different place entirely. If it is running, the #209 leaves Stone Town at 7am, and turns back in Pongwe at 10am, unfortunately ruling out the possibility of a day-trip. There are two **hotels**. Both use generator power for electricity, which is switched off at night, so rooms can get rather hot when ceiling fans are still.

Nature Safari Lodge ☎0747/415613 or 0747/419070, ⓦwww.pongwevillage.com. On a low shady cliff beside a small sandy cove, the beach here lacks palm trees but is still gorgeous.

Rooms, slightly dilapidated, are in two rows of four bungalows. The three at the front are used by the staff, so there's only one with a sea view ("Pongwe III", with three beds). There's a cheap bar and plain restaurant (Tsh3500–5000 a plate) with an entirely African menu (order 2–3hr before), including vegetarian options such as beans cooked in chilli, cumin, tomato and spinach, served with coconut basmati rice. Canoe rental costs Tsh10,000 per day (for two people). Free transport from Stone Town if prebooked. Breakfast included. ❸

🏃 **Pongwe Beach Hotel** 100m south of *Nature Safari Lodge* ☎0748/336181, ⓦwww.pongwe.com. The tight security here comes as an unpleasant shock (intended, it seems, to deter the handful of day-trippers that used to come – entry now depends on your willingness

to spend at least Tsh15,000 on a meal), but if you can live with that, the beach really does just blow everything else away. Scattered around the mature gardens are thirteen spacious rooms in thatched bungalows, with carved wooden doors and *semadari* beds, but where the place comes into its own is its restaurant, for exquisite seafood (Tsh15,000–20,000 for three courses). There's also a bar, pleasant lounge area, and various pricey tours and activities including snorkelling (from $15 per person), which should be arranged the day before. Often full, so book ahead. Breakfast included. ❻

Kiwengwa and Pwani Mchangani

As Zanzibar's main package-holiday resort, **KIWENGWA** is dominated by enormous all-inclusive resorts catering almost entirely to the Italian package-tour market. The clientele cocooned inside the resorts has little chance to experience the "real" Zanzibar, and local sensibilities are too often ignored (topless sunbathing, which is actually illegal, being but one example). The destructive excesses of development are glaringly apparent: erosion during the rains and a dusty atmosphere in the dry season that have been caused by wholesale land clearance, and typify the environmental and ethical nightmare that is beginning to afflict other parts of the coast, as the Zanzibari government continues to prefer short-term gains from foreign investors to less profitable but sustainable long-term development with local participation. Residents have not remained indifferent to all this however: two resorts were torched early in 2001 in the aftermath of the government's bloody crackdown on opposition supporters, and there's no guarantee of it not happening again. That said, there are a few places here that are more in tune with local life, and these are reviewed below.

Kiwengwa is actually rather difficult to pin down, seeing as it sprawls along almost 10km of coastline. The package-hotel strip fizzles out a couple of kilometres south of **PWANI MCHANGANI** (also called Kwa Pangaa). This is still very much a traditional fishing village, and has so far managed to avoid selling its shoreline – and soul – to the developers, surviving instead on fishing, coconut cultivation and the farming of seaweed, which you'll see hung out to dry everywhere. The village receives few visitors, though Italians have left their mark in the way local kids greet you: the habitual "Jambo!" is being replaced by "Jao!", their way of saying "Ciao!"

Practicalities

Kiwengwa is 40km northeast of Stone Town along a good surfaced road. Route #117 **daladalas** finish at Kiwengwa village. Others go to Pwani Mchangani, the last 8km being unsurfaced. Both start at "Nungwi stand" in Stone Town, being the west side of Creek Road just north of the Central Market. The ones to Kiwengwa run every ten minutes or so throughout the day, but those to Pwani Mchangani are infrequent, so find out about them the day before. At Kiwengwa, the daladalas stay on the asphalt, so if you're heading to *Bluebay Beach Resort* or *Shooting Star Lodge*, try and get the daladala driver to drop you there – an extra Tsh2000 or so should suffice; if not, you face a long, dusty and very hot walk. If you're **driving from Pongwe**, note that the unsurfaced road to Kiwengwa is extremely rocky in places and may require 4WD in some sections.

Bluebay Beach Resort 2km north of Kiwengwa ☏ 024/224 0241, ⓦ www.bluebayzanzibar.com. Similar in size to the brash all-inclusives on either side, this slick five-star resort has made some efforts to minimize its environmental impact. There's a fine stretch of beach, a nice swimming pool, and a wide range of activities on offer, while accommodation is in 88 luxurious rooms. Perhaps inevitably with a place this size, service – and indeed food – can be variable, and prices for services like taxi rides are inflated. Water sports and diving are offered here by One Ocean (see p.171). Day visitors are admitted on condition of buying lunch. Rates include windsurfing, tennis and fitness centre. Half-board. ❼–❾

Ocean Paradise Resort 2km south of Pwani Mchangani ☏ 0747/439990, ⓦ www .oceanparadisezanzibar.com. Newest and best of the big five-star beach resorts on this part of the coast, this is very stylish and makes good use of local materials in both its rooms and common areas. Facilities include Zanzibar's largest swimming pool, tons of water sports including scuba diving, a fitness centre and tennis courts, ocean-view restaurant, various bars and disco. Half-board. ❽–❾

Paradiso Risturante & Bungalow Behind the school in Kiwengwa village (no sign) ☏ 0747/415351, ⓔ alimcheni@hotmail.com. Two very good-value bungalows with two rooms in each, all en-suite doubles, on a scrubby patch of land next to a beach lined with coconut palms. There are also two huge houses for monthly rental

(from $500), each with two bedrooms. *Ngalawa* trips ($10 per boat including snorkelling equipment) are available, and food and drinks can be arranged (usually Tsh4000 for a plate of fish; prawns Tsh8000). Breakfast included. ❷

Reef View Hotel 1.5km south of Kiwengwa at Kumba Urembo ☏ 0747/413294. The southernmost of Kiwengwa's hotels, somewhat seedy these days but still good value for its five thatched *bandas* with shared bathrooms, and one two-room bungalow, all with sea views through strange *mikadi* palm trees. Facilities include a pleasant bar and a good restaurant: full lunches go for Tsh6000, and the evening buffet costs Tsh7000. Breakfast included. ❷–❸

🏃 **Shooting Star Lodge** 4km north of Kiwengwa ☏ 0747/414166, ⓦ www .zanzibar.org/star. Occupying a cliff top with wonderful sea views (the beach is accessed down a steep flight of steps), this is Kiwengwa's most romantic, intimate and effortlessly stylish option, and benefits from a small but lovely "infinity" pool (it has no raised edge, so the horizon just goes on and on), the absence of nearby resorts to spoil views or the silence, and one of Zanzibar's best restaurants (Tsh15,000–20,000 for three courses, or Tsh35,000 with lobster). All fifteen rooms are attractively furnished, though at this price level, invest in a cottage with private sea-view verandah rather than in a "garden lodge" room. Day guests can use the pool if they buy lunch. Activities are run through *Bluebay Beach Resort*. Closed from mid-April to mid-June. Half-board. ❼–❽

Matemwe

The beautiful palm-fringed beach either side of the fishing village of **MATEMWE**, 5km north of Pwani Mchangani, is the last of the northeast coast resorts, and one of the more intimate. **Accommodation** is not cheap, however. Along with much of the east and northeast coast, **swimming** at low tide is impossible unless you fancy a very long walk, but no matter – the walks across the lagoon to the barrier reef a kilometre offshore are part of the attraction. The hotels have kayaks and can organize sailing trips, though it's cheaper to arrange things yourself with locals. The main reason for coming here is for the superb **diving and snorkelling**, both in the lagoon and around Mnemba Atoll; see p.171 & p.180.

Practicalities

Matemwe lies 50km from Stone Town, with #118 **daladalas** running throughout the day from Stone Town's "Nungwi stand" on Creek Road, just north of the Central Market. The road is all asphalt, and ends at the shore. The rough and sandy road from Pwani Mchangani, 5km to the south, can be slow going, and there's no public transport along this stretch.

There are only a handful of **hotels** at present, though the latest – the large *Zanzibar Beach Resort & Hotel* – may be indicative of further large-scale development. Book ahead for *Matemwe Beach Village* or *Matemwe Bungalows*, both of which fill up quickly in season.

Matemwe Beach Village 1km north of the village ℡024/223 8374 or 0747/417250, ⓦwww .matemwebeach.com. Located amid palm trees on a large beachside plot, this welcoming place is considerably cheaper than the rest but could still do with a bit of work (a lot's been done already), as its seventeen spacious *makuti*-thatched bungalows (few if any with sea views) are rather basic and spoiled by an insidious smell of mould. There's a cosy bar and good restaurant, and water sports and diving are offered by One Ocean (see p.171). No swimming pool. Free transfers from Stone Town. Half-board. ❻–❼

Matemwe Bungalows 3.5km north of the village ℡0747/425788, ⓦwww.matemwe.com. Upmarket yet personal and unpretentious place on a rocky outcrop overlooking Mnemba Atoll, and the beach at one end. The fourteen rooms, all suites, are in individual thatched cottages strung out along the coast, each with a verandah, hammock and dreamlike views. All have solar-powered light and hot water. Superb seafood is the speciality of the gloriously positioned restaurant. Non-guests are welcome for lunch but should book ahead. There's a swimming pool, kayaks, and boat trips or snorkelling can be arranged; diving is run through *Zanzibar Beach Resort & Hotel*. Closed April & May. Full-board. ❾

Mohamed Restaurant & Bungalows 2km north of the village ℡0747/431881. Finally, a budget hotel in Matemwe. Don't expect much of the rooms, which are definitely tatty if adequate and clean (big blue mosquito nets, "cold" water only, and neither fans nor views), and the plot is narrow and cramped. But the gate in the fence at the end opens on to a beach that was surely made in paradise. It's also one of the few beaches that isn't "cleaned" of seaweed, a plus if you're not keen on the overly sanitized versions elsewhere. Also has good, fresh and simple food (including fish with coconut sauce, crab with salad; main courses around Tsh5500), snorkelling equipment and motorbikes. Breakfast included. ❶

Zanzibar Beach Resort & Hotel 2km south of the village ℡0747/417784, ⓦwww .zanzibarbeachresort.com. Matemwe's newest and largest hotel lacks the intimacy of the other options, but is very well endowed, coming with a raft of amenities (including lots of stuff for kids), a beautiful swimming pool (and of course the beach), and several restaurants and bars. It's also the base of a recommended scuba-diving outfit. Accommodation is in smallish chalets or four villas (up to six people in each) with kitchens, some of them with a distinctly prefabricated appearance. All are decorated in a neo-colonial theme, have a/c and balconies, most with sea views. It should be just right for families. Rates include non-motorized water sports. Half-board. ❽

Mnemba Atoll

Off the coast between Matemwe and Nungwi, **Mnemba Atoll** is a shallow expanse of coral reef with a tiny heart-shaped island on its western fringe. Contrary to Zanzibari law which states that beaches cannot be privately owned, landing on the island itself is not allowed unless you're super-rich and are staying at the obscenely priced *Mnemba Island Club* ($1700 a double). No matter – the atoll is a "must do" for many visitors, especially if snorkelling or scuba diving appeals (see p.171). Day-trips can be arranged from both Matemwe and Nungwi. The fairly standard price of $30–35 includes transport, lunch, snorkelling equipment, and a $5 entry fee paid to the Mnemba Island Marine Conservation Area.

The north coast

Life for most tourists on Unguja's **north coast** centres on the beach at **Nungwi**, a favourite with backpackers that combines beautiful beaches with Zanzibar's liveliest nightlife, excellent seafood restaurants, snorkelling and scuba diving. There's also a tidal aquarium, village tours, and dhow cruises at sunset. If the place feels too touristy, or hotel rates surpass your budget, there's an equally beautiful stretch of beach a few kilometres to the south at **Kendwa**, which has become famous for its monthly full-moon parties. Like Nungwi, it has good seafood restaurants and bars, and a laid-back atmosphere. The dagger-shaped **Tumbatu Island**, off the west coast, is one of Zanzibar's most traditional places, whose inhabitants lay claim to being the "original" Swahili – with some justification too, especially as the island contains the ruins of one of East Africa's oldest towns. Tumbatu's pride in its heritage also means that tourists are generally not welcome unless they have a genuine interest in history or culture. Easier to visit are some sixteenth-century ruins at **Fukuchani**, south of Nungwi.

Nungwi

From humble beginnings as a little fishing village and dhow-making centre known only to a handful of hippies, **NUNGWI** has become, in little more than a decade, Zanzibar's most popular beach resort. The place is positively infested with **tourists** – it's a firm fixture on the overland and round-the-world circuits, and the tourist dollar has inevitably attracted a range of hangers-on, including a surprising number of wannabe gigolos, and a handful of Maasai warriors in all their red-robed glory, who mine the lucrative ethnic-photography market.

Much of the western flank of Ras Nungwi ("Nungwi headland") has been overrun by a flurry of development, behind which the actual village is practically invisible. But things aren't as bad as they sound: the buildings are for the most part modest, locals remain unfazed by the invasion, and the atmosphere is remarkably easy-going, with little hassle. As long as you're not pursuing the "real" Zanzibar, you're almost guaranteed to have a good time.

The **beach** is of course the main enticement; it's narrower on the western side and gradually gets wider as you round the cape to the east, while the sea is resplendent in all directions, especially when dhows drift into view. As along the northeast coast, the wide tidal range here, especially around the top and to the east of the cape, means that swimming at low tide requires a long walk across the sands to get to deep water, and note that the shoreline east of *Smiles Beach Hotel*, including the entire eastern cape, can be covered in **seaweed** between November and January. Apart from the beach, there's a natural tidal aquarium that is home to **marine turtles**, plus a number of other activities including sunset dhow cruises, scuba diving and snorkelling. When swimming, be wary of treading on **sea urchins** at low tide.

Arrival

Nungwi is 59km from Stone Town, 8km beyond the end of the asphalt. **Dala-dalas** (#116) run there throughout the day (roughly 2hr; Tsh1200–1500) from the west side of Creek Road, north of the Central Market. Most

Diving and snorkelling off Unguja's north coast

For an introduction to scuba diving and snorkelling in Zanzibar, see p.46.

Strong currents, patchy coral cover and damage from fishermen, coral miners and careless anchoring means that the reefs just off Nungwi aren't the best for **diving and snorkelling**. However, with a boat, there are over a dozen much better reefs within easy reach.

Swimming out to the reef on the western shore for **snorkelling** is not recommended due to the potentially dangerous current; boat trips are offered by virtually everyone, though for locations on the east coast or beyond the northern tip of Tumbatu Island, safety considerations mean you should go through one of the dive centres reviewed below. Prices depend on location and duration, and also whether you can tag along with a group of divers, which works out cheaper. Trips to reefs just offshore, where Kendwa Coral Garden is the highlight, cost $15; a day-trip to Mnemba Atoll (average price $30–35; see p.171 & p.180) is highly recommended.

For **scuba diving**, there are a handful of reasonable reefs just offshore, though visibility is a modest 15m. The best of these is **Hunga Reef**: its soft and hard corals contain a wide variety of schooling tropical fish, and give occasional sightings of reef sharks, blue-spotted stingrays and barracuda. The water is clearer off **Mnemba Atoll** (see p.171 for reef descriptions), trips to which are offered by all of Nungwi's dive centres. Together with Mnemba, the one reef that's touted everywhere is the spectacular **Leven Bank** in the Pemba Channel. However, its depth and **dangerously strong currents** limit it to experienced divers only (don't believe less-ethical operators who say it's not a problem), and even with the best preparations there's always a risk of getting swept out to sea, so for this one – more than others – choose your dive centre with safety in mind. Safer locations are scattered along the **barrier reef** to the east, and include Ametatu, Mbwangawa (good for novices, with occasional reef sharks), Haji and – best of all – Kichafi Reef (8–18m), suitable for all levels and good for night dives too, as well as being home

tourists, however, come on **shared minibuses** (see p.123). These leave Stone Town at 8am and sometimes also at 3pm, most dropping their passengers at *Amaan Bungalows*, whose services the drivers (and *Amaan*'s "bouncers") can be extremely pushy in plugging. A **taxi** from Stone Town costs $50–60; renting a daladala (minibus) costs the same and works out cheaper if you're in a large group. **Day-trips** to Nungwi are offered by a number of Stone Town tour operators; see p.129.

Accommodation

Nungwi has almost two dozen **hotels**, mostly clusters of whitewashed bungalows with standard-issue *makuti*-thatched roofs. Most are pretty bland, overpriced even by Zanzibar's standards, and sometimes not especially welcoming. Don't be swayed by recommendations from minibus drivers or touts, who only push hotels that pay them commission. Most places also want payment in dollars: although you can legally pay in Tanzanian shillings, the hotel's conversion rates are so bad that you'll end up paying fifteen to twenty percent more. Still, it's not all gloom: the good news is that there's still a handful of more decent places to choose from, though if you're on a budget, neighbouring Kendwa (see p.188) is looking ever more enticing. Incidentally, the presence or absence of water sports in a hotel doesn't really matter as you can arrange them virtually anywhere.

to all sorts of life including blue-spotted stingrays, marbled groupers, turtles and crocodile fish.

Dive centres

The following **dive centres** are PADI-accredited and reliable. Use others at your own risk. When comparing prices, check for VAT (twenty percent) and per dive or per day supplements for Mnemba Atoll ($15–40) and Leven Bank ($15–20).

East Africa Diving & Watersports Center *Jambo Brothers Bungalows*, Nungwi ℡ 0747/416425 or 0747/420588, ⓦ www.diving-zanzibar.com. A cheap German-run company running courses up to Dive Master. Basic costs excluding supplements: Open Water $350, ten dives $230.

Ras Nungwi Diving *Ras Nungwi Beach Hotel*, Nungwi ℡ 024/223 3767, ⓦ www .rasnungwi.com/diving. Experienced with novice divers, and, though expensive, you get high safety standards and well-equipped boats. Basic costs without supplements: Open Water $430, Advanced Open Water $330, ten dives $390.

Scuba Do Between *Kendwa Rocks* and *Sunset Bungalows*, Kendwa ℡ 0747/417157 or 0748/415179, ⓦ www.scuba-do-zanzibar.com. Kendwa's only dive outfit, and highly recommended. Courses up to Instructor, using prescriptive computer-teaching methods. Good equipment and very safety-conscious. They also dive on the south coast from *Fumba Beach Lodge* (p.153). Basic costs without supplements: Open Water $385, Advanced Open Water $275, ten dives $300.

Sensation Divers Opposite *Amaan Bungalows*, with a branch at *Nungwi Village Beach Resort*, Nungwi ℡ 0745/863634, ⓦ www.sensationdivers.com. Read the small print here: prices exclude VAT, and the supplements for Leven Bank and Mnemba can be considerable. They have private guest houses in Bagamoyo and Pemba for overnight trips, and also have Nitrox facilities enabling longer dives. Basic costs without supplements: Open Water $360, Advanced Open Water $300, ten dives $270, Nitrox course $198.

The cheaper options are scattered along the cape's **western shore**, which is good for sunsets, eating out and nightlife. Unfortunately, the stretch of beach from *Union Beach Bungalows* to beyond *Nungwi Village Beach Resort* has been trashed by clumsy attempts at hindering erosion; concrete seawalls and piles of stones aren't really what the doctor ordered. The **eastern cape** has more upmarket hotels, better beaches and benefits from sunrises. It's generally quieter than the western side but has no restaurants or bars other than those in the hotels, and walking along the beach east of the lighthouse can be unsafe at night. All hotels include breakfast in their rates. See the map on p.184 for locations.

Amaan Bungalows ℡ 024/224 0026, ⓦ www .amaanbungalows.com. An extensive sprawl of closely spaced bungalows in the central area of the western cape, neither charming nor particularly welcoming, and the rooms – even the priciest ones – are very basic. The best, just five, have shared balconies right over the sea with superb views, but smell like they have plumbing issues; others, lacking sea views, have little going for them, and the very cheapest "D" rooms should be avoided unless you can't find anywhere else for $30 a night. No sea view ❷–❹, sea view ❺

Baobab Beach Bungalows ℡ 024/223 6315 or 0747/429391, ⓦ www.baobabbeachbungalows .com. At the south end of the western shore next to a beautiful little cove and nice stretch of sand, this contains fifty decent if unexciting rooms, most set well back from the beach on an uninteresting lawn – check them out before paying, as some can be smelly. The cheapest, in rows of bungalows at the back, have verandahs. Next up are lodge rooms, in thatch-roofed two-storey buildings containing four rooms each, all with satellite TV, whilst the spacious deluxe rooms at the front have sea-view verandahs,

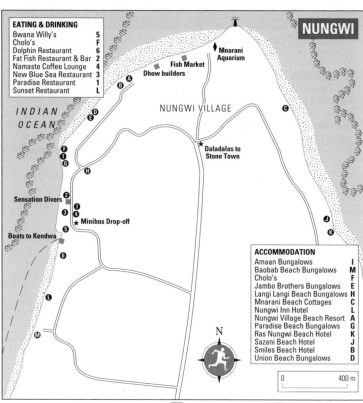

EATING & DRINKING

Bwana Willy's	5
Cholo's	F
Dolphin Restaurant	6
Fat Fish Restaurant & Bar	2
Namaste Coffee Lounge	4
New Blue Sea Restaurant	3
Paradise Restaurant	1
Sunset Restaurant	L

NUNGWI

INDIAN OCEAN

NUNGWI VILLAGE

Mnarani Aquarium

Fish Market

Dhow builders

Daladalas to Stone Town

Sensation Divers

Minibus Drop-off

Boats to Kendwa

ACCOMMODATION

Amaan Bungalows	I
Baobab Beach Bungalows	M
Cholo's	F
Jambo Brothers Bungalows	E
Langi Langi Beach Bungalows	H
Mnarani Beach Cottages	C
Nungwi Inn Hotel	L
Nungwi Village Beach Resort	A
Paradise Beach Bungalows	G
Ras Nungwi Beach Hotel	K
Sazani Beach Hotel	J
Smiles Beach Hotel	B
Union Beach Bungalows	D

N

0   400 m

▼ *Kendwa, Matemwe, Mahonda & Stone Town*

a/c and fridges. All have good bathrooms and ceiling fans. There's also Internet access, and the superbly positioned *Sunset Restaurant* (and bar). ④–⑥

Cholo's ☎ 0748/705502, ✉ fox708@yahoo .com. Run by a friendly bunch of Rastas, this is Nungwi's most chilled-out set-up, right on the beach (not on a small cliff like places to the south). Accommodation is in just three small, open-fronted *bandas* (security doesn't seem to be a problem) and there's a great *Mad Max* style bar, with good food. The music goes on till late, so it's not ideal for early risers. ①

Jambo Brothers Bungalows ☎ 0747/498380. One of Nungwi's oldest hotels, with a lovely nearby beach, but the reception staff are rather frosty and there's a lingering weariness throughout. The rooms too are tired, with cracked toilet seats and holey nets. Still, it's cheap, and most rooms have limited sea views. ②

Langi Langi Beach Bungalows ☎ 024/224 0470, ✉ langi_langi@hotmail.com. The "beach" bit is

actually across the road past their restaurant, but the fourteen rooms in semi-detached bungalows have clean modern bathrooms, a/c, fans and balconies, and the management are friendly. ④

Mnarani Beach Cottages ☎ 024/224 0494, ⓦ www.mnaranibeach.com. There's always a warm welcome at this small, intimate and efficiently run mini-resort on the quieter eastern flank of the peninsula, set beside a wonderful cove-like beach in lush gardens full of labelled plants and trees. The twelve smallish *makuti*-thatched cottages have private bathrooms, a/c and sea views. Larger, and better for families, are four two-storey apartments with kitchens and open-air upstairs bedrooms. There are sun loungers and hammocks on the beach, a bar nestled among coconut palms, and a wonderful restaurant specializing in seafood – dine on a terrace or, at night, on the beach. Snorkelling equipment is available and they have a motorized dhow for cruises and fishing. Good value. ⑤

Nungwi Inn Hotel ☏024/224 0091. An unexceptional place on the west side where you'll have to haggle to get a decent price, with a jumble of small cottages scattered around a dishevelled "lawn" doubling as a car park. Still, the rooms are well kept, have good bathrooms, and the beds even have cotton sheets. There's actually no size difference whatsoever between their standard and "large" rooms; the latter have a/c and hot water, but are within earshot of the adjacent dive centre's air compressor. One or two rooms have limited sea views, and there's a basic restaurant. ❸–❹

Nungwi Village Beach Resort ☏022/215 2187 (Dar es Salaam), ⓦwww.nungwivillage.com. Facing a broad and formerly picturesque stretch of beach, this is now fronted by an unsightly concrete seawall, against which the waves collide at high tide. This design malfunction aside, it's a pretty good place: the staff are friendly and helpful, and the rooms – all with a/c – are reasonable, standard ones in a courtyard at the back, and – at almost twice the price – sea-view ones in a number of two-storey thatched buildings by the beach, in front of a garden with hammocks slung between palm trees. The restaurant and bar are both good. ❹–❻

Paradise Beach Bungalows ☏0747/418860 or 0747/416308, ⓔshaabani_makame@hotmail.com. No bungalows here, just a two-storey block facing the ocean. It's the most popular "budget" hotel after *Amaan Bungalows* and, like it, has a less than felicitous atmosphere, thanks mainly to irritating hangers-on. The building work's not completely finished either, but outweighing most of this is the wonderful sea view from the top-floor balcony (shared by eight rooms). Rooms on the ground floor overlook a dusty parking lot. The rooms are tatty, with ripped linoleum floors, but acceptable despite the pure-nylon bedsheets. The separately managed *Paradise Restaurant* overlooks the ocean. ❸

Ras Nungwi Beach Hotel ☏024/223 3767 or 024/223 2512, ⓦwww.rasnungwi.com. Nungwi's most expensive option and only proper resort (it's the only place with a swimming pool), this 32-room complex is set on a palm-dotted outcrop beside a lovely stretch of sand. Prices depend on room size and proximity to the beach – at these prices, you might as well cough up the extra for a sea-view chalet. All rooms have a/c, fans and balconies, and are attractively decorated. The hotel also boasts several bars and restaurants (occasional live music, and seafood buffets twice a week), Internet access, and a pricey but safety-conscious dive centre (see p.183) which also offers water sports. Closed April to mid-June. Half-board. ❽–❾

Sazani Beach Hotel ☏0747/491747, ⓦwww.sazanibeach.com. A small, relaxed place on a lovely east-coast beach, but miles from the western tourist hub. There are ten well-equipped, en-suite rooms (they call them "snuggeries") in the colourful gardens, most with sea views from their verandahs. There's also a good beachside bar and restaurant. Half-board. ❻

Smiles Beach Hotel ☏024/224 0472, ⓔsmilesbeachhotel@zanzinet.com. An amusing foray into kitsch, with four two-storey Toytown houses with red tin roofs and external spiral staircases facing the sea (the beach lies beyond an unsightly seawall, as with *Nungwi Village* next door). The sixteen rooms, including triples, have a/c, sea views, phone, satellite TV and spotless bathrooms. There's a restaurant by the ocean, a boat for snorkelling or sunset cruises ($10 including drinks), and the staff are helpful and friendly. Closed April & May. ❺

Union Beach Bungalows ☏0747/454706. Next to *Jambo Brothers Bungalows* and similarly run-down but more welcoming, with ten basic twin-bed rooms, and a small restaurant (no alcohol). The ugly scatter of rocks on the top edge of the beach is a clumsy attempt to stop beach erosion. ❷

Along the western shore

In spite of the tourist trade, Nungwi itself is still very much a traditional fishing village, whose history of seafaring and dhow building remains a source of pride to many. The **dhow builders** use the stretch of beach beyond *Nungwi Village Beach Resort*; the craftsmen are used to inquisitive tourists, but ask before taking photos. Nearby, at the back of the beach, is a cluster of wooden structures that become the daily **fish market** whenever the fishermen return (times depend on the tides). Moored just offshore here are dozens of *ngalawa* outriggers.

At the northernmost tip of Unguja, Ras Nungwi, stands a **lighthouse** built in 1886, which is out of bounds. Just before the lighthouse is **Mnarani Aquarium** (daily 9am–6pm; Tsh2000), a small natural pond surrounded by porous coral ragstone into which seawater seeps at high tide. It contains dozens of endangered hawksbill and green turtles (*ng'amba* and *kasakasa* respectively), whose populations in the wild have declined dramatically over the last two decades, a direct result of the introduction of *jarife* shark nets for fishing (which have also greatly reduced shark and ray populations), and subsequent habitat damage by the use of beach seine nets and dynamite fishing. Until recently, female turtles were also traditionally hunted during their nesting periods, while their eggs were taken by fishermen for food.

The first turtles were brought to the aquarium in 1993, both for study and to provide a sanctuary for injured animals. New arrivals are bought from fishermen who occasionally catch them in their nets. Males are retained, whilst females are released when sexually mature. There's a walkway over the pond from where you can feed seaweed to the denizens; the murky water, whose level varies according to the tide, also contains grey mullet and trevally.

All these attractions are included in the locally run **Nungwi Cultural Village Tour**, which you can book at a hut outside the aquarium ($10 per person; ☏0747/863611, Ⓔnungwicvt@yahoo.com). The two-and-a-half-hour walk includes visits to old mosques, medicinal trees and plants, markets, basket-weavers, and a curious haunted saltwater well, much used for washing in the morning – the spirits evidently being late risers.

Water sports and cruises

All of Nungwi's hotels can arrange **snorkelling trips** or find you equipment to rent ($5 a day is about right), though for longer trips it would be safer to go through one of the **dive centres** reviewed on p.183. As to other water sports, it's really just a question of asking around, as outfits start up and disappear on an almost seasonal basis. For an idea of maximum prices, *Ras Nungwi Beach Hotel* charges $20 an hour for **kayaking** or **windsurfing**, and $40–65 for half- or full-day trips to **Mnemba Atoll** for snorkelling. You should be able to get the same things for about half those prices elsewhere. *Ras Nungwi Beach Hotel* is the only place to offer **water-skiing** however: $50 for fifteen minutes.

A place on a **sunset dhow cruise** can be booked through any hotel; the cost is generally $10–15 without drinks or snacks, $15–20 with.

Eating and drinking

Nungwi's **nightlife** is Zanzibar's liveliest, with plenty of bars to choose from along the western cape, and impromptu moonlit drumming sessions on the beach. The string of **restaurants** along the same section are one of Nungwi's main attractions, where – unlike the hotels – competition has succeeded in keeping standards high and prices low. Overall, they're quite similar both in their *makuti*-roofed appearance and menus (pizzas, pasta, seafood with rice), so choose by location. The best are directly on the beach or on small rocky headlands with wooden terraces, both with beguiling views. Most restaurants have daily specials chalked up on boards by the beach. Order early for things not on the menu (in the morning for dinner, for example), as the cook will have to tell the fishermen

Buying souvenirs

Please do not buy seashells, sea horses or other **marine souvenirs** in Nungwi, or elsewhere, no matter what the growing number of vendors might tell you. Apart from the trade being illegal, both internationally and in Zanzibar (not that you'd ever guess it), the collection of shells for the tourist trade kicks off a very damaging chain reaction on the already brittle coral ecosystem.

what to catch. If you're really on a budget, there's an unnamed local bar serving unexceptional chips with over-fried fish (Tsh1000) just north of *Cholo's*.

Bwana Willy's On wooden decking extending over the beach from a low headland on the western shore, this is a great bar for chilling out: delicious views, great cappuccino, huge comfy sofas, and even swings at the bar. Food should be available once the adjacent *Kigoma Hotel* is rebuilt.

Cholo's Right on the beach, this is Rasta heaven, and easily Nungwi's weirdest and funkiest place, constructed almost entirely from flotsam. The seats are canoes, the bar is a dhow's prow, and there's a cool "chill-out" zone on stilts above it. Drinks, including beers, fresh juices and cocktails (including a very good "Banana Blowjob") are reasonably priced, and the limited seafood menu is good, whether for lunch (Tsh4000–6000 a plate, including *pilau* with fish of the day) or, better, for dinner, when you can eat on the beach by a campfire (Tsh7000) or in the chill-out zone above (Tsh10,000) – dinner should be booked by lunchtime.

Dolphin Restaurant One of the cheaper places for eating out with Swahili favourites like banana curries, together with seafood and pizzas (mostly around Tsh3000–3500), and toasted sandwiches. There's also a bar, and reggae prevails.

Fat Fish Restaurant & Bar Wonderful views from the wooden terrace, and – if you're missing it – satellite TV. This tends to be one of the main nightspots in high season (discos most likely Tues & Fri). The menu isn't too spectacular, and slightly more expensive than elsewhere, with burgers or sandwiches at Tsh4000–5500 and pizzas Tsh6000–7000, though the half-kilo grilled lobster is reasonable value at Tsh17,000. It also offers a number of Indian dishes.

Namaste Coffee Lounge Next to *Amaan Bungalows* on the land side of the road (no views), this is a fine place for breakfast or snacks (up to 8pm), with juices and smoothies, freshly ground Kilimanjaro Arabica (one of the world's most subtle coffees), also served as espresso or cappuccino, lots of North American-style cookies, brownies and cakes, including a famous chocolate cake (all around Tsh2000), and a pleasant "ethnic"-style dining lounge in which to indulge.

🏃 **New Blue Sea Restaurant** Like the adjacent *Fat Fish*, this enjoys a wonderfully romantic view from its wooden terrace, and has plenty of tables with unobstructed sea views. The big speciality is pizza, courtesy of a wood-fired oven (mostly Tsh4500), though other dishes (around Tsh5500) are alluring too, including a wide variety of barbecued fish, Thai-style calamari (with lemongrass, garlic and soy sauce), typical mainland Tanzanian *mishkaki* (grilled skewers of goat meat) served with peanut butter or hot sauce, and half-lobsters from Tsh13,000 to Tsh23,000 depending on size. Drinkers are welcome, and they also do cocktails. Closed May.

Paradise Restaurant *Paradise Beach Bungalows*. The menu here is identical to that at *New Blue Sea* and by and large similarly priced, though crab or prawns will cost you Tsh8000. Particularly good is the grilled seafood platter, which includes lobster, crayfish, crab, calamari, octopus and fish (Tsh20,000; enough for two people). The sea-view terrace, looking north and west, is smaller than at other places, so come early for a table right at the edge. It also functions as a bar, with a preference for Tanzanian sounds.

Sunset Restaurant *Baobab Beach Bungalows*. Another gorgeously sited place under a huge *makuti* roof by the beach and with sweeping views. There are also tables under parasols on the low bluff beside it, and sun loungers on the beach. Drinks are slightly over the odds for Nungwi, but meals cost a little less, and include an excellent three-course seafood platter (Tsh17,000; or Tsh27,000 for four courses including lobster) and good starters (Tsh2500–3000: the pumpkin soup and crab or bisque soup are both worth trying). Good selection of French and South African wines, at a fairly standard Tsh20,000 per bottle.

Listings

Bicycles can be rented cheaply from locals and hotels. Tourist prices average $10 a day – more reasonable would be $5.

Car and motorbike rental Nungwi Travel, *Amaan Bungalows* (daily 8am–6pm; ☏024/224 0026, ⓦwww.amaanbungalows.com) sublets vehicles: $50/day for a car ($65 with driver), $35/day for a motorbike. Needs to be arranged at least a day in advance to give them time to sort out licenses.

However, they're not transparent about insurance arrangements in case of an accident – read the small print carefully, and ensure that everything that has been agreed is explicitly mentioned in the contract.
Health The larger hotels have doctors on call. For anything complicated go to Stone Town.

Internet Internet Club, *Amaan Bungalows* (daily 8am–8pm; $1 for 30min).

Money Exchange rates in Nungwi are ten to fifteen percent worse than in Stone Town. If you're stuck, Internet Club at *Amaan Bungalows* changes cash and travellers' cheques (daily 8am–8pm). Cash advances on credit cards, at similarly bad rates plus seven percent commission, are made at Nungwi Cards Assistance Point beside *Nungwi Inn Hotel* (Mon–Sat 9am–5.30pm) – you're paid in shillings. Credit cards are accepted by the more expensive hotels.

Supermarkets No supermarkets as such, but touristy things like sun lotion, shades and imported snacks (Pringles, chocolates) are sold at Haala Shop at *Nungwi Inn Hotel*.

Telephones Nungwi Cards Assistance Point at *Nungwi Inn Hotel* (Mon–Sat 9am–5.30pm) charges $3/min for international calls, Tsh300–500 for national.

Travel agent Nungwi Travel, *Amaan Bungalows* ☎024/224 0026, ⓦwww.amaanbungalows.com (daily 8am–6pm).

Kendwa

Compared to Nungwi, **KENDWA** – a few kilometres southwest – is refreshingly low-key, with a lovely wide beach deep enough for swimming at all tides, several hotels geared to budget and mid-range travellers, and famed full-moon beach parties. There are no noisy water sports, and nothing much to do except swim, snorkel or dive, and lounge around in a hammock. It's the place to head to if Nungwi feels too busy, brash or expensive, although things may not remain like this forever: one developer has seen it fit to blot the northern part of the beach with an all-inclusive package resort (thankfully largely out of sight). With Zanzibar running ever faster after tourist dollars, enjoy Kendwa now before it's too late.

Practicalities

Kendwa lies 1km west of the road to Nungwi along a very rocky track. Daily tourist **minibuses** are operated by *Kendwa Rocks* and *Sunset Bungalows* (both Tsh5000); they leave Stone Town in the morning at 8am, and turn back at 10.30am. Cheaper is to catch a #116 Nungwi **daladala** from the west side of Creek Road in Stone Town (roughly 2hr; Tsh1200–1500); get off at the sign-posted junction for Kendwa and walk the remaining kilometre.

Getting there **from Nungwi**, 3.5km to the north, is easiest on *Kendwa Rocks'* motorboat, which leaves from the beach next to *Bwana Willy's* between 10am and 10.30am, coinciding with the arrival of tourist minibuses from Stone Town (it leaves Kendwa at 9am). It's free if you stay with them, Tsh1000 otherwise. Private boats – just ask around – sometimes sail to Kendwa (Tsh3000 per person). There are no boats when sea conditions are rough. **Walking along the beach** is possible at low tide, but tourists have been mugged in the past, so don't walk if you're carrying valuables.

Accommodation

With the exception of the ugly *La Gemma Dell' Est* all-inclusive resort in the north, Kendwa's **hotels** are all quite intimate, even if they've been busy adding more bungalows and edging up their prices, and a good deal of the old hippy-bliss style still survives. For snorkelling and **scuba diving**, there's the recommended Scuba Do dive centre (see p.183). The hotels can also arrange snorkelling, and dhow cruises with local fishermen. **Internet access** is possible at *Kendwa Rocks* (Tsh2000/30min).

The following hotels are listed from north to south, and cover just under one kilometre of beachfront. Breakfast is included in room rates.

Les Toits de Palme ☏0747/418548. Kendwa's cheapest, with eight or nine basic, palm-thatched beach *bandas* (four of which are for guests) sharing a bathroom, plus six rooms in three small and spartan en-suite bungalows on the coral bluff, facing the sea. Cheap meals available (Tsh2500–3500). ❶–❷

White Sands Beach Hotel ☏0747/480987, ⓦwww.zanzibar-white-sands-hotel.com. A nicely relaxing, unpretentious and well-run place with stylishly decorated if rather bare rooms. There are three kinds, all on top of the coral bluff behind the beach: small and cosy ones in thatched cottages at the back with "cold" water, slightly bigger cottages with hot water, and – the biggest – four rooms in two cottages at the front with huge double beds and good views. There are hammocks slung between tamarisk trees on the beach, and a beautifully designed restaurant and bar. ❸–❹

Sunset Bungalows ☏0747/414647, ⓔinfo@sunsetbungalows.com (can also be booked through *Malindi Lodge* in Stone Town; see p.90). Six two-room bungalows facing each other at the back of the sandy beach (no real sea views though, as they're side-on), and more on top of the coral bluff. The rooms, decorated with colourful *kangas*, are small but have enough space for four-poster

beds. Triples cost just $5–10 more. Bar and restaurant on the beach. ❸–❹

Kendwa Rocks ☏0747/415475 or 0747/415527, ⓦwww.kendwarocks.com. Mellow Rastafarian-run place for a quiet and affordable getaway, with a range of accommodation including cheap "dorms" ($10–13 per person) in very basic palm-thatch *bandas*, the best being the two at the back of a sandy clearing behind the beach. Also in the clearing are eight coconut-wood bungalows on stilts, whilst on the coral headland at the back are slightly more expensive stone bungalows (some triples too) with the benefit of fans, reproduction antiques, four-posters with box nets and verandahs, but not all with sea views. The bar and restaurant is on the beach. "Dorms" ❶, bungalows ❸

Amaan Kendwa Beach Resort ☏0747/492552, ⓔamaankendwa@hotmail.com (can also be booked through *Jambo Guest House* in Stone Town; see p.87). Thirty-eight rooms, most in large two-room cottages sharing terraces in a scrubby garden on the coral cliff above the beach. Although the hotel claims that most rooms have sea views, only ten in the front row (also with a/c) are worth spending the extra $15 on. Good beach restaurant and bar (the *Titanic*), Internet access ($2/hr) and a forex with bad rates except for dollars cash. ❹–❺

Eating and drinking

Each hotel has its own bar, restaurant and musical tastes; you're welcome at any. The following are directly on the beach, and have wonderful views from their open sides. **Full-moon beach parties** are held at *Kendwa Rocks* (free entry), who also offer a distinctly provocative "booze cruise" most evenings at 5.30pm, for $15. As with hotels, the following restaurants are listed from north to south.

Sunset Bungalows Another good beach-restaurant-cum-bar with a youthful vibe, the menu here – just four or five dishes (usually Tsh5000) – is displayed on a blackboard. Dishes are well picked: things like grilled calamari in ginger sauce, marinated chicken skewers, or pan-fried beef (beef being something of a novelty on Zanzibar), and there's chocolate cake to finish. In addition to tables and comfy sofas, there are lounges and hammocks under the thatched roof, and a pool table.

Kendwa Rocks Run by reggae-loving Rastafarians, this youthful split-level *makuti*-thatched bar and restaurant is surprisingly plush in appearance, though prices remain in touch with the roots (around Tsh4000–4500 for main courses). The limited menu is based on the day's catch, and makes full use of Zanzibar's spices, though you can also be less adventurous and just go for fish and chips or seafood pasta. Barbecue buffets are held on the beach whenever it's busy. The starters are

refreshingly different, and include falafel, and fish-stuffed chapati. There's always a vegetarian dish too. The attached *Mermaid Bar* is well stocked, so perfect for cocktails (Tsh3000), and has South African wines. There's also a pool table, darts, and a traditional *bao* game.

Titanic Restaurant *Amaan Kendwa Beach Resort*. This has tables on the sand (for that sinking feeling?) rather than on a wooden terrace, and a menu (averaging Tsh6000–8000) ranging from pasta, burgers, sandwiches, grills and curries to the rather more inventive "Surf & Turf", which is tuna stir-fried with coconut, peanuts, cashews, pineapple and oyster sauce. The music is middle of the road.

White Sands Beach Hotel A very stylish place with upbeat music split into three areas: the bar, which also has swings; dining tables on the circular building's perimeter; and a wonderful lounge around a sand pit in the centre, with big rustic-style cushions, comfy loungers, and drapes for lampshades to create a magical nocturnal mood. Tingatinga painters ply their art in an adjacent building. The menu is short but well thought out, and always includes a decent vegetarian option (lasagne, for example). Expect to pay Tsh6500–8000 for things like crab claws with chilli, baked sea perch, or octopus in coconut sauce. To start, try the pleasingly tingly marinated fish, whilst to finish there's cake with whipped cream. Cocktails available.

Fukuchani

A good excuse for a bicycle trip from Nungwi is the **Fukuchani ruins**, 11km to the south. The ruins are signposted across a football field facing Tumbatu Island, just beyond Fukuchani village on the west side of the road. Whilst not overly impressive, the remains of a large sixteenth-century coral ragstone house are in good condition; most of the thick defensive walls still stand and carved door-arches and musket slots remain visible. Locals say the house was built by Portuguese (ask for *Nyumba la Wareno* – the Portuguese house – if you can't find the site), but archeologists ascribe them to the Swahili civilization. The site is believed to occupy that of a much older settlement, perhaps dating back to the ninth century.

Tumbatu Island

A few kilometres off the northwestern seaboard of Unguja is the eight-kilo-metre-long, dagger-shaped **Tumbatu Island**, whose inhabitants are famed for their pride and aloofness when dealing with strangers. Tumbatu's society is tightly knit, as typified by the closely built houses of its two towns, Jongowe and Kichangani, and in the curious fact that the towns – barely 3km from each other – have somehow evolved their own separate dialects.

Their inhabitants' claims to be direct descendants of ancient Persian kings and to speak the purest form of Kiswahili have some justification. Oral histories say that a Persian people by the name of Bin Umayr arrived in the ninth century, and indeed Tumbatu's southeastern corner contains extensive ruins of Persian-style buildings, including a mosque, the oldest of which may possibly date back to that time. But the Persian heritage is confusing when viewed through manu-scripts, which have a flotilla led by a prince named **Yusuf bin Alawi** arriving from Basra (now in southern Iraq) in the year 1204. The confusion stems from the prince's family name, Alawi, which is Arabian rather than Persian. The extensive ruins of **Makutani**, a stone town that may have been Zanzibar's first capital, date from that time.

Around the same time, a group of mainland Africans led by a man named **Chongo** settled in the south of the island at Jongowe (formerly Chongowe). Stormy early relations between the two groups of settlers gradually disappeared through intermarriage, which has created the present-day Tumbatu people. By the twelfth century, Tumbatu was one of the most important settlements on the East African coast, and for much of its history functioned as an independent state, distinct from Unguja and the mainland, only finally losing its independence in 1856. Indeed, Tumbatu ruled over northern Unguja for several centuries, and even now many people in Tumbatu consider that Unguja belongs to them.

Visitors with a genuine interest in the history and traditions of Tumbatu – and with more than a smattering of Kiswahili – will find the place fascinat-ing, but the majority of tourists are definitely not welcome. Day-trips are best arranged through Blue Dolphins Tours & Safaris in Stone Town (see p.129).

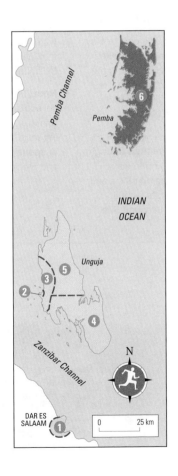

6

Pemba

CHAPTER 6 # Highlights

* **Indian Ocean flights** The twenty-minute flight to Pemba from Unguja or the Tanzanian mainland is short but glorious, giving spectacular views of coral reefs, mangroves and sandbanks. See p.195 & p.215

* **Scuba diving** The coral reefs encircling Pemba are ranked by many as being among the western Indian Ocean's finest and most exciting for scuba-divers. See p.196

* **Misali Island** Gorgeous beaches, nature trails through mangroves, flying foxes, snorkelling, sacred caves and, perchance, pirate Captain Kidd's buried treasure. See p.201

* **Pujini ruins** One of several sets of ruins on Pemba, these of a medieval tyrant's citadel. See p.204

* **Bullfighting** The most enter-taining reminder of two centu-ries of Portuguese rule, and with no violence other than that inflicted on the hapless bullfighters. See p.206

* **Ngezi Forest** The biggest of several surviving patches of primeval forest, with walk-ing trails and the possibility of spotting flying foxes, owls and monkeys. See p.211

△ Moored boat, near Chake Chake

Pemba

The island of **PEMBA**, 48km northeast of Unguja and little more distant from the Tanzanian mainland, is Zanzibar's forgotten half, traditionally conservative, deeply religious, and far removed from Unguja's commercialization. Measuring 67km from north to south and 22km from east to west, Pemba's highest point is no more than 100m above sea level, yet with its low hills gouged by gullies and entered by snaking, mangrove-lined creeks, the island presents a lush and fertile contrast to much of Unguja, and aptly fits the name given to it by the Arab geographer Yakut ibn Abdallah al-Rumi (1179–1229), who called it *Jazirat al-Khadhra*, the Green Island – which holiday brochures have since changed to the Emerald Island.

Sadly, whilst Unguja is experiencing an economic boom, Pemba – which has always been peripheral to the concerns of Zanzibar's Unguja-based government – is going back in time, and **poverty** is widespread. Per capita income is Tanzania's lowest, and the child mortality rate among the country's highest. Meanwhile, the island's lamentable infrastructure continues to deteriorate: most roads are pitted with potholes, the airport's only fire tender recently bade the world adieu, and there's not a single working streetlight on the island. Power cuts too are a daily reality, and the water supply is more likely to be trucked in than arrive through pipes. Not surprising, then, that Pemba is the main stronghold of the opposition party, the **Civic United Front (CUF)**, support for which has only deepened Pemba's marginalization. **Political unrest** and related violence as a result of all these factors has been considerable, especially in the run-up to elections, the next of which are due in 2010.

Pemba has three main towns, all on the west coast: the capital **Chake Chake** in the centre close to the airport; **Mkoani** in the south, where most ferries tie up; and **Wete**, a dhow port in the north. There's not an awful lot to do in any of these, but they do contain most of Pemba's accommodation and are good bases for exploring further afield. Rewarding targets include the primeval **Ngezi Forest** in the north, a scatter of atmospheric **ruined cities** which together tell the story of much of the Swahili coast, a handful of deserted if difficult to access beaches (part of their charm), beautiful offshore islets, and great scuba-diving.

Changing money on Pemba

Change all the money you'll need before coming, as changing cash can take half a day, and there's no way of changing travellers' cheques or getting cash advances on credit cards; though payment for scuba diving and upmarket accommodation can be made by cheque or plastic as long as this is arranged beforehand.

Despite this wealth of attractions, there are rarely more than a few dozen tourists on the island at any one time, and **tourist facilities** are extremely limited. Almost half the island's **restaurants** have closed down over the last few years, leaving barely more than a dozen, and by any standards Pemba is a gastronomic wilderness for those without a *mama* to cook for them, in complete contrast to Unguja. Given that affordable bed-space is limited, too, **accommodation** – and indeed scuba diving – should be booked before arrival. Public **transport** is

limited to shared pick-ups and minibuses along the main asphalt roads; beyond these, you'll need to walk, or rent a car, taxi or bicycle. Pemba's **opening hours** are notoriously capricious, even for banks: the best time for finding things open is in the morning. The **long rains**, during which time it can pour constantly for weeks, fall between March and June, a little later than on Unguja.

For information on **flying to Pemba**, see p.77 & p.215; for information on **getting there by ferry**, see p.123 (from Stone Town) and p.77 (from Dar es Salaam).

Chake Chake and around

If you're flying in, you'll land at Karume Airport close to Pemba's capital, **Chake Chake**. It's the most interesting of the island's three towns, and even has a modest but fascinating **museum** in an Omani fortress. For most visitors, Chake Chake serves only as a base for **scuba diving and snorkelling**, both of which can be exceptional around **Misali Island** – an unspoilt gem of a place said to have been where Captain Kidd buried his loot. Other good excursions include the ruins of a medieval tyrant's citadel at **Pujini**, the ancient ruined city of **Quanbalu** on Ras Mkumbuu peninsula, and a lovely series of **beaches** on the east coast near Vitongoji.

Chake Chake

Pemba's capital and largest town, **CHAKE CHAKE** ("Chake" for short), lies about halfway up the west coast at the end of a long and silty mangrove-lined creek. The town is lively by Pemba's standards, and contains a small and busy **market** along with a well-preserved **Arab quarter** that resembles a very miniature Stone Town (two streets and a few alleyways). Chake's history dates back at least to the Portuguese occupation, as evidenced by the style of the town's **fortress** – now a museum – which was rebuilt by the Omanis on the original Portuguese foundations.

Arrival and information

All flights to Pemba – from Stone Town, Dar es Salaam and Tanga – land at **Karume Airport**, 6km southeast of Chake Chake; taxis wait outside and charge Tsh3000–5000 for a ride into town. There are also a few daladalas (#105 or 106 marked "U" or "U. Ndege") to Chake Chake, but no guarantee of your arrival coinciding with them. Arriving by **daladala** from Wete or Mkoani, you'll be dropped in Chake Chake either at the junction by the Esso petrol station, or at the stand behind the market.

The guest book at the *Old Mission Lodge* is a good source of **information**, as is the management there (on Pemba in general as well as matters sub-aquatic). A detailed government-produced **map** of Pemba containing a mass of useful contextual information on the reverse (plus useless tourist listings from 1992) can

For an introduction to scuba diving and snorkelling in Zanzibar, see p.46.

Surrounded almost entirely by reefs, innumerable atolls and coral-fringed isles, Pemba's spectacular underwater kingdom – which contains almost half of Tanzania's coral reefs – is one of the world's most exhilarating **scuba-diving** destinations. The caverns, drop-offs, swim-throughs and immense coral gardens contain a bacchanalian profusion of marine life, all of which attracts the larger **pelagics** (open water fish) in abundance. Big schools of surgeonfish, shoals of barracuda and chevron, kingfish, wahoo, tuna and jacks, giant trevally, giant groupers and Napoleon wrasse can all be found, and diving companies will know the best places for turtles (all year), dolphins (best Dec–April), and – with a good deal of luck – migrating whale sharks (June–Aug) or whales (Aug–Sept). The **best time for diving**, offering the calmest conditions and clearest visibility, is from October to March. **Snorkelling** is best off Misali Island and at Uvinje Gap and Njao Gap in the north, though it's not cheap as all snorkelling reefs require a boat for access: count on $40 per person for a half or full day.

Underwater **visibility** is generally excellent, averaging 20–40m and often increasing to 60–70m on incoming tides, even during the rains. However, the steep drop-offs and strong currents that make such exciting drift dives out of most of Pemba's sites are also **potentially dangerous**, and mean that beginners or inexperienced divers should stick to Unguja, whose reefs are considerably more sheltered. The tragic disappearance of five divers off Pemba's Misali Island in 2005 was a sad reminder of the dangers inherent in scuba diving.

Probably the best reef for novices is **Uvinje Gap** southwest of Wete, which has lots of fish around shallow coral heads (bommies), and magnificent gorgonian sea fans lower down. Another good all-round site is **Njao Gap** in the north, which gives good odds on seeing green or hawksbill turtles. For experienced divers, Pemba has two indisputable highlights. The dreamlike **Manta Point** west of Wete is the tip of an underwater mountain that rises to within five to eight metres of the surface; its dense coral formations, including brittle leaf and gorgonian sea fans, attract a teeming profusion of life including turtles and the occasional reef shark, though unconscionable fishermen from Kojani Island on Pemba's east coast have annihilated the eponymous giant mantas that used to scratch their bellies on the peak to rid themselves of parasites. Also good, but with strong currents lower down are a number of places around **Misali Island**, which enjoy exceptional visibility, pristine corals and the chance of spotting sharks, manta rays and either green or hawksbill turtles. Although this is where the divers were lost in 2005, the sites had been dived virtually every day for years before then without incident, so you shouldn't let safety fears prevent you from diving here. Exhilarating **drift dives** include Emerald Reef

be bought at the Survey Department of the Commission for Lands & Environment (Ofisi ya Mazingira; Mon–Fri 7.30am–3.30pm; Tsh3500) in Machomane; turn right at the junction 2km north of Chake Chake, and right again at *Pattaya Guest House*. Swahili Divers (see above) may have a copy to consult.

Accommodation

Bucket showers are the norm as Chake Chake's water supply, pumped up from bore holes, depends on the sorry antics of the electricity company. Room rates include breakfast.

Government Hotel (*Hotel ya Chake Chake*) In the centre ☎ 024/245 2069. Seven twin-bed rooms, often full, all with fans and nets. There's also a bar, and an achingly slow restaurant. You might not be pleased to know that locals pay three times less for a room. ❷ in the very south (giant barracuda and hammerhead sharks), the southern wall of Fundo Reef southeast of Manta Point (superb corals, shallow caverns and spectacular overhangs from 5m to below sport-diving depth), and Kokota Reef in the same area, which lends itself to **night-time drift dives** for spotting Spanish dancers, a species of nudibranch (sea slug) that gets its name from its reddish fringed "skirt" and graceful movements.

Lastly, there are a couple of **wrecks** at Panza Point in the south, the more photogenic one – a Greek freighter that foundered in 1969 – lying in shallow water. Strong currents are present at both sites.

Dive centres
Pemba has four PADI-accredited **diving centres** offering tuition, and one live-aboard. Single dives average $40–50, and two dives in one day $80–100.

Dive 710 *Fundu Lagoon*, Wambaa Beach in the south ⊕024/223 2926, ⊛www .fundulagoon.com. Solid reputation, state-of-the-art equipment and good instructors for PADI courses at all levels, but you'll have to stay at the sadistically expensive *Fundu Lagoon* (see p.207). Closed mid-April to mid-June.

One Earth Diving *Manta Reef Lodge*, Ras Kigomasha in the far northwest ⊕0747/423930, ⊛www.mantareeflodge.com. Very well-regarded and reliable operator offering the full range of PADI courses; staying at the lodge is expensive (from $240 a double), but Jambo Tours & Safaris (p.201) can arrange daily transport from Chake Chake. Open Water costs $465; Advanced Open Water $340; ten-dive package (accommodation not included) $350.

Pemba Afloat Moored at Njao Inlet west of Wete ⊛www.pembaisland.com. Based in three twenty-metre ketches, this is a great live-aboard operation (with good dive sites almost under your feet) where full-board accommodation costs $100 per person. Diving is extra: $40–60 per dive, or $350 for Open Water tuition, $250 for Advanced Open Water.

Swahili Divers *Old Mission Lodge*, Chake Chake ⊕024/245 2786, ⊛www .swahilidivers.com. Experienced and reliable, and reasonably priced if you buy a package that includes accommodation. They offer all PADI courses up to Dive Master, and tuition in underwater photography. Prices are quoted in euros: Open Water with five nights full board costs €500 (approx $600); a combined Open Water and Advanced Open Water course with seven nights full board is €750 (approx $900); and a ten-dive package with six nights full board costs €445–545 (approx $535–655). They also have a dhow for live-aboard diving trips over three to seven days.

Le-Tavern Hotel 200m north of the *Government Hotel* ⊕024/245 2660. This modern two-storey place is a reasonable option, despite its non-communicative staff, with en-suite or shared bathrooms, the better rooms with views over town. ❶

Mamy Hotel & Restaurant Machomane; turn right at the junction 2km north of town, right at *Pattaya Guest House*, left after 200m ⊕0747/432789. A little out of the way, this basic but pleasant and friendly family-run guest house is one of Zanzibar's cheapest, and perfectly decent if you can live with its horrid green lightbulbs. There are just four large rooms, all with big beds, round nets and small ceiling fan. The one en-suite room

isn't worth spending double on, especially as its bathtub serves as the hotel's water tank. Also has safe parking, and food to order. ❶

Old Mission Lodge (Swahili Divers) 300m north of the *Government Hotel* ⊕024/245 2786, ⊛www.swahilidivers.com. Set in a restored Quaker Mission, this is Chake's most atmospheric choice, though the dorm beds are very pricey at approximately $24 (prices are in euros). Other rooms are much better value and it's these that are recommended. Facilities include a bar, massage, use of bicycles, an excellent library, good food, and – above all – their diving centre. Dorm ❸, rooms ❹–❺

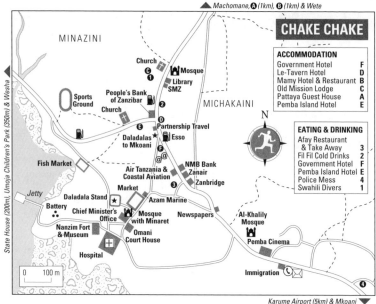

Machomane, Ⓐ (1km), Ⓑ (1km) & Wete

MINAZINI

CHAKE CHAKE

ACCOMMODATION
Government Hotel	F
Le-Tavern Hotel	D
Mamy Hotel & Restaurant	B
Old Mission Lodge	C
Pattaya Guest House	A
Pemba Island Hotel	E

EATING & DRINKING
Afay Restaurant & Take Away	3
Fil Fil Cold Drinks	2
Government Hotel	F
Pemba Island Hotel	E
Police Mess	4
Swahili Divers	1

MICHAKAINI

Church
Mosque
Library
SMZ
Sports Ground
People's Bank of Zanzibar
Church
Partnership Travel
Daladalas to Mkoani
Esso
Fish Market
Air Tanzania & Coastal Aviation
Zanair
NMB Bank
Market
Zanbridge
Jetty
Daladala Stand
Azam Marine
Battery
Chief Minister's Office
Mosque with Minaret
Newspapers
Al-Khalily Mosque
Nanzim Fort & Museum
Omani Court House
Pemba Cinema
Hospital
Immigration

State House (200m), Umoja Children's Park (350m) & Washa

0   100 m

Karume Airport (5km) & Mkoani ▼

Pattaya Guest House Machomane; turn right at the junction 2km north of town and it's 100m on the left ☎0747/852970. Six largish twin-bed rooms with fans and decent-sized nets, all but one room sharing bathrooms. It's a bit run-down and nylon bedsheets aren't too clever in this climate, but it's okay and the Western-style toilets still have their seats. ❶

Pemba Island Hotel 50m west of the People's Bank of Zanzibar ☎024/245 2215, ✉islandhotelevergreen@hotmail.com. A clean, modern four-storey building with lots of en-suite rooms (smallish mosquito nets); those with two beds are $10 and have better bathrooms. All have a/c, fan, fridge and satellite TV, but creature comforts hardly compensate for the hiked-up rates, and some of the toilets are missing their seats. ❸–❹

The Town

Chake Chake contains a strange but attractive fusion of buildings and is well worth a wander. The atmosphere is relaxed and friendly, and people are genuinely pleased – and curious – to see tourists poking around. Starting in the centre, head for the **market** (daily from 7am). Aside from a selection of herbs and spices, you can buy aromatic essential oils and tasty clove honey (*asali*). You can also purchase colourfully painted straw plate-covers that look like hats, and aromatic *halua* – a sticky boiled goo (think Turkish Delight) inherited from the Omanis, made from wheat gluten, nuts, spices, and a whole lot of sugar. At one corner of the market is an **old mosque** with a softly rounded minaret. Following the narrow road past the mosque brings you to the **Chief Minister's Office**, a bizarre, pale blue building dominated by a round tower studded with protruding hollow cylinders. Opposite is the glorious colonial-era **Omani Court House**, with an impressive carved door and clock tower with a defunct clock.

Continuing along the same street and turning right at the junction brings you to the diminutive **Nanzim Fort**, with its commanding view over the creek. The fort was built in the eighteenth century by the Omanis, but incorporates the foundations of a Portuguese fortress built in 1594. The square towers are an indication of the Portuguese influence, as the Omanis generally preferred round ones. Much of the fort was demolished in the early 1900s to make way for the present hospital; the remainder saw use as a prison and then police barracks before falling into disrepair. Part of what's left has been converted into a charming **museum** (Mon–Fri 8.30am–4.30pm, Sat & Sun 9am–4pm; Tsh2000), its entrance through a battered but sturdy wooden door. The museum, which also houses the Pemban national archives, consists of just three small rooms containing very well presented displays in both English and Kiswahili on most aspects of life in Pemba. Room 1 covers the island's archeological sites in surprising detail, and has medieval pottery, some coins and other finds; Room 2 is dedicated to dhows and seafaring; and Room 3 covers Zanzibar's rulers, the accent being on their work – or lack of – in Pemba.

Walking downhill from the fort towards the creek are the remains of the fort's battery on your right, comprising some rubble and a couple of rusty cannons. Further along, past a small football ground, is the **State House**, hidden behind a lush garden (no admission or photography). Beyond this, on the left, is a strange blue concrete archway embracing the gate to a **funfair**. Officially called Umoja Children's Park, this is only open for fifteen evenings a year: five each for the Idd al-Fitr celebrations at the end of Ramadan, the Idd al-Haj, and Christmas and New Year.

Eating and drinking

The following **restaurants** and **bars** are pretty much all there is apart from street-food vendors. That said, the cheapest and some of the best eats are indeed at the **street-food stalls** on the main road between *Old Mission Lodge* and the *Government Hotel*. Busiest at night, this is where you can find everything from the usual *chipsi mayai* (chip omelette) and goat meat (*mishkaki*; served, if you're lucky, with a spicy potato stew) to grilled octopus (*pweza*), bite-sized fish cakes, various juices (try tamarind: *kwaju*), and grilled squid and fish. To finish off, track down one of the **coffee vendors** who serve scaldingly hot and bitter coffee in tiny Omani-style porcelain cups for Tsh50 or less.

Afay Restaurant & Take Away In the town centre, this is the only local restaurant in Chake. It makes good simple food (little over Tsh2500), but the menu is in the weary "rice with fish, chicken with chips" tradition. Order early for a little more choice or for special requests. No alcohol.

Fil-Fil Cold Drinks On the main road near *Le-Tavern Hotel*. Does what it says on the tin, and nothing more. No alcohol.

Government Hotel Meals here require at least half a day's notice, but most people (well, a handful) come for its relatively cheap beer – it's one of only three bars in town. More fun when there's a power cut and people can't tell you're a tourist.

Pemba Island Hotel 50m west of the People's Bank of Zanzibar. The third-floor restaurant here has good views and its typically Swahili menu is

reasonably priced (mostly Tsh4000–5000), including octopus with coconut sauce and chicken *pilau*. No alcohol.

Police Mess 1km along the Mkoani road. Has beer, Konyagi (papaya gin) and a limited selection of other local spirits. Don't indulge too much as you'll have to walk back, and keep your opinions on Zanzibari politics under your hat. May not admit tourists whenever the political situation is incendiary.

Swahili Divers Run by a friendly bunch of *wazungu* well attuned to foreign tastes, with meals taken at a long table on the verandah. Lunch is limited to a salad and sandwich (Tsh5000). Dinners (Tsh11,000) are more substantial three-course affairs: nothing fancy, but filling and always with a vegetarian option. Tasty seafood buffets feature on Wednesday and Saturday. Beer available, making this the town's finest bar.

Listings

Airline tickets Coastal Aviation is opposite NMB bank (☎0747/418343); ZanAir is beside the bank (☎024/245 2990 or 0747/420760, ✉zanairpemba@zanzinet.com). Air Tanzania has its office beside Coastal (☎024/245 2162). See also Jambo Tours & Safaris and Partnership Travel on p.201.

Cinema Pemba Cinema, despite its mind-bogglingly dilapidated appearance, is still open and provides a unique and highly recommended experience. Amazingly, it still manages to get hold of real celluloid: weekday evenings (6pm) feature Bollywood flicks and weekends have third-rate American dross; a great night out for Tsh500.

Ferry tickets The one-stop shop is Partnership Travel on the main road near the *Government Hotel* (☎024/245 2278), who deal with all ferries, though you may pay a small mark-up. To book direct: SMZ (☎024/245 2349) next to the library, for the MV *Mapinduzi* and MV *Maendeleo*; Zanbridge (☎0747/420132), 200m south of the Esso filling station, for the MV *Sepideh*; Azam Marine (no phone) by the market for the MV *Serengeti*.

Football The local team, Manchester, plays at the imposing Chinese-built Gombani Stadium 3km along the Wete road. There are no fixed match days; entrance is a few hundred shillings.

Hospital The government-run Chake Chake Hospital beside Nanzim Fort (☎024/245 2311) is very run-down; the one in Mkoani is better. There's a good pharmacy nearby. For diagnostic tests, the Public Health Laboratory in Machomane (☎024/245 2473) is reliable.

Internet access Adult Training Centre, on the main road just north of Air Tanzania (daily 7.30am–4pm; Tsh1000/hr); ZCF Internet Café, beside the *Government Hotel* (erratic hours; Tsh1000/hr).

Library The public library (Mon–Fri 8am–4pm, Sat 8am–2pm; Ramadan closes 2 hrs earlier; free) has lots of English-language works on Zanzibar and Tanzania.

Money Chake's banks are dog-slow, and can chew up to half a day for changing cash. The "best" is NMB bank on the main road. Tanzania Postal Bank at the post office handles Western Union money transfers.

Telephones TTCL is on the main road near the Esso petrol station (Tsh2500/min for international calls).

Around Chake Chake

Given Pemba's relatively small size, Chake Chake is a good base for **excursions** to virtually anywhere on or off the island. The easiest (and cheapest) beaches to get to lie beyond **Vitongoji** on Pemba's east coast, but for that desert island paradise thing, **Misali Island** is the place to go. Along with gorgeous beaches, it offers nature trails through mangroves, a rare colony of flying foxes, snorkelling, and some of East Africa's best **scuba diving** (see p.196). For the historically inclined, Misali Island could be combined with a trip to the ruined city of **Quanbalu** on the western tip of Ras Mkumbuu peninsula. Dating back over a thousand years, Quanbalu was one of East Africa's earliest towns and its first major Islamic settlement. Medieval times are represented by a fortified citadel at **Pujini**, southeast of Chake Chake, which was constructed by a wealthy tyrant.

Vitongoji

The nearest good beaches to Chake Chake are a series of sandy coves beyond **VITONGOJI** on the east coast, which offer excellent swimming at high tide and reef walking at low tide. Chake's tour operators can arrange transport, but it's much cheaper and more fun to rent a **bicycle** from one of the tour operators. Heading out from Chake Chake, take the road to Wete for 2km and turn right (southeast) at Machomane. At the end of the sealed road (1km from the junction) turn left. Vitongoji village is 5km further on. Follow the main track beyond Vitongoji to get to Liko la Ngezi beach, or branch left 2km beyond the

When arranging half- or full-day trips, go through one of the companies below, as Chake's self-appointed guides are far from reliable, and reports of theft by some of them circulate. The following also offer full days in the north, combining Ngezi Forest and Vumawimbi Beach with Tumbe fish market and nearby ruins. Prices are pretty standard, and are based on the cost of car rental ($50–60 a day including fuel and driver) plus lunch and additional expenses. The following can also fix you up with a motorbike (*pikipiki*) for around $25 a day excluding fuel.

Jambo Tours & Safaris Under *Le-Tavern Hotel*, 200m north of the *Government Hotel* ☏0747/437397 or 0747/468809. Well priced and reliable; can also book scuba diving at *Manta Reef Lodge* on Ras Kigomasha in the northwest for no mark-up. Daily 8am–4pm.

Partnership Travel On the main road near the *Government Hotel* ☏024/245 2278. Long established; negotiable prices but not unreasonable to start with. Daily 8am–4pm.

Swahili Divers *Old Mission Lodge*, 300m north of the *Government Hotel* ☏024/245 2786, ⊛www.swahilidivers.com. More expensive but the most experienced for matters aquatic; a day's snorkelling at Misali Island costs around $40. They can help you find a reliable driver-guide for terrestrial tours.

village to reach Liko la Vumba and Makoba beaches. The alternative approach is by #316 **daladala** from Chake Chake to Vitongoji, but this leaves you with a 3km walk to the nearest beach.

Misali Island

The island of **MISALI**, 17km west of Chake Chake, is a tiny fragment of coral rag rock that emerged from the ocean some fifteen thousand years ago. It's one of Pemba's highlights, offering idyllic beaches, nature trails for spotting flying foxes (bats), good snorkelling and superb diving. It also has a touch of historical romance, as the legendary pirate **Captain Kidd** is said to have used the island as a hideaway, and to have buried booty here.

A more certain treasure is Misali's rich **ecosystem**, which boasts 42 types of coral, over three hundred species of fish, a rare subspecies of vervet monkey, endangered colonies of flying foxes, nesting sites for green and hawksbill turtles, and a large if rarely seen population of nocturnal coconut crabs. In 1996, the island and its reefs became Pemba's first (and as yet only) **marine sanctuary**; in exchange for a portion of tourist revenues, local fishermen have agreed to abandon destructive fishing techniques, to respect no-go zones established for restocking and to protect the turtle nesting sites. The island is uninhabited except for the sanctuary's rangers and passing fishermen. The sanctity of the island, and its name, are explained by the legend of a **prophet** named Hadhara (meaning "knowledge" or "culture"), who appeared before Misali's fishermen and asked them for a prayer mat (*msala*). There was none, so Hadhara declared that since the island pointed towards Mecca, it would be his prayer mat.

A $5 **entrance fee**, generally not included in quotes for tours, is payable on the island. The island's **visitor centre** is on Baobab Beach where the boats pull up, and has good displays on ecology and wildlife plus information sheets that you can take with you while snorkelling or walking the trails. There's no accommodation and camping is prohibited, as is alcohol.

Snorkelling

The shallow reef around Misali is good for snorkelling, though the current can be trying for weaker swimmers and you should stay close to the shore as currents further out can be dangerously strong; ask the folks at the visitor centre for advice. For confident swimmers, a **submerged coral mountain** off the western shore is an extraordinary place; the mountain, one of four in the area, is 3–5m below sea level: you'll need a boat to get there. More accessible is the shallow reef flanking Baobab Beach, which starts a mere 10–40m from the shore. The shallower part features **conical sponges**, traditionally collected by fishermen for use as hats; further out, the reef is cut by sandy gullies and teems with life.

Nature trails

A series of nature trails has been established around the island; pick up one of the information sheets from the visitor centre. The **Mangrove Trail** can be done on foot at low tide or in combination with snorkelling. The **Intertidal Trail** (low tide only) starts at Turtle Beach on the west side of the island, and includes a

Zanzibar and the monsoon

Quanbalu is but one of several sites on Zanzibar, indeed along the entire East African coastline from Somalia to Mozambique, which owed its existence to the Indian Ocean's age-old, monsoon-driven dhow trade. The **monsoon** – its name deriving from the Arabic word for season, *mausim* – is characterized by the annual reversal of prevailing winds and ocean currents in the Indian Ocean, causing the alternation of wet and dry seasons. In East Africa, the northerly and very humid **kaskazi** monsoon blows strongest from November to March, bringing with it stifling heat and humidity, which in turn may be followed by occasional cyclonic tropical storms. The drier southerly **kusi** monsoon winds, strongest from August to October, accompany the long dry season. The monsoon's effects though are most apparent when the winds reverse direction, bringing heavy rains. In Zanzibar, the **short rains** fall in November or December, and the **long rains** (*masika*) peak in March and April, which Zanzibar's more poetic hoteliers prefer to call the "Green Season". As the rains drag on, the land becomes cooler than the ocean's surface and the winds begin to swing again, eventually sweeping across the Arabian Sea to join another monsoon wind from the Bay of Bengal, to become India's famous summer monsoon.

For many tourists, the word monsoon carries with it the promise of ineffable romance, but the reality is rather different. Rain it does, in metronomic afternoon **downpours** that drench everything, that occasionally flood entire districts (Ng'ambo, adjacent to Stone Town, is a frequent victim), that mix drinking water with sewage and cause outbreaks of cholera, and whose mildewed fingers infiltrate creaking nineteenth-century houses to bring a handful of them tumbling to the ground every year. All this is the price of Zanzibar's monsoon-gifted fertility.

The monsoon-driven trade

Historically, the rhythmical ebb and sway of the monsoon's winds and ocean currents has long facilitated seaborne **trade** in the western Indian Ocean, linking East Africa to Arabia and India, China, Malaysia and Indonesia, and even with the ancient Mediterranean empires. The monsoon trading cycle started with the *kaskazi* which swept down from Arabia and the Indian Subcontinent, bringing with it merchants and immigrants. On arriving in East Africa, the traders had several months in which to conduct business before the southerly *kusi* gathered sufficient strength to take them home. The word *kusi* itself stems from ancient times. Egypt's Queen Hatshepsut small isle connected by causeway that is popular with nesting seabirds. Mangroves and low-tide pools also feature. Another trail takes you past one of Misali's three **sacred caves**, believed by locals to be the abode of benevolent spirits. Each cave has a specially appointed traditional guardian (healer), and people leave offerings to the spirits (or to Allah) to seek intercession in worldly matters. The caves' sacred nature means that tourists should not enter if scantily dressed.

There's also a trail from Baobab Beach to Turtle Beach and to Mpapaini, whose caves contain roosts of **Pemban flying foxes** (an endangered species of bat). Go with a guide to avoid disturbing them. If you can get to Misali very early in the morning (leave before sunrise), you stand a slim chance of spotting a rare and shy subspecies of **Pemba vervet monkey**; your best bet is on the western beaches where they hunt for ghost crabs.

Ras Mkumbuu and Quanbalu

The long and narrow peninsula north of Chake Chake Bay is **Ras Mkumbuu**, its name, meaning a belt or sash, aptly describing its shape. Close to Ngagu

(reigned c.1472–58 BC) sent seaborne expeditions to "Kos" in search of gold, ebony, myrrh and animals, and the Assyrian Empire (Mesopotamia, now Iraq) knew East Africa as Kusu. Their forebears, the **Sumerians**, were trading extensively with East Africa almost five millennia ago, and bequeathed linguistic traces still discernable in contemporary Kiswahili.

The **Phoenicians**, from what's now Lebanon, were also well acquainted with what they called Azania (possibly from "Zanj", meaning Africans), having first ventured down the East African coast three thousand years ago. The anonymous *Periplus of the Erythraean Sea* (c.130–140 AD) vividly recounts the considerable trade that flourished along the coast at the time, and provides the earliest known written evidence that traders had circumnavigated the African continent – at least 1500 years before Vasco da Gama "discovered" the same. It also states that Zanzibar and the coast were subject to Arabian sovereignty, alluding to the Queen of Sheba's (Saba, now in Yemen) dalliance with **King Solomon**, whose not-so-legendary gold mines were most likely located in what's now Zimbabwe. In return for lances, hatchets, daggers and awls, and various kinds of glass, East Africa exported great quantities of ivory, rhinoceros horn, tortoiseshell (from marine turtles) and palm oil. The **Greeks**, too, came here: a report by the geographer Marinus of Tyre recounting the journey of a Greek merchant named Diogenes was referred to in Claudius Ptolemy's *Geography*, written a century or so after the *Periplus*.

Even the **Chinese** came; in 1414, East Africa received one of the most extraordinary flotillas ever seen: the **Star Raft Expedition**. Consisting of almost two hundred vessels, the largest weighing ten times more than the galleons used by Columbus in 1492, it was both a voyage of discovery, and – through the symbolic exchange of goods – a cosmic means of asserting the Ming Dynasty's Emperor's status as sovereign of the world. For much of the last millennium though, the western Indian Ocean monsoon routes were dominated by **Persians and Arabs**, whose dhows came to East Africa bearing both merchants and refugees fleeing the internecine conflicts that had taken hold of the Middle East. Naturally enough, the traders' enforced stay in East Africa led to the establishment of trading centres and East Africa's first cities. Intermarriage and the fusion of different cultures was equally inevitable, and led to the creation of the **Swahili**: a people, a language, a culture and a civilization. Lying at the heart of the Swahili world, Zanzibar could really be said to be a child of the monsoon.

village at its far western tip are the remains of East Africa's oldest known Muslim town, **Quanbalu** (or Qanbalu), which may have been founded as early as the eighth century. The town was mentioned by several early writers as one of two major trading centres on Pemba, the other being Matambwe Island, 30km north. Both sites were excavated in 1995 by a team from the British Institute in Eastern Africa who came up with radiocarbon dates for the ninth and tenth centuries.

In his historical encyclopaedia, *Meadows of Gold*, the Arab traveller Ali ibn Husayn **al-Masudi**, who stayed in Quanbalu in 916 AD, described its population as being a mixture of Muslims and "Zanj infidels", the latter with "no religious law ... every man worships what he pleases, be it a plant, an animal, or a mineral." The Muslim rulers were descendants of religious refugees from the eighth century who achieved power through force, and the extent of Quanbalu's early prosperity and importance was shown by finds of Persian and Arab pottery, Madagascan soapstone bowls and a Chinese coin.

The **ruins**, mostly from the thirteenth and fourteenth centuries but built on older foundations, include a large congregational mosque which was the largest in sub-Saharan Africa until the Great Mosque at Kilwa Kisiwani on the Tanzanian mainland pipped it in the fourteenth century. Quanbalu's mosque has an especially fine arched *mihrab*, as well as a minaret. Other remains include houses and at least fourteen tombs, some of them surmounted by chimney-like pillars and decorated with Chinese porcelain. Both the pillars and inclusion of chinaware are common throughout the Swahili coast. For reasons as yet unknown, the town fell into decline in the sixteenth century and was eventually abandoned.

Access is cheapest by road from Chake Chake (upwards of $30–40 per vehicle), though the extremely rocky trail along the peninsula means that many drivers are reluctant to take you. Your best chance is through Jambo Tours & Safaris (p.201). More romantic but much more expensive (up to $150 per group) is to come by sea: Swahili Divers (p.201) can sort you out. Quanbalu could also be combined with a snorkelling trip to Misali, as long as all people in the boat agree.

Pujini ruins

Some 10km southeast of Chake Chake, the **Pujini ruins** provide an enjoyable and fascinating half-day excursion. Pujini is the site of a citadel built during the heyday of the **Diba tribe**, who ruled eastern Pemba from the fifteenth to seventeenth centuries, and whose influence at one time spread as far as Pate in northern Kenya, Kilwa on the Tanzanian mainland, and the Comoros Islands in the Indian Ocean. The Diba are believed to be descendants of Shirazi settlers from Diba in the Persian Gulf, possibly from Diba in the present-day UAE.

Pujini was built by the tyrant Muhammad bin Abdulrahman, a merchant and pirate whose nickname, **Mkama Ndume**, means "grasper of men". The ruins (also known as Mkama Ndume) are defensively located on a hilltop and are now mostly rubble, though the presence of several old tamarind and baobab trees makes them singularly photogenic. The **mosque** is the best-preserved building, drawing worshippers from as far as Unguja. Also noteworthy is the **well**, half-filled with rubble, in the enclosure's northeastern corner. Legend has it that Mkama Ndume had two wives who were jealous of each other, so to prevent them meeting at the well he had a dividing wall built inside it. One of the wives would use a bucket and rope whilst the other descended by a staircase – still partially visible – to reach the water. More likely though is that the small chamber at the foot of the staircase was a shrine to spirits (*majini*). Carved out of the soft limestone, it contains a lamp niche and a small plaster relief of a **siwa horn**. Long, heavy and frequently ornate, they were made from ivory, brass or wood and were symbols of sovereignty and authority all along the Swahili coast and on the Arabian Peninsula. Another **staircase** leads up to the battlements, beyond which what looks like a dried moat was actually a canal that enabled dhows to be pulled inland for loading and offloading.

The ruins aren't signposted and are difficult to find without a guide – just make sure that whoever accompanies you knows the place. **Renting a car** is the simplest approach; half-day rental with driver costs $30–35 from Chake Chake. Alternatively, rent a **bicycle**. From Chake Chake head towards the airport along the road and turn right after 5km (1km before the airport). Pujini village lies 4km along a rough dirt road. **Guides** can be hired informally in Pujini, though few people speak English, and they'll need their own bicycle. The site lies a few kilometres southeast of the village, in a grove of baobab and tamarind trees south of a football field.

Southern Pemba

Coming to Pemba by ferry from Stone Town, you'll arrive at the southern port of **Mkoani**. There's nothing much to the town itself, but it does have a good cheap guest house where you can arrange a variety of enjoyable **boat trips** for snorkelling, sun bathing and perhaps spotting **dolphins**. There's an upmarket hotel at **Wambaa Beach**, and that's about it. Between September or October and February, don't miss the **bullfights** at Kengeja village on the south coast. For trips further afield, things are cheaper if arranged in Chake Chake.

Mkoani

MKOANI is where most visitors arrive, as all ferries from Unguja and Dar es Salaam dock here. In spite of being Pemba's biggest port, the town itself is very dull, though the fish and produce market on the beach south of the jetty is always worth a look. On land, there's a lovely sandspit 4km north of town at **Ras Mkoasha**. To get there, follow the road from the port towards *Jondeni Guest House* and keep on walking. The people you'll meet along the way are unfailingly friendly, making the walk itself part of the pleasure.

Practicalities

Ferries dock at the port 1km downhill from the centre along Uweleni Street. **Daladalas** drop you along Uweleni Street (there's no stand); leaving Mkoani, #603 daladalas run frequently throughout the day to Chake Chake (Tsh700–800). Given the limited hours and slothsome endeavour of The People's Bank of Zanzibar (Tues & Thurs 8.30am–1.30pm), forget about **changing money**

Boats to Makoongwe Island ▲ **Ⓐ** *(700m) & Ras Mkoasha (3.5km)*

0 100 m	N

Customs

Mosque

Port & Ferry Terminal

Mosque

Immigration

Market

People's Bank of Zanzibar

Police

MKOANI

Chake Chake

Mosque

Hospital ✚

UWELENI STREET

ACCOMMODATION
Government Hotel   **B**
Jondeni Guest House   **A**
EATING & DRINKING
Jondeni Guest House   **A**
New Haroub Restaurant **1**

– Chake Chake is better. If you get ill, the town's **hospital** (☎024/245 6075 or 024/245 6011) is Pemba's best.

With precisely two **hotels**, one **restaurant**, and a couple of stalls selling grilled and fried fish in the market, Mkoani doesn't exactly spoil its visitors. Local culinary passions centre around octopus (*pweza*).

Government Hotel (*Hotel ya Mkoani*) 1km uphill along Uweleni St ☎024/245 6271. Identical in every respect to the government hotels in Chake Chake and Wete, giving a weird sense of déjà vu. Rooms are tatty twin-beds (and no single rates, at least officially), but they do have private bathrooms, fans and nets, and it's the only place that serves alcohol. Breakfast included. **❷**

Jondeni Guest House 1km north of the port ☎024/245 6042,

Ⓔjondeniguest@hotmail.com. Set on a hill high above the sea, this is Pemba's best-value budget hotel, and is well used to backpackers, offering a wide range of affordable boat and snorkelling excursions. Accommodation ranges from dorms ($8 per person) to rooms with bathrooms, all with big *semadari* beds. There's a pleasant garden at the back with inspiring sea views, and there's always something cooking for lunch and dinner ($5): the spiced octopus in coconut with mashed potatoes

Bullfighting, Pemba style

The village of **Kengeja** in Pemba's deep south would be unremarkable were it not for the curious spectacle of **bullfighting**, which traditionally takes place in the months following the main clove harvest, meaning from September or October to February. The fights are a relic of the Portuguese presence in East Africa, and unlike their Spanish counterparts, don't result in the death of the animals. Pre-fight preparations have spiritual significance. The evening before, villagers hold a dance called *umund* and visit graves to receive help from their ancestors and request the arrival of the rains. The fights themselves feature up to six specially trained bulls. Initially tethered, the bulls are provoked by jostling crowds and *tandaa* pipe music until they are sufficiently enraged, after which they are untethered, the crowd scatters and the "matador" takes over. Completely unarmed, he goads the bull with a white cloth, his skill lying in artfully avoiding the bull's charges and in overt displays of machismo, while the pleasure for the spectators lies both in the deft movements of the fighter, and in seeing him scamper up the nearest tree whenever things get hairy.

To get there, catch a #215 **daladala** from Mkoani marked "Mwambe". From Chake Chake, take a #603 daladala towards Mkoani but get off at Mtambile junction and change there for a #215. **Tickets** for seats in the sexually segregated grandstands cost a few hundred shillings; it's free to join the crowds around the arena. There's no accommodation.

is particularly good, and they're happy to conjure up something fancier like prawns if you order a few hours before. Breakfast included: dorms ❶, rooms ❶–❷

Boat tours and snorkelling from Mkoani

Mkoani is ideal for day-trips by boat as there are several places within an hour's sail: **Makoongwe Island**, 3km offshore, has a roost of rare flying foxes (bats), whilst minuscule **Kwata Islet**, 7km west off Mkoani, is practically all beach and has decent snorkelling and a patch of mangroves nearby. Ignore Mkoani's handful of *papasi* and arrange things instead at *Jondeni Guest House*, which has its own *mashua* dhow (with twin outboard motors and sun canopy) for trips. The isles can be visited individually, or combined as one trip for $20 per person (minimum two). Snorkelling at Misali Island (see p.201) costs $35 per person including entrance fee, and snorkelling over a shallow wreck at Panza Point in the south is $45. *Jondeni* also offers high-tide **mangrove tours** by dugout canoe ($5 per person) for birding and swimming, and **sailing** in *ngalawa* outriggers ($10 per person).

Wambaa Beach

The sheltered western shore of **Wambaa Peninsula**, north of Mkoani, has several kilometres of dreamy white sand of the kind that upmarket lodge developers dream about, though at present there's only one such place. In addition, the untouched mangrove forests at either end are a bird-watcher's delight. The place is most easily visited on a boat trip arranged through Mkoani's *Jondeni Guest House*, which gives you the chance to spot dolphins along the way. You could conceivably also reach Wambaa by **bicycle**, though it's 25km each way from Mkoani across a lot of hills and sandy tracks. Public transport is limited to infrequent #230 daladalas from Mkoani, and #330 daladalas from Chake Chake.

Staying on the cheap is not possible unless you arrange something with a local family in Wambaa village (ask at *Jondeni Guest House*), as the only **hotel** is the woefully expensive *Fundu Lagoon*, 2km north of the village (☎024/223 2926, ⓦwww.fundulagoon.com; $530–1050 depending on the room and season; closed mid-April to mid-June). The ultimate in "barefoot chic", it's a stylish but over-the-top place with fourteen tented bungalows similar in style to those in mainland safari parks, and a huge pier that rather spoils the view and the Robinson Crusoe desert-island illusion. There are lots of water sports; rates include drinks but exclude diving and motorized activities.

Northern Pemba

North of Chake Chake, the land is flatter but just as lush, with extensive patches of forest surviving between cultivated areas. Rice is the staple crop here, although cloves are also grown – as your nostrils will tell you. The main town is the dhow port of **Wete**, which has several good guest houses accustomed to budget travellers, and serves as a handy base for a series of **attractions** in the area, including Ngezi Forest, beautiful deserted beaches on Ras Kigomasha in the far north, and several medieval ruins.

Wete

The entrance to the port town of **WETE** is marked by a dual carriageway and a cluster of socialist-era apartment blocks. The friendliest and most likeable of Pemba's main towns, Wete counts a dhow port and two markets among its attractions. The reason for its having two markets, incidentally, is to divide local fishermen from competitors from Tumbe in the northeast: the former occupy the central market, the latter the one near the *Government Hotel*; both are open daily from 10am to 6pm.

Wete's **port** is at the bottom of a steep hill just past some government buildings, and still receives the occasional *jahazi* trading dhow, and – should the service not have been suspended yet again – a weekly ferry to and from Tanga on the Tanzanian mainland. Other than arriving or attempting to leave Pemba by dhow (see p.38), the main reason for coming here is to visit Ngezi Forest, the beaches further north, and a number of fascinating ruins to the northeast.

Practicalities

There are **two roads** from Chake Chake to Wete: the old and more direct one (30km; daladala #606 marked in red) to the west, whose surface has all but vanished, and the fast Pemba North Feeder Road (35km; daladala #606 marked in black), which starts 7km north of Chake Chake at Melitano junction. The drive takes about an hour. Wete's **daladala** stand is next to the market near *Sharook Guest House*; you can also catch vehicles along the main road. The

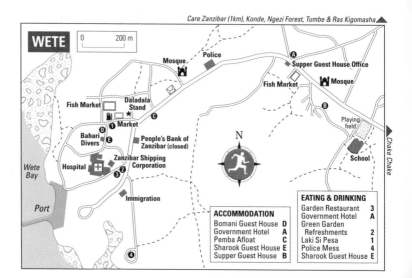

Care Zanzibar (1km), Konde, Ngezi Forest, Tumbe & Ras Kigomasha

WETE

0   200 m

Police
Mosque
Supper Guest House Office
Fish Market
Mosque
Fish Market
Daladala Stand
Market
Playing field
Bahari Divers
People's Bank of Zanzibar (closed)
Zanzibar Shipping Corporation
School
Wete Bay
Hospital
Immigration
Port
Chake Chake
N

ACCOMMODATION
Bomani Guest House   D
Government Hotel   A
Pemba Afloat   C
Sharook Guest House   E
Supper Guest House   B

EATING & DRINKING
Garden Restaurant   3
Government Hotel   A
Green Garden
   Refreshments   2
Laki Si Pesa   1
Police Mess   4
Sharook Guest House   E

Zanzibar
and the Sea

Zanzibar, that blissful-sounding name, comes from the ancient Persian *Zang-I-Bar*, meaning the sea or the coast of the blacks. Since antiquity, Zanzibar has been washed by tides from Arabia, India and beyond, and has long been a fulcrum for trade. Intermarriage between the indigenous Africans and Persian and Arab settlers created the Swahili: the people, the language and the culture. The sea is also why tourists come – apart from the postcard-perfect beaches, the isles are blessed with extraordinarily rich marine habitats, from primeval coastal forests and swampy mangrove forests to some of the finest coral reef systems on earth.

Dhow cruise, Nungwi

Dhows

Cradled by the monsoon winds, East Africa has been trading with the outside world for at least five millennia, though it was the Persians who introduced the lateen-rigged vessel that became the maritime emblem of East Africa: the dhow.

The earliest account of East African boats dates from the second century AD, when *Periplus of the Erythraean Sea* mentioned sewn boats on the island of Menouthias (probably Pemba), and a mainland port called Rhapta, its name – from the Greek *rhapton ploiarion* – also meaning sewn boats. This ancient method of construction survived until the 1930s; myth has it that iron nails were not used for fear of the supposed magnetic effects of the ocean floor. Instead of nails, even wooden ones, vessels were sewn or lashed together using coconut-fibre, the gaps being filled with pounded fibre, mangrove bark and lime. The slanted triangular sails were made of woven palm leaves called *miyaa*.

At up to fifteen metres in length, long-prowed jahazi dhows were the largest and grandest of East Africa's sailing ships. Construction took up to half a year, and launches were accompanied by animal sacrifices and much celebration. Few *jahazis* are built today, but one or two examples can still be seen afloat, including one at Nungwi that has been converted for sunset cruises; there's also a life-size reconstruction of a sewn *jahazi* in the atrium of Stone Town's House of Wonders. More common these days are smaller mashua dhows that still shuttle between Zanzibar and the mainland, and the delightful sail-powered ngalawa outriggers, a design said to have come from Indonesia. Lowliest of the lot, but from which the Europeans adopted the name, are paddle-powered dau canoes (also called *mitumbwi*), traditionally dug out of a single trunk, but nowadays more likely to be made from planks.

Dhow-building, Nungwi

You can watch the fascinating process of dhow construction along Nungwi's western cape, and off Gulioni Road in Stone Town. Apart from iron nails, modern methods and tools remain unchanged from those used two thousand years ago.

Coral reefs

Far and away the coast's richest habitats are coral reefs, which form a fringing barrier around most of Zanzibar's islands. Corals thrive in warm, shallow tropical waters, and are a strange mix of animal and mineral: the coral we know as jewellery is actually an external skeleton (exoskeleton) excreted by microscopic animals called polyps. Growing together in colonies of billions, the polyps eventually form gigantic reefs, providing a perfect habitat for all kinds of marine life, from micro-organisms, sea cucumbers, sea stars and crustaceans, to a dazzling and colourful array of fish, dolphins, sea turtles and whales.

Corals are very vulnerable to small changes in ocean temperature however. The 1997–98 El Niño event, which fractionally increased ocean temperatures, killed off large numbers of symbiotic algae called zooxanthellae, without which the coral polyps died – in places this wiped out up to ninety percent of corals. Zanzibar's reefs have recovered well, however, indicating that corals are perhaps more resilient than was once thought.

Mangrove forests

Much of Zanzibar's intertidal zone is covered by tropical mangrove forests, whose dominant trees (*mikoko*) are among the world's most specialized plants – a necessity, given that their bases lie mostly submerged. Many species have a surrounding carpet of curious spike-like aerial roots called pneumatophores, which provide the trees with oxygen when the tide is up. The tangle of roots also traps fallen leaves, whose decomposition supports fish and shellfish nurseries, and provides a permanent habitat for many other species too, including comical sideways-skittering ghost crabs, and mudskippers – fish on the evolutionary road to becoming amphibians.

Mangrove trees, Misali Island

Snorkelling and scuba diving

Caressed and nourished by the warm South Equatorial Current, Zanzibar's fringing coral reefs offer exhilarating scuba diving and snorkelling, with an abundance of colourful and sometimes heart-stopping marine life to be seen within a short boat ride of most beaches. **Scuba diving** is most spectacular off Pemba, though the strong currents that add spice to so many dives also mean it's safer for novices to learn the ropes in Unguja. **Snorkelling** is also best off Unguja, whose eastern barrier reef encloses a series of shallow and sheltered tidal lagoons. If you're exceptionally lucky, migrating whales (*nyangumi*) can be seen – or more often heard singing – when you're diving; the best times are August and September for Pemba, and September or October for Unguja. Dolphins can be seen year-round, especially off Kizimkazi which has developed a veritable dolphin tour industry. Detailed information, including what you can expect to see, is given on pp.46–49, and in boxes within individual chapters.

Healthy mangroves are an essential part of coral reef ecology, as they act as filters for water washed in from land: micro-nutrients eventually wash through and on to the mangroves, but anything larger which might suffocate coral polyps gets trapped. By anchoring sand and calming surrounding waters, mangroves are also a natural defence against coastal erosion.

Giant coconut crab, Chumbe Island

Unfortunately, Zanzibar's mangroves have been heavily depleted over the last few decades for use as building poles (*boriti*) in the hotel industry, and as fuel for both domestic use (for boiling sea water to obtain salt), and for firing coral rock to make lime. The establishment of marine reserves such as Jozani–Chwaka Bay National Park and Menai Bay Conservation Area give reason for hope, however.

Mangroves can be seen, either by boat or on foot at low tide, at Jozani–Chwaka Bay National Park (see p.147), Jambiani's cultural tourism programme (p.158), Chumbe Island Coral Park (p.134), and from various hotels in Bwejuu, Kae and Chwaka. On Pemba, boat trips to Misali Island (p.201) or the islets off Mkoani provide easy access.

best source of **tourist information** is the *Sharook Guest House*, who also run a variety of excursions in the area.

Change **money** before coming as there's no bank. **Plane** and **ferry tickets** can be bought at a number of ever-changing agents along the main road. If you're **ill**, Wete Hospital (☎024/245 4001) between the centre and the port is in reasonable shape, and Clove Island Pharmacy opposite *Garden Restaurant* is well stocked.

Accommodation

You should bargain at all of Wete's accommodation options to get reasonable room rates. Electricity and water supplies are erratic throughout town. All except *Bomani* include breakfast in their rates.

Bomani Guest House Between the market and *Sharook Guest House* ☎024/245 4384. A sleepy, friendly and pleasingly prim and proper Muslim place with eight rooms (singles and doubles), all but one sharing bathrooms. All have good box nets, ceiling fans, and a table and chair. **①–②**

Government Hotel (*Hotel ya Wete*) Junction of the Chake Chake and Konde roads ☎024/245 4301. The third of Pemba's identikit government-run hotels, this one still with some broken windows from a bomb blast following the 2000 elections. All rooms are large en-suite twins, rather dilapidated but acceptable if you get one with a decent net and clean sheets; there's also a TV lounge, bar and restaurant that requires plenty of patience on your part. **②**

Pemba Afloat ⓦ www.pembaisland.com. Not exactly *in* Wete, this is a trio of yachts moored in Njao Inlet, two of which have berths for overnight guests. Mainly used by scuba-divers (see p.197), other excursions are also available, and the food's good. Full-board. **⑧**

Sharook Guest House In the centre ☎024/245 4386 or 0747/431012. Run by a friendly and very helpful local family, this calm place is used to tourists, and offers a range of tours. Rooms are large and have fans, most also have bathrooms complete with toilet seats and paper. Check the nets for size though. There's satellite TV in the entrance, and very good food if ordered early. **①**

Supper Guest House (aka *North Lodge*) Behind the Soviet-style apartment blocks west of the Chake Chake road ☎0747/427593 or 0748/427459. Half-asleep staff and just four rooms, two (same price) with showers and cleanish squat toilets, but the mosquito nets are too small, and some rooms are stuffy. All have ceiling fans and a table and chair. Food available. **①**

Eating and drinking

There's not a lot of choice for **eating out**, but one or two good places turn up trumps if you order several hours before you intend to eat. Best of the lot is *Sharook Guest House*, with a good range of very well prepared dishes for around Tsh5000. Several basic restaurants along the main road provide cheaper meals, the best being *Garden Restaurant* (for full meals) and *Green Garden Refreshments* (better for snacks), both at the west end of town. Near the western market, the dingy-looking *Laki Si Pesa* is reliable for *pilau* and *supu ya kuku* (chicken broth). Food stalls by the post office sell juice, octopus, meat balls, fish and chapati, and there's a place with fresh sugarcane juice facing the *Government Hotel*. **Drinkers** are catered for by the *Government Hotel* and the *Police Mess*, the latter likely to be closed to visitors at times of political tension.

Around Wete

Northern Pemba contains a scattering of atmospheric medieval **ruins**, of which those at Hamisi near Chwaka are especially beguiling. There are plenty of **beaches** too, Pemba's best (all spectacularly wide, blindingly white and just about perfect), but getting to them can be a bit tricky. Easiest to reach is Vumawimbi on Ras Kigomasha peninsula, just north of Ngezi Forest, another worthwhile destination. As Wete is Pemba's main dhow harbour, there are lots of possible day-trips by **boat**, notably to the casuarina-covered Uvinje Island, Fundo Island (overnight stays possible), Misali Island for snorkelling, and the ruins of Quanbalu at Matambwe Mkuu (3hr sailing). **Scuba diving** is offered by Pemba Afloat (see p.197), a trio of twenty-metre ketches moored at Njao Gap.

Tours can be arranged through the *Sharook* and *Supper* guest houses, who offer much the same trips at much the same prices. The standard cost for visiting Ngezi Forest is $25 per vehicle plus entrance fees; spice tours, at a farm south of Wete, are no more than $40 per person including lunch and transport. Wete's speciality, though, is a trip to **Fundo Island** by *mashua* dhow; you can either camp for the night or stay with a family for around $50–60 per person (this can also be arranged through Jambo Tours & Safaris in Chake Chake; see p.201). Both guest houses can arrange **vehicle rental** ($40 a day for a car with driver, excluding fuel; $25 for a motorbike) or fix you up with a **bicycle** (Tsh5000/$5 a day).

Matambwe Mkuu

About 1km southwest from Wete harbour lies **Matambwe Mkuu** ("Great Peninsula"), actually a small island connected to the main island by a trail through mangroves at low tide. There's only a small fishing village here now, but the thirteenth-century Arab geographer Yakut mentioned Matambwe as Pemba's second most important town after Quanbalu, and excavations here have unearthed gold coins from the ninth century (possibly minted at Cairo), and an indigo-dyed cotton pouch under the floor of a merchant's house that contained over 2500 silver coins, the most recent dated 1066. The foundations of a mosque date from the same period. Admittedly, the ruins are little more than rubble and it takes an especially vivid imagination to picture them in their prime, but there are good views over Wete, and the short crossing by dhow – arranged through the *Sharook* or *Supper* guest houses – is always fun.

Cloves

Pemba's low hills, fertile soil and tropical climate are ideal for growing **cloves** (*karafuu*) – the island's estimated three and a half million clove trees account for ninety percent of world production. Cloves were first brought to Africa in the eighteenth century, when French traders had the bright idea of smuggling fresh cloves from the Dutch East Indies to Madagascar. In 1818, Seyyid Saïd transplanted several thousand saplings to Zanzibar, and by the 1850s Zanzibar had become the world's largest clove producer. Unguja's plantations exceeded Pemba's until 1872, when a **cyclone** destroyed two-thirds of Unguja's clove trees and the balance shifted.

Recent times have been hard for Pemba's clove producers however, due to the Zanzibar State Trading Corporation's monopoly. With the corporation paying well under open-market rates for the crop, a large proportion of each harvest is smuggled by dhow to Mombasa in Kenya, where producers receive up to three times as much. The smuggling is the reason for the many roadblocks north of Chake Chake.

Unfortunately, the only visible signs of the government revenue from cloves are the seaside mansions built by local politicians and "big men", while the islanders themselves are left with a collapsing infrastructure.

△ Woman drying cloves, Pemba

Ngezi Forest

Until the introduction of clove cultivation, sixty percent of Pemba was covered by indigenous forest. Nowadays the only sizeable remnants are small patches at Ras Kiuyu and Msitu Mkuu in the northeast, and in the 29-square-kilometre **Ngezi–Vumawimbi Nature Reserve** straddling the neck of Ras Kigomasha peninsula in the northwest. Protected as a forest reserve since the 1950s, Ngezi (also written Ngesi) is a veritable ecological island, of which about a third is incredibly lush tropical forest characterized by unusually tall hardwood trees – notably endangered *mvule* teak species, that grow to over 40m. Most of the trees are festooned with vines and creepers, and their canopies conceal a thick tangle of undergrowth as well as a few small ponds. Other habitats in the reserve include coastal evergreen thickets, mangroves, swamps and a central heathland, the latter dominated by a species of heather (*Philippia mafiensis*; in Kiswahili, *ndaamba*) unique to the islands of Pemba and Mafia.

The major attraction for naturalists is the chance of spotting the endemic Pemba **flying fox**, which is a large species of bat (*popo*) that feeds on figs, mangoes, papaya and tree blossoms, and thereby plays an important pollinatory role. Other mammals include the **marsh mongoose** – Pemba's only indigenous carnivore – and the endemic Pemba **vervet monkey** (or green monkey, locally called *tumbili*). With luck, you might also see the diminutive **Pemba blue duiker** (*chesi* or *paa wa Pemba*), feral pigs introduced by the Portuguese, and the Zanzibar **red colobus**, introduced in 1970 when fourteen monkeys were relocated from Unguja's Jozani Forest. Unfortunately the monkeys never really took to Pemba, and the population has remained constant over the decades. Another exotic species is the **Javan civet cat**, believed to have been brought to the island by traders from Southeast Asia for musk production. The ancient Indian Ocean trading links are also evidenced by the presence of several plant and tree species native to both Asia and Madagascar. The forest's **birdlife** also has more than enough to interest keen twitchers, including the threatened

Russets scops owl, the Pemba white-eye, Pemba green pigeon and the violet-breasted sunbird.

Locals consider the forest sacred, and Ngezi contains at least six **ritual areas** called *mizimu* that are periodically swept clean for the benefit of the ancestral spirits who dwell there. Two of these, containing the tombs of *shariffs* (people claiming descent from the Prophet Muhammad), lie along the road that transects the reserve and can be visited as part of a two-kilometre **nature trail** from the gate, which also passes by ponds that are popular with birds. With time for arranging things, you could also go looking for flying foxes (two days' notice required), or scouting for scops owls at night (half a day's notice).

Practicalities

Getting to Ngezi is easiest on an organized tour; around $30 per person including entrance fees from Wete, or $40 through Chake Chake's tour operators or *Jondeni Guest House* in Mkoani. Access by daladala is awkward, as they terminate in the scruffy market town of **Konde**, 4km short of the reserve (#601 from Wete, #602 from Chake Chake); there's neither accommodation there or in the reserve. Daladala drivers are usually happy to earn a few thousand extra shillings by taking you up to the gate though. Alternatively, you could cycle from Wete, a 36-kilometre round-trip.

The office at the gate (daily 7.30am–4pm) collects a Tsh4000 **entry fee**; there's no charge if you're cycling or driving through to get to the top of Ras Kigomasha peninsula. Although you can walk around Ngezi unaccompanied, it's best to hire a **guide** at the gate, both for their knowledge and for security, as there have been muggings in the forest in the past. The guides are free, but reasonable tips are expected; something like Tsh5000 would suffice. There are a few interesting leaflets posted on the walls inside but nothing to take away. For more **information**, contact the nature reserve's office at Care Zanzibar, 2km along the Konde road from Wete (℡024/245 4126, ℮cnrpemba@redcolobus .org), which is also the place to ask about their planned **community-based tourism** project.

Ras Kigomasha

Passing through Ngezi Forest, the forest ends almost as suddenly as it began, giving way to scrub, patches of cultivation, a neglected rubber plantation started by the Chinese, and a couple of fabulous and virtually deserted beaches on either side of Pemba's northernmost point, **Ras Kigomasha** (*ras* means "head", hence peninsula). On the western side is a fabulous five-kilometre stretch of sand known as **Panga ya Watoro**, a curious name meaning "the knife of the refugees". To the east, **Vumawimbi** ("roaring surf") beach consists of 4km of gently curving bay. There are no facilities whatsoever so bring everything you'll need.

Practicalities

Public transport stops at Konde, so access is limited to car hire or organized tours. Cycling isn't really a possibility unless the sixty-kilometre round-trip from Wete leaves you unfazed; remember that camping is illegal on Zanzibar. There are just two **hotels** in the area, both with delightful beaches.

Kijiwe Beach Resort Ngezi Beach, southwest of Ngezi Forest ℡0747/866027. A new locally run hideaway, with basic *bandas* on the beach, and better-appointed cottages behind. Also has a restaurant (meals Tsh3000–4000). A day-trip here from Wete, arranged through *Supper Guest House*, costs $20 per person including lunch. Beach *bandas* **❶**, bungalows **❷**.

Manta Reef Lodge Panga ya Watoro beach, Ras Kigomasha ℗0747/423930, ⓦwww.mantareeflodge.com. Sitting on a completely unspoiled and utterly magical beach that's worth the asking price alone, this is particularly recommended if you've come to Pemba for scuba diving or snorkelling – the hotel has an excellent dive centre (One Earth Diving; see p.197), a relaxed and unpretentious atmosphere, and fifteen marvellous and very large, open-fronted (breezy) timber-floored cottages lining the hillside between the ocean and forest, most with sea views. Meals are served in a thatched restaurant by the beach patronized by vervet monkeys, and bushbabies at night. There's also a beach bar, hammocks, and a welter of activities (most $25–60), including nature and bird walks, fishing from inflatable kayaks, road and sea excursions, and of course diving and snorkelling (also possible just offshore, no boat required). Full-board. ❸

Tumbe

Heading east from Konde, a sandy track to your left after 6km leads to the sprawling village of **TUMBE**, known for its lively fish market and skilful dhow builders. Beyond the village, the road heads on to the beach, where Tumbe's fishermen land and auction their catch. The best times to visit are at low tide (especially in the afternoon) and early in the morning, when there's a lively assortment of traders from Wete and elsewhere.

As you approach the village, keep an eye out for a small black sign on the right reading "SMZ Historical Monument", indicating the remains of **Old Tumbe** – Tumbe Mjini. The signpost itself leads precisely nowhere, but the elderly shopkeeper beside it can have someone guide you to the "site", which is little more than a few fragments of pottery scattered around the fields near an old but certainly not ancient mosque. Closer inspection reveals a few clumps of lemongrass (*mchaichai*) scattered among the crops. These have been left untouched as planting lemongrass was the traditional – and very fragrant – way of marking the graves (*kaburi*) of ordinary people. The **graves** of more important folk are given away by pairs of massive baobab trees (see p.147). The only other trace of the old village are the carved wooden doors in the present village, which are visibly much, much older than the houses they guard, and often in better condition too.

Tumbe lacks **accommodation**, so has to be visited as a day-trip, either from Wete or Chake Chake. Tour operators in Chake Chake include Tumbe in most northern itineraries. By **public transport**, things are easiest from Chake Chake: catch a #602 daladala and get off at the junction 1.5km beyond Chwaka. From Wete, catch a #601 daladala to Konde and change there for a #602, and get off at the same junction. The village is 1km from there, and the beach another 1km beyond.

Hamisi ruins

Several medieval ruins lie between the road and the coast east of Tumbe, of which the sixteenth-century **Hamisi ruins** (also known as the Haruni or Chwaka ruins), close to the bay, are the most impressive and easiest to find. Tradition has it that the fortified town and palace, which replaced Old Tumbe, were the seat of Harun bin Ali, son of Muhammad bin Abdulrahman (see p.204). Tyranny appears to have been a family trait, as hinted at by Harun's nickname, *Mvunja Pau*: *mvunja* means destroyer, and *pau* is the pole that takes the weight of a thatched roof.

Hamisi is **signposted** on the main road about 2km east of the junction for Tumbe. From here, walk down the footpath from the sign into a depression with lush vegetation on your right. Turn right at the first fork so that you're walking parallel to the road, passing some temporary pools on your

△ Hamisi ruins

right which are used by locals to wash in. The track eventually veers left and up towards some tall coconut palms. Walk through the coconut palms into an area of cassava fields, from where the bay is visible. The first of the ruins – part of a palace – can be seen on the left. The track disappears a few hundred metres further on in another cassava field. The bulk of the ruins lie another 100m further on.

The first building you see is a small **mosque**, much of it reduced to blocks of collapsed masonry. The *mihrab* remains more or less intact, in spite of a tree root growing into it. The mosque was built for Harun's wife and gets its nickname of *Msikiti Chooko* ("Mosque of the Green Bean") from the ground beans or peas that were blended with the mortar to strengthen it. Some 100m southeast of the mosque are the remains of a particularly large **tomb**, surmounted by a ten-sided pillar bearing curious upside-down shieldlike indents on one side. On the other side of the pillar is an incised eight-petalled floral motif, oddly off-centre. The tomb is said to be that of Harun.

Fifty metres south of here is a large **Friday mosque** that appears to be raised by a metre or so above the ground, a false impression caused by the amount of rubble covering the original floor. Its *mihrab* is in almost perfect condition; the five circular depressions on either side of it originally held Chinese porcelain bowls, and people still leave offerings here.

Moving on from Pemba

Daladalas

Pemba's **daladalas**, also known as *gari ya abiria* ("passenger vehicles"), operate during daylight hours, usually 7.30am–5pm, and connect Chake Chake, Mkoani and Wete with each other. The main routes are as follows:

#1 Chake Chake–Ole
#3 Chake Chake–Mkoani
#5 Chake Chake–Wesha
#6 Chake Chake–Wete (old road)
#10 Chake Chake–Wingwi/Micheweni
#11 Wete–Pandani
#16 Chake Chake–Vitongoji
#24 Wete–Konde (old road)
#33 Wete–Micheweni
#34 Chake Chake–Wete (new road)
#35 Chake Chake–Konde

Flights

Pemba's **airport** is 6km southeast of Chake Chake; taxis to there from town shouldn't cost more than Tsh5000. Departure taxes, paid in cash, apply if not included on your ticket: $6 or Tsh6000 including safety levy on flights within Tanzania, or $25 plus $8 safety levy on international flights. The only companies flying to and from Pemba are Coastal Aviation (CA) and ZanAir (ZA). Their offices in Chake Chake are listed on p.200. From **Pemba** there are flights to: Dar (ZA, CA: 2–3 daily; 1hr); Saadani (ZA, 1–2 daily; 30min); Tanga (CA: 1 daily; 20min); Zanzibar (ZA, CA: 3 daily; 30min).

Ferries from Mkoani

Note that ferry schedules to and from Pemba change, or are cancelled, with amazing frequency, and travel agents outside the port towns themselves are often ill-informed, so don't rely on them. **Mkoani** is Pemba's main ferry port, with sailings most days to Stone Town, and some boats carrying on to Dar es Salaam, albeit after a long wait in Unguja, so you might as well break the journey there. Vessels and days of departure change frequently, but sailing times are usually 10am. The **ferry offices** are by the port entrance, most in converted shipping crates; they're closed when no arrivals or departures are imminent. For what it's worth, at the time of writing the services were as follows: the fast MV *Sepideh* (Megaspeed Liners) departs on Tuesday, Thursday and Saturday at around 1pm; the government-run MV *Mapinduzi* or MV *Maendeleo* on Saturday at 10am; and the MV *Serengeti* (Azam Marine) on Wednesday, Friday and Sunday at 10am. **Tickets** on the MV *Sepideh* cost $50 in first-class, $40 in second; the rest are $25 in first-class, $20 in second, and $15 in third.

Wete, in the north, is primarily a dhow port, but since 2004 a weekly passenger ferry has replaced the rickety cargo boat between Wete and **Tanga** on the Tanzanian mainland. However, if history be a judge, this is liable to be suspended at any time, as indeed it was in the run-up to the 2005 general elections. The vessel is either the MV *Mudathir* or the MV *Aziza I* or *II*. Sailing times change on an almost weekly basis, the mostly likely being Sunday morning at either 7.30am or 9am. Also worth enquiring about is the MV *New Happy*, which occasionally continues from Stone Town via either Mkoani or Wete to Tanga. From **Mkoani**, ferries run to: Dar es Salaam (3 weekly; 6hr); Stone Town (8 weekly; 3–6hr by day, 8–10hr overnight). From **Wete**, they run to: Stone Town (1 weekly; 8hr 30min); Tanga (1–2 weekly; 6hr).

Contexts

Contexts

History

Zanzibar's turbulent and often brutal history has been shaped by its **geographical location**. On the edge of Africa, yet within the ebb and flow of the western Indian Ocean's **monsoon** winds and ocean currents, its position brought it within reach of sailing ships from Arabia, India and the Far East, and also obliged traders to spend part of the year in East Africa before the monsoon switched direction and garnered sufficient strength for the journey home.

The first link between Zanzibar and the African mainland was the **immigration** of African fishermen five to six thousand years ago. Since then, relations have primarily been of a mercantile nature, whether with ancient empires, during the heyday of the **Swahili civilization** in medieval times, or more recently through the Zanzibar-controlled **ivory and slave trade**, which scaled its wealthiest heights (and plunged to its most inhumane depths) in the nineteenth century. Following a comparatively brief interlude of European rule, which heralded the end of the slave trade and of Zanzibar's power, 1964 saw the union of Zanzibar with mainland Tanganyika to create the present **United Republic of Tanzania**. A marriage of convenience, some say, and indeed the united parties have shown little affection towards one another over their four-decades-old partnership.

Early trade

The first non-Africans to call at Zanzibar, around 2000–3000 BC, were **Sumerian traders** from Mesopotamia, who may have bequeathed linguistic characteristics that eventually found their way into Kiswahili. The Sumerians were followed, three thousand years ago, by **Assyrians** and **Phoenicians**, who used Zanzibar as a stopover en route to Sofala in Mozambique, which provided much of the gold, silver and ivory used by successive ancient Mediterranean empires, and may have been the site of the original **King Solomon's Mines**. According to Herodotus, Phoenician ships were also the first to circumnavigate Africa, when they were sent on a three-year voyage of exploration by the Egyptian Pharaoh Necho II (610–595 BC). The earliest coins found on Zanzibar are over 2000 years old, and come from ancient Parthia (northeast Iran), Sassania (Iran/Iraq), Greece and Rome. Egyptian coins and a dagger have also been found, as have Roman glass beads.

The second-century *Periplus of the Erythraean Sea*, based on the account of an anonymous Greek mariner, calls the coast **Azania** and mentions both a busy trading town called **Rhapta** on the mainland and the island of **Menouthias**, probably either Pemba or Unguja. Both places, said the *Periplus*, were under Arabian sovereignty – presumably Sabaeans from the **Kingdom of Sheba** (modern Yemen), who bartered ivory, turtleshell, ambergris, mangrove poles, ebony and other rarities in exchange for imported weapons, wheat, wine, cloth and Chinese porcelain.

The **Chinese influence** is a curious and often understated factor in African history, mainly thanks to five centuries of silence and isolation imposed by the Ming Dynasty in 1443. Before then, contact was in fact quite substantial: a shipment of silk and porcelain certainly reached Zanzibar in 138 BC, and the

219

Chinese also came in person, most famously in 1414 as part of the extraordinary "Star Raft Expedition" (see p.203), its two hundred vessels said to have carried 35,000 sailors. Chinese influence went beyond trade too: Kenya's Bajuni tribe, from the Lamu Archipelago, claim descent from shipwrecked Chinese sailors. Apart from ambiguous ancestry, the Chinese left numerous written accounts, coins, and the tradition of embedding porcelain into the tombstones of dignitaries. **Malay and Indonesians** also came, and may have been responsible for the introduction of coconuts, bananas, and possibly the Polynesian-style outrigger canoes (*ngalawas*) still used today; in 945, a Malay flotilla was also reported laying siege, unsuccessfully it turned out, to the town of Quanbalu on Pemba. Clearly, East Africa was far from being a peaceful backwater, and even in the eighth century, the Chinese chronicler Tuan Ch'eng-shih noted that Arabs were continually raiding the African mainland – a hint of the slave trade to come.

Swahili civilization

As the centuries rolled on, Zanzibar and East Africa became ever more firmly entwined in the broader Indian Ocean trading network. For the most part, traders were just passing by but, in due course, **trading towns** grew up along the coast. The first outsiders to establish a permanent presence were the **Persians**, who by the end of the first millennium AD ruled a series of settlements along the coast of *Zang-I-Bar* ("the sea of blacks"), from Somalia in the north to Mozambique in the south – including Kizimkazi on Zanzibar, whose mosque, dated to 1007, is the oldest standing mosque in East Africa. In similar vein are the tales of **Sindbad the Sailor** in the *Arabian Nights*, whose fanciful "island of cannibals" may have been loosely based on Zanzibar. Whatever the historical truth of the tales, Persian traders were already well acquainted with the East African coast, and the influx of a ruling class encouraged many to settle: an especially attractive proposition at a time when war and internecine strife plagued Arabia and the Islamic heartland.

In intermarrying with the locals, the Persians gave rise to East Africa's **Shirazi culture** – a blend of African, Persian and Muslim elements that was later to receive sizeable Arab input, becoming the **Swahili**. The birth of the Swahili (from the Arabic *sahel*, meaning "coast") coincided with an upsurge in the Indian Ocean trading network. **Gold** and **ivory** were the main African exports, though slaves, turtleshell, leopardskin, rhinoceros horn, indigo and timber also found ready markets. The Swahili civilization reached its peak in the fourteenth and fifteenth centuries, when its coastal towns controlled the flow of gold from mines near Sofala.

The Portuguese period

The growth and prosperity of the Swahili came to an abrupt end on the arrival of the **Portuguese**, the first being Vasco da Gama in 1498 en route to "discovering" the sea route to India. Although Portuguese involvement in East Africa was initially limited to its use as a staging post, the riches of the Swahili trade soon kindled a more avaricious interest. In 1503, southern Unguja was sacked by the Portuguese captain **Ruy Lourenço Ravasco**, who exacted annual tribute in gold from Unguja's traditional ruler, the Mwinyi Mkuu. Kilwa Kisiwani on the mainland – by then East Africa's most prosperous city – was sacked two years later, and within a decade the Portuguese had conquered most of the Swahili coast. However, the Portuguese presence disrupted the ancient western Indian Ocean trading network so badly (the city of Mombasa was burned to the ground five times, for example) that the entire coast fell into decline, and formerly prosperous cities were simply abandoned and crumbled away.

The collapse of the trade network deterred further Portuguese interest in East Africa other than maintaining a number of harbours to act as stepping stones along the route to India. This lack of attention, coupled with their increasingly stretched military resources, opened the way for a new power to take control of the abandoned trade routes – **Oman**. In 1606 Pemba was taken by Omanis based in Malindi, Kenya, and in 1622 the Portuguese suffered a monumental defeat at the **Battle of Hormuz**. The defeat signalled the *de facto* ascendancy of Omani power in the region, although the Portuguese held onto Unguja until 1652, when the Omani sultanate sent a fleet at the request of Zanzibar's Mwinyi Mkuu. The modest Portuguese garrison at Stone Town was captured and burned, and the Europeans expelled. The last Portuguese stronghold in East Africa north of Mozambique, Mombasa's Fort Jesus, fell to the new rulers in 1698.

Omani domination and the slave trade

Having ejected the Portuguese, Oman was the western Indian Ocean's major trading and military power, and was swift to assert its control over East Africa. The only real threat to Omani sovereignty was from a rival Omani dynasty, the Mazrui family, based in Mombasa. The Mazruis seized Pemba in 1744, but were unsuccessful in their attempt to take Unguja eleven years later. In spite of the rivalry, Zanzibari trade flourished, and key to its wealth was the **slave trade**. The establishment of sugar and clove plantations in European Indian Ocean possessions boosted demand, and by 1776 – when the French joined the trade – some three thousand slaves were being traded annually at Zanzibar and Kilwa. The increased demand, and rocketing prices for ivory, encouraged Oman to extend its control over the mainland trade routes.

Given its increasing economic independence, Zanzibar was becoming politically autonomous from Oman. The pivotal figure in Zanzibari history was **Seyyid Saïd** (ruled 1804–1856; full name Saïd bin Sultan bin Ahmad bin Saïd al-Busaïdi), who at the age of 15 assassinated his cousin to become the sole ruler of the Omani empire. The sultan (*seyyid*) recognized the economic potential of Zanzibar and East Africa, and spent most of his reign developing and consolidating it, encouraging merchants to emigrate from Oman, and continuing incursions on the African mainland. In 1811 he opened Stone Town's notorious **slave market**, which during the following sixty years traded over a million lives. Shrewd diplomacy with the British – who were increasingly pushing for the abolition of the slave trade – allowed Seyyid Saïd to wrest Mombasa from the Mazruis in 1827. The sultan also cultivated trading relationships far beyond the Indian Ocean: the United States opened a consulate in Stone Town in 1837, and European nations were swift to follow. With the entire East African coast now under his control, and backed by the Western powers, Seyyid Saïd took the unusual step of moving the Omani capital from Muscat to Zanzibar in 1841, and a short-lived but immensely prosperous golden age began, bankrolled not just by ivory and slaves, but by cloves – for which Zanzibar accounted for four-fifths of global output.

Seyyid Saïd was succeeded by **Sultan Majid**, and after a brief power struggle between him and his brother, the Omani empire was split into two: the Arabian half, and the vastly more prosperous African one centred on Zanzibar. In spite of the efforts of the British to stop it, the slave trade was now booming, as was the clove trade, and Omani control of the inland trade routes also made Zanzibar the logical base for European explorers of the "dark continent".

The age of exploration

Apart from a trip to Lake Nyasa by the Portuguese explorer Gaspar Bocarro in 1616, the first Europeans to travel through Tanzania were the German missionaries, **Johann Ludwig Krapf** and **Johannes Rebmann**. In the 1840s, they tried to convert several tribes to Christianity, without much success, and their reports of snow-capped mountains near the equator (Mount Kenya and Mount Kilimanjaro), were met with ridicule back home. Hot on their heels though came a train of other explorers and missionaries, among them such Victorian heroes as Sir Richard Francis Burton, James Augustus Grant, Joseph Thomson, Samuel White Baker and John Hanning Speke. Many of them set out to locate **the source of the Nile** (see p.100), a riddle that had baffled Europeans since Herodotus in the fifth century BC. The search for the Nile's source was not merely an academic exercise, but had geopolitical importance: whoever controlled the Nile's waters would control Egypt and from 1869 the Suez Canal, giving quick access to India and the Far East. The "riddle of the Nile" was finally solved by the British explorer, **John Hanning Speke**, who reached the shore of Lake Victoria in 1858, and went on to sail down the great river. The most famous explorers to have graced East Africa though are a duo whose names have become inseparable: the journalist-turned-adventurer **Henry Morton Stanley**, and the missionary-turned-explorer **Dr David Livingstone**. Their famous "Dr Livingstone, I presume?" encounter took place in 1871 at Ujiji, on the shore of Lake Tanganyika in western Tanzania.

Although Livingstone was careful about how he went around preaching the gospel of the Lord, he was very much an exception among a motley bunch of conceited missionaries who believed that Africans were primitive and inferior and therefore in need of being "civilized". But with competition heating up between rival European powers for new markets and natural resources, the supposedly backward nature of Africans and the handy excuse of wanting to stamp out the slave trade (in which Europeans had freely participated) gave them the perfect reason to begin the conquest of the continent by force.

The British Protectorate

In 1870 Sultan Majid's successor, **Sultan Barghash**, inherited vast wealth – much of it squandered on opulent palaces and civic buildings that grace Stone Town today – but also an empire that had little real power, not least over the mainland trade routes that had made its fortune. Barghash's accession also coincided with a devastating cholera epidemic that killed ten thousand people in Stone Town alone, whilst in April 1872, a violent cyclone swept across Zanzibar, destroying all but one ship in Stone Town's harbour (around three hundred in all), and levelling 85 percent of Unguja's clove plantations. This string of disasters was compounded in 1873 when the sultan was forced by the British to ban the slave trade between the African mainland and Zanzibar (slavery itself was only abolished in 1897). With both its main sources of income in tatters, it became increasingly clear that Zanzibar was at the mercy of the British. Barghash tried briefly to reassert his authority on the mainland, but by 1882 European plans for the colonization of Africa were in full flow. Barghash's protests fell on deaf ears, and he retreated from international affairs, while Europe proceeded with the **partition of Africa**. Zanzibar's mainland possessions – with the exception of a six-kilometre coastal strip – were taken from it in 1886 by Germany.

Barghash died in 1888 a bitter man, to be succeeded by his son, Khalifa bin Saïd, who had little choice but acquiesce in whatever the Europeans wanted. He died just two years later, and on November 1, 1890, Zanzibar was declared a **British Protectorate**. The sultanate was allowed to continue in a ceremonial capacity, but the real shots were called by the British – quite literally, in August 1896, upon the death of Sultan Hamad bin Thuwaini bin Saïd. Two hours after the sultan's death, the palace complex in Stone Town was seized by Khalid, a son of Sultan Barghash, who, urged on by 2500 supporters, proclaimed himself sultan. The British, who preferred Thuwaini's cousin, Hamud ibn Mohammed, issued an ultimatum which Khalid ignored. At precisely 9.02am on August 27, the **shortest war in history** began when three British warships opened fire on the palace complex. By 9.40am the British had reduced two palaces to rubble, killed five hundred people and forced the surrender of Khalid, who took refuge in the German consulate from where he fled into exile.

The road to Independence

At the end of **World War I**, the British were given control of Tanganyika, though the administration remained separate from that of Zanzibar, which was nominally still a sultanate. The British nevertheless set about consolidating their administration in Zanzibar with a new judicial system, refinements to the rubber-stamping parliament and the installation of a sewerage system for Stone Town.

World War II was a major turning point for Africa. Many Tanzanians and Zanzibaris had been conscripted as soldiers and porters for the British and expected something in return when the war was over. Opposition to colonial rule began across the continent, and with the new world order now dominated by the United States and the Soviet Union, change was inevitable. In Tanganyika, the Independence movement was headed by the Tanganyika African National Union – **TANU** – founded as the Tanganyika African Association in 1929. From 1954 onwards, TANU was led by **Julius Kambarage Nyerere**, a mild-mannered former schoolteacher from northern Tanganyika, and graduate of Edinburgh University. Professing a peaceful path to change inspired by Mahatma Gandhi, Nyerere's open-minded and down-to-earth style won TANU widespread support, and the grudging respect of the British, who, faced with the inevitability of Independence, saw in Nyerere a figure that they could trust. Following a number of legislative elections in which TANU were kept at bay with a rigged system of "reserved seats", in August 1960 mounting tension finally forced free elections for 71 seats of the Tanganyika Legislative Council. TANU won all but one, Nyerere became chief minister, and in that capacity led the move towards **Tanganyikan Independence**, which was officially proclaimed on December 9, 1961.

Zanzibari Independence – and revolution

In Zanzibar the situation was more complicated, as there were effectively two colonial overlords: the British, who wielded political and judicial power, and the Omanis, who still owned the land and the island's resources, and whose sultans retained their importance as heads of state. The first rumblings of **discontent** came in 1948, when African dockers and trade unionists publicly protested against both British and Arab domination. Britain eventually allowed the formation of political parties to dispute elections held in 1957 for the Legislative Council. Africans were represented by the **Afro-Shirazi Party (ASP)**, while the Arab minority supported the Zanzibar Nationalist Party (ZNP). Between 1959 and 1961 a series of increasingly rigged elections gave the ZNP, in coalition with the Zanzibar and Pemba People's Party (ZPPP), disproportionate representation in the council, while the ASP was consistently denied power. Heedless of the rising tension, the British instituted limited self-government in June 1963, and the following month another round of elections was held, which again saw the ASP lose, despite having polled 54 percent of the vote. Nonetheless, Britain went ahead with plans for Independence, and on December 10, 1963, the **Sultanate of Zanzibar** came into being.

African resentment of the Arabs on Zanzibar – who made up just twenty percent of the population but controlled most of the wealth and power – grew steadily until, on January 12, 1964, barely four weeks after Independence, **John Okello**, a Ugandan migrant labourer and self-styled "Field Marshal", led six hundred armed supporters in a bloody **Revolution**. In one night of terror, some twelve thousand Arabs and Indians were massacred, and all but one percent of Stone Town's Arab and Indian inhabitants fled the country. Among them was Zanzibar's last sultan, Jamshid ibn Abdullah, who ended up in exile in England. Despite having started the Revolution, Okello lacked the support to create a government, and the ASP's leader, Sheikh Abeid Amani Karume made himself Prime Minister of the Revolutionary Council of the **People's Republic of Zanzibar and Pemba**.

The United Republic of Tanzania

As President of Tanganyika, Nyerere's first moves were to promote a sense of national consciousness: Kiswahili was made the official language and was to be taught in every school, while tribal chiefdoms – a potential source of divisive conflict – were abolished. In 1962 Tanganyika adopted a republican constitution, and elections returned Nyerere as president. The following year, Tanganyika became a **one-party state** under TANU.

The chaos of the Zanzibari Revolution coincided with the height of the **Cold War**, and came shortly after Nyerere had survived an army mutiny, for which he had recourse to help from British marines. Feeling threatened by the possibility of extremists taking power in Zanzibar, Nyerere sought to defuse the threat through an **Act of Union** between Tanganyika and Zanzibar, which would give him the power to intervene militarily on the Isles. Karume, for his part, was in a quandary, as the exodus of Arabs and Indians after the bloody revolution instantly devastated Zanzibar's economy, and few international organizations were willing to help a left-wing regime that had come to power through such violent means. The solution, which he soon came to regret, was to accept Nyerere's overtures for the Union, which was signed on April 26, 1964, bringing into existence the **United Republic of Tanzania**. Nyerere became Union president and Karume one of two vice-presidents. Zanzibar retained political and economic autonomy, a separate administration and constitution, and its own president and judicial system, while gaining fifty of the 169 seats in the Tanzanian National Assembly. In spite of these concessions, Karume came to view the Union as a mainland plot to take over the island, and even now – four decades down the road – few people on either side are happy with the marriage.

Ujamaa

As first President of the Union, Nyerere faced huge challenges. The entire country was one of the poorest on earth, with just twelve doctors and 120 university graduates to its name. Life expectancy was 35, and 85 percent of the adult population was illiterate. The outside world was willing to help out, but the inevitable strings would compromise Tanzania's independence. The task of developing the country was made harder as over ninety percent of the population lived in remote rural settlements.

In February 1967, at the height of an extended drought, Nyerere delivered a famous speech that became known as the **Arusha Declaration**, in which he laid out his vision of self-reliant, non-Marxist "African socialism" for Tanzania: "The development of a country is brought about by people, not by money. Money, and the wealth it represents, is the result and not the basis of development... The biggest requirement is hard work. Let us go to the villages and talk to our people and see whether or not it is possible for them to work harder."

In practice, those noble ideals translated into "villagization": the resettlement of rural households into centralized and collective **Ujamaa villages**, *ujamaa* being the Kiswahili word for brotherhood or familyhood – togetherness. Until 1972 the resettlement programme was voluntary, and around twenty percent of the population had moved. This, however, wasn't enough, so **forcible resettlement** started and by 1977 over thirteen million people, or about eighty percent of the population, resided in some eight thousand Ujamaa villages.

Unfortunately, the policy was an **economic disaster**. Vast areas of formerly productive land were left untended, the communal system proved to be more fertile for corruption and embezzlement than for agriculture, and by 1979 Tanzania's jails contained more political prisoners than in apartheid South Africa. Yet the policy did have its successes: access to clean water, health care and schools was vastly improved, and by the 1980s adult **literacy** had soared to over ninety percent. Equally important, throwing everyone together in the same, sinking boat, forged a strong and peaceful sense of **national identity** that completely transcended tribal lines, and created a nation of people justifiably proud of their friendly relations with each other, and with outsiders – with the exception of Zanzibar, unfortunately.

Depression, collapse and conciliation

Over on Zanzibar, **President Karume**, who had courted the USSR, Cuba and China for help in establishing state-run plantations (many of which now lie abandoned), had brought about similar ruin but without much sense of unity: the Isles remained, and still remain, bitterly divided, the most obvious political gulf mirroring geography, with pro-government Unguja Island and pro-opposition Pemba Island. Karume became increasingly paranoid and dictatorial. He deported Asians whom he believed were "plotting" to take over the economy, elections were banned, arbitrary arrests and human-rights abuses became commonplace and there were even allegations that Karume himself had arranged the murder of leading politicians and businessmen in the late 1960s. In April 1972, after two previous attempts on his life, an **assassin's bullet** finally found its mark.

The failure of *Ujamaa* to address Tanzania's economic problems had become glaringly apparent, and in 1977 the **East African Community** between Tanzania, Kenya and Uganda, founded in 1967, was finally buried when rock-bottom relations with capitalist Kenya closed the border between the two countries. With both sides of the Union increasingly isolated, closer ties between them seemed to be the way forward. In February 1977, the Afro-Shirazi Party – under Karume's more moderate successor, Aboud Jumbe – merged with Tanganyika's TANU to form **Chama Cha Mapinduzi** (CCM – The Revolutionary Party), which remains in power today. Nyerere became chairman, and Jumbe vice-chairman.

While relations with Kenya were bad, things were worse with Uganda's brutal dictator, **Idi Amin**, whose troops invaded Tanzania's northwestern **Kagera Region** in October 1978. Tanzania barely had an army worth the name, so it took a few months to train up a force of some fifty thousand men, who responded, assisted by armed Ugandan exiles, with a counter-attack in January 1979. Much to the surprise of seasoned military observers, they completely routed the supposedly better-equipped and better-trained Ugandan army, and pushed on to Uganda's capital, Kampala, driving Idi Amin into exile. The war, although brief, was something that Tanzania could ill afford, and the estimated $500-million cost ensured further economic misery back home.

As Tanzania sank deeper into **debt** and resorted to international donors for aid, Nyerere found himself increasingly at odds with his stated socialist ideals. Far from being self-reliant, Tanzania was more dependent than ever. The economy had collapsed, agriculture barely sufficed for subsistence, and the country was saddled with a crippling debt burden. In 1985, with the donors demanding economic reforms, **Nyerere resigned** from the Union presidency. It was time for change.

The multiparty era

The **1985 elections** ushered in a Union government headed by pragmatic reformer **Ali Hassan Mwinyi**, whose ten-year tenure was characterized by the wholesale desertion of Nyerere's *Ujamaa* policies. Instead, capitalist economic reforms and liberalization were the order of the day – literally so in the case of IMF-imposed austerity measures. Another condition of donor support was the scrapping of the one-party political system. Independent Tanzania's first **multiparty elections** were held in 1995. There were two polls: one for the

Union parliament and presidency, the other for Zanzibar's separate executive. On the mainland, things passed off smoothly with the ruling CCM and their presidential candidate, former journalist **Benjamin Mkapa**, easily winning the race. Steady economic improvement since then, and a hopelessly divided mainland opposition, handed Mkapa and the CCM a second term in 2000, whilst – to no one's surprise – the 2005 elections once again saw the CCM romp to power, this time under the charismatic leadership of **Jakaya Kikwete**.

Things could not have been more different over on **Zanzibar**, its experience of multiparty politics marred by bitterly disputed elections, condemnation from international observers, withdrawal of foreign aid, outbursts of violence, political repression, and a whole lot of bad blood between the two feuding parties, CCM and CUF.

Zanzibar since 1995

While the **1995 election** on the mainland was generally free and fair, the contest for Zanzibar's separate executive plunged the Isles into chaos. There, the CCM was pitted against a formidable foe, the **Civic United Front (CUF)**. As heir to the ZNP and ZPPP parties that had given way to the ASP in 1963, CUF favoured looser ties with the mainland, even secession, and had at one time vaunted the possible imposition of Islamic sharia law. Needless to say, CCM viewed their challengers as extremists to be kept out of power at all costs. The run-up to the elections was marred by unrest, and although polling itself was peaceful, violence erupted again when CCM was declared victorious by the slenderest of margins: winning 26 seats in Zanzibar's parliament to CUF's 24. Despite condemnation from international observers, who reported serious discrepancies, **Salmin Amour** was duly reinaugurated as Zanzibari president, responding to his critics with police harassment and arbitrary arrests, causing around 10,000 CUF supporters to flee and the European Union to cut off aid.

After the election, CUF activists were charged with treason after speaking out against police harassment. Amnesty International adopted the accused as prisoners of conscience. Arrests of CUF MPs followed in 1998, and international pressure mounted against the repeatedly postponed **treason trial**, which finally got under way in March 1999. As was becoming habitual with Zanzibar's embattled leaders, Amour claimed that the Isles' troubles were being orchestrated by an external "plot". More arrests followed in 1999, despite which CCM and CUF signed a Commonwealth-brokered **reconciliation pact** to resolve their differences through peaceful means. It was not to be.

There had been high hopes that the **2000 elections** would be free and fair but, in a repeat of 1995, the Zanzibari vote was a dangerous farce. Trouble erupted immediately after polling, with both CUF and CCM claiming irregularities, and international observers calling the vote a shambles. The new Zanzibari president, **Amani Karume** – son of Zanzibar's first president – attempted to defuse the tension by acquitting the treason-trial suspects. The gesture was not enough to appease CUF, who felt they had been cheated once again and demanded a rerun. Tensions increased when CUF issued a ninety-day ultimatum in November calling for fresh elections, failing which, "extraordinary action" was promised.

In **January 2001**, just days before CUF's ultimatum was to expire, mass demonstrations in Zanzibar and Dar es Salaam were held, and the ensuing violence saw the deaths of at least 26 demonstrators and one policeman. News footage clearly showed police brutality, but Karume went on the offensive, blaming CUF for having started the violence, and publicly praising the police for their handling of the "heavily armed demonstrators". Mass arrests were widely reported, as were allegations of intimidation, torture and rape, especially in the CUF stronghold of Pemba. Public condemnation of the killings came from all sectors of Tanzanian society, finally prompting the government to talk with CUF. Much to everyone's surprise this resulted in a peace accord. Called the **Muafaka** ("Agreement"), CCM agreed to incorporate other parties in their government, release political detainees, and reform the judiciary and widely derided Zanzibar Electoral Commission. And, as a possible sop to CUF's nationalist leanings, Zanzibar has had its own flag, and international soccer team to boot, since 2004.

Sadly, the **2005 elections** – which again saw CCM claim a slender victory on the Isles – were a predictably chaotic, contentious and violent affair, inevitably so given that CCM had failed to incorporate CUF in its government as agreed under the *Muafaka* accord, and that for much of the year CCM and CUF had traded inflammatory threats during which the spirit of *muafaka* was all but buried. The Electoral Commission had indeed been reformed, but unfortunately for CUF, so had constituency boundaries: three seats were transferred from their Pemba stronghold to Unguja, CCM's powerbase – which appears to have been decisive in handing CCM its one-seat majority. The establishment of a **permanent voters' register** was not without controversy either, with allegations that mainland police and soldiers – traditionally CCM supporters – had been drafted into the Isles to be inscribed as voters. Still, at least this time international observers were able to compare the poll to previous ones, and came out with the verdict "not perfect but better than last time".

Doubtless the two parties will eventually be pushed back to the negotiating table to hammer out yet another ineffectual accord, but as yet there has been little real change on either side to give any cause for hope. The two parties are as bitterly divided as ever, corruption is pervasive, the Isles' basic infrastructure remains inadequate, freedom of the press is not all that it could be, and the gap between the haves and have-nots has widened: the average Zanzibari is poorer than his Tanganyikan cousin, earning well under a dollar a day. At some point the status of Zanzibar as part (or not) of the Union will have to be renegotiated or clarified. In the meantime, for the islands to have any chance of lasting peace and prosperity, it's perfectly clear that CCM and CUF will have to work together in that noble but so easily ignored spirit of *muafaka*, whether they like it or not.

Books

There's woefully little published about Zanzibar other than glossy coffee-table tomes, the best being the output of Zanzibar's own Gallery Publications. Tanzania's best **bookshops**, which can also order titles for you, are A Novel Idea in Dar es Salaam (p.77; ⊛www.anovelidea-africa.com) and The Zanzibar Gallery in Stone Town (p.120). You can usually also find a decent selection of titles in the gift shops of larger beach hotels. A good online store is ⊛www.africabookcentre.com. Most of the books reviewed below can also be bought through ⊛www.amazon.co.uk or ⊛www.amazon.com. Books marked with ⚡ are highly recommended.

Coffee-table books

⚡ **Javed Jafferji** *Images of Zanzibar* (Gallery, Zanzibar). Superb photos by Zanzibar's leading photographer.

Javed Jafferji & Gemma Pitcher *Zanzibar Style: Recipes*. Designer recipes from Zanzibar's upmarket hotels and restaurants.

History

⚡ **British Institute in Eastern Africa** *Azania* (BIEA, Kenya/London). Annual academic journal containing a wealth of research articles, abstracts and book reviews about all aspects of East African archeology. Subscribe at ⊛www.britac.ac.uk/institutes/eafrica.

Heinrich Brode *Tippu Tip – the Story of His Career* (Gallery, Zanzibar). The semiautobiographical story of East Africa's most notorious slave trader, who lived out his retirement as a respected gentleman in Stone Town.

⚡ **Richard Hall** *Empires of the Monsoon* (HarperCollins, UK). A recommended sweep across the history of the western Indian Ocean.

Christopher Hibbert *Africa Explored: Europeans in the Dark Continent 1769–1889* (Penguin, UK). An entertaining read, devoted in large part to the "discovery" of East and Central Africa.

⚡ **John Iliffe** *Africans: the History of a Continent* (Cambridge UP, UK). Available in abridged form in Tanzania, this is the standard and recommended overview of Africa's history.

⚡ **I.N. Kimambo & A.J. Temu** (eds) *A History of Tanzania* (Kapsel, Tanzania). A comprehensive roundup from various authors, and the only one widely available in Tanzania. The modern period finishes at *Ujamaa* (1967), making it a little dated, but it's still a great resource.

Roland Oliver & J.D. Fage *A Short History of Africa* (Penguin, UK/Viking, US). Dated, but still the standard paperback introduction.

Kevin Patience *Zanzibar: Slavery and the Royal Navy*; *Zanzibar and the Bububu Railway*; *Zanzibar and the Loss of HMS Pegasus*; *Zanzibar and the Shortest War in History*; *Königsberg – A German East African Raider* (all self-published, ⊛www.zanzibar.net/zanzibar/zanzibar_books). Various short, informative and pleasurable reads about Zanzibar. Most are available in Zanzibar and Dar.

Emily Ruete *Memoirs of an Arabian Princess from Zanzibar* (Gallery, Zanzibar). The extraordinary memoirs of the runaway Princess Salme, who eloped in the 1860s with a German merchant. Also available in the German original, and translated into French, Italian and Spanish.

Abdul Sheriff *Slaves, Spices and Ivory in Zanzibar* (James Currey, UK/ Ohio University, US). Covers the immensely profitable eighteenth- and nineteenth-century slave trade. Abdul Sheriff is also editor of *Zanzibar under Colonial Rule* (James Currey, UK) and *Historical Zanzibar – Romance of the Ages* (HSP, UK), being an insightful collection of well-annotated archive photographs.

Explorers' accounts

Copies of nineteenth-century explorers' journals are difficult to track down unless they've been recently reprinted, or scanned and posted on the Internet (try ⑩www.gutenberg.org or ⑩www.blackmask.com). Apart from the following, ask your bookshop for anything on or by David Livingstone, Richard Francis Burton, John Hanning Speke, James Augustus Grant, Verney Lovett Cameron, Ludwig Krapf or Johannes Rebmann.

Richard Francis Burton *The Lake Regions of Central Africa: From Zanzibar to Lake Tanganyika* (Narrative Press, US); *Zanzibar: and Two Months in East Africa* (o/p; ⑩www.wollamshram .ca/1001/Blackwood/zanzibar.htm); *Zanzibar: City, Island and Coast* (o/p). Entertaining but extremely bigoted accounts of the explorer's adventures.

Martin Dugard *Into Africa: The Epic Adventures of Stanley and Livingstone* (Broadway, US). A compelling, blow-by-blow biographical account of the explorers' travels before and after their famous meeting. The text relies heavily on both the explorers' published and unpublished works, and is a riveting read.

David Livingstone *Missionary Travels and Researches in South Africa*; *The Last Journals of David Livingstone* (both at ⑩www.gutenberg.org). Livingstone's writings deal mainly with his travels on the mainland, and have little of the prejudice and arrogance so common among his contemporaries. His last journals contain the famous

tirades against the slave trade which were invaluable in pushing European public opinion against it.

Alan Moorehead *The White Nile* (Penguin, UK/Harper Perennial, US). A riveting account of the search for the source of the Nile, and European rivalries for control in the region. Good for a quick portrayal of nineteenth-century European attitudes towards Africa, with plenty of contemporary quotes and extracts from explorers' journals.

Henry Morton Stanley *Autobiography of …* (Narrative Press, US). Subtitled "The Making of a 19th-Century Explorer", this is a suitably bombastic autobiography by the famous explorer. The title of his bestseller, *How I Found Livingstone* (Epaulet, US; also ⑩www .gutenberg.org), needs no explanation.

Colum Wilson & Aisling Irwin *In Quest of Livingstone* (House of Lochar, Scotland). Detailed account, with the authors following the trail of Livingstone's last expedition.

The Swahili

James De Vere Allen *Swahili Origins* (Nkuki na Nyota, Tanzania). Masterful treatment of a potentially thorny question: exactly what, or who, are the Swahili?

 Sarah Mirza & Margaret Strobel *Three Swahili Women*

(Indiana UP, UK/US). Born between 1890 and 1920 into different social backgrounds, these biographies of three women document enormous changes from the most important of neglected viewpoints.

Visual arts and architecture

Aga Khan Trust for Culture *Zanzibar: A Plan for the Historic Stone Town* (Gallery, Zanzibar). A hefty but entertaining academic tome covering architecture and history in great detail.

 Anon *Tribute to George Lilanga* (East African Movies, Tanzania). Gorgeously illustrated tome collecting many works by one of Tanzania's leading Tingatinga painters.

 Yves Goscinny (ed) *East African Biennale* (Tanzanian Publishers, Tanzania); *Art in Tanzania*. (East African Movies, Tanzania). Gloriously illustrated catalogue for the East African Biennale contemporary art exhibition (formerly "Art in Tanzania"): fantastic and inspiring stuff, from Tingatinga to the brilliant woodcarvings of Bagamoyo's artists.

Javed Jafferji & Gemma Pitcher *Zanzibar Style*. Inspiring eye-candy for budding interior decorators; this lavish tome contains photos of furnishings and architectural details from leading hotels and historic buildings.

Uwe Rau & Mwalim A. Mwalim *The Doors of Zanzibar* (Gallery, Zanzibar/HSP, UK). The title says it all. Gorgeously illustrated.

Abdul Sheriff (ed) *The History and Conservation of Stone Town* (James Currey, UK/Ohio University, US). A collection of illustrated essays on Stone Town, covering pretty much every aspect of its history and architecture.

Abdul Sheriff & Javed Jafferji *Zanzibar Stone Town: An Architectural Exploration* (Gallery, Zanzibar). A short and colourful guide.

Swahili literature: poetry, orature and proverb

Zanzibari literature is, like all things Swahili, an eclectic mixture. From the Arab side comes classical poetry and a good many fables virtually identical to those told by Sheherazade to Harun al-Rashid in the *Arabian Nights*.

Typical of the African mainland is Zanzibar's vibrant tradition of orature – oral literature – which encapsulates every aspect of myth, morality and reality using ogres, flying trees, strange worlds and lots of talking animals to symbolize vices and virtues – hare is cunning, hyena greedy and stupid, the elephant powerful but gullible, the lion a show-off ...

George Bateman *Zanzibar Tales: Told by the Natives of East Africa* (Gallery, Zanzibar). A delightful collection of fables and legends first published in 1908.

Ali A. Jahadmy *Anthology of Swahili Poetry* (Heinemann o/p). Rather wooden translations of classical compositions, and pertinent background.

Jonathan Kariara & Ellen Kitonga (eds) *An Introduction to East African Poetry* (Oxford UP). An accessible collection categorized into broad subjects like "love and marriage" and "yesterday, today and tomorrow".

Jan Knappert *Myths & Legends of the Swahili* (East African Educational Publishers, Tanzania). An entertaining selection of tales similar to stories told across the Muslim world, with strong echoes of the *Arabian Nights*.

Amir A. Mohamed *Zanzibar Ghost Stories* (Good Luck, Zanzibar). A collection of weird and wonderful ghost stories from Zanzibar. Available in Zanzibar only.

Shaaban Robert (tr. Clement Ndulute) *The Poetry of Shaaban Robert* (Dar es Salaam UP, Tanzania). The only English translation of works by Tanzania's foremost poet and writer, with the Kiswahili original on facing pages; a great tool if you're learning the language.

Various *Summons* (Tanzania Publishing House, Tanzania). The only collection of modern Tanzanian poetry written originally in English, offering an intimate insight into the concerns of post-Independence Tanzania.

Wildlife guides

Anton Koornhof *The Dive Sites of Kenya and Tanzania* (New Holland, UK). A little dated (1997) but still highly recommended if you're at all interested in snorkelling or diving, this is beautifully illustrated, also covers snorkelling sites, and has thoughtful commentaries on environmental matters.

Ewald Lieske & Robert Myers *Coral Reef Fishes: Caribbean, Indian Ocean, and Pacific Ocean* (Princeton University Press, US). Another beautifully illustrated guide, although not everything applies to Zanzibar.

Ber van Perlo *Collins Illustrated Checklist of the Birds of East and Southern Africa* (HarperCollins, UK). An essential pocket guide, providing clear colour illustrations and distribution maps for every species in East Africa, though little in the way of descriptive text.

Dave Richards *Photographic Guide to the Birds of East Africa* (New Holland, UK). Over three hundred colour photos.

Nigel Wheatley *Where to Watch Birds in Africa* (Helm, UK/Princeton UP, US). Tight structure and plenty of useful detail make this a must-have for serious birders in Africa.

John Williams *The Field Guide to the Birds of East Africa* (Collins, UK). The most commonly used book on safari, also available in German, but outdated.

Music

A millennium of contact and intermarriage with peoples from around the Indian Ocean has produced extremely cosmopolitan and eclectic **musical traditions** in Zanzibar, ranging from traditional African drum-based *ngoma* still used in ceremonies far from tourist eyes, to distinctly Oriental-sounding *taarab* orchestras (a blend of *ngoma* with Indian and Arabian chamber orchestras), Cuban-influenced dance bands playing brassy *jazzi*, chilled-out reggae, and contemporary suburban genres such as rap, hip-hop, and a fusion of these with R&B called Bongo Flava.

Ngoma ya kiasili – traditional music

Music, songs and dance play a vital role in traditional African cultures, not least as a cohesive force as they involve everyone present, whether as singers, dancers, instrumentalists or just hand-clappers. The Kiswahili name for traditional music, **ngoma ya kiasili** (*ngoma* for short), means "music of the ancestors".

Often drum-based (*ngoma* also means drum), the poetic **lyrics** – making full use of traditional riddles, proverbs and metaphoric language – are used to transmit all kinds of information, from reciting family histories and advising youngsters of their responsibilities, to informing newlyweds of the pains and pleasures of married life. There's often also a **spiritual** or supernatural

△ Sidi Goma, performing at the 2005 ZIFF festival

233

The best time for catching live music on **Zanzibar** is early February for the Sauti za Busara Festival, and early July for the Festival of the Dhow Countries; more information on both is given on p.117. The Muslim celebration of Idd al-Fitr, at the end of Ramadan (dates on p.45), is also a great time to be around; it can last up to five days, with much music, feasting and dancing. The rest of the year, a handful of Stone Town's restaurants and clubs oblige with performances of *kidumbak* (a slimmed-down version of *taarab*) or more anodyne touristic bands whose repertoire invariably includes the initially pleasant but eventually irritating tourist favourite, *Jambo Bwana*. If you're very lucky you may be invited to a wedding – a fine time to experience *taarab* in its most enjoyable context.

If you're passing through **Dar es Salaam**, it's well worth sampling its nightlife at least once: dozens of dance bands perform in an ever-changing rota across the bars and clubs in the city's suburbs, providing a hugely enjoyable and sweaty start or end to any holiday.

significance, for instance in seeking the intervention of spirits to bring rain, and *ngoma* is still used – albeit furtively – in witchcraft and initiation ceremonies on Zanzibar. The powerful **hypnotic quality** characteristic of many *ngomas* has a purpose: mesmerizing work rhythms help reduce fatigue, while the ethereal rhythms and intricate harmonies of ritual dances aim to bring the living and the dead together to communicate in a mental limbo: an astonishing shifting of the senses. The underlying idea is that of **continuity**, that a person is never completely "dead" until forgotten by the living – a crucial concept for understanding the basis of virtually every traditional African society.

Other than at traditional weddings – colourful and passionate affairs in which *taarab* or *kidumbak* also figure – Zanzibari *ngomas* are rarely performed in public, welcome exceptions being Stone Town's two **annual festivals** (see p.117), and year-round evening concerts at Stone Town's Ngome Kongwe (the Omani Fort; see p.118), though the medley of Tanzanian *ngomas* there is far from authentic. Of the many Zanzibari *ngoma* styles, the one you're most likely to come across is **chakatcha**, whose drums provide a fine rhythmical base for dancing. **Unyago**, traditionally played for girls' initiation ceremonies, has been popularized by the *taarab* singer Bi Kidude. Other dances worth enquiring about include *msondo, beni, msewe, bomu, lelemama, kyaso, gonga, tukulanga* and *kirumbizi*. If you're around during Ramadan, the drumming and singing you might hear between midnight and 4am is **daku**, which urges people to take their last meal of the night before the next day's fast begins.

Taarab and kidumbak

Taarab (*tarab, tarabu*) is the quintessential music of the Swahili coast, from Somalia in the north to Mozambique in the south. It's actually barely a century old, but has roots stretching way back to pre-Islamic Arabia, Persia and India – a quixotic synthesis easily discernible in its sound. The soloist – in Zanzibar usually female – sings in a high-pitched and clear if tense nasal twang (a sinuous wailing, perhaps, to the unattuned ear) along the lines of Indian sung-poetry called *ghazal*, and is accompanied by an orchestra of up to fifty musicians often dressed in full European-style dinner suits (the name *taarab* derives from the

Arabic for "civilized"). *Taarab's* main centres are Stone Town on Zanzibar, and Mombasa and Lamu in Kenya.

Instruments

The instrumental composition of a traditional *taarab* orchestra is based on that of the Egyptian *firqam* string orchestra. In its purest form, *taarab's* main instruments are the Arabian **lute** (*udi*, *oud* or *kibangala*) on which the medieval European lute was based, Arabian/North African-style **goblet drums** (*dumbak*, *darbuk* or *darabbukah*), a **frame drum** (*bendir*), **violins** (*fidla*) tuned to Arabic scales, a 72-string **Egyptian zither** (*qanun* or *taishokoto*), **tambourines** (*rika* or *riqq*) and, occasionally, clarinet-like reed-blown **pipes** (*zumari ney* or *nay*).

Of course, *taarab's* nature is far from static. By the 1940s Cuban rhythms were beginning to make themselves heard, as were rhythmical swashes imported from Indian and Egyptian movies, Indian *tabla* particularly. Nowadays, most *taarab* groups also feature accordions, synthesizers, electric bass and guitars, and even saxophones, at times lending modern *taarab* an uncannily "Sonic the Hedgehog goes to Bollywood" kind of quality.

Lyrics and performances

Taarab is traditionally performed at weddings and other social gatherings, fine occasions for women to dress up and dance, when men may be excluded altogether. Even in more public affairs, *taarab* is danced to almost exclusively by **women**, who shuffle along in a snaking conga while shaking their bottoms in a complex rhythmical movement called *kukata kiuno*, meaning "to cut the waist" – it looks lazy, but drives men crazy. Dealing with love, jealousy and relationships, the poetic lyrics are often composed specially for the occasion. A man may request, or even pen, a **love song** for his flame. For these, the man dances a few steps and makes a donation to the singer, and may then dance with the object of his affection for the following number. The combination of dancing and lyrics also provides women with a subtle means of making social statements that would not be permissible in other contexts: a woman can get a point across by dancing up to the singer or giving her money (*kutunza*) during lyrical passages she particularly agrees with, whilst deliberately offensive **grievance songs**, called *mipasho*, can be requested to tease, criticize or upbraid another. Although the "accused" is never named, his or her identity is easily understood by the parties involved, and the real feelings lie simmering just beneath the surface.

Performers

The doyenne of Zanzibari *taarab* was the hugely influential **Siti Bint Saad**, Zanzibar's first female *taarab* singer and also the first to perform in Kiswahili rather than Arabic. In so doing, she did more than anyone else to popularize *taarab* across the social spectrum, reaching the peak of her fame in the 1930s and 1940s, when her voice became synonymous with Swahili culture. Equally beloved, and still going strong after a career now spanning eight decades, is **Bi Kidude** (real name Fatuma Binti Baraka), who began her career in the 1920s under the tutelage of Siti Bint Saad. Like her mentor, Bi Kidude was not afraid to broach controversial topics in her songs, including the abuse of women, and as her fame grew, she did away with the veil that she and Siti Bint Saad had been obliged to wear for public performances. Old age has done nothing to temper her independence: she has experimented with *taarab* and jazz/dance fusion, and has also popularized drum-based *unyago* (which she plays in "hobby horse" style), formerly reserved for girls' initiation ceremonies. With her deep, bluesy and mesmerizing voice, the "little granny" (her nickname) is a giant among African musicians. *Taarab*'s big male star is the Kenyan-born **Zein L'Abdin**, who's been singing and playing lute since 1951.

The main *taarab* orchestras are based in Stone Town, where the big two are the traditionalist **Nadi Ikhwan Safaa** (also known as Malindi Taarab) founded in 1905, who remain close to the traditional roots of *taarab*; and **Culture Music Club** (Mila na Utamaduni), the largest and most successful, who began life in the Afro-Shirazi Party in the years before Independence. In Dar es Salaam, the two big orchestras – both contemporary in style – are **Zanzibar Stars Modern Taarab** and **East African Melody**, whose raunchy *rusha roho* wedding lyrics invariably cause a stir.

Kidumbak

Hiring a full *taarab* orchestra is an expense that most cannot afford. A cheaper alternative is a smaller **kidumbak** orchestra, which features more drums (*dumbak*; hence the name) and a peculiar bass made from a tea-chest, giving it a much more African feel. **Makame Fakis**, the leader of Sina Chuki Kidumbak, is the main exponent of this genre, and is widely considered to possess the sweetest male voice on Zanzibar. Other groups and singers worth asking about include Sosoliso Kidumbak, led by Mohamed Othman, and Hakina Ubaguzi.

Rap, hip-hop, R&B and Bongo Flava

It's taken a decade for hip-hop and rap to establish themselves as a major force in East African music. The scene is constantly changing: whilst you'll hear plenty of it on the radio, live performances are rare, not helped by the fact that crews form, split, rename, disappear or even emigrate with bewildering frequency.

Hip-hop is the purest, most underground form of the styles, sometimes with no backing track at all, and its socially-conscious lyrics often broach controversial issues such as poverty, AIDS, politics and identity – all of them particularly sensitive on Zanzibar. **Rap** is more commercial, its lyrics – usually over US-inspired or imported backing tracks – leaning more towards love songs and postured "gangsta rap" copied from MTV – nothing you can't hear anywhere else. But the huge commercial hit, propelled by ample airtime on FM radio stations, has been **Bongo Flava**, which combines rap with R&B. Perhaps the most eclectic of the styles, the sound varies greatly between performers – sometimes irritatingly sugary and repetitive "I love you so" type dirges, other times mind-bendingly inventive in its combination of traditional rhythms, samples and computer-generated riffs.

Given the ever-changing scene, attempting to recommend current **performers** is a thankless and rather pointless task for a guidebook, as a crew ruling the airwaves one month might be completely forgotten the next. As a result, performances are difficult to locate. One name definitely worth enquiring about though is **DJ Cool Para**, the daddy of Zanzibari rap and inventor of "taa-rap", a blend of rap and *taarab*. For the lowdown on the rest: try www.africanhiphop.com for upcoming events, a welter of band reviews, features and a webcast; or go to www.afropop.org for lots of excellent feature articles, including reviews of festivals and gigs. The subject of www.bongoflava.com is self-evident, and has audio and video clips, and an events section; there's also a good introduction to the genre at www.artmatters.info/bongo.htm. In Stone Town, ask at the **Dhow Countries Music Academy** (see p.96), who should be up to speed on the latest.

Dance music – muziki wa dansi

On the Tanzanian mainland, the most immediately enjoyable musical genre is *jazzi* or **muziki wa dansi** – dance music. The usual line-up includes several electric guitars and basses, drums, synthesizers, a lead singer (often also a guitarist), and a welter of female dancers whose contortionist stage antics leave little to the imagination. Band sizes can be big – anything up to thirty members – a necessity given the almost nightly performances, and all-too-frequent defections of musicians to rival bands. Most bands are known by two names: their proper name, and their *mtindo*, or dance style.

Congolese and Cuban styles have had an especially pervasive influence on the scene since its inception in the 1930s, especially Cuba's pre-Revolution big bands and Congo's enormously successful Afro-Cuban brand; styles like rumba, cha-cha-cha, salsa, marimba, *soukous, kwasa kwasa, ndombolo* and *mayemu* are recognized everywhere. The Congo connection reached its height in the 1970s, after a number of Congolese musicians fled their war-torn country to settle in Tanzania and Kenya, where they established a number of extremely popular bands. The greatest of the lot – gathering the cream of Congo's expatriate musicians – was **Maquis du Zaïre**, which later became **Orchestre Maquis Original**.

A throw-back to traditional *ngomas* and their competing dance societies is the habit of dance bands to come in rival pairs. The biggest are veterans **OTTU Jazz Band** (or "Msondo", after their *mtindo*), founded in 1964, and **DDC Mlimani Park Orchestra** ("Sikinde"), both of whom perform three times a week in Dar. Another eminently danceable pair of rivals are **African Stars** ("Twanga Pepeta") and their stable-mates, **African Revolution Band** ("Tam Tam"), also based in Dar es Salaam. Zanzibar has little of Dar's jazz scene, though the **Police Band** south of Stone Town always attracts a lively crowd; also worth seeking out is **Beni ya Kingi** (or "Mbwa Kachoka"), blending jazz with *taarab*.

Discography

A good **Internet store** with a decent selection of Zanzibari music is www.natari.com. A good compilation is the two-volume *Music from Tanzania and Zanzibar* (Caprice). The following are all CDs.

Ngoma

The best place for buying **cassettes** of traditional *ngoma* is **Radio Tanzania** in Dar es Salaam (shop inside Ubungo bus terminal; Mon–Fri 8am–3.30pm)), who have almost eighty different tapes for sale, but sadly nothing from Zanzibar.

Zanzibar *Imani Cultural Troupe: BAPE, Songs and Dances from Zanzibar* (Felmay).

Taarab and kidumbak

The following, and much more, can be bought at Stone Town's Dhow Countries Music Academy; see p.96.

Bi Kidude *Zanzibar* (Retro Afric); *Machozi ya Huba: Bi Kidude, Zanzibar 2003* (HeartBeat).

Culture Music Club *The Music of Zanzibar* (Globestyle); *Spices of Zanzibar* (Network Medien); *Bashraf: Taarab Instrumentals from Zanzibar* (Dizim); *Waridi – Scents of Zanzibar* (Jahazi Media/ EMI).

Kidumbak Kalcha *Ng'ambo – The Other Side of Zanzibar* (Dizim).

Makame Fakis Various locally-produced CDs available in Zanzibar.

Nadi Ikhwan Safaa *Taarab: The Music of Zanzibar, Vol. 2. Ikhwani Safaa Musical Club* (Globestyle); also locally-available cassettes.

Various artists *Soul & Rhythm: Zanzibar* (2 CDs, Jahazi Media/ EMI); *Zanzibar: Music of Celebration* (Topic).

Jazz and muziki wa dansi

The best place for buying cassettes of dance classics is Radio Tanzania in Dar es Salaam (see p.237), which has over a hundred recordings.

Beni ya Kingi *Beni ya Kingi* (Dizim).

Mlimani Park Orchestra *Sikinde* (World Music Network/ Africassette); *Sungi* (Popular African Music).

Various *Dada Kidawa, Sister Kidawa – Classic Tanzanian Hits from the 1960s* (Original Music); *The Tanzania Sound* (Original Music); *Musiki wa Dansi: Afropop Hits from Tanzania* (World Music Network/Africassette); *The Tanzania Sound* (Original Music).

Rap, hip-hop and Bongo Flava

Various artists *Bongo Flava – Swahili Rap from Tanzania* (out | here rec).

The Swahili

Zanzibar's tumultuous history can easily be read on the faces of its inhabitants: black, white, and every shade in between. Through the intermediaries of commerce and Islam, foreign ideas have shaped every aspect of life here for over a millennium, creating a rich **synthesis** of culture and history, language and literature, music and architecture. Zanzibar is where Africa meets Arabia, Europe and the Orient. Traders would arrive each year on the *kaskazi* monsoon, and return on the *kusi*. Some, by choice or mishap, would be left behind, but others came and stayed deliberately: religious refugees fleeing persecution in Arabia, or people simply seeking a better life in faraway climes. Subsequent **intermarriage** created two distinctly Afro-Arabian civilizations, first the Shirazi, and then the Swahili, of which Zanzibar – together with Kenya's Lamu Archipelago – is the cradle. It's fitting, then, that the name of the Swahili should derive from the Arabic *sahel* or *sawahil*, meaning coast. In a metaphorical sense, the Swahili really are a shore, lapped by the tides and currents of peoples and cultures from all around the Indian Ocean – Africa, Arabia and Persia, India and Pakistan, Indonesia, Malaysia, and even China.

Swahili and Shirazi identity

For all of Zanzibar's well documented history over the last thousand years, determining who is and isn't Swahili can be tricky, as the Swahili are not a "tribe" in any definable sense, nor are they – or have ever been – a unified nation or political entity. Their **language**, Kiswahili, isn't restricted to them alone, having been spread all over eastern and central Africa by slavers and traders, and then by European colonial regimes to become the lingua franca

---

Kangas and kitenges

The colourfully-printed cotton wraps worn by many Zanzibari women are called **kangas,** named after the guinea fowl whose polka-dotted plumage resembled the first designs that were imported by Portuguese merchants in the mid-nineteenth century. At the start of the twentieth century they began to acquire the **proverbs** and riddles (*neno*, literally "statements") that are now such a characteristic feature of the design. The proverb is a way of making public sentiments that would be taboo expressed in any other form. So, for instance, a wife wishing to reprimand her husband for infidelity or neglect might buy a *kanga* for herself with the proverb, "The gratitude of a donkey is a kick", while one reading "A heart deep in love has no patience" might be bought for a woman by her lover, expressing his desire to get married. And one reading "I may be ugly, but I'm not for sale" is self-explanatory.

A double-pane *kanga* is a **doti**, and is often cut in two, one part being worn around the body, the other around the head or shoulders. Similar to a *kanga*, but without the proverb or riddle, is a **kitenge**, made of thicker cloth and as a double-pane; their size also makes them ideal for use as bedlinen. Women will be happy to show you some ways of tying it. For more ideas, winkle out a copy of *Kangas: 101 Uses*, by Jeanette Hanby and David Bygott, or *The Krazy Book of Kangas* by Pascal Bogaert, both available in Stone Town and Dar es Salaam.

of that vast region, and the official language of Kenya and Tanzania. Like all old languages used by trading peoples though, Kiswahili contains clues about whom they mixed with. Based on African Bantu, it's full of words derived from Arabic and peppered with others of Indian, Portuguese and English origin. The language aptly betrays the Swahili's eclectic multicultural blend.

Swahili architecture and Zanzibar's doors

The tropical sun's midday sting, and the virtue of modesty extolled by the Qur'an, condition the logic behind traditional Swahili architecture. In urban settings, such as Stone Town, houses have always been built in tightly-packed huddles accessed off narrow alleyways, keeping the heat and glare at bay. Privacy then was of vital importance, and the houses – like Swahili women – were traditionally veiled. Buildings looked inwards on to a cool courtyard, whilst external balconies, essential for keeping houses cool, were bounded by intricately carved wooden filigree screens called *uzio*, shielding the occupants from public view.

A house's most obvious "veil", of course, is its door, beyond which a narrow passageway called a *daka* limits the scope of any furtive glances from the street. At the height of Stone Town's growth in the nineteenth century however, modesty mattered little to Stone Town's richer inhabitants. **Social standing**, largely determined by wealth, was far more important, and thus doors and their frames became a favoured means of expressing the opulence and grandeur of one's mansion inside. Unsurprisingly, Zanzibar's largest and heaviest door guards the entrance to Sultan Barghash's House of Wonders, whose interior contains another twelve spectacular examples.

The longevity of Swahili doors – often outlasting the houses whose entrances they once guarded – is the result of the wood used, including teak and sesame imported from India (the use of sesame perhaps lending sense to Ali Baba's "Open Sesame"). The **brass studs** are said to have been intended to repel marauding elephants, but as elephants are most unlikely ever to have lived on Zanzibar, it seems the story came from India along with the doors, or from linguistic confusion: when, in 916, the Arab chronicler al-Masudi reported that Zanzibar abounded in elephants, Zanzibar – "sea of the blacks" – would also have meant the mainland. Wherever the tale stems from, by the nineteenth century the studs had come to symbolize the protection of a house. Further symbolic protection is often given by a chain or rope motif carved around the door frame, to guard against bad luck and the evil eye.

Residential doors are the most elaborate. Divided into two panels, the male (*mlango mdume*) on the right and female (*mlango jika*) on the left, many also have a smaller door inset into the left-hand panel for the use of children. The oldest, in the Persian or Omani style, are characterized by carved rectangular frames, massive plain panels and rectangular lintels with floral and geometric patterns. Over time, the frames and lintels became more intricate and ornate, often with an Arabic arch or semicircular panel above. The arch usually contains a frieze bearing a date, the owner's monogram and a Qur'anic inscription. **Decorative motifs** include fish (a symbol of fertility), smoke (prayers rising to heaven) and lotus flowers, which represented fertility in ancient Egypt and peace in India. More common are doors in the plainer and smaller Indian style, many of them serving as entrances to shops. Their abundant floral motifs represent God's presence in the natural world: pineapples are a variation of the fish symbol, and palm leaves are another ancient symbol, inferring good health and plenty. A startling variant of the Indian style are **Gujarati doors**, invariably made of teak imported from Kutch, distinguished by their coffered panels, many studs and delicately carved frames.

For more on the subject, get a copy of *The Doors of Zanzibar* by Uwe Rau and Mwalim A. Mwalim, available in Stone Town's bookshops.

Given the mix, and the slave trade's historical importance in East Africa, questions of family background and **status** loomed large in Zanzibari society. Families that traced their roots – not always very plausibly – to foreign shores in the distant past, particularly to **Shiraz** in what's now Iran, claimed superior social status, in counterpoint to their darker-skinned compatriots, some of whom would have descended from slaves. As late as the nineteenth century, the ruling elite – the Ungwana or "Civilized" – preferred to call themselves Shirazi even if they knew better. According to one legend recounted in the sixteenth-century *Chronicle of Kilwa*, the first of them arrived in 975 AD after the sultan of Shiraz, Hassan bin Ali, dreamt that a giant iron rat destroyed the foundations of his palace. Taking it as a bad omen, the king along with his six sons sailed south in seven dhows. Separated in a storm, each founded a city along the East African coast, from Mogadishu in Somalia to Kilwa in southern Tanzania, and – on Zanzibar – Quanbalu on Pemba, and Kizimkazi on Unguja. The legend carries with it a good deal of historical truth. From the eighth to the eleventh centuries, trade in the western Indian Ocean was largely dominated by the Persian state of Shiraz, and the Persian influence on Zanzibar is still plain to see, whether in the style of architecture at now ruined cities such as Quanbalu, in the Persian inscription at Kizimkazi's mosque (dated 1107), or at Makunduchi, whose annual Mwaka Kogwa festival celebrates Persia's pre-Islamic, Zoroastrian New Year in a most exuberant manner.

Historians dispute the extent of the Persian immigration, and the course it took: the legend mentioned above suggests they took a direct route, but some Zanzibaris say that their "Shirazi" forebears came from a mysterious and long-lost city called **Shungwaya**, which was probably located in southern Somalia. Either way, it seems certain that the migrations were gradual affairs over many centuries, whose composition also reflected the shifting cultural make-up and political changes around the Red Sea and Persian Gulf.

Whatever their exact origins, the Shirazi gave their name to East Africa's first great trading civilization, controlled by a series of coastal city-states including Unguja Ukuu on Zanzibar, and Kilwa on the mainland. The Shirazi civilization reached its literally golden height – based on control of the gold trade from mines in Mozambique – in the fourteenth century. Nowadays, the distinction between Swahili and Shirazi is difficult even for Zanzibaris to make (there are no certain visual clues); intermarriage is a great leveller, and with slavery and the old elitist structures long gone, the term Shirazi itself is now disappearing.

Religion and beliefs

Arabia's influence on Zanzibar permeates most aspects of life, and it's no surprise to learn that virtually all Zanzibaris are Muslim, mostly **Shafiites** belonging to Islam's broad-based Sunni branch. Given the eclectic blend characterizing all things Swahili, Zanzibar's take on religion is far from rigid, and has even made room to accommodate some **popular beliefs** such as the existence of ancestral spirits, spirit possession and various forms of magic including sorcery and divination, that would be guaranteed to offend in the more orthodox corners of the Islamic world. That said, the last fifteen years or so have witnessed an upsurge in more **fundamentalist** beliefs, particularly on Pemba Island whose continuing alienation from the Zanzibari mainstream, deeply-ingrained poverty, and sense of having been repeatedly cheated at election time, has also robbed some people of their faith in democracy. Mosques on Fridays are busier, the imam's sermons more keenly heard, and more women wear headscarves or *buibuis* – black gowns that cover the head but not the eyes.

Islam

The religion of **Islam** – an Arabic word meaning "to surrender" (to the will or to the law of God, Allah) – was founded in the year 622 of the Christian calendar, year zero for Muslims, when the Prophet Muhammad arrived in Medina, having been chased out of Mecca by unbelievers, and began his successful conversion of the citizens to the new religion.

The book of Islam, **the Qur'an** (or Koran), was revealed to Muhammad over a period of 22 years by the Archangel Gabriel. For Muslims, the Qur'an is the literal word of God, not a collection of accounts and commentaries penned by humans, like the Bible. Muhammad though, far from being divine, was merely the messenger, although the respect paid him by Muslims means that his face is never depicted in images. The Qur'an divides into 114 chapters called *suras*, each consisting of astonishingly perfect poetic Arabic – the language of God.

Stemming from the Middle Eastern monotheistic tradition, Muslim cosmology and the Islamic conception of a person's role within it is not very different to that of Judaism and Christianity: behave and do well to others and you'll go to Heaven; if not, the fires of Hell await. That said, the Qur'an is a far more legalistic guide to life than is the Bible. It provides the foundation for **sharia law**, and as such is read as God's writ. For instance, rather than *suggesting* that it would be good to give alms, it states that each Muslim who can afford it *must* give away ten percent of his wealth to the poor and needy. One of the problems though is that, in some cases, the Qur'an appears to contradict itself, for instance with respect to alcohol. In some *suras*, alcohol is simply forbidden (*haram*), whilst other *suras* state that one should not be drunk while praying, or that it would be better not to drink, but there's no outright ban or promise of damnation if you do. For this reason, each of the main branches or sects of Islam has its own interpretation of the Qur'an, which are taken together with **collections of sayings** (*hadith*) attributed to Muhammad or his close companions.

Tolerance

Islam is often pictured by its detractors as a religion of obligation or imposition, for instance, regarding the veiling of women. However, Muslims do not see this as an obligation but rather the voluntary acceptance of God's commands; it's this acceptance (you'll hear *insha Allah*, "God willing", all over Zanzibar) that actually makes Islam a remarkably tolerant religion, an aspect too easily forgotten through the actions of murderous fanatics. Christians, Zoroastrians and Jews are considered to "share the book" (the Qu'ran), and Islam recognizes their Prophets in return. People in lands conquered by followers of Islam were not obliged to convert, in contrast to the bloody proceedings of the Catholic Inquisition, for example.

The Pillars of Islam

The Qur'an spells out five duties that each Muslim must fulfil, the so-called Pillars of Islam. These are: the heart-felt profession of faith (the Shahadah: "There is no God but Allah and Muhammad is his Prophet"); recitation of five daily prayers facing the holy city of Mecca (before sunrise, early afternoon, late afternoon, after sunset, and at night); almsgiving (zakat); fasting, unless travelling or if fasting would be physically damaging, from sunrise to sunset during the month of Ramadan; and – as long as the devout can afford it – a pilgrimage ("Haj") to Mecca, at the centre of which is the Kaaba stone (possibly a meteorite) that was the object of veneration for a pre-Islamic cult, replaced by Islam in 632.

Islamic festivals

Coinciding with the pilgrimage to Mecca is **Idd al-Haj** (or Idd al-Adha), the one-day feast of the sacrifice during which every family with the means sacrifices a sheep or goat to commemorate the unquestioning willingness of Ibrahim (Abraham) to sacrifice his son Isaac for the love of God.

A more personal sacrifice is the month-long fast of **Ramadan**, which must be observed by all Muslims except for children, the infirm and those travelling. Between dawn and dusk throughout that month, people may not eat, drink, smoke or indulge in sex. Ramadan is a hiatus in the normal way of things, a suspension of normality, as indeed it is intended to be. It marks the passage of the old to the new, the revitalization of one's faith and morality, and it performs – ultimately – a spiritual cleansing similar to that provided by Carnival and Christmas for Christians before commercialization took over the show.

The first sighting of the sliver-thin crescent new moon marks the end of Ramadan, and the start of **Idd al-Fitr** (Idd al-Fitri, or Sikukuu), two to four days of merrymaking when the streets resound to the cries of excited children decked out in new clothes, and the explosions of firecrackers and cap guns. It's a time for giving gifts and charity, visiting friends and relatives, and dancing to *taarab*. In more sacred spirit is **Maulidi** (or Maulid an-Nabi), the Prophet Muhammad's birthday, which is a time for prayer and of giving praise to the Prophet, often through poetry or music.

Traditional religion and beliefs

Inevitably, given Zanzibar's cosmopolitan nature, Swahili Islam has found space to accommodate less orthodox religious beliefs and practices, such as making offerings to ancestral spirits.

Crucial to these beliefs, which are common throughout Africa, is that a person does not die completely when his or her heart stops beating. This is only the end of the physical aspect of life. The **spirit** – either as a real if invisible thing, or as a memory – lives on, usually in a kind of limbo, near to the living yet far away, and close to God. As such, they act as intermediaries between God and the living, and can play an important part in "convincing" God to bring rain, call off floods, or heal disease. **Bad luck**, which expresses itself in mishaps such as accidents, illness or sudden death, may be caused by spirits irked at having been neglected or forgotten. Indeed, several houses and alleyways in Stone Town are said to be haunted, including that of the nineteenth-century slave trader, Tippu Tip. Most of these ghosts appeared after the Revolution, when locals took over the townhouses and mansions abandoned by the elite; times were hard, so ghosts proved handy scapegoats.

The remedy to any kind of spiritually-induced misfortune is to make some kind of propitiatory **offering**, such as leaving food on a rooftop, or coins, food or drink in shrines or graves. This is not "ancestor worship", a term coined by missionaries who completely misunderstood the concept. More appropriate would be to say that the living venerate and respect, and sometimes fear, their dead relatives. Only when the spirits or memories of the deceased are truly forgotten by the living, do they pass away into the void that is nothingness or death. The belief neatly encapsulates probably the most important aspect of many African philosophies, namely the principle of **continuity**. In continuity – from the past through the present to the future – lies unity, prosperity and life.

In general, the habits of the spirit ancestors follow in exaggerated form those when they were physically alive. Thus, a kind-hearted person will become a similarly public-minded and benevolent spirit. On the other hand, the spirit of a murderer will predictably have bad effects on the living unless frequently placated with offerings. Yet good or bad, it does appear that if they are in danger of being overlooked, all spirits can become a nuisance: no one likes to be forgotten.

Diviners and soothsayers

Some people can hear or see the ancestors in their dreams, and become diviners or soothsayers – **waganga** (singular: *mganga*). Usually old men and women, they're feared about as much as they're valued for their supernatural skills. Mental illness, physical ailment, depression, loneliness, unhappiness or bad luck, nothing is beyond their remedy. But behind the clouds of incense, the *mganga*'s agitation, the dubious preparations, the bloodshot eyes and talking in tongues, there's reason, too. The psychological duality of fear and expectation of relief, the religious combination of Islam and the spirit world, all combined with natural drugs prepared from local plants, is indeed effective. The Kiswahili term for all this is *dawa moto* ("hot medicine"), as opposed to the "cold medicine" (*dawa baridi*) sold in pharmacies.

Proverbs (*methali*) are an important part of daily life, and find all sorts of uses. Proverbial knowledge is respected, and speakers alluding to appropriate proverbs at the right time are much lauded. The following is a selection that you might find useful yourself. The pithier ones also find their way onto **kangas** – the cotton wraps worn by women – which are used to display a woman's disapproval of her husband's actions, as a reminder of a woman's worth, or as a declaration of tenderness from a lover who gave the *kanga* as a present.

Asifuye mvuwa imemnyea. He who praises rain has been rained on.

Atangaye na jua hujuwa. He who wanders around by day a lot, learns a lot.

Fadhila ya punda ni mateke. The gratitude of a donkey is a kick.

Fumbo mfumbe mjinga mwerevu huligangua. Put a riddle to a fool, a clever person will solve it.

Haba na haba, hujaza kibaba. Little and little, fills the measure.

Haraka haraka haina baraka. Hurry hurry has no blessings.

Hata ukinichukia la kweli nitakwambia. Hate me, but I won't stop telling you the truth.

Heri kujikwa kidole kuliko ulimi. Better to stumble with toe than tongue.

Kila ndege huruka na mbawa zake. Every bird flies with its own wings.

Kizuri chajiuza kibaya chajitembeza. A good thing sells itself, a bad one advertises itself.

Maji ya kifufu ni bahari ya chungu. Water in a coconut shell is like an ocean to an ant.

Mama nipe Radhi Kuishi na Watu Kazi. Mother, give me your blessings, living with people is really tough.

Mchumia juani, hilla kivulini. He who earns his living in the sun, eats in the shade.

Mgeni ni kuku mweupe. A stranger is like a white fowl (ie noticeable).

Mjinga akierevuka mwerevu yupo mashakani. When a fool becomes enlightened, the wise man is in trouble.

Moyo wa kupenda hauna subira. A heart deep in love has no patience.

Msema kweli hana wajoli. The speaker of truth has no friends.

Mtumai cha ndugu hufa masikini. He who relies on his relative's property, dies poor.

Mwenye moyo wa furaha humzaidia raha. The owner of a cheerful heart will find his joy increasing.

Mwenye pupa hadiriki kula tamu. A hasty person misses the sweet things (because they cannot wait for the fruit to ripen).

Nazi mbovu harabu ya nzima. A rotten coconut in a heap spoils its neighbours.

Ndovu wawili wakisongana ziumiazo ni nyika. When two elephants fight, it's the grass that gets hurt.

Ngalawa na iwe juu wimbi chini. May the boat be on top, the waves below ("safe journey").

Pekepeke za jirani, hazinitoi ndani. Unwarranted spying by a neighbour does not take me out of my house.

Penye nia ipo njia. Where there's a will there's a way.

Tulia tuishi wazuri haweshi. Calm down and live with me, pretty ones are never in short supply.

Ulimi unauma kuliko meno. The tongue hurts more than the teeth.

Usisa firie Nyota ya Mwenzio. Don't set sail using somebody else's star.

Vita vya panzi (ni) furaha ya kunguru. War among grasshoppers delights the crow.

Swahili cuisine

Given the cosmopolitan nature of Swahili society, **traditional cuisine** features a wide and invariably mouthwatering range of ingredients inherited from Africa, Arabia, India, China and Indonesia, plus Zanzibar's famous spices and extremely fresh seafood. Just one glance at the "flavour enhancers" used in most recipes is enough to get your taste buds fired up: garlic, ginger, lemongrass, celery, lemons and limes, sweet basil, coriander, chilli, onion, tomato, tamarind, soya sauce, oyster sauce, green mangos ...

If just one ingredient is absolutely typical of Zanzibar though, it's **coconut milk**, which is the base for many a sauce and goes well with almost anything. Its preparation, ideally from fresh (green) coconuts rather than the familiar hairy brown ones, is somewhat wasteful as it's not the liquid inside (coconut juice) that's used, but a pressed preparation of coconut flesh. In brief, you need to grate the coconut rind (ideally using a Swahili "goat board" – *mbuzi ya kibao* – which is a kind of stool fitted with a serrated blade at one end), mix the shredded fresh with lukewarm water, squeeze out the "milk" with your hand, and repeat two or three times. The resulting creamy liquid is then sieved through cloth before being ready to use. You might wish to use only the creamier "first press", which has more flavour.

Food staples and recipes

Zanzibar's starchy staple is **rice** (*wali*), which can be a dish in itself depending on how many extra ingredients you throw in (see the recipe for pilau rice on p.248). The usual variety is relatively short grained and sticky (so put that basmati away), which makes it easier to roll into balls for eating. To make **coconut rice**, simply replace one third of the water you'd normally use with

△ Shopkeeper with a selection of spices, Stone Town

The recipes given here should give you a feeling for the practicalities of Swahili cooking but don't necessarily have to be followed to the letter. Much more important is your own taste and intuition, and the use of fresh, authentic ingredients. **Fish** typically used in Zanzibari cooking includes kingfish, sea bream, rock cod, grey mullet, shark, tuna and sailfish, together with octopus and squid. **Shellfish** is generally limited to large prawns, shelled or whole, though crabs are sometimes used; lobster appears to be a recent introduction to tourist plates and palates. As for meat, **chicken** is most commonly used, free-range if possible. Goat meat is also common, but can be difficult to find back home; mutton and lamb are good substitutes. Needless to say, pork is never used, and lemon tends to replace vinegar. For commonly used **spices**, see the box on pp.130–131.

coconut milk; the usual measures, to ensure there's no liquid left by the time the rice is cooked (so it's not soggy), is one cup of rice to two cups of liquid, plus a tablespoon of oil and salt to taste. Add the rice to the liquid when boiling, reduce the heat and cover with a lid.

The most popular staple on the Tanzanian mainland, and increasingly so on Zanzibar, is **ugali**, a stiff polenta-like porridge made from ground cornflour (maize meal). It's rather bland on its own, but as it's always eaten with some kind of stew or vegetables, it absorbs other flavours nicely. To make it, boil up a litre of water in a pan, add half a kilogram of cornflour and salt to taste, and wait until it returns to the boil before stirring. And stir you must, continuously, until the mixture stiffens and becomes smooth. Then reduce the heat and leave covered with a lid (or, better, with banana leaves) for a couple of minutes. *Ugali* is eaten by hand: the usual method is to roll a bite-sized ball between the fingers or palm of your right hand, then dip it in whatever sauce the *ugali* is accompanied with and pop it in your mouth.

Also good, and distinctly African, are **cooked bananas** (or plantain; *ndizi* in Kiswahili). Tanzania boasts over one hundred varieties, each with a particular use and method of preparation. Some are ideal for grilling, others for roasting, boiling, stewing, mashing, frying, steaming, using in desserts, or being eaten fresh. In Swahili and African cooking, they take the place of potatoes. Back home, don't use normal bananas for cooking, as they're so soft and sweet that you'll end up with a textureless if tasty sludge. Instead, ask for plantain. Bananas and plantain go well with cardamom.

Sweet potatoes (*viazi vitamu*) also serve as a staple, prepared the same way you'd cook potatoes, or simmered in coconut milk. Another popular staple, especially on account of its easy cultivation (just cut up a stem into 30cm lengths and stick them in the ground) is **cassava** (*muhogo*), a sweetish floury tuber related to yams and mandioca/tapioca. Be careful when preparing it as **the skin is poisonous** if eaten. There are two main methods of preparation. The easiest is simply to peel and parboil them, before mashing, frying or – best – roasting. Whichever way you choose, cassava can be rather mouth-drying, so it's best doused in a light chilli sauce (water, finely chopped fresh chilli, finely chopped onion and tomato, lemon and salt), or with butter, salt, and black or white pepper. The alternative preparation for cassava is time-consuming but results in a far more delicious dish: peel the cassava and parboil it, then leave it covered in water overnight. Once it starts fermenting, grate it and leave for several days to dry. The flakes are then cooked in the same way as *ugali* (sometimes also mixed with cornflour and palm oil), making a greenish, delightfully gloopy and finely aromatic alternative to plain *ugali*.

Courtesy of India come **chapati** pancakes, which are eaten throughout the day, including at breakfast. Preparation is more haphazard than the other staples but easy once you get the hang of it. Place half a kilogram of flour in a bowl, make a well at the centre and pour in one egg that's been beaten with a cupful of lukewarm water. Mix well, adding small amounts of water as required to make a thick dough. Once you've got dough, add a tablespoon of ghee, butter or indeed any old kind of fat, knead it in well, and repeat once. Now take a handful of dough, roll it into a thin pancake roughly 3mm thick, and drop into a very hot, thick-based frying pan. If you've got the heat and amount of fat right it shouldn't stick, but to be sure you could rub a little fat on to the chapati before cooking, or add a small amount to the pan. Fry the chapati on both sides until it fills up with little bubbles, and serve hot.

Pilau rice

A simple and tasty way of making full use of Zanzibar's spices is **pilau rice**, which has nothing to do with the Indian rice of the same name. There are many recipes for this, so let your nose and imagination guide you in the selection of spices. Pilau tends to be served on its own.

Ingredients:
500g diced goat meat (or lamb or beef)
2 cups rice
1 small onion, chopped
4 cloves garlic, peeled and crushed
1 level teaspoon of each of the following powdered spices, more if fresh: coriander, cloves, cumin, cinnamon, black pepper, turmeric, curry leaves, aniseed, optionally fenugreek (powdered or leaves)
1 tomato (chopped)
500ml water
oil for frying

Preparation:
The trick here is to boil the meat first until tender (ten to twenty minutes depending on the size of the pieces) and keep the resulting stock. Then heat up the fat in a pan and add the spices, stirring continuously. After 30 seconds or so, add the onion and garlic, and continue stir-frying for five minutes or until the onion starts turning brown. Then add the tomato, meat, stock and the rest of the water, and once boiling add the rice. Turn down the heat and simmer until the rice has absorbed all the water.

Octopus in coconut sauce

This is a lunchtime classic (*pweza na nazi*), featuring on virtually every restaurant's menu, big or small. If you don't like or can't find fresh octopus, the recipe works just as well with any white-fleshed fish, though it'll need less time to cook. It can be served with any of the staples mentioned above, and also goes well with mashed potatoes.

Ingredients:
500g octopus
1 onion, finely chopped
2–3 cloves garlic

1 teaspoon curry powder
pinch of chilli powder (or one fresh)
1/2 cup of creamy coconut milk (or grated coconut mixed with milk)
juice of half a lemon
1 cup water
salt to taste
oil or ghee for frying

Preparation:
Clean the octopus, removing the ink sac from the head, then boil over a moderate heat until soft (around ten minutes). You can use the water later to cook rice, though it'll be loaded with iodine so ensure you're not allergic. Cut the body and tentacles into bite-sized pieces. Heat the oil and add the onion and spices. Fry until the onion becomes golden, then add the water and coconut milk. When simmering, add the octopus and cook for another two minutes. You could optionally add finely chopped tomato.

Curried fish with cashews

This is one of several variants; you can use peanuts (groundnuts) instead, and the fish could just as easily be prawns or chicken.

Ingredients:
500g white-fleshed fish (cod, bream or similar)
1 large onion, chopped
250g tomatoes, skinned and chopped
2 teaspoons curry powder
5 cardamom pods
1/2 cup toasted cashew nuts or peanuts
500ml water
oil for frying
salt and pepper to taste

Preparation:
Fry the onion until it begins to turn brown, then add the curry powder and cardamom pods and cook for five minutes, stirring continuously. Add the tomatoes and cook another five minutes. Cut the fish into bite-sized chunks and add to the pan, add the water and bring back to the boil. Simmer for five to ten minutes, then add the cashews, stir well and you're done.

Garlic prawns

Chances are that the prawns in your local supermarket come from East Africa, where prawns (*kamba*) are an appreciated delicacy. The following recipe – in which the marinade is the important bit – goes particularly well with coconut rice.

Ingredients:
500g fresh prawns, unpeeled
2–3 cloves garlic, peeled and puréed
2 onions, finely chopped
1 green chilli, finely chopped
1 teaspoon of fresh ginger, finely chopped
1 spring onion, chopped

1 tomato, finely chopped
lemongrass (fresh), one stem finely chopped
dash soy sauce
dash vinegar
1 teaspoon unrefined sugar or half teaspoon molasses
coriander leaves to garnish
oil for frying
salt and pepper to taste

Preparation:
The marinade is the trick here: soak the prawns in garlic, ginger, pepper, salt and soy sauce for at least an hour before cooking. When done, stir-fry the onions in oil until golden brown, add the chilli and cook for two minutes. Add the remaining ingredients except the prawns, stir well, then – once it's cooking nicely – add the prawns and cook for a further five minutes.

Beans in coconut sauce

This frequently accompanies a main dish, but is nutritious enough to serve as a full meal together with rice or chapati.

Ingredients:
500g red beans or kidney beans
1 large onion, chopped
1 green pepper, chopped
2 carrots, grated
1 cup creamy ("first press") coconut milk
oil for cooking
salt and pepper to taste

Preparation:
The trick here is to soak the beans overnight before cooking. To minimise the risk of flatulence, boil them at a lively heat for ten minutes, then skim off the scum on the surface before reducing to a simmer, covering the pan and cooking until soft. Then drain them. Now heat the oil in the pan, add the onions and fry until golden, then add the pepper, carrot and salt, and cook for four minutes. Then increase the heat and add the beans, stirring well. After a couple of minutes, add the coconut milk and cook until the sauce thickens.

Language

Language

A beginner's guide to Kiswahili

Kiswahili – the language of the Swahili, the official tongue of Tanzania and Kenya, and lingua franca throughout eastern and central Africa – is primarily a Bantu language, enriched with thousands of foreign "loan words", the majority of them Arabic. Zanzibar is acknowledged as being the source of the standard dialect of Kiswahili that is spoken throughout East Africa, even if the inhabitants of Kenya's Lamu Island would beg to differ.

Kiswahili can be a very beautiful and expressive language, a fact not lost on the explorer Henry Morton Stanley, who noted that Kiswahili "has words to paint her [nature] in every mood. English rich as it is, is found insufficient." Once you get the hang of basic grammar, Kiswahili is quite easy to learn, and locals are delighted if you make the effort. Even with limited knowledge you can make yourself understood, and you'll rarely have problems in tourist areas with English. The best **phrasebook** is the *Rough Guide Swahili Phrasebook*. A good **dictionary**, available in the better bookstores in Stone Town (p.121) and Dar es Salaam (p.77), is the two-volume edition published by Oxford University Press. For **language courses** and tuition in Stone Town, see p.121.

Pronunciation

Kiswahili is pronounced exactly as it's written, with the stress nearly always on the penultimate syllable. Each vowel is syllabic, and odd-looking combinations of consonants are often pronounced as one syllable, too. **Shauri** (advice) for example, is pronounced "sha-oo-ri". Nothing is silent. Where an apostrophe precedes a vowel, eg **ng'ombe** (cattle), the vowel is accentuated, something like a gulping sound.

A as in appetite
AO sounds like "ow!"
B as in bed
CH as in church, but often sounds like "dj"
D as in donkey
DH like a cross between dhow and thou
DJ as in pyjamas
E between the "e" in bed and "i" in bid
F as in fan
G as in good

GH at the back of the throat, like a growl; nearly an "r"
H as in harmless
I as in happy
J as in jug
K as in kiosk
KH as in loch
L as in lullaby. Often pronounced "r"
M as in munch; preceding a consonant, it's one syllable, eg **mnazi** (coconut), "mna-zi"

N as in nonsense; preceding a consonant, it gives a nasal quality	T as in tiny
NG as in bang	TH as in thanks
O as in orange	U like oo, or "ou" in the French "tous".
P as in paper	V as in victory
Q Same as K	W as in wobble
R as in rapid, or rolled. Often pronounced "l"	Y as in you
S as in silly	Z as in zero

Elementary grammar

Kiswahili **grammar** is confusing at first, but relatively simple once you grasp (and memorize) the basic building blocks. The main idea is that nouns, adjectives and verbs change their prefixes according to the context. The following sections cover the most common grammatical rules. Don't worry about getting things wrong; Zanzibaris are invariably delighted to hear visitors making an effort, no matter how botched.

Nouns and adjectives

Nouns fall into eight or nine classes, each with different prefixes for their singular and plural forms, and with the same prefix applied to any associated adjective.

Each class covers certain areas of meaning. For example, words beginning "m" (singular) or "wa" (plural) are people, eg **mtalii/watalii** tourist/s. Also beginning "m" (singular) or "mi" (plural) are trees and plants or things connected with life, eg **mti/miti** tree/s. Words beginning "ki" or "ch" (singular) or "vi" or "vy" (plural) are generally "things", eg **kiti/viti** chair/s. Most abstract nouns, and place names derived from a people's name, begin with "u", eg **uhuru** freedom, **Uingereza** England.

The same noun prefixes are added to the associated **adjective**, so you get **mtalii mzuri** – a nice tourist; **miti mizuri** – lovely trees; **viti vizuri** – good chairs.

Pronouns

mimi	I, me		yeye	he/she, him/her
wewe	you (sing.)		sisi	we, us
ninyi	you (pl.)		wa	they, them

Verbs

The **verb** system is reasonably simple, though there's a lot to memorize at first. You begin with a personal prefix, then a marker for the tense, then the verb root, eg I (**ni-**) am (**-na-**) be happy (**furai**) is **ninafurai**.

Personal prefixes

I ni- (negative si-)
you (sing.) u- (negative hu-)

you (pl.) m- (negative ham-)
he/she a- (negative ha-)
we tu- (negative hatu-)
they wa- (negative hawa-)

Tenses

-na-	present
-li-	past
-ta-	future
-me	just past, or still going on

Some verb roots

The following are common verb roots. Except for irregular verbs, the infinitive gets a "ku" prefix (eg **kutaka** to want, **ninataka** I want).

fanya	do
wa	be/become
weza	be able (can)
wa na	have
taka	want
jua	know, understand
fikiri	think
penda	like
kupenda (irregular)	love
tazama	look
sikia	hear
sema	say or speak
ona/onana	see/meet
kuja (irregular)	come
toka	come from
kwenda (irregular)	go
kaa	stay
nunua	buy
leta	bring
pa	give

kula (irregular)	eat
nywa (irregular)	drink
sikia njaa	be hungry
wa na kiu	be thirsty
choka	be tired
lala	sleep
ota	dream
andika	write
soma	read
cheza	play
furai	be happy

Examples of pronouns, verbs and tenses

The hyphens in the examples below illustrate how the word is constructed. Hyphens are not used in written Kiswahili.

a-li-taka	she wanted
ni-me-choka	I am tired
tu-ta-lala	we will sleep
u-li-sikia?	Did you hear?
wa-na-penda ...	they like ...
m-na-enda?	are you (pl.) going?
a-me-kuja?	has he come?
wa-me-kwenda?	have they gone?
a-li-sema...	she said ...
ni-na-weza ...?	can I ...?
ni-ta-leta	I will bring
tu-na-kaa ...	we are staying (at/in)
ni-na-ju	I know

Words and phrases

Greetings and general phrases

Jambo; reply **Jambo.**   Hello
 Used mainly for
 tourists. The correct
 form is **Hujambo;** reply
 Sijambo ("problems?",
 "no problems")

Salaam or **Salamu**   Peace

Salaam mualaikum;   Peace be on you
 reply **Mualaikum**   (a very respectful
 salaam   way of greeting
   elders)

Shikamoo, or   I show my respect
 Shikamooni when   (a very polite way
 greeting several.   of greeting elders
 Usually qualified by a   on the mainland).
 title (eg **Shikamoo**
 bibi for an old woman).
 Reply **Marahaba.**

Sabalkheri/Masalkheri   Good morning/
   evening

Habari? ("news?"); can be qualified, eg Habari gani? ("your news?"), Habari yako? ("what news?"), Habari za kazi? ("news of work?") or Habari za safari? ("news of the safari?"); reply mzuri ("good"), mzuri sana ("very good"), or other adjective — How are things?

Vipi? or Mambo? reply Poa, Bomba or Gado (all slang, meaning "cool") — What's up? (informal)

Hodi! or Hodi hodi! (said on knocking or entering) — Hello? May I come in?

Karibu (Karibuni when speaking to several) — Come in, enter, welcome (also said when offering something)

Jina langu .../ Nina itwa ... — My name is .../ I am called ...

Unatoka wapi? — Where are you from?

Ninatoka ... — I am from ...

Mimi Mwingereza/ Mwirlanda/ Mwamerika/ Mkanada/ Mwaustralia/ Mnuzilandi/ Mjerumani/ Mwitalia/ Kaburu/ Mwafrika ya Kusini — I'm British/ Irish/ American/ Canadian/ Australian/ Kiwi/ German/ Italian/ South African (white) South African (black)

Sifahamu — I don't understand

Samahani — sorry, pardon

Samahani, sifahamu Kiswahili — Sorry, I don't understand Kiswahili

Kiswahili changu ni kibaya — My Kiswahili is bad

Unasema kiingereza? — Do you speak English?

Unasemaje kwa kiswahili ...? — How do you say ... in Kiswahili?

Sema tena (literally "speak again") — Could you repeat that?

Sijui — I don't know

nataka piga picha — I want to take a photo

Naomba nikupige picha? — May I take your picture

Naomba nipige picha? — May I take a picture? (not a person)

sawa or sawa sawa — OK

Shukran, Shukrani, Ushukuru or Asante (Asanteni when speaking to several) — Thank you

Na wewe pia — And the same to you

tafadhali — please

Hebu — Excuse me (let me through)

hamna shida, hakuna matata or wasiwasi — No problem

Si kitu — It's nothing

I say? (one of the funnier English loan words) — really?

Kwaheri (Kwaherini when speaking to several); literally "with blessings" — Goodbye

Usiku mwema — Good night (when leaving)

Lala salama — Sleep well

Rudi tena — Come back again

Tutaonana — We shall meet again

Inshallah (Mungu akipenda for non-Muslims) — God willing

Alhamdullilah (Tunamshukuru mwenyezi Mungu for non-Muslims) — Praise God

Basics

na	and/with	hii	this/these
kwa	with	langu	mine
za or ya	of	siyo?	isn't it?
ya	by	kweli?	really?
au	or	kabisa (used as positive emphasis)	exactly
naam	yes		
la or hapana (a general negative)	no	labda	maybe
		sana (follows adjective)	very
hakuna or hamna	none, there isn't		
nani?	who?	-zuri (with prefix)	good, pretty, tasty
nini?	what?	-baya (with prefix)	bad
gani?	which?	si mbaya	not bad
kwa nini?	why?	-kubwa/-dogo (with prefix)	big/small
wapi?	where?		
lini?	when?	-ingi (with prefix)	a lot
kwa sababu ...	Because ...	safi	clean, pure, fresh
ni	(it) is/(they) are	moto/baridi	hot/cold

People and titles

baba (also used for a man)	father	mtoto (pl. watoto)	child
		rafiki	friend
mama (also used for a woman)	mother	bwana	mister
		mzee (a term of respect for an old or important man); pl. wazee	sir
kaka	brother		
dada	sister		
babu (also an old man or elder)	grandfather		
		mwalimu	teacher (also a term of respect)
bibi (also an old woman or elder)	grandmother		

Getting around

Iko wapi ...?	Where is ...?	dau or mtumbwi (pl mitumbwi)	canoe
lini?	when?		
gari (pl. magari)	vehicle	ngalawa	outrigger (with sail)
teksi	taxi	jahazi	trading dhow (large)
daladala or gari ya abiria	communal minibus	mashua	trading dhow (smaller)
		ndege	plane
kituo cha teksi/basi/ daladala	taxi/bus/daladala stand	uwanja wa ndege (lit."stadium of birds")	airport
baisikeli	bicycle	manamba	ticket tout
mvuko (pl. mivuko)	ferry	dereva	driver
kivuko	ferry port/landing	petroli, mafuta	petrol, oil
chombo (pl. vyombo)	boat	fundi	mechanic

257

barabara	highway
njia or ndia	road, path
njia panda ya ...	junction for ...
kwa miguu	on foot/walking
Inaondoka lini?	When does it leave?
Tutafika lini? or Tutafika saa ngapi?	When will we arrive?
pole pole	slowly
taratibu	carefully, methodically
haraka	fast, quickly
Ngoja!/Ngoja kidogo	Wait!/Wait a moment
Simama!	Stop!
Unaenda wapi?	Where are you going?
Mpaka wapi?	To where?
Kutoka wapi?	From where?
Kilometa ngapi?	How many kilometres?

Ninaenda ...	I'm going to ...
Songa kidogo	Squeeze up a little
Twende	Let's go
Twende tu	Keep going
moja kwa moja	straight ahead
kulia	right
kushoto	left
juu	up
chini	down
kaskazi/mashariki/ kusini/magharibi	north/east/south/west
Nataka kushuka hapa	I want to get off here
Gari imevunjika	The car has broken down
Safari njema	Have a good journey

Accommodation

hotel, nyumba ya wangeni or gesti	hotel
Naweza kukaa wapi?	Where can I stay?
Naweza kukaa hapa?	Can I stay here?
mapokezi	reception
chumba (pl. vyumba)	room
Napenda kuona chumba	I'd like to see a room
Nataka chumba kwa wasiku mbili	I want a room for two nights
self containa or chumba self	en-suite room
common	room sharing bathroom

Choo/bafu kiko wapi?	Where's the toilet/ bathroom?
maji moto/baridi	hot/cold water
kitanda (pl. vitanda)	bed
shiti	bedsheet
mto	pillow
chandarua	mosquito net
kiti na meza	table and chair
televisheni	television
mshumaa	candle
ufuaji	laundry
kuni	firewood

Shopping

duka	shop
machinga	street vendor
biashara	business, commerce
fungua	open
funga	closed
mfuko/rambo	bag/plastic bag (slang)
pesa or hela	money
Ngapi?	How much? (quantity)
Pesa ngapi? Bei gani? or Shillingi ngapi?	How much? (price)

Mingi zaidi	That's too much
ghali sana	expensive
rahisi	cheap
Punguza kidogo!	Reduce the price!
Nipe ...	Give me (can I have?) ...
Nataka ...	I want ...
Naomba ...	May I have ... (more polite)
Sitaki ...	I don't want ...
Sitaki biashara	I don't want to do business

Health and toiletries

Mimi mgonjwa or Ninaumwa	I'm ill
homa	fever
daktari	doctor
hospitali	hospital
duka la dawa	pharmacy
kidonge	pills
dudu	insect
dawa ya wadudu	insect repellent
dawa (dawa baridi Western, dawa kali traditional)	medicine
sembe	razor
sabuni	soap

Numbers (namba)

moja	1
mbili	2
tatu	3
nne	4
tano	5
sita	6
saba	7
nane	8
tisa	9
kumi	10
kumi na moja	11
kumi na mbili	12
ishirini	20
ishirini na moja	21
thelathini	30
arbaini	40
hamsini	50
sitini	60
sabaini	70
themanini	80
tisini	90
mia or mia moja	100
mia moja na ishirini na moja	121
elfu	1,000
milioni	1,000,000

Time and calendar

Saa ngapi?	What time?
Saa ngapi sasa?	What time is it now?
saa kumi	ten o'clock (4am or 4pm)
saa kumi na robo	quarter past ten
saa kumi na nusu	half past ten
saa kumi kasorobo	quarter to ten
dakika	minutes
leo	today
jana	yesterday
jusi	day before yesterday
majusi	several days ago
kesho	tomorrow
kesho kutwa	in two days
kila siku	every day
alfajiri	dawn
asubuhi	morning
mchana	daytime
usiku	night time
wiki ilioyopita/hii/ijayo	last/this/next week
mwaka huu	this year
mwezi huu	this month
sasa	now
bado	not yet, still
sasa hivi	soon
baadaye	later
-subiri (has prefix)	wait
Jumatatu	Monday
Jumanne	Tuesday
Jumatano	Wednesday
Alhamisi	Thursday
Ijumaa	Friday
Jumamosi	Saturday
Jumapili	Sunday
Januari	January
Februari	February
Machi	March

259

Aprili	April	Septemba	September
Mei	May	Oktoba	October
Juni	June	Novemba	November
Julai	July	Desemba	December
Agosti	August		

Signs

Hatari	Danger	Mbwa mkali (literally "sharp dog")	Fierce dog
Angalia/Onyo	Warning	Hakuna njia	No entry

Food and drink

chakula	food	kopo	can
hoteli	restaurant	kiroba	sachet (contains a tot of spirits)
mgahawa	tea house (very basic restaurant)	moto/baridi	hot/cold
mama/baba lisha or mama/baba ntilie	streetfood vendor	barafu	ice
Mnauza chakula hapa?	Do you serve food here?	bia (commercial); pombe or busa (local brew)	beer
Nakula mboga tu	I am vegetarian	gongo or changaa	local spirits
meza	table	tuwi	coconut juice
Iko ...? or Kuna ...?	Is there any ...?	kahawa	coffee
Iko ... or Kuna ...	Yes, there is ...	juice (pronounced "juwiis")	juice
Haiko ... or Hakuna ...	No, there isn't	maziwa	milk
nusu	half (portion)	mtindi or maziwa mgando	curdled milk
tosha/basi	enough		
choma	grilled	chai (ginger tea chai tangawizi, spiced tea chai masala, black tea chai rangi, tea with milk chai maziwa)	tea
mchemsho	boiled		
rosti	stewed		
kufurahia chakula or karibu chakul	enjoy your food		
kinywaji	a drink	maji (drinking water maji ya kunywa)	water
glasi or bilauri	glass		
chupa	bottle		

Menu Reader

Snacks

andazi	doughnut
biscuti	biscuits
chapati	chapati, a floury pancake
chop	mincemeat or egg in a mashed potato pasty, or a rib of mutton or chicken leg in batter
kababu	fried meatball
kitumbua	deep-fried rice cake
mahindi	maize cob

mantabali	"Zanzibari pizza", stuffed chapati like a spring roll
mayai	eggs (singular *yai*)
mishkaki	grilled goatmeat skewers
sambusa	samosa (triangle of pastry stuffed with minced meat, onion and pepper, or vegetarian)

Meat (nyama) and fish (samaki)

dagaa	tiny freshwater sardines, sun-dried
filigisi	tripe, innards, sweetmeats
kamba	prawns
kamba coach	lobster
kolekole	kingfish

kondoo	lamb
kuku	chicken
maini	liver
ngisi	squid
ng'ombe	beef
pweza	octopus
sangara	Nile perch

Vegetables (mboga)

batata	potatoes
biringani	aubergine (eggplant)
chipsi	chips
dengu	lentils
kabichu	cabbage
karoti	carrots
kitunguu	onion
mabamia or mabinda	okra
maharage or maharagwe	beans
mahindi	maize

mchicha	kind of spinach
mdewere	spinach
mtama	millet
muhogo	cassava
ndizi	banana (plantain)
nyanya	tomatoes
pilipili mboga	sweet pepper
saladi	salad or lettuce
tango	cucumber
ujaka	kind of spinach
viazi vitamu	sweet potatoes
wali	rice

Typical dishes

biryani	peppery and highly spiced dish of meat and rice
chipsi mayai	chip omelette
matoke	banana stew

mchanganyiko	a mixture of more or less everything
mtori	a light banana soup, in Arusha and westwards

nyama choma	chargrilled meat, best accompanied with grilled bananas and chilli	supu	spicy meat broth served with lemon and chilli, eaten for breakfast (and as a hangover cure): **supu ya makongoro** is with animal hooves, **supu ya utumbo** is with intestines
pilau	rice spiced with cardamom, cinnamon, cloves and pepper, and whatever else comes to hand		
pweza na nazi	octopus cooked in gently spiced coconut sauce (Zanzibar)	ugali	East Africa's staple, a stodgy cornmeal polenta usually served with stew.
		uji	millet porridge, eaten for breakfast

Condiments, herbs and spices

See also the box on spices and herbs on pp.130–131.

chumvi	salt	mchaichai	lemongrass
gigiri	sesame	mdalasini	cinnamon
gilgilani	coriander	mrehani	sweet basil
hiliki	cardamom	pilipili hoho	chilli pepper
karafu	cloves	pilipili manga	black pepper
kungu manga	nutmeg	sukari	sugar
limao	lemon	tangawizi	ginger
mafuta	oil	uzile	cumin
manjano	turmeric		

Fruit (matunda)

chenza	tangerine	nazi	coconut
chongoma	Indian plum	dafu	a young coconut for drinking
chungwa	orange		
danzi	sour orange	ndizi	banana
duriani	durian	papai	papaya
embe	mango	pasheni	passion fruit
fenesi	jackfruit	pea	avocado
korosho	cashew	pera	guava
kungu	Indian almond	sheli sheli	breadfruit
kungumanga	pomegranate	shoki-shoki	lychee
kwaju	tamarind	stafeli	soursop
limau	lemon	tende	date
mratab	sapodilla	tikiti	watermelon
mtopetope	sweetsop (custard-apple)	tunda la kizungu	apple
nanasi	pineapple	zabibu	grape

Glossary

askari security guard, soldier

banda any kind of hut, usually rectangular and with a sloping thatched roof (pl. **mabanda**)

baraza stone bench, a sitting or meeting place

benki bank

boriti mangrove poles used in building

buibui the black cover-all cloak and veil of Shia Muslim women

chai a tip or bribe, literally "tea"

choo toilet (**wanaume** is gents, **wanawake** is ladies)

imam the man who leads prayers in a mosque

jengo building (pl. **majengo**)

kabila tribe (pl. **makabila**)

kanga or **khanga** printed cotton sheet incorporating a proverb, worn by women

kanisa church

kaskazi northeast monsoon (Dec–Mar)

kitabu book

kitenge double-paned cotton cloth (pl. **vitenge**)

kofia embroidered cap worn by Muslim men

kusi southwest monsoon (June–Sept)

makuti palm-leaf thatch, used for roofing

malaika angel

malaya prostitute

mama kubwa big lady

mchina Chinese or oriental-looking person (pl. **wachina**)

mhindi Indian person (pl. **wahindi**)

mihrab prayer niche set in a mosque's qibla wall facing Mecca

msikiti mosque

mtaa ward or neighbourhood; street

mtalii tourist (pl. **watalii**)

Mungu God

murram red clay and gravel road

muziki music

mzungu white person (pl. **wazungu**)

ngoma dance, drum, music, celebration

ngoma ya kiasili traditional music

panga machete or knife

polisi police

posta post office

rondavel round hut or cottage, often thatched

safari any journey

sahil coast

semadari traditional four-poster bed

serikali government

shamba farm

shisha water pipe for smoking

skule (**shule** on the mainland) school

sigara cigarette

simu telephone

soko market; **soko kuu** main market

Ulaya Europe

Travel store

TRAVEL

& MORE

Visit us online

www.roughguides.com

Information on over 25,000 destinations around the world

- **Read** Rough Guides' trusted travel info

- **Share** journals, photos and travel advice with other readers

- Get exclusive Rough Guide **discounts** and travel deals

- Earn membership points every time you contribute to the

  Rough Guide community and get free books, flights and trips

- Browse thousands of **CD reviews** and artists in our music area

ONLINE

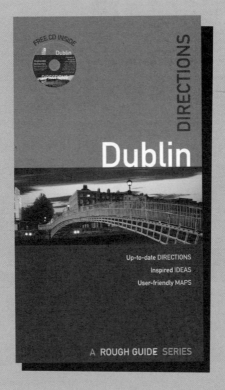

stay in touch!

Rough Guides' FREE full-colour newsletter

News, travel issues, music reviews, readers' letters and the latest dispatches from authors on the road

If you would like to receive roughnews, please send us your name and address:

Rough Guides, 80 Strand
London, WC2R 0RL, UK

Rough Guides, 4th Floor, 345 Hudson St
New York NY10014, USA

newslettersubs@roughguides.co.uk

ROUGHNEWS

ROUGH GUIDE MAP

France

1:1,100,000 · 1 INCH: 17.3 MILES · 1 CM: 11 KM

Plastic waterproof map
ideal for planning and touring

★ **waterproof**

★ **rip-proof**

★ **amazing value**

MAPS

Rough Guides To A World Of Music

'stick to the reliable Rough Guide series'
The Guardian (UK)

Tanzania is the new music capital of East Africa and from the spice islands of Zanzibar to the shores of the great lakes, *The Rough Guide To The Music Of Tanzania* explores the diversity of the country's culture as expressed in its popular music. This album features hip-hop with a Maasai tinge, Haya vocal rhythms from Lake Victoria, acoustic *taarab* sounds from the Indian Ocean, together with the guitars and horns of Dar Es Salaam's most famous dance bands.

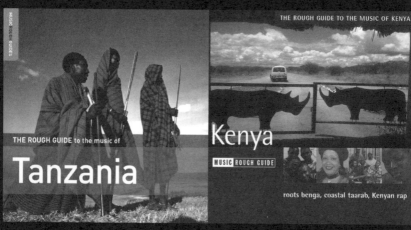

THE ROUGH GUIDE to the music of

Tanzania

THE ROUGH GUIDE TO THE MUSIC OF KENYA

Kenya

MUSIC ROUGH GUIDE

roots benga, coastal taarab, Kenyan rap

High-energy *benga* music, with its pulsating beat and funky interlocking guitar riffs, has been at the forefront of Kenyan pop since the late 1960s. More recently, contemporary artists, such as Gidi Gidi Maji Maji and Nyota Ndogo, have been exploring the possibilities of merging traditional melodies, instruments and rhythms with new sounds from R&B and other international genres. In addition, *taarab* music – a mixture of Indian Ocean and coastal traditions – and rumba-based Swahili and Lingala music are phenomenally popular. *The Rough Guide To The Music Of Kenya* spans these styles from classic *benga* gems, to sparkling new *taarab* compositions, with a sampling of the most innovative sounds of Kenya's hip hop generation.

Hear sound samples at WWW.WORLDMUSIC.NET

Rough Guides Radio

Now you can visit **www.worldmusic.net/radio** to tune into the exciting Rough Guide Radio Show, with a new show each month presenting new releases, interviews, features and competitions.

NOTES

NOTES

Small print and
Index

A Rough Guide to Rough Guides

Published in 1982, the first Rough Guide – to Greece – was a student scheme that became a publishing phenomenon. Mark Ellingham, a recent graduate in English from Bristol University, had been travelling in Greece the previous summer and couldn't find the right guidebook. With a small group of friends he wrote his own guide, combining a highly contemporary, journalistic style with a thoroughly practical approach to travellers' needs.

The immediate success of the book spawned a series that rapidly covered dozens of destinations. And, in addition to impecunious backpackers, Rough Guides soon acquired a much broader and older readership that relished the guides' wit and inquisitiveness as much as their enthusiastic, critical approach and value-for-money ethos.

These days, Rough Guides include recommendations from shoestring to luxury and cover more than 200 destinations around the globe, including almost every country in the Americas and Europe, more than half of Africa and most of Asia and Australasia. Our ever-growing team of authors and photographers is spread all over the world, particularly in Europe, the USA and Australia.

In the early 1990s, Rough Guides branched out of travel, with the publication of Rough Guides to World Music, Classical Music and the Internet. All three have become benchmark titles in their fields, spearheading the publication of a wide range of books under the Rough Guide name.

Including the travel series, Rough Guides now number more than 350 titles, covering: phrasebooks, waterproof maps, music guides from Opera to Heavy Metal, reference works as diverse as Conspiracy Theories and Shakespeare, and popular culture books from iPods to Poker. Rough Guides also produce a series of more than 120 World Music CDs in partnership with World Music Network.

Visit www.roughguides.com to see our latest publications.

Rough Guide travel images are available for commercial licensing at www.roughguidespictures.com

Rough Guide credits

Text editor: Helen Marsden
Layout: Umesh Aggarwal, Jessica Subramanian
Cartography: Maxine Repath, Karobi Gogoi
Picture editor: Harriet Mills
Production: Aimee Hampson
Proofreader: Diane Margolis
Cover design: Chloë Roberts
Photographer: Suzanne Porter
Editorial: London Kate Berens, Claire Saunders, Geoff Howard, Ruth Blackmore, Polly Thomas, Richard Lim, Clifton Wilkinson, Alison Murchie, Karoline Densley, Andy Turner, Keith Drew, Edward Aves, Nikki Birrell, Alice Park, Sarah Eno, David Paul, Lucy White, Joe Staines, Duncan Clark, Peter Buckley, Matthew Milton, Tracy Hopkins, Ruth Tidball; **New York** Andrew Rosenberg, Richard Koss, Steven Horak, AnneLise Sorensen, Amy Hegarty, Hunter Slaton, April Isaacs, Sean Mahoney
Design & Pictures: London Simon Bracken, Dan May, Diana Jarvis, Jj Luck, Mark Thomas; **Delhi** Madhulita Mohapatra, Ajay Verma, Amit Verma, Ankur Guha, Pradeep Thapliyal

Production: Sophie Hewat, Katherine Owers
Cartography: London Ed Wright, Katie Lloyd-Jones; **Delhi** Manish Chandra, Rajesh Chhibber, Ashutosh Bharti, Rajesh Mishra, Animesh Pathak, Jasbir Sandhu, Karobi Gogoi, Amod Singh
Online: New York Jennifer Gold, Suzanne Welles, Kristin Mingrone; **Delhi** Manik Chauhan, Narender Kumar, Shekhar Jha, Lalit K. Sharma, Rakesh Kumar, Chhandita Chakravarty
Marketing & Publicity: London Richard Trillo, Niki Hanmer, David Wearn, Demelza Dallow, Louise Maher, Jess Carter; **New York** Geoff Colquitt, Megan Kennedy, Katy Ball; **Delhi** Reem Khokhar
Custom publishing and foreign rights: Philippa Hopkins
Manager India: Punita Singh
Series editor: Mark Ellingham
Reference Director: Andrew Lockett
PA to Managing and Publishing Directors: Megan McIntyre
Publishing Director: Martin Dunford
Managing Director: Kevin Fitzgerald

Publishing information

This second edition published July 2006 by
Rough Guides Ltd,
80 Strand, London WC2R 0RL, UK
345 Hudson St, 4th Floor,
New York, NY 10014, USA
14 Local Shopping Centre, Panchsheel Park,
New Delhi 110017, India
Distributed by the Penguin Group
Penguin Books Ltd,
80 Strand, London WC2R 0RL, UK
Penguin Putnam, Inc.
375 Hudson Street, NY 10014, USA
Penguin Group (Australia)
250 Camberwell Road, Camberwell,
Victoria 3124, Australia
Penguin Books Canada Ltd,
10 Alcorn Avenue, Toronto, Ontario,
M4V 1E4, Canada
Penguin Group (New Zealand)
Cnr Rosedale and Airborne roads
Albany, Auckland, New Zealand
Cover concept by Peter Dyer.

Typeset in Bembo and Helvetica to an original design by Henry Iles.
Printed and bound in China.

288pp includes index.
A catalogue record for this book is available from the British Library.
ISBN 978-1-84353-567-6

Help us update

We've gone to a lot of effort to ensure that the second edition of **The Rough Guide to Zanzibar** is accurate and up to date. However, things change – places get "discovered", opening hours are notoriously fickle, restaurants and rooms raise prices or lower standards. If you feel we've got it wrong or left something out, we'd like to know, and if you can remember the address, the price, the time, the phone number, so much the better.

We'll credit all contributions, and send a copy of the next edition (or any other Rough Guide

if you prefer) for the best letters. Everyone who writes to us and isn't already a subscriber will receive a copy of our full-colour thrice-yearly newsletter.

Please mark letters: "**Rough Guide Zanzibar Update**" and send to: Rough Guides, 80 Strand, London WC2R 0RL, or Rough Guides, 4th Floor, 345 Hudson St, New York, NY 10014. Or send an email to **mail@roughguides.com**

Have your questions answered and tell others about your trip at
www.roughguides.atinfopop.com

Acknowledgements

Jens Finke I would especially like to thank Maria Helena, for being there and keeping up with my insane working hours, and Helen Marsden at the other end of the line for both her superb (and for me enjoyable) work as this book's editor, and for her patience in dealing with my infamous inability to stick to deadlines while under pressure from the almighty "big potatoes". All well worthwhile, I hope. In Zanzibar, particular thanks – in no particular order – go to Amin and Jaffer Machano, Ally Keys, Rod Kayne (glad you finally got rid of me?), Abbas Juma Mzee, and – as ever – the folks at Swahili Divers.

SMALL PRINT

Readers' letters

A big thank-you to all the readers who wrote in with comments and suggestions about the first edition, and grovelling apologies to those whose names I've either misspelled or missed off entirely (things got very hectic):

Johan Vanden Abeele, Nick and Sarah Atkinson, Ian Chisholm, James Clarke, Erika Cule, Claude David, Simon Davies, Leicester Fosse, Rahel Hardmeier, Mike Hartwell, Michael Hell, Gerard Hettema, Professor James Hough, Marije Jongejan, Mussa Hassan Mussa Kitambulio, Belia Klaassen, Joyce Klaassen, Maisy Luk, Michela Mazier, Dr Paul McAndrew, Kris Mizutani, Kristina Pentland, Alberto Poli, Val Presten, Liisa Riihimaki, Amanda Sangorski, Gillian Scoble, Mansuetus Setonga, Jo Slater, Ype Smit, William Visser, Mary Taylor, Adam and Anne White, Murray White, Stephanie Wynne-Jones, Andreas Zahner.

Photo credits

All photos © Rough Guides except the following:

Introduction
p.4 Women of Uroa watching the dhow race at the eighth ZIFF Festival of the Dhow Countries © Peter Bennett/www.ziff.or.tz
p.5 Stone Town street © Steven Marks/Cape Photo Library/iAfrika
p.7 Watmon Cultural Club performance © Chiara Gallo

Things not to miss
08 Hawksbill turtle, Indian Ocean © Peter Pinnock/Alamy
09 T.I.D performing at the eighth ZIFF Festival of the Dhow Countries © Chiara Gallo/www .ziff.or.tz
13 Bottle-nosed dolphins © Jeff Rotman/naturepl. com
15 Makunduchi Festival © Chiara Gallo
18 Traditional bullfighting, Gombani Village, Pemba © Peter Bennett

Colour insert: Zanzibar and the Slave Trade
"Slaves in the Hold", engraved by Deroi, published by Engelmann & Cie, 1827–35 (hand-coloured litho), artist Johann Moritz Rugendas (1802–58) © Michael Graham-Stewart/ Bridgeman Art Library

Convoy of slaves, Zanzibar, 1889 © Mary Evans Picture Library/Alamy
Tippo-Tip, Zanzibar, c.1890, E.C Dias © Bridgeman Art Library

Colour insert: Zanzibar and the Sea
Giant pink gorgonian fan and jackfish, Indian Ocean © Geoff Spib/iAfrika Photos
Dhow building, Nungwi © Ariadne Van Zandbergen
Dugong © Doug Perrine/naturepl.com
Snorkelling trip, Zanzibar © Jeremy Jowell/iAfrika Photos
Giant Coconut Crab, Chumbe Island © Ariadne Van Zandbergen

Black and white pictures
p.62 Lutheran Church, Dar es Salaam © Ariadne Van Zandbergen
p.134 Snorkelling off Chumbe Island © Cozzi Guido/4cornersimages.com
p.168 Aerial view of Mnemba Island © Regis Colombo/www.diapo.ch
p.233 Sidi Goma performing at 2005 ZIFF Festival © Peter Bennett/www.ziff.or.tz

SMALL PRINT

281

Index

Map entries are in colour.

R

S

INDEX